JStor
Gale databases.

# Afro-Creole

# Afro-Creole

POWER, OPPOSITION, *and*
PLAY IN THE CARIBBEAN

✦

Richard D. E. Burton

CORNELL UNIVERSITY PRESS
Ithaca and London

Copyright © 1997 by Cornell University

All rights reserved. Except for brief quotations in a review, this book, or parts
thereof, must not be reproduced in any form without permission in writing
from the publisher. For information, address Cornell University Press, Sage
House, 512 East State Street, Ithaca, New York 14850.

First published 1997 by Cornell University Press

Printed in the United States of America

⊗ The paper in this book meets the minimum requirements of the American
National Standard for Information Sciences—Permanence of Paper for Printed
Library Materials, ANSI Z39.48-1984.

Library of Congress Cataloging-in-Publication Data

Burton, Richard D.E., 1946–
    Afro-Creole : power, opposition, and play in the Caribbean /
Richard D.E. Burton
        p.    cm.
    Includes bibliographical references (p.      ) and index.
    ISBN 0-8014-3249-9 (cloth : alk. paper)
    1. Jamaica—Civilization—African influences.   2. Trinidad and
Tobago—Civilization—African influences.   3. Haiti—Civilization—
African influences.   4. Slavery—West Indies—History.   5. Creoles—
Jamaica—Religion.   6. Creoles—Trinidad and Tobago—Social life
and customs.   7. Creoles—Haiti—Religion.   8. Government,
Resistance to—West Indies—History.   9. West Indies—Race
relations.   I. Title.
F1874.B8      1997
303.48'272906—dc21                                                      96-50046

        Cloth printing        10  9  8  7  6  5  4  3  2  1

        Paperback printing    10  9  8  7  6  5  4  3  2  1

# Contents

# Illustrations

# Acknowledgments

Since my primary discipline is French, and since almost all of my previously published work on the Caribbean concerns Martinique, writing a book that focuses on Jamaica, Trinidad, and Haiti and attempts to bring together as wide a range of historical, anthropological, and political materials, as *Afro-Creole* does, has taken me into areas of Caribbean studies in which I am more than usually dependent on the ideas and scholarship of others. In these circumstances I am all the more eager both to acknowledge the major intellectual debts I have incurred while working on this project and to absolve the authors concerned of responsibility for any tendentious use to which I may have put their ideas. Every idea I have taken over is, I hope, correctly attributed, and I have derived particular inspiration from the work of the following people, whom, whether I know them personally or not, I list in uncontroversial alphabetical order: Roger Abrahams, Mervyn Alleyne, Diane Austin-Broos, Karen McCarthy Brown, Barry Chevannes, Carolyn Cooper, Michael Craton, Robert Dirks, Lisa Douglass, Barry Gaspar, Richard Hart, Gad Heuman, Barry Higman, Errol Hill, Thomas Holt, Michel Laguerre, Earl Lovelace, Anthony Maingot, Frank Manning, Daniel Miller, Errol Miller, Sidney Mintz, Ken Post, Richard and Sally Price, Gordon Rohlehr, James Scott, Elisa Janine Sobo, Paul Sutton, Peter Wilson, Carole Yawney, and Kevin Yelvington.

All illustrations are credited in the proper place, and I am particularly grateful to Gerry Besson, Judith Bettelheim, John P. Homiak, James Houk, William Wedenoja, Dolores M. Yonker, and not least Raphael de Leon (the Roaring Lion), who have permitted me to use material in their personal collections.

A place apart belongs to Ross Chambers, who, in addition to countless personal kindnesses, introduced me, through his work in nineteenth-century French literature (which is where, intellectually, I began), to Michel de Certeau's distinction between resistance and opposition on which much of the argument of this book depends. It is also a particular pleasure to thank Nigel and Ellie Bolland, whom I knew at the University of the West Indies in Jamaica in the early 1970s but with whom I had had no subsequent contact, for the warmth with which they received me into their home while I was writing this book: there is nothing Caribbeanists like more than swapping stories, memories, and ideas about the Caribbean, and these were good times, spent in wonderful surroundings in upstate New York.

I am also extremely grateful to Peter Agree of Cornell University Press for the positive way responded to the project from the first and for his patience in shepherding me and my manuscript through the various stages of publication.

Three other debts: to Henning Pape-Santos, who word processed the manuscript with speed, aplomb, and precision; to David Robinson, dean of the School of African and Asian Studies at Sussex University, who generously provided me with financial support; and above all to Dominick LaCapra, director of the Society for the Humanities at Cornell University, and to his predecessor, Jonathan Culler, who jointly enabled me to write this book in the optimum conditions afforded by Cornell and its superb Olin Library. *Honneur et respect à tous,* as they say in the French Caribbean.

R. D. E. B.

*Ithaca, New York*

# A Note on Terminology

Throughout this book "colored" is used in the standard Caribbean sense of "mixed race." Used as an adjective it is lowercased and spelled in the conventional American English manner; as a noun it is capitalized, and I use the standard British English spelling, "Coloured." In general, "white" and "black" are used as adjectives, "White" and "Black" as nouns, and many similar terms follow this pattern. Spellings in quotations are as in the originals, apart from some minor standardization in quotations from twentieth-century works. I have not attempted to standardize the spelling of either *patwa* (patois) or French Creole terms. Translations are mine unless otherwise indicated in the references, and italics in quotations are present in the original unless attributed to me. A glossary of terms not otherwise identified in the text or footnotes is provided at the end of the book.

Afro-Creole

# Introduction

My focus in this book is on two related issues, both of fundamental importance to an understanding of the Caribbean. The first concern is to rethink historically one of the most perennially controversial issues not merely in academic discourse but in day-to-day discussion about the Caribbean: How "African" or, alternatively, how distinctly "Caribbean" or "creole" is (are) Afro-Caribbean culture(s)? Was the experience of the Middle Passage, followed immediately by forced initiation into the slave plantation, so traumatic that, as one influential theory has it,[1] African-born slaves were in effect stripped of all their cultural assets and compelled to piece together a culture out of what they could beg, borrow, or steal from their European-born masters? Or as maintained by a rival, and equally influential, theory first coherently argued in Melville J. Herskovits's seminal *Myth of the Negro Past* of 1941, did slave culture and the postemancipation Afro-American cultures derived from it remain African in underlying structure if not in all their surface expressions? As this position has it, much, if not all, of the slaves' ancestral cultures was transported with them across the Atlantic and either survived intact or was reformulated or reinterpreted in resistant response to the radically new conditions the slaves encountered. Accordingly, many African cultural forms not merely were preserved in the New World but flourished there, often concealed beneath a European shell. The African-derived Vodou spirits of Haiti, Damballa, Legba, and Erzilie, for instance, are conventionally represented as Saint Patrick, Saint Peter, and the Virgin Mary. Or finally, as a

1. The theory of "culture stripping" is particularly associated with E. Franklin Frazier's *The Negro Family in the United States* (1939). For a brief summary of the debates between Franklin Frazier and Herskovits, see Mintz and Price 1992:62–65.

1

third, mediating, theory contends, did there take place some form of cultural miscegenation between Africa and Europe, corresponding to the sexual miscegenation of black and white? According to this theory, starting from the very formation of slave colonies in the Caribbean, African and European cultural elements were merged, married, blended, or combined into a new and quintessentially Caribbean synthesis, a tertium quid to which the appropriately composite term "creole" is widely given.[2]

In formulating these three principal approaches to the study of Afro-Caribbean culture(s), I have highlighted their differences as well as glossed over or omitted the many distinctions and qualifications that the best of their proponents bring to their analyses. In practice each of the three—which I will label the Eurogenetic, Afrogenetic, and creativity or creolization hypotheses[3] —has variants that commonly overlap with those of rival hypotheses, producing an interpretative continuum corresponding to the continuum of cultures that have coexisted and competed in the Caribbean ever since slavery. Thus not even the most passionate advocate of the Afrogenetic hypothesis maintains that *everything* in slave culture or contemporary Afro-Caribbean culture is a survival or reinterpretation of some African cultural form, that nothing was borrowed or stolen from the dominant culture or that no new cultural forms were created by the slaves and their descendants. Similarly, the once widely held view that enslavement obliterated Africanity among the slave population and that slave and Afro-Caribbean cultures are no more than a bricolage of borrowed bits and pieces has now been largely abandoned in the English-speaking world, though more sophisticated versions of it survive in France and the French West Indies.[4]

---

2. The word "creole" is commonly, if somewhat fantastically, said to derive "from a combination of two Spanish words *criar* (to create, to imagine, to establish, to found, to settle) and *colon* (a colonist, a founder, a settler) into *criollo*: a committed settler, one identified with the area of settlement, one native to the settlement though not ancestrally indigenous to it" (Brathwaite 1974:10). For a valuable and succinct discussion of the meanings of the word in different societies, see Bolland 1992b:50–52.

3. I have taken the terms "Eurogeneticist" (*eurogénétiste*) and "Afrogeneticist" (*afrogénétiste*) from Chaudenson 1992:39. The term "creativity hypothesis" (or "creation model") is used by Mervyn Alleyne (1988:22) in his discussion of the "creativity vs. continuity debate" (19) in Afro-American studies.

4. One such survival is the work of the linguist Robert Chaudenson (1992), who argues that creoles are essentially "restructurations" of the parent European languages from which any significant African substratum is absent. Another is the anthropologist André-Marcel D'Ans's daring insistence, in the face of near unanimity to the contrary, on the "fundamental non-Africanness of Haitian culture" (1987:254). A third, in Martinique, is the polemical work of the militantly anti-Afrocentrist proponent of *créolité*, Raphaël Confiant, for whom not the slightest "fragment of Africanness" (*une quelconque pépite d'africanité*) remains in the Martinican conscious or unconscious (1993:131). For him, what little Africanness survived the Middle Passage has passed into and been deconstructed by the new creole culture, whose governing principles are essentially French derived (37). For a brief discussion of the idea of *créolité* in contemporary Martinique, see Burton 1993b:19–25.

In practice, therefore, almost all contemporary approaches to Afro-Caribbean culture(s) stress its (their) syncretistic or mosaic character, though there remain significant differences of emphasis and interpretation concerning both the way syncretization took place and how far the primary cultural components—above all the African component—were preserved, either intact or "reformulated." While accepting that there can be no question of whole African cultures' having survived in the New World, even among the descendants of Maroons, a sophisticated but representative Afrogeneticist such as Mervyn Alleyne (*Roots of Jamaican Culture*, 1988) is nonetheless able to argue persuasively for great continuity between African and Afro-Jamaican cultures. If cultural creation has taken place, he contends, it is upon the infrastructure of an African-derived habitus or *mentalité* that was able to survive the multiple disruptions of capture, transportation, and induction into the plantation. Contrary to received opinion, tribal identities were not entirely destroyed by the planters' alleged policy of mixing different ethnic and linguistic groups for security reasons. In any case, the cultures of West African from which the vast majority of Jamaican slaves were seized constituted a common matrix. Furthermore, the underlying Africanness of Afro-Jamaican culture was reinforced by the arrival of substantial numbers of African indentured laborers after emancipation.[5] Whatever cultural superstrata may have been formed through interaction with Whites, the substratum of the Jamaican masses remains durably African to this day, and it is this cultural substratum that informs all its most characteristic expressions: language, music, dance, and perhaps above all, religion. What Alleyne offers is an essentially Herskovitsean interpretation of Afro-Jamaican culture, sharpened and reinforced by his use of linguistics-derived concepts, most notably that of a cultural continuum corresponding to the language continuum of acrolect ("upper language"), mesolect ("middle language"), and basilect ("lower language"), which will structure my own argument in much of what follows.[6]

The position argued by Sidney Mintz and Richard Price in their widely admired *The Birth of African-American Culture: An Anthropological Perspective* (1992) could not, at least on the surface, be more different from that of *Roots of Jamaican Culture*. For Mintz and Price it is axiomatic that no human group, let alone an enslaved one, "can transfer its way of life and the accompanying beliefs and values intact from one locale to another" (1992:1). Furthermore,

5. For a discussion of the impact on Trinidadian culture of postemancipation African arrivals, see Warner-Lewis 1991.

6. See Alleyne 1980, passim, for the general concept of a linguistic continuum in Caribbean societies and 1988:91–96 for an application of this concept to the range of religious variations in Jamaica. An ambitious application of the concept of a linguistic continuum to the analysis of nonlinguistic cultural phenomena in Guyana has been made by Drummond (1980), drawing on Derek Bickerton's seminal *Dynamics of a Creole System* (1975), and the idea has also been applied suggestively to Haiti by D'Ans (1987:273).

while acknowledging that the Africans transported to the New World "shared a certain number of underlying cultural understandings and assumptions, insofar as their societies were related to one another, both historically and by virtue of intense contact," they query whether the arrivants "can be said to have shared a *culture*, in the sense that European colonists in a particular colony can be said to have done so" (2).[7] Far from constituting even a rudimentary community, arriving slaves formed no more than "*crowds*, and very heterogeneous crowds at that" (18), and they "became a *community* and began to share a *culture* only insofar as, and as fast as, they themselves created them" (14). Nowhere in the Caribbean—indeed nowhere in the New World—can a functioning African or neo-African culture be said to survive; even the Maroon cultures of Surinam and French Guiana, often viewed (not least by Herskovits) as oases of Africanity in the Americas, turn out on closer inspection to involve new cultural creations as much as retentions from the past (52–55) and are thus essentially creole cultures, though their mode of creolization differed significantly from that obtaining among Africans who remained on the plantation. But unlike the extreme Eurogeneticists, Mintz and Price do not believe that enslavement produced in its victims a complete cultural tabula rasa that could be inscribed only with European-derived values, customs, and beliefs. Rather, a process of cultural creation began on the very ships that brought the slaves from Africa to the New World (43–44); as they interacted with each other and with the various categories of Whites they came in contact with, disparate cultural materials were recombined according to certain "unconscious 'grammatical' principles, which may underlie and shape behavioral response" (9–10); the idea of an underlying "grammar of culture" common to all West Africans is taken explicitly from Herskovits (11), and Mintz and Price's use of it may not differ greatly from Alleyne's concept of a shared West African substratum. But whereas for Alleyne the existence of this common cultural grammar is the basis of the alleged continuity between Africa and Afro-America, for Mintz and Price it forms the infrastructure on which a new culture, not neo-African but creole, was constructed. Rather than simply transposing African cultural forms—adapting or reinterpreting them according to circumstances—slaves are said to have drawn on *all* the cultural resources available to create a cultural system that could not be other than "highly syncretistic in terms of its diverse African origins, as well as in terms of inputs from European (and often other) sources" (62). The ingredients may have been African, European, Amerindian, or whatever, but the way they were combined was solely and quintessentially West Indian. Furthermore, it was not just the slaves whose culture was transformed by the experience of slavery. Like most proponents of

7. I borrow the term "arrivants," so much more expressive than "arrivals," from Brathwaite 1973.

the creativity hypothesis, Mintz and Price insist that creolization was bilateral during slavery, before becoming multilateral as indentured laborers were imported from India and elsewhere after emancipation. Plantation life involved a multiplicity of "nodal points of contact and flow" (32)—between Whites and their domestic, skilled, and privileged slaves, between white men and black women, between white children and black nurses—leading to the emergence of a dominant "white" variant of creole culture that coexisted in latent or overt tension with the dominated "black" variant. Mintz and Price do not see a graduated continuum of creole cultures, but their insistence that cultural transformation on the plantation was a two-way process clearly points in that direction.

Faced with issues of such complexity and contentiousness, I have attempted in chapter 1 to do what to my knowledge no study of the Anglophone Caribbean has done—to trace the *stages* whereby, in the specific case of Jamaica, Africans were transformed (or not transformed, as the case may be) by the experience of slavery, through their interaction with each other, with the slaves, both locally and African born, they encountered on their arrival in Jamaica, and with the various categories of Whites they confronted on and off the plantation. By examining slave culture in cross section at a series of critical junctures—roughly 1700, 1730, 1780, and 1820—I combine synchronic and diachronic approaches and argue that the passage from African to Afro-Creole, which I see as being far advanced if not complete by the time of emancipation, involved at the same time cultural loss, cultural retention and reinterpretation, cultural imitation and borrowing, and cultural creation. *All* these processes must be given their proper place and weight if the full complexity of culture making in the Caribbean is to be understood. It seems to me self-evident that *both* "continuity" and "creativity" are involved in creolization, which I see as taking place at least as much *within* the slave community as between that community and the Whites. Throughout, I attribute a determining importance to the ever-growing proportion of creole (locally born) slaves who, much more than the Whites themselves, seem to have been the direct and decisive agents of cultural transformation on the plantation. While concentrating on the elaboration of an Afro-Creole culture, I also discuss the parallel processes simultaneously at work among Whites in Jamaica, though I reject the idea that anything like a unified creole culture was created, or could have been created, under the conditions of slavery. Rather, I believe that what took place was a "segmentary" rather than "synthetic" creolization,[8] to use Orlando Patterson's valuable distinction. What progressively emerged

8. "The major difference between synthetic and segmentary creolization is that whereas in the latter each group develops its own local culture, with synthetic creolization the group attempts to forge a local culture that combines elements from all the available cultural resources" (Patterson 1975:318).

in slave society in Jamaica (and would be further developed after emancipation) was a continuum of overlapping and competing cultural forms, all of them creole or creolized, that I label "Euro-Creole," "Meso-Creole" (the "middle culture," corresponding to the mesolect of "middle language," of the free colored classes and certain sections of the slave elite), and "Afro-Creole." It should be stressed that these indicate no more than "zones" on the cultural continuum, each differentiated from its neighbors and competitors rather than totally different, and each further subject to a range of important internal variations. While using the concept of a cultural continuum, I try to avoid what Nigel Bolland (1992b:64) has called "the portrayal of creolization as a 'blending' process, a mixing of cultures that occurs without reference to structural contradictions and social conflicts." This view, as he rightly says, "obfuscates the tension and conflict that existed, and still exists, between the Africans and Europeans who were the bearers of these traditions." Bolland's general conclusion (1992b:72) that creolization is "not a homogenizing process, but rather a process of *contention*" between different racial and social groups, is one I fully endorse.

With chapter 2 the focus shifts to the second major theme of the book, a consideration of cultural resistance in the Caribbean, first in the case of Jamaica (chapters 2 and 3), then of Trinidad (chapter 4), and finally Jamaica, Trinidad, and Haiti combined (chapter 5). I say "resistance" in deference to standard usage, but in fact, as readers will quickly discern, I draw an important distinction, derived from the work of Michel de Certeau (1980),[9] between "resistance"—those forms of contestation of a given system that are conducted from *outside* that system, using weapons and concepts derived from a source or sources other than the system in question—and "opposition," by which term de Certeau designates those forms of contestation of a given system that are conducted from *within* that system, using weapons and concepts derived from the system itself. Michel Foucault makes a similar point in the first volume of *The History of Sexuality* (1978:95–96) when he writes that "where there is power, there is resistance, and yet, or rather consequently, this resistance is never in a position of exteriority in relation to power." Obviously "resistance" in this sense corresponds to what de Certeau means by "opposition." It follows that though there are "points of resistance ['opposition'] present everywhere in the power network," there is, according to Foucault, "no single locus of great Refusal, no soul of revolt, source of all rebellions, or pure law of the revolu-

9. For earlier applications of de Certeau's opposition/resistance distinction to the Caribbean, see Burton 1993a and 1993b. Partly based on these studies, Kevin Yelvington (1995a:228–30) has used de Certeau's theory to illuminating effect in his discussion of labor relations in a Trinidadian factory, published after this book was completed, and has also applied it to West Indian cricket in an essay (Yelvington 1995b) likewise published after the completion of my work, whose conclusions echo those in chapter 4.

tionary. Instead there is a plurality of resistances, each of them a special case: resistances that are possible, necessary, improbable; others that are spontaneous, savage, solitary, concerted, rampant, or violent; still others that are quick to compromise, interested, or sacrificial; by definition, they can only exist in the strategic field of power relations." It further follows, says Foucault, that "great radical ruptures, massive binary divisions" occur only very occasionally in human history, in the case of the Caribbean perhaps only in Saint-Domingue between 1791 and 1804 and in Cuba in the late 1950s. Otherwise "resistances" ("oppositions") are "distributed in irregular fashion" as the "odd term in relations of power," as so many "points, knots or focuses of resistance" that are "spread over time and space at varying densities, at times mobilizing groups of individuals in a definitive way, inflaming certain points of the body, certain moments in life, certain types of behaviour." It is this problem of the relation between opposition and resistance (using both those terms in de Certeau's sense), and of the passage from the former to the latter, that is studied in chapter 2 with relation to the great slave uprising in Jamaica in 1831–32, generally known as the Baptist War, which is here seen as poised on the brink of a "great radical rupture" or "massive binary division" that failed, finally, to take place.

A further implication of the distinction between opposition and resistance is that Afro-Creole cultures—especially after 1800 when in almost every slave colony (Saint-Domingue being "free" by that time) creole slaves clearly outnumbered those of African origin—tend to be much more *cultures of opposition* than *cultures of resistance*,[10] in that they draw heavily on materials furnished by the dominant culture—notably language and religion—that they contrive, in the multifarious ways described in this book, both to modify (without transforming them entirely) and to turn against the dominant culture in order to contest that culture. Or as Emilia Viotti da Costa (1994:xvii) puts it in her fine study of the Demerara slave rebellion of 1823, which appeared just as I was completing my manuscript: "In their day-to-day interactions with masters and

10. In de Certeau's terms, the last extended acts of *resistance* in British West Indian slave colonies would be Tacky's uprising in Jamaica in 1760 and Cuffee's in Berbice in 1763: both were African dominated and aimed at nothing less than a "war of racial extermination and the establishment of an ethnic autocracy on Ashanti lines" (Craton 1982:122; see also Geggus 1983:22). At the time of the foiled Jamaican slave plot of 1776, creole slaves were clearly the leading participants (see Craton 1982:172 and chapter 2, n. 1 below), and, despite Edward Kamau Brathwaite's ingenious attempts to show otherwise (1977), the 1831–32 Baptist War in Jamaica was clearly Afro-Christian rather than "African" in inspiration, with creole slaves providing the bulk of the uprising's cadres and also the majority of its participants (see Higman 1976:227). The Saint-Domingue slave rebellion was essentially an act of *resistance* in that, though most of its most important leaders were Creoles, its participants were predominantly of African origin, and neither Christianity nor, until it was well under way, French Revolutionary ideals seem to have played a significant part in its inception: its aim was from the outset to overthrow slavery, though it was only after Napoleon's attempted reimposition of slavery after 1802 that the further goal of national independence seems to have emerged.

missionaries, [slaves] appropriated symbols that originally were meant to subject them and wrought those symbols into weapons of their own emancipation. In this process they not only transformed themselves and every one around, but they also helped to shape the course of history." This is an admirable summary of the problem I am concerned with, but Viotti da Costa does not, I think, bring out sufficiently the ambiguity of such forms of opposition, which not only enable the dominated to oppose the dominant group on the latter's own ground but draw the dominated, willy-nilly, further into the dominant group's worldview. In other words, I see cultural opposition in the Caribbean as double-edged to the extent that an (Afro-)Creole culture cannot, by dint of its very creoleness, get entirely outside the dominant system in order to *resist* it (in de Certeau's sense of the word) and so tends unconsciously to reproduce its underlying structures even as it consciously challenges its visible dominance. I explore this paradox through a series of examples ranging from the various forms of Afro-Christianity in Jamaica, Rastafarianism, Trinidadian carnival, Haitian Vodou, and cricket in the Commonwealth Caribbean as a whole, always focusing on the ambivalence of cultural forms, which seem unable to oppose the dominant system without simultaneously confirming, and even reinforcing, the latter's hegemony. Anthony Maingot (1994:120) has written that "the masses in the English-speaking Caribbean have always tended to be politically radical but sociologically conservative," with the further implication that in the final analysis the sociological conservatism always wins out over the political radicalism. Part of the reason for this, I suggest, is that Afro-Creole cultures are themselves a paradoxical amalgam of the radical and the conservative that, to repeat, simultaneously challenges and confirms the dominant order by turning the latter's resources against it in a complex double game of oppositionality—a game that can lead into, but also often militates against, the possibility of actual *resistance*, in the more circumscribed sense in which I am using that term. In short, an oppositional culture, precisely because it opposes the dominant order on the dominant order's own ground, is always likely, sooner or later, to be "recuperated" by it, as I believe the examples of Afro-Christianity, Rastafarianism, Vodou, carnival, and cricket, among others, demonstrate in the case of the Caribbean.

Having explained how I am using the term "opposition" in this book, I will now say something about the other two concepts in my subtitle, "power" and "play." Taking my lead from slave terminology, which designated as "plays" any weekend celebration involving music, dance, food, and drink, I use the word "play" in a very broad sense to refer to all nonutilitarian activities in the Caribbean, ranging from the religious (Afro-Christianity, Vodou), through the festive (Jonkonnu, carnival) to the more narrowly ludic (stickfighting, cricket), all of which I situate within the broader context of a "play culture" that I describe at the beginning of chapter 4. The basic thesis is that in the Caribbean all play is oppositional and all oppositionality is "playful" or contains a "play element"—which most definitely does *not* mean that it is not intensely serious at the same time, as anyone who has seen or taken part in a cricket match involving West Indians—even a game of street or beach cricket—will know well. "Power" I also use very broadly, to include both the external sources of power that from the beginning of European colonization have acted on and in large part determined the Caribbean's evolution right up to this day, and the internal structures whereby that external power is transmitted and refracted. Sometimes I capitalize "Power" to indicate its external source, keeping lowercase "power" for its internal operations, but I have not been fully consistent in this. That the external structures of Power are implicitly present rather than explicitly discussed in this book should be seen not as reflecting a desire to minimize their importance, but rather as a consequence of where my main focus lies, namely on the cultural responses to the experience of domination and disempowerment by the Afro-Creole populations of Jamaica, Trinidad, and Haiti from the period of slavery up to the present.

That experience and the range of cultural responses to it have, I believe, been paradoxical in the extreme, and, as I researched and wrote this book I was struck by the recurrence of one image that seems to embody both power and counterpower in the Caribbean and, above all, the ambivalent relation between them. This image or symbol comes in a multiplicity of guises that I foreground in the last chapter. Its first and most sinister manifestation is the slave driver's rod, described by the all too aptly named Thomas Roughley in his *Jamaica Planter's Guide* of 1823 as "the emblem of his rank and dignity, a polished staff or and, with prongy crooks on it to lean on, and a short-handled tangible whip" (quoted in Walvin 1993:240). After the abolition of slavery, the rod and the whip did not disappear as implements of physical authority— far from it—but gradually evolved into internalized forms of coercion. Often the form was religion, with the missionary taking the place, as it were, of the slavemaster of old and, in the words of the Rev. J. A. James's *Sunday School Teacher's Guide* of 1818, using Bible and sermon to "put the rod into the hand of conscience, and excite a trembling dread of the strokes which are inflicted by this internal censor."[11] But the rod of religion is a characteristically double-edged weapon, for if it is used by the dominant order to sanctify and shore up its power, it is also turned against it time after time by dominated groups in society, in the form of the shepherd's crooks, swords, and scepters of Revival, the rods and staffs of Rastafarianism, and all the swords, flags, and other physical "props" of the living theater that is Vodou. The slavemaster's rod also appears, transmuted and transformed into an instrument or symbol of counter-

11. Quoted in Viotti da Costa 1994:94. *The Sunday School Teacher's Guide* would have been widely read, and its instructions taken to heart, by many nonconformist missionaries in the British West Indies in the first half of the nineteenth century.

authority, in the stickfighter's baton (which, I suggest, later mutates into the flashing willow blade of the batsman), and in all the innumerable staffs, staves, swords, banners, and other emblems of popular counterpower that are ritualistically displayed during carnival. And of course the rod is also present, though turned against its original bearer and his successors, in all the machetes, sharpened sticks, and other improvised weapons with which, throughout their history, oppressed West Indians have physically challenged their oppressors. Thus the rod in its multiple manifestations becomes the symbol of both power and popular opposition to power in the Caribbean with, forever looming in the background and sometimes being wielded with implacable force, the big stick of ultimate Power in the region.

This, as I imagine is now clear, is a very wide-ranging book, but I should stress that it is not a survey of Afro-Caribbean culture but rather an argument, or a series of linked arguments, concerning some of its salient features, primarily religion, festivities, and the general phenomenon of play. It is the nature of the argument that has determined the inclusion of certain cultural forms and themes and the exclusion of others and that has led to the concentration on Jamaica, Trinidad, and Haiti, with only occasional references, where appropriate, to other Caribbean countries. By juxtaposing two countries with different imperial and religious traditions—British and primarily Protestant in the case of Jamaica, French and primarily Catholic in that of Haiti—with one, Trinidad, that historically has combined both the French and the British (and the Spanish) traditions as well as the Catholic and the Protestant, I hope I have brought out the fundamental unity of the Afro-Creole complex as well as the important variations that exist within it. But I have not given each country equal attention, nor have I treated all in the same way. Rather, I have dwelt on what in each is most germane to my overall argument in order to create a suggestive mosaic of cultural parallels and contrasts. Thus what progressively emerges as the unifying theme of the opening three chapters on Jamaica is religion in the form of Afro-Christianity and its derivatives: first as a specific instance of the general phenomenon of creolization (chapter 1), then as a principal focus of cultural opposition to slavery during its final decades (chapter 2), and finally, as the bedrock, in a variety of forms (Revival, Pocomania, Bedwardism, Pentecostalism, Rastafarianism), of Afro-Jamaican culture from emancipation to the present. With chapter 4 the geographic focus shifts from Jamaica to Trinidad, but the central theme remains cultural opposition, now in the form not of religion but of "play," both as a general concept and in certain of its most significant institutionalized expressions: stickfighting and cricket, the verbal play that is calypso, and the changing content and meaning of Trinidad carnival. The further shift to Haiti in the opening sections of chapter 5 reintroduces religion in the form of Vodou. I use the links between Vodou and the processions and ceremonies known collectively as Rara to investigate the connections between the religious culture of possession and secular culture of masquerade, and to link both to the structure of political power in postindependence Haiti. The discussion of Vodou, Rara, and politics leads into a more general consideration of the relation between power and counterpower in the Caribbean as figured in the emblem of the rod. And using the image of the double-edged sword brandished by the warrior spirit Ogou in Vodou, the book ends with a number of necessarily double-edged judgments concerning the relation between political leaders and their followers in the recent history of the Caribbean.

The focus on the culture of opposition in primarily its religious, festive, and ludic forms has led me to underplay certain aspects of Afro-Creole culture and history and to omit other aspects entirely. I discuss the whole complex issue of maroonage in another book I am writing about Martinique (where an intricate historically based but ideologically motivated "myth" of the Maroon lies behind much contemporary literature and thought), and I justify the absence of direct and detailed treatment here on the grounds that by 1800, when my discussion of opposition and resistance to slavery in Jamaica begins, long-term maroonage was no longer the major threat to the slave system that it had been before the signing of the treaties of 1739, which transformed the established Maroon communities into adjuncts and allies of the system.[12] I have also more or less completely omitted the question of "East Indians" in Trinidad and elsewhere; to have considered their variant of creoleness and their forms of oppositionality would have taken me far beyond the Afro-Creole of my title and led to a book of Brobdingnagian dimensions. The question of gender is more complex. I refer to it repeatedly—to the prominence of women in Revival, Pentecostalism, and Vodou, to the tension between men and women manifest in Rastafarianism, to the place of women in the culture of respectability that is so often contrasted to the male-dominated culture of reputation and play that provides the book's primary focus—but I have not dwelt explicitly on the oppositional culture of West Indian women (often as oppositional to West Indian men as to the dominant "white" power structures) or on specifically female ways of living the processes of creolization and the composite culture they fashion. In particular, I have said very little about family structures. My explanation, if not my justification, for this omission is that to concentrate, as this book mainly does, on areas of West Indian male culture from which women are almost systematically excluded is ipso facto to fail to give West Indian female culture the attention it merits. On the other hand, I have highlighted all those instances where, especially in recent years, West

12. On the ambivalent position of Maroons in Jamaican slave society, see the summary in Campbell 1988:250–60. The "Second Maroon War" of 1795–96 was essentially a rebellion by one of the Maroon communities (that of Trelawny Town) and in no way threatened the slave system as such.

Indian women appear to be moving out of the private world of the yard to which custom confines them and in to the traditionally male-dominated world of the street, understood both literally and metaphorically. The conventional dichotomy of male/outside and female/inside culture spheres discussed at length in chapter 4 appears at last to be breaking down, and though I am not sure that "the end of patriarchy has already begun in the Caribbean" and that in due course "women's power in society will replace men's power in society" (see Miller 1988:20), I do see current shifts in gender relations as potentially the most dynamic force for change in the Caribbean since universal suffrage and political independence, and conceivably even since emancipation.

*Afro-Creole* is best seen, therefore, as a mosaic of themes, images, and ideas, but like creole culture itself it is an "unstable mosaic" (Confiant 1993:116), and I have not tried to impose order and pattern where they do not appear to exist, or to fit every piece of the argument into a single all-embracing conclusion. I have throughout preferred suggestiveness to completeness and paradox to affirmation or negation. The ideas I have tried to express are sometimes complex and contentious, and some of my conclusions regarding the "culture of resistance" in the Caribbean run against orthodox thinking on this matter. If it serves to highlight the double-edgedness of what, as will now be clear, I prefer to call the culture of opposition in Jamaica, Trinidad, and Haiti and to stimulate debate about how that culture both challenges and reinforces the status quo, then *Afro-Creole* will more than have fulfilled its purpose.

# From African to Afro-Creole:
# The Making of Jamaican Slave Culture,
## 1655–1838

"*S*e *Kreyòl no ye / Pa genyen Ginen ankò:*
We are creoles / Who have Africa no longer" (quoted in Brown 1991:280–81).
So runs a well-known Haitian Vodou chant probably dating back to slavery,
to which a Jamaican *jamma*, or work song, of 1790 adds its doleful and sar-
donic appraisal of what it means to have lost one world and to have not yet
fully gained, or created, another:

| *Bomma (leader)* | *Bobbin (response)* |
|---|---|
| If me want for go in a Ebo, | Me can't go there! |
| Since dem tief me from a Guinea, | Me can't go there! |
| If me want for go in a Congo, | Me can't go there! |
| Since dem tief me from my tatta, | Me can't go there! |
| If me want for go in a Kingston, | Me can't go there! |
| Since massa gone in a England, | Me can't go there! |

(quoted in Cassidy 1961:274)

It is this passage from "Guinea" to "creole," as lived by the slaves of Jamaica,
that this chapter sets out to explore as rigorously and completely as the available historical accounts permit. I attempt to chart, stage by stage, what losing
"Guinea" meant in cultural terms and how slaves began, from the very moment
of arrival on the farther shore (indeed even earlier, from the moment of capture and embarkation on the slave ship), to adapt and create in response to the
radically different human and physical contexts in which they now found
themselves. What was lost, what was retained, and what, painfully and partially, was created? In an attempt to answer these questions, and at the risk of

an overrigid periodization, we can discern four successive phases of development: first, the establishment of the British colony and the rapid formation of a plantation society based on slavery (1655–1700); second, the half-century of consolidation and expansion that followed (1700–1750); third, what I call the "fulcrum period" (1750–80) when for the first time the demographic balance began to shift in favor of creole as opposed to African-born slaves; and finally, the last fifty years or so of slavery (1780 to 1834–38) when, thanks in some large measure to the impact of Christian missionaries (more black, as we shall see, than white), existing tendencies toward the creolization of slave culture were significantly intensified and accelerated. The analysis is both synchronic and diachronic: it attempts to describe a cross section of Jamaican slave culture during each of the phases above, and also to show how particular cultural forms—notably language, food, dress, music, and funeral customs—evolved (or failed to evolve) from one phase to the next. The emphasis is as much on permanence as change, and though slave culture provides the principal focus throughout, the parallel but distinct processes of creolization undergone by Whites and Free Coloureds form an essential part of the emerging mosaic. By 1838, as Jamaican society stood on the brink of the most revolutionary change in its history, a culture had been forged that was certainly no longer "African" (though it retained many more African elements than are commonly allowed) but had become Creole, or more precisely, Afro-Creole. Despite all the changes and creations of almost two hundred years, slave culture remained radically different from the other forms of creolized culture present in the colony—the "Euro-Creole" of the white elite and the "Meso-Creole" of the Free Coloureds. A continuum had emerged, with the soon-to-be-liberated and numerically dominant black masses occupying both the most disparaged and the most dynamic basilectal zone, which would undergo further transformations after emancipation.

## Phase One: The Formation of Plantation Society, 1655–1700

"The inhabitants of *Jamaica* are for the most part *Europeans*, some *Creolians*, born and bred in the Island *Barbados*, the Windward Islands, or *Surinam*, who are the Masters, and *Indians*, *Negros*, *Mulatos*, *Alcatrazes*, *Mestises*, *Quarterons*, &c. who are the Slaves." Thus wrote the great naturalist Hans Sloane (1707:1:xlvi) of the Jamaica he had visited in 1689, when in just over three decades the colony had already left behind its small-scale farming origins to embrace the monocrop—sugar—and the institution—plantation slavery—that together would dominate its history for the next century and a half. In 1673 the number of Whites (7,768) and Blacks (9,504) had been roughly equal. Twenty years later the white population (disproportionately reduced, it is true, by the destruction of Port Royal by an earthquake in 1692) remained much the same, but the number of Blacks had risen precipitously to 40,000, exclusively as a result of massive importation of slaves directly from Africa or from elsewhere in the Caribbean (D'Costa and Lalla 1990:17). Valuable though it is, Sloane's breakdown of the colony's population conceals its bewildering diversity during these early years. Between 1655 and 1700 the white population alone included, at any one time, some or all of the following linguistic and ethnic subgroups: soldiers, officials, merchants, farmers, and planters from England, speaking a range of regional and class variants of English; sailors and buccaneers with their distinctive seafarers' tongue; indentured laborers from London and from Devon, Somerset, and Cornwall, the first—mainly jailbirds and prostitutes—speaking, one imagines, some low-life argot, the second broad West Country dialects, perhaps even in some cases the nearly extinct Cornish; more indentured laborers from Scotland, Ireland, and Wales, for many, perhaps most, of whom Gaelic or Celtic would have been their first and often their only means of communicating;[1] planters, farmers, and laborers from Barbados, Surinam, Virginia, Bermuda, and elsewhere in the Caribbean (Montserrat, Nevis, St. Kitts), all speaking some variety of New World English; and Portuguese-speaking Sephardic Jews who had arrived from Brazil via Surinam (D'Costa and Lalla 1990:13). There were even, in the early years, groups of Romany-speaking gypsies shipped out from England to toil alongside Africans on the farmsteads and in the canefields.[2]

Facing this array of the deracinated, the deranged, the debauched, and the desperate was the much larger nonwhite population, itself divisible into several subcategories, one of which—the Indians mentioned by Sloane—had effectively disappeared by the end of the century. Standing apart from the enslaved population, but still interacting with it, were the three Maroon communities that had formed under the Spaniards and whose languages reflected their already partially creolized character: Afro-Hispanic, Afro-Arawak, plus a range of surviving African languages (D'Costa and Lalla 1990:13). Also set somewhat apart were those slaves—850 in 1680, perhaps 2,500 by 1692—who administered to the needs of the buccaneer community at Port Royal and who, given the much greater number of Whites they lived among (2,000 in 1680, about 6,500 in 1692), were probably heavily creolized by the time the

1. In the anonymous novel *Marly* (1828), set in the last years of slavery, the hero is told on his arrival in Jamaica of one Scottish planter whose practice is not "to employ any person whatever, unless they are from the Highlands, and can talk Gaelic." "The very negroes," Marly is told, "so well understand his predilection for the language of his clan, that when they see a walking buckra seeking employment on any of the estates under his charge, they accost him with the question, 'Can you talk Gaelic? for if you can't, massa no employ you'" (Anon. 1828:9).

2. An act of Parliament of 1661 required shipping out gypsies to the West Indies, though whether as slaves or as indentured laborers is unclear. The act was still in force in 1715, and as late as 1793 J. B. Moreton claimed to have known "many gipsies" in Jamaica who had been "taken into keeping by gentlemen, who paid exorbitant hire for their use" (see Hancock 1982:76–77).

earthquake engulfed them.[3] The slave population itself was clearly divided, as it always would be throughout slavery's existence, between African-born slaves and those Sloane calls *"Creolians,"* who "born in the Island, or taken from the *Spaniards,* are reckoned more worth than others in that they are season'd to the Island" (1707:1:xlvii). In fact, Sloane's "Creolians" were less likely to have been born in Jamaica than to have come to the island via Barbados[4] where, whether they had been born there or had arrived from Africa, they would have had "ample daily access to the vernacular of the island as spoken by a labour force of predominantly West of England, Irish and lower-class London provenance" (Le Page and Tabouret-Keller 1985:42). It is reasonable to assume that by the time they were transshipped to Jamaica they were speaking a language not far removed from the regional English of white Barbardians.[5] By 1700, however, the bulk of the slave population would have been imported directly from Africa, first from among the Akan and Ga-Andangme peoples of the coastal strip of Ghana and then, after 1680, from Dahomey and—somewhat surprisingly—from as far south as Angola (Patterson 1967:142). The Angolans apart, most of the African-born slaves would speak mutually unintelligible but structurally related languages of the Kwa group, of which Akan in its different forms (Twi, Asanti, and Fanti) and Ewe were undoubtedly the most widespread (Alleyne 1988:66). Finally, as Sloane notes, there is already evidence, in the form of "Mulatos," "Mestises," "Quarterons" and the mysterious "Alcatrazes," of extensive miscegenation between the white men and black women: some, at the very least, of this mixed-race population must have spoken a form of Creole or creolized English.

Jamaica about 1700 confronts us, then, with a situation not of diglossia, triglossia, or even heteroglossia but of panglossia, a state of "generalized multilingualism" (Fleischmann 1993:42) in which no fewer than seven principal strata, plus numerous substrata, may be discerned: (1) the official language of the colonizers; (2) the dialects/languages of indentured laborers; (3) the dialect of the "Creolian" or "Barbadian" slaves and of the emerging colored class, probably not far removed from (2) above; (4) the Portuguese of the important Jewish community; (5) the Afro-Arawak, Afro-Hispanic, and perhaps Afro-

---

3. Buisseret and Pawson, from whom these figures are taken (1975:98–99) find "little evidence of 'creolization'" at Port Royal, where "food, clothes, buildings, and recreations all obstinately followed English norms, however unsuitable these might be" (119). They are speaking, however, of the town's *white* population: it is difficult to see how the slaves could have remained unaffected by this "English" environment.

4. See Patterson 1967:145–46. The first slaves on the Drax Hill plantation at St. Ann's Bay studied by Douglas V. Armstrong were probably also, like their owner, of Barbadian provenance if in many cases of African birth (Armstrong 1990:36–37).

5. According to both Le Page and Tabouret-Keller (1985:44–45) and D'Costa and Lalla (1990:105), seventeenth-century Bajan (Barbadian), spoken by Blacks and Whites alike, should be regarded as a dialect of English rather than as a Creole.

Portuguese of the Maroon communities; (6) African languages; and (7) the emerging Creole(s). As we shall see, all of these layers, with the probable exception of (5), are surprisingly durable, and African languages in particular will be attested until late in the eighteenth century and may still have been spoken by a handful of slaves when emancipation finally came. Nonetheless the emerging pattern of language is clear: level (1) will hold out (though the everyday speech of white Jamaicans and, still more, of Jamaican Whites will be progressively creolized),[6] and level (7) will gradually absorb and transform level (6) so that by 1800 the linguistic chaos of the origins will have been reduced to a graduated continuum ranging, through various interlectal forms, from English "at the top" to Creole "at the bottom," combined with a sprinkling of surviving marginal languages (African, Portuguese, possibly Gaelic).[7] How this process (may have) occurred will be discussed in the pages that follow, but it is already clear by 1700 that a key role would devolve on the important minority—perhaps as much as a quarter—of "Barbardian" slaves who, in Patterson's words, "were already seasoned and were well placed, both historically and socially, to impose their own patterns of behavior and speech on the creole slave society which was then in its nuclear stage" (1967:142). Their creoleness strengthened and developed through interaction with lower-ranking Whites, such "Barbardians" soon formed a creolized core around which successive waves of arrivants from Africa would in due course accrete, though the way they did so, as well as the extent, was anything but symmetrical and continuous.

Turning to the material culture of the earliest Jamaican slaves, it is not its "creoleness" but its "Africanness"—or at least its radical otherness from the norms and values of those who described it—that will strike us most. In dress, housing, music, and dance and in their funerary customs, the slaves were most emphatically "them," not "us" or even distantly related to the world of "us." Thus, despite being issued at Christmas "a little Canvas Jacket or Breeches," the slaves, male and female alike, go about "almost naked," says Sloane, "their Cloths serving them but a very small part of the year." They live in "small,

6. A "white Jamaican" is a locally born person of "pure" European ancestry; a "Jamaican White" is an "apparently white person with a partially black ancestry" (Douglass 1992:8).

7. The Maroon communities, which in 1655 were already multiethnic and partially creolized (see Campbell 1990:16), do not seem to have played a major part in the creolization of plantation slaves, though the "semipermeable membrane" (Craton 1982:64) that both separated and linked the two groups certainly permitted all manner of cultural and other exchange. It was only *after* 1665 that, thanks to fresh waves of African-born runaways, the Maroons acquired the markedly "African"—and specifically Akan—character that despite undergoing significant recreolization after emancipation, they have not lost to this day. Perhaps, as Craton says (1982:64), the importance of the Maroons is that they offer "a rival version of creolization [that] in some respects . . . resembled that which occurred within the plantation" but that "depended on freedom and free enterprise, not on constraint and an alien form of agricultural exploitation." For a recent discussion of the mutations of Maroon culture from the seventeenth century up to the present, see Bilby 1994.

oblong, thatch'd Huts, in which they have all their Moveables or Goods, which are generally a Mat to lie on, a Pot of Earth to boil their Victuals in, either Yams, Plantains, or Potatoes, with a little salt Mackerel, and a Calabash or two for Cups and Spoons." They "take great pleasure in having their woolly curled Hair, cut into Lanes or Walks as the *Parterre* of a Garden," something that Sloane has observed them doing "for want of a better Instrument, with a broken piece of a Glass Bottle." At one time the slaves "were allowed the use of Trumpets after their Fashions, and Drums made of pieces of a hollow Tree, covered on one end with any green Skin, and stretched with Thouls or Pins." But "making use of these in their Wars at home in *Africa*, it was thought too much inciting them to Rebellion, and so they were prohibited by the Customs of the Island": they are now limited to "several sorts of Instruments in imitation of Lutes, made of small Gourds fitted with Necks, strung with Horse hairs, or the peeled stalks of climbing Plants or Withs." It is these, plucked or bowed, that accompany the songs—"all bawdy, or leading that way"—that they sing when they forgather "at nights, or on Feast days," while other slaves dance with "Rattles ty'd to their Legs and Wrists, and in their Hands, with which they make a noise, keeping time with one who makes a sound answering it on the mouth of an empty Gourd or Jar with his Hand." It is a first mention of the weekend "plays" that in the century to come will form the spiritual heart of Jamaican slave culture.

Surprisingly, in view of the sudden influx of thousands of "saltwater" slaves into the colony, slave family life is in Sloane's account impressively stable, perhaps thanks to the planters' decision to "buy Wives in proportion to their Men, lest the Men should wander to neighbouring plantations." Whatever the reason, the slaves are strongly monogamous, and "so great a love" do they have for their children that "no Master dare sell or give away one of their little ones, unless they care not whether their Parents hang themselves or no." But such solidarity went well beyond family to embrace the whole slave community and was enshrined in the burial rites on which all white observers would comment for more than a century to come. "The *Negroes* from some Countries think they return to their own Country when they die in *Jamaica*," writes Sloane, "and therefore regard death but little, imagining they shall change their condition by that means from servile to free, and so for this reason often cut their own Throats" (all quotations from Sloane 1707:1:xlvii–lviii). To this end, wrote John Taylor in 1688, when Jamaican slaves place a corpse in its grave, they bury along with it "casadar bread, roasted fowles, sugar, rum, tobacco, & pipes with fier to light his pipe withall" to sustain it on its homeward journey to Africa. Then they "fill up the grave, and eat and drink thereon, singing in their own language [and] very dolefully desiring the dead corpse (by kissing the grave) to acquaint their father, mother, husband and other relations of their present condition & slavery as he passes thru their country towards the pleasant mountain, which message they bellow out to the dead corpse in a dolefull sound, and goe kiss the grave & depart" (quoted in Handler and Lange 1978:199, 202–3). Clearly no "deep, amnesiac blow"[8] had obliterated these slaves' memory of their native land, nor would it obliterate that of African-born slaves through the duration of slavery.[9]

Despite the existence of a core of creolized "Barbadian" slaves, therefore, the bulk of the slave population of late seventeenth-century Jamaica remained thoroughly wedded to its African origins. Signs of incipient creolization are few but are present nonetheless. The good placed in the grave are not African but quintessentially Jamaican; the slaves' "victuals" appear to combine local vegetables (yams, plantains, calabash) with additional ingredients of European origin (salt mackerel), and the resultant dish is "creole" in at least the minimum sense that it is not identifiably African or European; the slaves' use of simples and "balm" is said by Sloane (1707:1:liv) to have been learned mainly from the surviving Arawak remnant, and one of the slave songs transcribed for Sloane by a French musician named Baptiste has been shown to combine two distinct African musical traditions in a way that suggests a meeting, if not yet a merging, of African cultures in the New World (see Rath 1993:724–25). Finally, it is possible to recognize in one of the slave dances recorded by Sloane (1707:1:xlvix) the African-derived nucleus of what by 1800 will have developed into Jamaica's first fully national art form, Jonkonnu: "Their Dances consist in great activity and strength of Body, and keeping time, if it can be. They very often tie Cows Tails to their Rumps, and add such other odd things to their Bodies in several places, as gives them a very extraordinary appearance." There was an African core, then, on and out of which, with the addition of other cultural materials, a syncretic Afro-Creole culture would in time be con-

---

8. The reference is to the well-known poem "Laventille" by Derek Walcott (1965:35), which concludes as follows:

> Something inside is laid wide like a wound.
>
> some open passage that has cleft the brain,
> some deep, amnesiac blow. We left
> somewhere a life we never found,
>
> customs and gods that are not born again,
> some crib, some grill of light
> clanged shut on us in bondage, and withheld
>
> us from the world below us and beyond,
> and in its swaddling cerements we're still bound.

9. Giving evidence to the parliamentary committee on slavery in the early 1790s, one slave-owner (Mark Cook) stated that he had heard his slaves "speak very much in favour of their own country, and express much grief at leaving it. I never knew one but wished to go back again" (quoted in Brathwaite 1974:40).

structed. But before this Jamaican slave life would, between 1700 and 1750, become still more obviously "African" thanks to the rapidly accelerating influx of "Guiney-birds" into the colony.

## Phase Two: Consolidation and Expansion, 1700–1750

Already seriously outnumbered by 1700, the white population of Jamaica had by 1750 shrunk to a still smaller fraction of the whole as more and more Africans were sucked into the colony to meet the plantation system's insatiable demand for labor. The disproportion between Whites and Blacks was greatest in the early 1720s (7,100 to 80,000), then adjusted somewhat in favor of the former: approximately 10,000 to 100,000 in 1739, 18,000 to 167,000 in 1768, 25,000 to 210,000 in 1787 (D'Costa and Lalla 1990:17). But these figures give little idea of the ratio of Whites to Blacks *on the plantations*, where one White to fifteen Blacks, rising on some plantations to one to twenty, was probably the norm by the 1750s. From the Whites' point of view, the problem was compounded because the white population was by now made up largely of transients. As their prosperity grew, plantation owners left the colony for lives of leisure in the metropole, and the running of plantations devolved more and more on attorneys, themselves without "roots" in the colony, whose interest in the long-term well-being of the plantations—and above all of the slaves—in their charge was nil: short-term profitability was all that concerned them. Lower down in the white class hierarchy, the pattern was the same: overseers, bookkeepers, and craftsmen were all birds of passage, working one year on this plantation, another year on that, before moving on to another colony or returning "home" to England or Scotland. In theory the Great House was the center of plantation existence, the sun all else revolved around. But by mid-century that center was frequently empty or a mere temporary residence for transient Whites, and the plantation's center of gravity—its moral core, so to speak—had shifted from Great House to Negro Village. By 1780 slaves would identify much more with "their" plantation than would the nomadic white personnel responsible for its day-to-day running.

Probably the distance between masters (or their surrogates) and slaves was never greater than between 1700 and 1760. On plantations of three to four hundred slaves, face-to-face contacts between Whites and the predominantly African-born field slaves would be comparatively rare: power was now mediated, for the most part, through the crucial figure—crucial in the literal sense, for he stood at the crux, the crossing point, of black-white relations—of the head driver, whence it would transit, via the driver's "team" of assistants (recruited, like their superior, from among creole slaves) to the slave population as a whole. On most plantations, after 1700 Whites would deal directly, at least in the day-to-day routine, only with house slaves (almost always Creoles,

and frequently colored) and skilled slaves who likewise belonged overwhelmingly to the locally born black and colored labor force. In particular,
few Whites would venture into the Negro Village, so that at night and on
weekends slaves were able to lead a quasi-autonomous existence, free at least
of direct white surveillance. A basic temporal binarism—daytime for Busha,
nighttime (plus weekends and feast days) for Neger[10]—came to structure the
whole slave experience, which in the interstices and intervals that plantation
labor vouchsafed it was comparatively free to develop according to its own
logic; and that logic, during the first half of the eighteenth century, appears to
have been preponderantly African.

There was, of course, one very good reason for this: between 1700 and
1750 the overwhelming majority of slaves in Jamaica were themselves first-
generation arrivants from Africa. On the Worthy Park estate studied by Michael Craton, no fewer than 80 percent of the 240 slaves in 1730 were African
born, and 130 of them retained African names, of which 60 were Akan day-
names (Craton 1978:54–55),[11] suggesting that, whatever official policy may
have laid down concerning the mixing, for security reasons, of slaves from
different "tribes," ethnic identities were at this stage well able to survive the
trauma of capture, transportation, and "seasoning." Moreover, new arrivants
were commonly assigned for such seasoning to established slaves of their own
ethnic group, and as late as 1785 Bryan Edwards could describe how settled
slaves would adopt such compatriots "because, amongst other considerations,
they expected to revive and retrace in the conversation of their new visitors,
the remembrance and ideas of past pleasures and scenes of their youth," while
the newcomers "considered themselves as the adopted children of those by
whom they were thus protected, calling them parents and venerating them as
such" (Edwards, 1806:2:341–42). Not only were old ties and solidarities not
entirely dissolved by the ordeal of the Middle Passage, but new ones were
formed in the very holds of the ships, and many observers stressed how "shipmate is the dearest word and bond of affectionate sympathy among the Africans . . . they look upon each other's children mutually as their own" (James
Kelly, 1838, quoted in Patterson 1967:150). Children addressed their parents'
shipmates as "uncle" and "aunt," and sexual intercourse between men and
women of the same boatload was viewed as incestuous on the grounds that

10. Cf. McDonald (1993:167): "The recent historiography of slavery has emphasized how
slaves differentiated between their lives from sunup to sundown, as plantation laborers, and their lives
from sundown to sunup, when, relatively free of planter control, they developed systems of family
and community relations and engaged in cultural, artistic and religious pursuits." Or as the slave
quoted by Bryan Edwards (1806:2:291) succinctly puts it, "Sleep hab no massa."

11. At Drax Hall at much the same time (1735), 178 out of 345 slaves had African names,
among which Akan day-names predominated (Armstrong 1990:37). It goes without saying that many
slaves with "official" European-style names would have used their "country names" among themselves
(see Hall 1989:124–25).

"they form an attachment for each other resembling that of brother and sister, and which is prohibitory of further intimacy" (William Sells, 1823, quoted in Dirks 1987:115). Not for nothing do the terms *sibi* (< *sippi* < *shippi*) and *mati* survive in the English-based Creoles of Surinam to designate especially close nonkin relationships (Mintz and Price 1992:43–44).

New slaves may therefore have arrived in the Caribbean as "crowds" or "aggregates" (Mintz and Price 1992:20), wrenched from any communal identities and structures, but the Jamaican evidence suggests a fairly rapid reincorporation into new social patterns that were in part African derived and in part newly created. But given the preponderance of African-born slaves, it is not surprising that the description of Jamaican slave culture given in Charles Leslie's *New History of Jamaica* (1740) does not differ substantially from Hans Sloane's account of slave life as it was half a century earlier. Slaves still go about seminaked (35), and neither their funerary customs (307–9)[12] nor their dances and music (310) show any significant impress of creolization: "They have two musical Instruments, like Kettle-Drums, for each Company of Dancers, with which they make a very barbarous Melody. They have other musical Instruments, as a *Bangil*, not much unlike our Lute in anything but the Musick; the *Rookaw*, which is Two Sticks jagged; and a *Jenkgoving*, which is a way of clapping their Hands on the Mouth of Two Jars: These are all played together, accompanied with Voices, which made a very terrible kind of Harmony." On the other hand, their diet is now thoroughly and recognizably creole, consisting of "Oglio's or Pepper-pots, which some here are exceeding fond of; they take Callilu . . . and boil it with beaten Maiz or *Indian* Corn (which they call *Fu-Fu*), Herring, salt fish, and red Pepper, and when 'tis ready, eat it as we do Broth" (33). Leslie confirms what Sloane says of the importance—economic, cultural, and psychological alike—of the slaves' own provision grounds and adds vital new intelligence concerning the growth of an "alternative" marketing system for vegetables and livestock that "some of them, who are more industrious than others . . . , carry to Markets on the *Sundays* (which is the only Market-day in *Jamaica*) and sell for a little Money, with which they purchase Salt-Beef, Fish, or Pork, to make their *Oglios* or Pepper-Pot" (306). This crucial innovation apart, the first half of the eighteenth century seems to have been static in terms of *cultural* creolization. What was

12. "When one is carried out to his Grave, he is attended with a vast Multitude, who conduct his Corps in something of a ludicrous manner: They sing all the way, and they who bear it on their Shoulders, make a feint of stopping at every Door they pass. . . . The nearest Relation kills [a hog], the Intrails are buried, the four Quarters are divided, and a kind of Soup made, which is brought in a Calabash or Gourd, and, after waving it Three times, it is set down; then the Body is put in the Ground; all the while they are covering it with Earth, the Attendants scream out in a terrible manner, which is not the Effect of Grief, but of Joy; they beat on their wooden Drums, and the Women with their Rattles make a hideous Noise: After the Grave is filled up, they place the Soup which they had prepared at the Head, and a Bottle of Rum at the Feet" (Leslie 1740:308–9).

"Slave Play on the Dombi Plantation [Surinam]," by Dirk Valkenburg (1707). Den kongelige Maleri- og Skulptursamling, Statens Museum for Kunst, Copenhagen.

"creole" (or creolized) in 1700 remained so in 1750, and what was "African" stayed "African." Otherwise there was no significant change.

The principal caveat to this judgment remains language, about which Leslie gives us only the sketchiest details. Loosely, and predictably, he tells us that *"Creolian* Negroes . . . all speak *English"*—presumably he means an at least partly creolized English—and, no less predictably, he says that "the Slaves are brought from several Places in *Guiney,* which are different from one another in Language, and consequently they can't converse freely" (310–11). On the other hand, it is difficult to imagine that the speaking of Creole would not have made some ingress into the mass of African-born slaves, the agents of transmission being once again the locally born slave elite, many of them descended from the original "Barbadian" core group, who, though "swamped by the greatly increased influx of African Negroes" (Patterson 1967:146), nonetheless retained the crucial positions of power and privilege on the interface between the white minority and the great mass of slaves. Drivers—those liminal beings who straddled both worlds—were obviously key figures in the diffusion of Creole, which, as Mervyn Alleyne has stressed (1980:184–85, 194), happened primarily and essentially *within* the slave community as a whole rather than *between* that community and the Whites. Or to put is more simply, African-born slaves were creolized through their regular interactions with creole slaves rather than through their sporadic encounters with Whites.[13] At the same time that Creole was spreading "downward" to the mass of African-born slaves, there is evidence from the 1730s that it was also spreading "upward" to locally born Whites and to those other Whites who remained in the colony long enough to be acculturated to its mores. Jamaican Whites, wrote John Atkins in 1736, are "half Negrish in the Manners, proceeding from the promiscuous and confined Conversation with their Relations, the Servants at the Plantations, and have a language especially pleasant, a kind of Gypsy Gibberish, that runs smoothest in swearing" (quoted in D'Costa and Lalla 1990: 23–24). By 1750 a pattern of diffusion had been established. From an original nucleus composed of "Barbadian" slaves and their offspring, the speaking of Creole spread to *some* of the first generations of Africans but to *all,* or virtually all, of their children.[14] Then, from this enlarged Creole-speaking nucleus, new arrivants from Africa learned to speak a heavily Africanized form of Creole whose most obvious African features would be eliminated from the speech of their children, which would then conform closely to the Creole of the foundational core. The process would be repeated with each new wave of arrivants, so that at any time a range of Creoles would be being spoken on the plantation. As Mervyn Alleyne has argued (1980:185, 198), a continuum of Creoles,

13. For evidence of a similar pattern of creolization in the French-speaking colonies, see Chaudenson 1992:117–21.

14. On the crucial role of children in the process of creolization, see Chaudenson 1992:90.

ranging through various interlectal forms from the Anglo-Creole of the elite to the Afro-Creole of the masses is not a recent development in Jamaica but is inherent in the original process of creolization itself. At any one time Afro-Creole was being learned and unlearned as slaves moved into and out of the state and stage of arrivant, so that though the number of African-born slaves grew continuously between 1700 and 1750, so, exponentially, did the number of Creole-speakers, who in due course ceased to be a core and became a majority. The hypothesis is that by 1750 the speaking of Creole had developed a momentum that, by stages, drew all new arrivants through an original Afro-Creole to something much closer to the mesolectal Creole of the slave elite. As Alleyne has explained, the development of a "stable" or "mature" Creole-speaking society involves a progressive loss of the Ur-Creole of the arrivant: in a curious way, creolization and decreolization become opposite but complementary sides of a single linguistic process. By 1760 *linguistic* creolization was without doubt well advanced. *Cultural* creolization, as we have seen, lagged significantly behind, but, as Creole-speakers became a majority, the conditions were created for the gradual transformation of a culture that up to that time had, despite certain creolized features (notably diet), remained essentially African in character.

## Phase Three: The Fulcrum, 1750–1780

The year 1760 represents a significant watershed in the evolution of Jamaican plantation society. In the first place that year the system sustained, and fought off, the most serious eighteenth-century threat to its survival in the form of a major insurrection led by the African-born, and probably Akan-speaking, slave Tacky. Tacky's rebellion was the last of the "old-style" African-dominated uprisings in Jamaica. Planned and largely manned by slaves of "Coromantee" (Akan) origin, it was preceded by the taking of oaths and by ritual dancing akin to the Ikem dance performed in Ashanti society on the eve of war and aimed, like similar African-dominated revolts before it, at a "war of racial extermination and the establishment of an ethnic autocracy on Ashanti lines" (Craton 1982:122). Although creole slaves were also involved, the traumatized Whites identified the uprising with Africans and African cultural practices and, the rebellion quelled, took steps to eliminate what they saw as its origin and focus, the practice of "Obeah." A law of 1760 prescribed death or transportation for "any Negro or other Slave, who shall pretend to any supernatural Power, and be detected in making use of any Blood, Feathers, Parrot Beaks, Dogs Teeth, Alligators Teeth, broken Bottles, Grave Dirt, Rum, Eggshell or any other Materials relative to the Practice of Obeah or Witchcraft, in order to delude and impose on the Minds of others" (quoted in Brathwaite 1971:162). Hitherto the planters and their surrogates had been largely indifferent to the cultural practices of their slaves. After 1760 they became "far more concerned about questions of standardization and control" (Craton 1978:55) and for the first time took an active interest, if not in their creolization, then at least in their de-Africanization. Significantly, it was only after 1760 that Thomas Thistlewood—of whom more shortly—began smashing his slaves' musical instruments as a matter of policy: "[3d February 1764] At night, about 11 o'clock, broke Job's banjar [banjo] to pieces at the mill house," "Saturday 20th November 1773: About 10 o'clock this night, got up and went to my Negro houses, where found Mrs. North's George playing upon the Banjar to Lincoln. I chopped all up in pieces with my cutlass, & reprimanded them" (Hall 1989:131, 182).

But it was not only, and not even primarily, from the Whites that the pressures toward de-Africanization were derived. Between 1750 and 1760 the demographic balance between creole and African-born slaves finally began to tip in favor of the former. On both the Worthy Park and Drax Hall estates, African names became progressively rarer after 1750, falling at Drax Hall from 51.6 percent of the slaves in 1735 (178 out of 345) to 24.6 percent (85 out of 325) in 1753 and 19.5 percent (66 out of 339) in 1780 (Armstrong 1990:37; cf. Craton 1978:156–57).[15] Nor should one assume that Whites alone were responsible for this onomastic revolution. Creole slaves not only gave "English" forenames to their own children but, as an aside in Thistlewood's diary reveals, were also actively involved in renaming African slaves: "Saturday 25th [May 1754]: p.m. Mr Cope sent an Ebo Negro man (a new Negro) he bought today. Our Negroes have named him Hector. I put him to live with London" (Hall 1989:63). More and more, the culture of locally born slaves was becoming hegemonic, and, if London was a creole, or even a creolized, slave, we may expect that he viewed the African-born "Hector" with something of the disdain described by the planter historian Edward Long in 1774: "The Creole Blacks differ much from the Africans, not only in manner, but in beauty of shape, feature, and complexion. They hold the Africans in the uttermost contempt, stiling them "salt-water Negroes" and "Guiney birds"; but value themselves on their own pedigree, which is reckoned the more honourable, the further it removes from an African, or transmarine ancestor" (Long 1774:2: 410). Their positions of (relative) power and prestige sometimes enhanced, as Long implies, by a relative lightness of skin, the creole slaves and their lan-

15. According to Craton (1978:156), "the gradual, and almost certainly voluntary, shift in the types of names—from a majority of African names to an increasing number of single English names, and to the first Christian names with surnames—provides a telling index of the decline of African influences and the increasing influence of Creole, Christian, and status norms." See, however, the cautionary observations in Higman 1984b:61. On African day-names in Jamaica and their gradual disappearance, see DeCamp 1967.

guage and culture acted as a cynosure and standard for incoming Africans.[16] This had been the case from the outset, but now that they were so many (by 1760, wrote Long, Africans were "chiefly awed into subjection by the superior multitude of Creole Blacks [2:444]), their power to influence and transform was that much greater. In other words, cultural creolization, like the linguistic creolization that preceded it and rendered it possible, took place primarily not between Whites and Blacks, but between one group of slaves and another. Not that the Africans always succumbed to the pressures placed on them; as we shall see, what is striking about cultural creolization is not just its speed and extent but that it should have left so much untouched or only barely transformed in its wake.

The potency of the Creole language was irresistible, however. African languages survived, creating considerable apprehension among Whites; wrestling with an African runaway named Congo Sam, Thistlewood calls out for assistance to two onlooking slave women, Bella and Abigail; but "he spoke to them in his language and I was much afraid of them" (Hall 1989:54).[17] The continued currency of African languages also gave slaves who spoke them the means of mocking their masters with impunity, as Thistlewood also reveals: "Egypt Negroes privately called me ABBAUMI APPEA, i.e. 'No For Play.' Mr John Hartnole they call CRAKRA JUBA, i.e. 'Crazy Somebody'" (146). Nonetheless, Creole in its different forms had clearly established itself as the most widely spoken, if not dominant, language in the colony, and it is from about this time that, again thanks to Thistlewood, we get our first authentic examples of Creole speech utterances, like the gleeful cry of the rebel slave Davie who, hoisted up on a gibbet to die of starvation, sees two white people fighting and exclaims delightedly, "'Tha's good, me love for see so'; and seeing a monkey leap upon a pail of water a Negro wench was carrying on her head, laughed heartily and said: 'That monkey damned rogue, true,' &c. &c." (107). Or again, the slave woman Margaritta who, asked by "a Buckrah . . . to go in the bush with him near the Styx bridge," tartly retorts "'Me bin say, heh, no me go, bin say warrah [what is this], &c.'" (137–38). These two utterances ring unmistakably true and, even if Thistlewood's transcriptions are only partially accurate, clearly belong to somewhat different "points" on the Creole continuum: Davie's somewhere in the mesolect, Margaritta's rather "lower," more in the basilect. Yet as Long indicates, there were modes of Creole far more "archaic" or "basic" than that spoken by Margaritta, namely the kind of proto-Creole used as a medium by newly arrived Africans and the creole slaves charged

16. By 1780 between 8 and 10 percent of the slaves at Drax Hall were of mixed race, and not one of them was listed as a field slave (Armstrong 1990:39–41).

17. This incident cautions against attaching too much significance to the bearing of English forenames: despite their names, Bella and Abigail appear to be African born.

with their "seasoning": "The Africans speak their respective dialects, with some mixture of broken English. The language of the Creoles is bad English, larded with the Guiney dialect, owing to their adopting the African words, in order to make themselves understood by the imported slaves; which they find much easier than teaching these strangers to learn English" (Long 1774:2:426). Despite what Long says, it is likely that, when speaking together, creole slaves would *switch codes* and, dropping the more obviously African features they used with arrivants, speak the kind of mesolectal Creole of which *The History of Jamaica* gives an early and valuable description: "In their conversation, [creole slaves] confound all the moods, tenses, cases and conjugations, without mercy: for example; *I surprise* (for, I am surprized); *me glad for to see you* (pro, I am glad to see you); *how you do* (for, how d'ye do?); *me tank you; me very well;* &c." Long goes on to make another valuable, if no longer surprising comment: "This sort of gibberish likewise infects many of the White Creoles, who learn it from their [black or colored] nurses in infancy, and meet with much difficulty, as they advance in years, to shake it entirely off, and express themselves with correctness" (2:427).[18] All this conforms Alleyne's hypothesis concerning the early existence *in Jamaica* of a graduated continuum of Creoles and further suggests the capacity that all but the newest arrivants possessed of switching codes and of moving, within limits, from one "zone" on the continuum to another. Mid-eighteenth-century Jamaica confronts us, then, not with a situation of diglossia, such as may have obtained in the French-speaking colonies by this time, but with a considerably more fluid linguistic space "across," "up," and "down" which many Creole speakers were, again within obvious limits, capable of moving as social context and expressive need required.

The situation regarding cultural creolization was considerably more rigid, though here too there is evidence of an emerging creole continuum in at least certain facets of life. Most notably, the creole cooking created by the slaves (possibly influenced by Arawak models) from the local vegetables they grew and the assortment of ingredients (salt fish and salt meat) they received from their owners had, doubtless in more elaborate forms, moved into the upper reaches of society, so that not only white Creoles but also the expatriate English are said by Long to have acquired a taste for the "olios and pepperpots" of the slaves (Long 1774:2:267). On arriving at his first plantation, the young Thomas Thistlewood ate "some Clucking hen broth, and also Tum Tum of plantain and fish beat together, with old Sharper who is a sensible Negro" (Hall 1989:14), and though as he got older his tastes, in food as in other things, became considerably more extravagant, the huge blowouts he enjoyed with neighboring plantation cronies—"stewed mudfish, and pickled

18. See also Long's comment (1774:2:278) on white creole children's "constant intercourse from their birth with Negro domestics, whose drawling, dissonant gibberish they insensibly adopt, and with it no small tincture of their awkward carriage and vulgar manners."

crabs, stewed hog's head, fried liver, &c. quarter of roast pork with paw paw sauce and Irish potatoes, bread, roast yam and plantains, a boiled pudding (very good), cheese, musk melon, water melon, oranges, French brandy said to be Cognac, punch and porter"—were still recognizably part of an emerging creole cuisine (170). The slaves' diet seems to have become somewhat more varied, incorporating now, in addition to the long-established root vegetables and salt fish, "jerked hog, or fowls" reared, no doubt, on the slaves' own small-holdings; roasted, stuffed cane rats, called "Sir Charles Price rats" by the slaves after the planter who had supposedly introduced them into Jamaica, were also much favored, though this was an aspect of the local cuisine that Long chose not to explore (1774:2:413–14). Although the distance from Thistlewood's boiled crabs and stewed snook to the field slaves' salt mackerel and shad was as vast as that from the Euro-Creole of the elite to the Afro-Creole of the first gang, all were located at widely separate points along a single embryonic continuum.

Dress too shows a certain narrowing, no doubt very marginal, of the distance between Whites and Blacks. In the first instance, there is no suggestion in Long or in Thistlewood, as there is in Sloane and Leslie, that slaves worked seminaked in the fields. They were supplied cloth by their masters—the familiar heavy "oznabrig"—and, at least on Thistlewood's plantation, were responsible for making it up themselves. Some slaves received cast-off clothing from Whites—when Thistlewood gets a new blue broadcloth coat, Solon gets his old brown one (Hall 1989:271)—but there is little in the published parts of his diary of the extraordinary explosion of slave elegance, ostentation, and style that we shall witness toward the end of the century. What is clear, however, is that certain privileged slaves could dress very much better than their less favored brothers and sisters, witness the good fortune of Thistlewood's black (and possible African-born) mistress Phibba, who receives from her lover regular gifts of "check, linen, handkerchiefs, needles, hat, cloak, &c." (231) and on one occasion no fewer than six pairs of shoes (225). "I never saw a Field Negro with a Shoe on," wrote one visitor to Jamaica as late as 1832 (John Baillie, quoted in Sheridan 1985:194).[19] Clearly the vestimental gap between privileged slaves and their inferiors was much more significant than that between them and their masters.

Turning to other areas of culture, there is some early evidence of the emergence of "mesolectal" musical forms in Long's remark that there are "Creole Blacks, who, without being able to read a single note, are known to play

19. Shoes were essential to health, protecting not only against burns, cuts, and bruises but above all against the dreaded jiggers, fleas that burrow into the soles of the feet and lay eggs, causing ulcerated swellings that required cutting out and sometimes amputation of the infected foot or leg (see Sheridan 1985:193–94). The slaves who most needed this protection—the field slaves—were the ones most likely to lack it.

twenty or thirty tunes, country-dances, minuets, airs, and even sonatas, on the violin; and catch, with an astounding readiness, whatever they hear played or sung, especially if it is lively and striking" (1774:2:262–63). But here more than ever caution is in order: there can be little doubt that the predominant form of music was still, and would long remain, the heavily African style of singing and playing that appears unchanged in its essentials from the account of Hans Sloane (1707) to that of William Beckford (1790:2:387). Likewise burial rites—"Every funeral is a kind of festival," says Long (1774:2:421)— show no significant change from 1700 to 1780. One slave woman was given leave by Thistlewood in 1771 "to Throw Water (as they called it) for her boy Johnie who died some months ago; and although I gave them strict charge to make no noise, yet they transgressed, by beating the Coombie loud, singing high, &c. Many Negroes there from all over the country" (Hall 1989:185–86). On the other hand, there are tantalizing glimpses in Thistlewood's diary of African-derived cultural forms that will pay vital roles in the syncretic creole cultures of the future: the "many diverting Nancy [Anancy] stories (as Negroes call them)" told by the slave woman Vine that, significantly if ironically, Thistlewood finds "entertaining enough" (160), or the "Boxing Stick" Thistle-wood confiscates from a slave called Paradise Sam, in which one can clearly discern the equivalents of the fearsome batons used by stickfighters in Trini-dad in the nineteenth and early twentieth centuries (233).[20] And as though to prove that creole cultures are not just of African provenance, Thistlewood makes a casual aside in his diary entry of 11 June 1778, of whose significance for the future he could have no inkling: "In the evening Mr Beckford & Mr John Lewis, &c. played at cricket" (256). Were there slaves watching? And if there were, did they think that here there was something of Buckra's that they could take over and not so much mimic as invest with their own meanings and style?[21]

However, it was not with bat and ball that Thomas Thistlewood made his most notable contribution to the future of *créolité*, but rather through the en-

20. "It is made of heavy hard wood, is about one inch square, & 20⁷⁄₁₀ inches long, rather tapering towards the end held in the hand, and rounded for better holding in the hand for near 10 inches, with a hole for string 3⁸⁄₁₀ inches from the end. This is a very unlawful weapon for Negroes to be permitted to have." On stickfighting in Trinidad, see chapter 4 below. Two forms of stick dance known as *warrick* and *kittiballi* are still performed in Jamaica (see Ryman 1978–79:9).

21. The discovery on the banks of the River Tweed in the 1980s of a belt buckle depicting a black man wearing a slave collar batting in what is clearly a West Indian setting (probably Barbadian) suggests that some slaves did play cricket as early as the 1780s (see Marcus Williams, "Mystery of a Mud-Covered Buckle," *Times*, 5 November 1986). That the slave in question appears to be connected with the Royal Navy is particularly significant given "the mutual confidence and familiarity" that were said to obtain between slaves and sailors: "In the presence of the sailor, the Negro feels as a man" (James Kelly, 1838, quoted in Brathwaite 1974:17).

counters he records in an arch mixture of English and abbreviated Latin on practically every page of the published parts of his diary:

> Friday, 9th May [1760]: In the morning *Cum* Warsoe *Sup*. Ladder top by the corn-loft side in the curing house. Stans! Backwd. . . . In the evening *Cum* Amelia (belonging Miss Sally Witter) *Sup. Lect.* She had been in the country selling soap, and would sleep in my house. (95)

> *Cum* Mountain Susannah. *Sup* Chest Lid TT No 2, Books & wearing apparel, *in me. dom.* (124)

> Thursday, 20th October [1768]: p.m. *Cum* Salley, *mea, Sup. Terr* at foot of cotton tree by New Ground. West north west from the house (*sed non bene*). (150)

Thistlewood's diary merely confirms, and describes with niggling precision as to time, place, and manner, what has always been known—that middle- and low-ranking plantation Whites had routine sexual access to the female slaves in their charge, regularly imposing themselves by force or by threat or, as was Thistlewood's usual practice, paying for their pleasure with two or three "bitts" or with promises of privileges, gifts, or whatever. Such sexual transactions were brief, casual, and in most cases utterly dehumanized, though with one female slave, Phibbah, Thistlewood had what turned out to be a lifelong association not, it seems, without respect and affection on both sides. The endless stream of Sukeys, Mirtillas, Sabinas, Egypt Susannahs, Violets, and Little Dolls who pass through the diary's pages seem to have been house slaves and field slaves indifferently: their speech and responses are never recorded, so we can only speculate on their response to Thistlewood's attentions. These brutish encounters in corn loft and canefield point not only to the violent, venal, and transgressive dimension of creolization, but to the ambivalent part often played in it by slave women who were both its most abused victims and, in a minority of cases (such as Phibbah's), among its most obvious beneficiaries. For Phibbah, as we have seen, undoubtedly profited from her association with Thistlewood, receiving regular gifts (including a pair of spectacles when she got older) for services rendered and able to sell the horse she owned to a slave on another plantation for seven pounds (94): clearly Long's claim that slaves held 20 percent of the currency circulating in Jamaica cannot be dismissed (see McDonald 1993:31). It is clear from Thistlewood's account that Phibbah was a woman of power, sometimes chastising female slaves in her charge (see Hall 1989:198) and, like many colored (or, more rarely, black) housekeepers of her kind, playing a "role in the subtle control of plantation slaves [that] should not be underestimated" (Brathwaite 1971:143). Thus the position of slave women in the history of creolization is paradoxical in the extreme. Some, mainly African-born women, were among its most active opponents, clinging to ancestral beliefs, customs, and memories (see Bush 1981:259) and, like the delirious "Old Sybil" on Thistlewood's plantation, "singing [their] country" (Hall 1989:34) in anger and anguish at what they had suffered. But others, mainly but not exclusively house slaves, lived closer to Buckra than all but the head driver and the most skilled of the specialized male slaves and absorbed from him (and when she was present, from his wife) ways of acting and thinking that they would in due course pass on to their offspring. Thus they became, at once or successively, victims, beneficiaries, and finally agents of assimilation. I shall return to these and related issues in my discussion of the "female" culture of respectability in chapter 4.

The picture that emerges from Thistlewood's extraordinary diary of Jamaica in the 1750s, 1760s, 1770s, and early 1780s, then, is one of a very relative narrowing of the cultural gap between Whites and Blacks and of the emergence of at least the first elements of a creole cultural continuum. The real but limited *cultural* creolization recorded in the diary, however, did not and could not undermine the fundamental reality of plantation slavery, namely the unbridgeable *social* and *political*—and beyond that *existential*—distance separating Buckra from Neger. Thistlewood's plantation, no less than the plantations described by Sloane and Leslie, was founded on the regular, routinized deployment of violence, often of the degenerate and sadistic kind that degrades instigator, agent, and victim alike: "Gave ['Port Royal'] a moderate whipping, pickled him well, made Hector shit in his mouth, immediately put a gag whilst his mouth was full & made him wear it 4 or 5 hours. Friday, 30th July 1756: Punch catched at Salt River and brought home. Flogged him and Quacoo well, and then washed in salt pickle, lime juice & bird pepper; also whipped Hector for losing his hoe, made New Negro Joe piss in his eyes & mouth &c." (72–73). This no amount of creolization of speech, dress, or diet could modify or mitigate, nor could it diminish the loathing of slaves who, on hearing of the death of Thistlewood's nephew John, released a salvo of gunshots "with a loud Huzza after each . . . , for joy that my Kinsman is dead, I imagine. Strange impudence" (133). Finally, toward the end of his life, stricken with rheumatism and perhaps fearing at last for his immortal soul, Thistlewood did something he had never previously done in Jamaica: he went to church. It was 7 March 1784, and Mr. Stanford "preached a very good sermon. Text 2nd Chap. Job 10th verse." The following night, he was, predictably, back "*cum Abba's Mary, mea. Sup Illa lect in illa dom.* Gave d° 4 bitts" (298). Whether it was *bene* or *non bene* he does not say, and it is to be doubted also whether at any time before, during, or after the act he gave thought to the fact that, at church the previous day, there had been "a good congregation, at least 150 *of all colours*" (ibid.; italics added). For Jamaica was changing, with

Christianity perhaps the greatest agent of change, and the process of creolization was about to enter a new, and for the first time truly revolutionary, phase of its history.

## Phase Four: Toward a Creole Synthesis, 1780–1838

In 1826 Alexander Barclay prefaced his contribution to the intensifying debate in Britain concerning "the West Indian question" by making a series of bold contrast between "Jamaica today" and "Jamaica yesterday" or, more precisely, Jamaica just twenty years earlier:

Twenty years ago, there was scarcely a negro baptized in Jamaica. Now they are nearly all baptized.

Twenty years ago, the churches were scarcely at all attended by the slaves. . . . [Now] they are all fully attended, and principally by slaves.

Twenty years ago, negroes were buried at midnight, and the funeral rites, in the forms of African superstition, were the occasion of continual excesses among those who attended. Negroes are now buried during the day, and in the same manner as the white people.

Ten years ago, the marriage rite was altogether unknown among the slaves. The number now married is not inconsiderable, and is fast increasing. (Barclay 1826:xxii–xxiii)

Each of the propositions above—to say nothing of the claim that Obeah "is now seldom heard of" (ibid.)—will be subject to qualification in the discussions that follow, but taken together they point to two indisputable truths: first, that in the twenty years following the abolition of the slave trade in 1807, Jamaica had changed more radically than at any time since the plantation revolution of the late seventeenth century, and second, that the spread of Christianity among both the slave and free colored populations was fundamental, as both cause and expression, to the transformation that had occurred.

As it happened, the Jamaican "revolution" began somewhat earlier than Barclay imagined, in the 1780s, with a series of developments that the abolition of 1807 would accentuate, accelerate, and bring to completion. The most obvious index of change was the relative, and then absolute, decline in the number of slaves imported from Africa. By the 1780s it became in general cheaper for planters to replenish their workforce from within than from without, and measures were taken, in the form of improved material conditions, threats, and incentives, to encourage the existing slave population to reproduce itself. This natalist policy had limited success, though it did not exclude a final desperate recourse to Africa in the last years of the trade. Between 1801 and 1807, no fewer than 63,000 "saltwater" slaves were shipped into the colony (Bakan 1990:51), so that as late as 1817 up to 35 percent of Jamaican slaves were African born, as opposed to a mere 7 percent in Barbados (Higman 1984a:121). Nonetheless, creole slaves now outnumbered Africans at least two to one on most plantations, and on many the proportion was much higher: at Drax Hall, for instance, only 64 out of 345 slaves (18.6 percent) were listed as African born in 1817, and only 21 (6.1 percent) had African names (Armstrong 1990:37).[22] An important consequence of the progressive creolization of the slave stock was an equalization in the ratio of males to females, which had been of the order of 150–80 to 100 in the last decades of the trade but, in the British Caribbean as a whole, fell to 101 to 100 by 1817 and 95 to 100 in 1834. There was, writes Higman (1984a:116), "a definite movement from male to female predominance" in the last twenty-five years of the slave regime.

Outnumbered, the African-born slaves were literally marginalized by the creole majority, their manners, language, and appearance stigmatized as "primitive" as in the Christmas celebrations described by James Kelly in 1838:

> [The] Africans took the sides and corners of the hall, whilst the Creoles occupied the centre and piazzas, and evidently considered themselves entitled to the best places, which the Africans cheerfully conceded to them, evincing the greatest deference to the superior civilization of the upstarts! The one class, forced into slavery, humbled and degraded, had lost everything and found no solace but the miserable one of retrospection. The other, born in slavery, never had the freedom to lose; yet did the Creole proudly assume a superiority over the African. (Quoted in Patterson 1967:152)

This sense of superiority manifested itself in all walks of life. Africans and Creoles "hate each other as cordially as the Guelphs and Ghibellines," opined M. G. Lewis in 1816 (1834:190), describing, inter alia, how creole slaves disdain to eat "a Cane-piece Cat roasted in the true African fashion" (241), how

22. At Worthy Park, on the other hand, the proportion of African-born slaves rose substantially (to 60 percent) thanks to massive imports in the 1790s, before dropping to 30 percent in 1821 and 10 percent in 1838. African names survived, but in a diluted, syncretized form, so that Akan daynames, which represented 26.3 percent of the total, fell to an average of 4.8 percent between 1783 and 1838, by which year they had disappeared completely, suggesting that the last generations of African imports "were born in places as far apart, and as different, as London and Moscow, Stockholm and Palermo" (Craton 1978:74, 156–57). Craton, however, may overstate his case, for there is evidence elsewhere of the survival of ethnic identities until the very end of slavery—for example, in James Kelly's statement in 1838 that at Christmas the different ethnic groups "formed into exclusive groups competing against each other in performing their national music" (quoted in Patterson 1967:152). On M. G. Lewis's plantation Eboe (Ibo) slaves occupied a separate area in the Negro Village (Lewis 1834:188).

they smirk as Africans bow and murmur "Tank, mass" as they receive jackets presented by Lewis (126), and finally how one creole slave woman, his cook, tells him straight out that "Massa ought to sell all the Eboes, and buy Creoles instead" (190). To the enduring split between creole and African-born slaves should be added the partly related separation of Coloureds from Blacks on the plantation and, linked but again not identical to that, the increasing disparity, in terms of lifestyle and mentality, between the (large) minority of skilled and domestic slaves (though their position was significantly different) and the mass of the field slaves. Finally, since black women were the most likely to work in the fields and the least likely to have skilled or privileged positions, an important distinction of gender ran through the entire slave community.

But the most important distinction in Jamaica remained, as ever, that between slave and free, though by 1800 the free part of society was considerably more complex and divided than it had been. There was first the divide between the expatriate British, especially colonial officials, and the local white population as a whole, which in the eyes of a snooty observer like Lady Nugent, wife of the governor, was only marginally different from the Blacks and the Coloureds: "The Creole language is not confined to the negroes. Many of the ladies, who have not been educated in England, speak a sort of broken English, with an indolent drawing of their words, that is very tiresome if not disgusting. I stood next to a lady one night, near a window, and, by way of saying something, remarked that the air was much cooler than usual; to which she answered, 'Yes, ma'am, him rail-ly too fra-ish'" (Nugent 1907:132).[23] Among the local Whites, "Town"—the white residents of Kingston, with many Jews among them—were increasingly at odds with "Country." But the most important demographic, social, and political phenomenon of the late eighteenth and early nineteenth centuries was the rapid rise of the free colored class; outnumbered in 1789 by Whites 18,000 to 10,000, it was by 1834 almost twice the size of the entire white community (31,000 to 16,000) and still more substantial if one adds the 11,000 Free Blacks in the colony (Heuman 1981a:7). A minority of the Free Coloureds were wealthy and owned slaves—perhaps as many as 50,000 all told in 1820 (Heuman 1981b:55)—but most occupied peripheral and parasitic positions in plantation society, visiting upon Blacks all the fear and contempt they themselves inspired among Whites. The position of this free colored buffer class was ambivalent in the extreme. "You brown man hab no country," say the black slaves in *Marly* (Anon. 1828:94), "only de neger and de buckra hab country," but it was precisely their "doubleness" that prompted Coloureds to consider themselves the only *true* Jamaicans. After all, as one of their spokesmen declared in 1833, "this

23. Similarly John Stewart, visiting Jamaica in the early 1800s, thought that local white women "exhibit much of the *Quashiba*," notably "an awkward and ungraceful sort of affectation in their language and manner" (Stewart 1808:160).

is our native country—we have nowhere to go" (Heuman 1981b:60). On the other hand, it was these living embodiments of creolization, combining "Africa" and "Europe" in their very physical being, who were most inclined to venerate the European, and specifically the English, at the expense of the creole and the local. In dress, manner, and sometimes speech, they set out to assimilate Englishness and so situate themselves in opposition both to white Jamaicans—who, whatever else they were, were undoubtedly creole—and to the black masses. It was they, not the Whites, who founded the Society for the Diffusion of Useful Knowledge or the St. James Institute for Promoting General and Useful Knowledge (Heuman 1981b:54) and they whose sons steadily displaced white boys at schools like Woolmer's Free School, where there were 3 colored pupils to 111 Whites in 1815, but no fewer than 360 to 90 by 1832 (Brathwaite 1971:173–74). Ironically, it was the most physically creolized section of the Jamaican population that would from the outset be the most powerful agent of cultural and linguistic *decreolization*.

By 1820, then, Jamaica was both overwhelmingly more creole and also more socially, politically, and culturally fragmented than ever before. There were at least three forms of cultural-political conflict in the colony, all interrelated and readily confused but in principle separate. First, within the white community (local and expatriate combined) there was bitter enmity between the slaveowning elite (broadly but not invariably supported by the colonial administration) and the island's most recent arrivants from Britain, the nonconformist missionaries who, since the 1790s, had been proselytizing in earnest among the nonwhite population, slave and free alike. Second, within the local community there was the conflict between slaveowner and slaves (with the free colored class peripherally and ambivalently involved) over the colony's, and indeed the empire's, question of questions: Could and should slavery survive? Finally, there was the conflict between white missionaries and slaves (and quite probably among slaves themselves) concerning the kind of Christianity the latter should follow: the moralistic, British-style nonconformism taught by the missionaries or the turbulent, charismatic Afro-Christianity autonomously created and espoused by the slaves. None of these was in any straightforward sense a conflict between "Europe" and "Africa," or even between Whites, Blacks, and Coloureds. The first was a social, political, and partly religious conflict among Whites over the social, political, and religious future of (colored and black) slaves. The second was a social, political, and partly cultural conflict among Creoles, each of the parties being no longer either "European" or "African," but communities at widely separated points on the creole continuum. Even the final conflict—between missionaries and slaves—was other, or more, than a conflict between "Europeans" and "Africans," since the slaves the missionaries proselytized were often significantly creolized before Christianization. As was widely attested, it was among *creole* slaves—and skilled, colored creoles at that—that missionaries frequently made their most important and influential converts.

There is, however, a further complicating factor. The first, and by all accounts the most successful, missionaries in Jamaica were not British but American, and more pertinent still, *black* Americans, former slaves like George Liele, Moses Baker, and George Gibb who came to the colony in the early 1780s and had already made substantial numbers of converts among slaves before serious *white* missionary activity began in 1789. Though the picture is unclear, the self-styled Black Baptists seem to have made most headway among the slaves first of Kingston and then on the plantations (Patterson 1967:210–11), whereas the white Wesleyan Methodists who followed them seen to have made their first converts mainly among the Free Blacks and Coloureds of Kingston who had previously been forced to sit in the back pews or organ loft of the city's Anglican church (Turner 1982:12). Both Black Baptists and white Wesleyan Methodists trained black and colored lay preachers for future proselytizing, but it seems clear that from the outset there was a split in style, form, manner, and church organization between the "Euro-Christianity" taught by the Whites and their nonwhite trainees and the "Afro-Christianity" taught by the Black Baptists. The political differences were still more marked. Even though in the eyes of the planter both groups were equally suspect, there can be little doubt that it was Black Baptist preachers who urged slaves to seek immediate freedom, while their Wesleyan Methodist counterparts enjoined them, in effect, to wait until freedom was given them (see Bakan 1990:57). The conflict between the two variants of Christianity was exacerbated, and complicated, when in 1813 the first white Baptist missionaries arrived in Jamaica from Britain and attempted to take over the Black Baptist church, which by then had enjoyed twenty years of autonomous existence. The Black Baptist preachers and their congregations split off to follow their own style of worship, which, giving a Christian form to long-established Myalist practices, emphasized music and dancing, "spirit possession," prophecy, and speaking in tongues. The white missionaries, however, continued to make converts, their styles of worship differing sufficiently to create significant variations among the kind of slaves and other nonwhites they appealed to, so that by the 1820s a religious version of the Creole language continuum was already in place, ranging from the Euro-Christianity—principally Methodist—of the free colored class through the "Creo-Christianity"[24] of the white-led Baptist churches to the black-led Afro-Christianity of the slave masses. All these religious forms were creolized to a greater or lesser degree; only the Anglican Church, which belatedly and ineffectively entered the battle for converts and

24. The expression is Edward Kamau Brathwaite's (1978:61), and I am using it in a somewhat different sense from his.

to which, equally belatedly, the planter class rallied for moral and spiritual sustenance, can plausibly be described as "European." Although Afro-Christianity and Euro-Christianity remained wide apart, slave religion, expressed in the form of "plays" and other burial rituals, which had been entirely outside the dominant culture before 1780, had now, thanks to the missionaries, been at least partially drawn into that culture. The "continuum of religious variation," like the "continuum of linguistic variation" it parallels, was inherently unstable, permitting new syncretic forms to appear and allowing individuals to move, as they did in their speech, from one "zone" on the continuum to another. After emancipation, as we shall see, the zone approximately designated "Afro-Christianity" would generate a further set of variant forms—Revival, Revival Zion, Pocomania, Convince, Kumina—all occupying overlapping positions on "the continuum of religious differentiation created by the meeting of Myalism and Christianity" (Alleyne 1988:91, 96, to which this whole argument is indebted).

Turning to other facets of slave culture in the last years of slavery, the evidence suggests a growing autonomy in all areas of slave life and an emergence within the very structures of plantation society of what Michael Craton (1982:332) has called a protopeasant culture and economy that the slaves would take with them when, in the years following emancipation, they left the estates en masse for the hills. According to John Blackburn, writing in 1807, slaves had "their houses, their provision grounds, their gardens and orchards which they consider as much their own property as their Master does his Estate" (quoted in McDonald 1993:19). It was not uncommon for huts, gardens, and other possessions to be bequeathed by one slave to another, and cash transactions for goods and services were part of everyday life. Slaves were virtually self-sufficient in food, and many sold their surplus at Sunday markets throughout the island where, as well as buying and selling food, clothes, housewares, tobacco, alcohol, and luxury items such as jewelry, scarves, and handkerchiefs, they could socialize with each other, drinking and gambling if they chose, effectively free of direct surveillance: in the 1790s, according to Bryan Edwards, ten thousand slaves attended Kingston market every Sunday (McDonald 1993:29; see also Mintz 1974:201–4). Even planters bought pigs and calves from their slaves, paying them in cash, especially at Christmas, since "money is more acceptable to them at this Period of the year as they wish to lay it out in little matters for finery etc. for Xmas" (David Ewart, 1807, quoted in McDonald 1993:21). Christmas, as we shall shortly see, was the focus and apogee of the whole of Jamaican slave culture.

Few Whites ever ventured into the Negro Villages, which by the early 1800s showed every sign of being autonomous, self-regulating communities, still essentially African in their physical form but beginning to incorporate European elements into an emerging, if still unstable, creole synthesis. Some

"Sunday Morning in the Country." A market-bound higgler woman meets a male acquaintance. From Richard Bridgens, *West India Scenery, with Illustration of Negro Character, the Processes of Making Sugar, etc.* (1836). Reproduced by permission of the Syndics of Cambridge University Library.

owners tried to introduce barrackslike accommodations for their slaves, but the latter resisted, preferring to construct their own homes, whose basic structure, said the *Jamaican Journal* in 1818, was "as in Sierra Leone, the Negro huts of Africa" (ibid., 97). Wattle-and-daub walls, thatched roofs, and earthen floors were the norm, though 11 of the 123 slave dwellings on the Old Montpelier estate in 1825 were built of stone and 17 had board walls: these were almost certainly owned by skilled slaves (93). The structure of slave villages, together with plantation records of slaves' patterns of kinship and residence, suggests a limited trend, in the last years of slavery, toward a combination of nuclear and extended families that, being neither African nor European, may be regarded as an authentically creole form of family structure. On the three adjoining estates owned by Charles Ellis—Old Montpelier, New Montpelier, and Shettlewood Pen—Barry Higman (1975:271) has shown that in 1825 "the most common family household unit, in terms of the number of slaves it accounted for, was that consisting of a man, his wife, and their children, or the nuclear family."[25] There were 50 such units in all (out of 252, 19.8 percent) involving 204 out of the 814 slaves on the estate (25.2 percent), and the proportion of "stable," "male-headed" households is raised still higher when one adds the 67 units, involving 169 slaves, in which a male slave was living with one or more females; on the other hand, there were 70 units, involving 328 slaves, that in their various forms could be described as "female-headed households" (Higman 1973:535). The evidence is hardly conclusive, suggesting at most that the long-held view that "the nuclear family could hardly exist within the context of slavery" (Patterson 1967:167) requires some qualification, at least during the last years of slavery. More suggestive is the indication, contained in a description of the Hope estate in 1818, that "in some instances whole families reside within one enclosure: They have separate houses, but only one gate. In the centre of this family village, the house of the principal among them is generally placed, and is in general very superior to the other" (Higman 1975:278). What proportion of slaves lived in such family compounds? And were they, as the description above suggests, only "slaves entrusted with duties of responsibility or skill"? We may at the very least conclude that a significant minority of slaves had, by the end of slavery (and perhaps long before), evolved a type of family structure that, whether male headed or female headed, showed a trend toward nuclearization combined with a continuing sense of extended family ties. It was this complex but stable family form that such slaves would take with them into freedom and that, reinforced by Christian precept and practice, would function as a model for family structures in the fifty years following emancipation (see Patterson 1982b).

The material culture of slaves in the last years of slavery suggests, like so much else, a complex gestation period during which African and European elements alternated and vied with each other as slaves, sometimes aided and sometimes hindered by their owners, groped toward some kind of practical solution to concrete problems of survival. It was, in short, a period of bricolage in which we find slaves fashioning wooden locks, keys, and bolts to protect what more and more they regarded as personal property (McDonald 1993:109), using needles, thimbles, buttons, buckles, and cloth supplied by their owners to make clothes that fulfilled their own practical and aesthetic desires (Armstrong 1990:177), or trying, apparently unsuccessfully, to apply European glazing techniques to their own forms of pottery (153). At Drax Hall, slave-made and European artifacts are found side by side, though the archaeological evidence points to a sharp reduction, from about 1750 onward, in the amount of slave-produced earthenware in use. By the end of the century, the African-

25. "Wife" here is presumably used in the sense of "common-law wife," since formal religious marriages were still exceptional. The male slaves on M. G. Lewis's Cornwall estate "have all so much decency as to call their sexual attachments by a conjugal name" (Lewis 1834:111).

style earthenware cooking pots known as yabbas (< *Twi ayawa* = earthen-ware vessel or dish) had been largely replaced by iron pots supplied by the owners, though food was still prepared and eaten communally in the "yard"; furthermore, the making and use of yabbas resumed after emancipation, when iron pots were no longer supplied (150–57). Overall, however, "the presence of large quantities of European artefacts" within the slave village at Drax Hall indicates "change from traditional patterns and assimilation of European prac-tices within the new context of Afro-Jamaican community" (271). We can infer a relative creolization of everyday life, then, with the proviso that much that the slaves made will not have survived, such as the calabash dishes de-scribed by Barclay (1826:315), many of them "carved with figures like those which are tattooed on the skins of the Africans."

Conditions in the slave huts were spartan indeed: only a minority of households had anything resembling a bed, and not all slaves possessed even a blanket. But there was one area—clothes—in which by 1800 slaves, or more precisely some slaves, seemed to be even lavishly supplied and through which, self-evidently, they were displaying all the creativity, imagination, and indi-viduality systematically denied them by the routinized ordeals of the planta-tion. Here is a typical description form 1797: "Mechanics are generally able from their own labour to buy good clothing: Broadcloth coats, linen waist-coats and breeches, a smart cocked hat, with a gold or silver loop, button and band, are common with them in the holidays; to which they sometimes add shoes and stockings. They frequently have their cloaths made in the newest English fashion and sometimes exceedingly fantastically" (*Columbian Magazine* 3 (1797), quoted in McDonald 1993:127). At their daily tasks slaves wore, as we have seen, a standardized uniform of osnaburg that made of them the anony-mous, almost sexless, human machines that the laws and codes governing their lives decreed them to be. At their weekend dances and on feast days, however, they appeared as if magically transformed, "the men in broadcloth coats, fancy waistcoats, and nankeen or jean trousers, and the women in white or fancy muslin gowns, beaver or silk hats, and a variety of expensive jewelry. . . . All of them who can afford to buy a finer dress, seldom appear, excepting when at work, in the coarse habitments given them by their masters" (Stewart 1969: 269). Their personalities restored and enhanced by the extravagance of their dress, the slaves then *performed* before each other, actors and spectators at once, vying with each other in what seems to have been a self-conscious ritual reversal of the structures that governed their workday lives: the projection and aggrandizement of selves normally reduced to near nothingness, the stylized and expressive display of bodies condemned during the week to remorseless, repetitive movement, the expenditure of energy for self, not for Buckra, all of these made each Saturday night "play" a carnival in miniature. And as we shall see, on at least one day of the year the slaves moved out of their village and into the Great House to perform before, and with, their masters and mistresses. This was at Christmas, Jamaica's first truly "national" festival, an occasion of the utmost ambivalence that, combining as it does this book's principal themes of inside and outside, reputation, style, and performance, opposition and accommodation, requires analysis in depth in the chapter that follows.

## Coda: Jamaica in 1838

By 1838, the year of final emancipation, both Jamaica's Whites and its Blacks had been significantly transformed by the experience of slavery, which had brought them together even as it held them radically and necessarily apart. The Whites had ceased to be "European" and the Blacks "African" in any "pure" or unequivocal sense, and both had been, to a significant though unequal degree, creolized; furthermore, a third "colored" group, with no "home" other than Jamaica, occupied an ambivalent intermediate zone between them. All three groups were creole, but this does *not* mean they shared a common creole culture; indeed, the Euro-Creole and Afro-Creole zones of the continuum remained so far apart that they seemed to be different cultures entirely rather than what they in fact were—the opposed extremities of a single but highly differentiated hybrid creole culture. It was, in short, a case not of *two* Jamaicas (see Curtin 1968) but of three—the Euro-, the Meso-, and the Afro-Creole, each "shading" racially, culturally, and linguistically into its neighbor—with a fourth entity, the hegemonic imperialist culture of Britain, capping and ultimately controlling the rest. Thus asymmetrically triangulated Jamaica moved out of slavery and into a new sociocultural order.

Just as the three zones of the continuum were differentiated from each other, so within each zone there were marked variations in what aspects of life had been creolized, to what extent, in what manner, and when. Such variations were particularly apparent in the religious beliefs and practices that characterized the Afro-Creole zone. Here, thanks to the work of black and white missionaries, the overwhelming majority of Blacks had by 1838 been at least nominally Christianized; on many plantations almost all slaves had received baptism, many had absorbed more than the formal rites and beliefs of the new faith, and some had been married according to the church they belonged to.[26]

26. The testimony of M. G. Lewis leads one, however, to be cautious about the profundity of the slaves' Christianity. Not only do many slaves display, according to Lewis, a marked "unwillingness to be christened," not least because "the conceive that the ghosts of their ancestors cannot fail to be offended at their abandoning an [African] appellation, either hereditary in the family, or given by themselves" (Lewis 1834:349, cf. 345), but even nominal converts are almost comically ignorant concerning their new faith, witness the slave who puts the following question to Lewis: "'Beg massa pardon, but want know one ting as puzzle me. Massa say "the child," and me want know, massa, one ting much; was Jesus Christ a boy or a girl?'" (230). Of course this could well be a case not of ignorance but of "puttin' on ole Massa."

Yet much Afro-Christianity remained at least as much "Afro" as "Christian,"
and in the marriage of Myalism and Christianity, much of the substance of the
former had received only the thinnest veneer of the latter. Despite Barclay's
"balance-sheet" of twenty years of systematic evangelization, with which the
previous section began, Obeah had most definitely not been eliminated
(though it may indeed have been less frequently heard of), nor had burial
rites—the core, as we have seem, of earlier slave religion—been more than
superficially transformed by the missionaries' teaching and example. According
to Barclay, night funerals were banned in 1816, and it became normal—at
least among the Anglican converts who concerned him—for a white person to
attend slave funerals and "read the service appointed by the church of England, in committing dust to dust." Yet as even Barclay admits, the "latent taint
of African superstition" which leads "negroes universally [to] attach greater
importance to having what they call 'a good burial'" also prompts them to
combine Christian and non-Christian practices in distinctly un-Anglican mixture: "As the negroes attach an importance to the burial of the dead, they
extend the same feelings to the graves, over which they erect tombs commonly built of brick, and neatly white-washed. The white-washing is carefully
repeated every Christmas, and formerly it was on these occasions customary
to kill a white cock, and sprinkle his blood over the graves of the family; but
this last part of the ceremony seems now to be little attended to, and is likely
to be soon extinct" (Barclay 1826:165–66). But if such vestiges of former
practice survived, probably much more extensively than Barclay imagined,
even among those few slaves who had been received into the highly Eurocentric Anglican Church, how much more strongly must the "African taint"
have impregnated the practices of Native Methodists, Black Baptists, and
other "Spirit Christians" "lower down" on the religious continuum?[27] In short, if
it is important to stress the *extent* of creolization under slavery, it is also necessary to stress its limits. The creole "synthesis" is in this sense no synthesis at
all, because it remains by definition incomplete and unstable, always becoming, never achieved, so that the creole never entirely absorbed or replaced the
African substratum even when, after 1838, fewer and fewer people of African
origin remained.

Given the multiplicity of its internal divisions—creole versus African
above all, but also skilled versus unskilled, domestic versus praedial, colored

27. Cf. the female slave mentioned by Lewis who, though of mixed race, "had imbibed strong
African prejudices from her mother, and frankly declared that she found nothing in the Christian
system so alluring to her taste as the post-obit balls and banquets promised by the religion of Africa."
It will be hard, Lewis avers, for the "'pulpit drum ecclesiastic' . . . to overpower the gumby," and for
the moment—he is writing in 1817—"the joys of the Christian paradise" are as nothing, in the
slaves' minds, beside "the pleasures of eating fat hog, drinking raw rum, and dancing for centuries to
the jam-jam and kitty-katty" (Lewis 1834:345).

versus black, all of them overlapping to a greater or lesser extent—the slave community that emerges from the accounts of Edwards, Stewart, Barclay, Lewis, and others shows remarkable cohesion and stability, and it is clear that by 1800 at the latest new forms of social structure had been evolved that to some extent cut across the dividing lines of plantation life the planters did their utmost to sustain. Even after the abolition of the slave trade, the term "shipmate" continued, in Edwards's words (1806:2:285), to signify "a relationship of the most endearing nature, perhaps as recalling the time when the sufferers were cut off together from their common country and kindred, and awakening reciprocal sympathy, from the remembrance of mutual affiliation"; it is also clear that the creole children of shipmates continued to recognize the potency of that bond.[28] Edwards also comments (2:289) on "the high veneration in which old age is held by the negroes in general" (it is, he says, "one of the few pleasing traits of their character"), stressing the way "in addressing such of their fellow-servants as are any ways advanced in years, they prefix to their names the appellation of parent, as *Ta* Quaco, and *Ma* Quasheba, *Ta* and *Ma* signify father and mother, by which designation they mean to convert not only the idea of filial reverence, but also that of esteem and fondness." In similar vein, Lewis (1834:258) noted that "among negroes it is almost tantamount to an affront to address by name, without affixing some term of relationship, such as 'grannie,' or 'uncle,' or 'cousin.' My Cornwall boy, George, told me one day, that 'Uncle Sully wanted to speak to massa.' 'Why, is Sully your uncle, George?' 'No, massa; me only call him so for honour.'" All this suggests a deliberate policy, on the part of the slaves stripped by their masters of every kind of human dignity, to rehumanize themselves and their fellows through an elaborate stylization of everyday relationships, to counter their systematic infantilization by an equally systematic cultivation of adult titles and modes of address: "The punctilio observed by negroes toward each other is past belief of those who never witnessed it," wrote A. C. Carmichael in 1833 (quoted in Dirks 1987:143). Could it be that the standard West Indian (and more generally Afro-American) appellation "man" began as a self-conscious retort to being addressed, routinely and contemptuously, as "boy"?

A sugar plantation, wrote William Beckford (1790:1:141), "is like a little town." By the early 1800s there is strong evidence that slaves had come to see themselves as "citizens" of that town or, at the very least, of the Negro Village that for them was its vital heart. They had created their huts and their provision grounds, both of which could be bought and sold or handed on by bequest; they were virtually self-sufficient in food; their burial grounds gave them a sense of continuity with the past; they had at the very least the linea-

---

28. Thus one of Lewis's domestic slaves, asked why he treats another elderly slave as a relative, replies, "He and my father were shipmates, massa" (Lewis 1834:350).

ments of a stable family structure and, beyond that, a strong sense of themselves as a community of "sufferers";[29] and their weekly "plays" gave their lives
both a communal focus and a vision of freedom before and beyond slavery.
They even, according to Stewart (1969:262), set up "a sort of bench of justice," presided over by the senior slaves, "which sits and decides, privately, and
without the knowledge of the whites, on all disputes and complaints of their
fellow-slaves." Not only were slaves increasingly citizens of their own little
town, but they created "federal" ties with the citizens of other plantations. In
theory introverted and self-contained, each plantation was in reality pervious
to others, and in a whole variety of ways—the regular exchange of visits at
weekends, Sunday markets, Christmas and other celebrations, and prayer
meetings, as well as the work that sometimes took them to other plantations—slaves established what Long (1774:2:414) called a "general correspondence" across the island through which they became "intimately ac-
quainted with affairs of the white inhabitants, public as well as private" and
also—though Long neither says nor probably knows this—developed the
sense of a broader collective identity over and against their oppressors. It is to
some inchoate sense of *national* identity that Long (ibid., 2:411) unwittingly
points when he says that slaves "seem also to feel a patriotic affection for the
island which has given them birth; they rejoice at its prosperity, lament its
losses, and interest themselves in the affairs and politics that are the talk of the
day." Not too much, perhaps, should be made of this, and above all of the
reasons Long implies for the slaves' protopolitical consciousness. If slaves took
an interest in the ups and downs of the local economy, it was because they
knew their well-being depended directly on it; and as we shall see in the next
chapter, what they learned from overhearing their masters talking about politics provided crucial intelligence for their own struggle against slavery. Yet
whatever their level of political consciousness (and the timing of revolts to
coincide with the Whites' periods of greatest weakness suggests it was high),
slaves clearly possessed a sense of themselves as a "we" that, on certain occasions such as the great uprising of Christmas 1831 discussed in chapter 2, was
capable of overriding the tendencies toward individual and group self-interest
that, with the planters' encouragement, continued to divide them. The tension
between individual, group, and collective identities and interests remained
strong, as the Anancy stories the slaves told each other often reveal, but the
pivotal institutions of Negro Village culture—funerals, "plays," extended family compounds and "grounds"—all worked toward overcoming the centrifugal
forces built into slave life. All four institutions were African derived, but all
equally bore the marks of progressive indigenization: they linked slaves to a

29. It is fascinating and ironic to find the modern Jamaican demotic prefigured in Edwards's
archetypally colonialist history of the British West Indies (see above; Edwards 1806:2:289).

shared past, expressed a shared present, and pointed forward to at least the possibility of a shared future. Finally, the spread of Christianity in its various creolized forms gave this inchoate sense of community a new and powerful framework in which to develop and lent it the added support of a supernatural sanction: not for nothing would Black Baptism come to be known as the "Black Family" in Jamaica (Bleby 1853:25). It was this emerging Afro-Creole synthesis that would provide the core of the postemancipation peasant culture discussed in chapter 3. But before that it would act inseparably as a focus of opposition and as a means of accommodation to slavery in its final decades, and it is the fundamental *doubleness* of slave culture that the following chapter addresses.

# Resistance and Opposition in Jamaica, 1800–1834

Studies of slave resistance in the Caribbean conventionally distinguish two categories of antislavery activity. On the one hand, usually referred to as "physical" or "violent" resistance, there are the many full-scale slave revolts that constituted the battles in what one historian (Beckles 1987:5) has called "the two hundred years" war waged by slaves in the West Indies against their masters, concerted, well-organized uprisings sometimes involving thousands of slaves and often known by the name of the slave who was the principal leader: Tacky's revolt in Jamaica in 1760, Cuffee's in Demerara in 1763, and Bussa's in Barbados in 1816. To these must be added the less personalized Demerara Rebellion of 1823, the Baptist War or Christmas Uprising in Jamaica in 1831–32, discussed at the end of this chapter, and above all the only fully successful slave uprising in Caribbean, or indeed world, history—the Saint-Domingue rebellion of 1791–94, followed by the war of independence (1801–4) waged by the self-liberated slaves against France when Napoleon sought to reimpose slavery by force. "Physical" or "violent" resistance would also include the two Maroon Wars in Jamaica (1729–39 and 1795–96), though these were not wars against slavery as such but struggles by the Maroon communities to preserve the autonomy they had already gained from and within the plantation system. Yet to dwell only on the "battles" is to lose sight of the continual skirmishes involving smaller numbers of slaves, even individual slaves acting alone, in less concerted or more narrowly focused acts of physical violence against their oppressors—above all attacks on detested overseers, bookkeepers, and other figures of authority. It is also to ignore the evidence of all the *attempted* acts of physical resistance that for one reason or another (usually betrayal) failed to get beyond the stage of conspiracy: the extraordinary Antigua slave plot of 1736 (see chapter 5 below) or, restricting ourselves to the most salient instances in Jamaica, the "Coromantyn" uprising planned for Christmas 1765, the conspiracy of 1776, which for the first time in Jamaica involved a majority of creole slaves (see Sheridan 1976),[1] or the Ibo conspiracy of 1815. Finally, the whole phenomenon of maroonage needs to be considered in all its ambivalence: Was it "revolutionary," "restorationist," or "isolationist" in its aims (see Campbell 1988:13), a form of resistance to slavery or, to the extent that it left the slave system intact, a form of accommodation to it or even, ultimately, after the treaties of 1739 in Jamaica, a form of complicity and open collaboration?

When one surveys the two-hundred-year history of West Indian slavery, it is clear that active resistance was most intense at the beginning of the period, when the slave system was not yet fully implanted, and at the end, when slaves knew that pressure for its abolition was building up in Britain. Many, as we shall see, believed then that it had already been abolished in law and was surviving only because the planters refused to put that law into practice. During the slave system's "zenith," however, say from 1740 to 1810, concerted armed resistance was much less frequent and, above all, much less effective. To take just the case of Jamaica, after the repression of Tacky's revolt in 1760[2] there was no major uprising involving plantation slaves until over seventy years later when the Christmas Uprising broke out. Even during the period of the French Revolutionary and Napoleonic wars, when Jamaican slaves knew full well of the successful uprisings in the neighboring colony of Saint-Domingue and when, it might be imagined, the masters were at their most vulnerable, there was no instance of a concerted uprising or even of a major conspiracy to foment one (see Geggus 1987:274–75). Yet all historians are agreed that the absence of uprisings does not indicate an acceptance of slavery or an accommodation to its horrors, and it is here that the second category of slave resistance comes into its own: what is variously known as "psychological," "nonviolent," "inward," or "cultural" resistance (see Geggus 1983:2–3), meaning the multiplicitous ways whereby, stopping short of actual physical confrontation with their oppressors, slaves could both enact and conceal their nonacceptance of the system, covertly defy those who operated it, or by manipulation, deceit, and maneuver concretely improve their position within it. This second category of resistance includes the following activities among

1. According to Thomas Thistlewood, writing to Edward Long, the 1776 conspiracy was hatched by "Drivers, Tradesmen, Old Worthy Men . . . and other favorites in whom the Utmost Confidence had been reposed, whereas, in all former disturbances it was among the Guinea, or Salt Water Negroes, that the Plots were Concerted" (quoted in Ward 1988:218). On the gradual "creolization" of resistance to slavery, see Craton 1982:293.

2. Tacky's revolt may be seen as the last of the African-led insurrections that "aimed at a war of racial extermination and the establishment of an ethnic autocracy on Ashanti lines" (see Craton 1982:120–25).

others: lying to or poking fun at Massa or Busha,[3] stealing (or as the slaves put it, "taking") plantation property, feigning illness and working slow (perhaps taking an inordinate time to "go to bush"), breaking tools, interfering with plantation machinery, and even—though here one is on the fringes of "physical" resistance—setting fire to the sugar fields just before they were to be harvested. In this context self-mutilation and suicide—acts whereby hostility to oppression is turned against the victim's own person—may be construed as resistance, as can the high incidence among women, acting alone or with the help of slave midwives, of what has been called "gynaecological resistance": infanticide and abortion. By dint of their proximity to Whites, domestic slaves deployed a particularly wide repertoire of such acts of resistance, from spitting in Buckra's food to lacing it with poison, though, since it involved the near certainty of detection and punishment, the latter act would be performed only in extremis. The whole point of "psychological" resistance was to show and not show nonacceptance of the system and above all *not to be caught* in the act of maneuver, deception, or defiance. What Carolyn Cooper (1993:141), cleverly echoing Jamaican pronunciation, has called "(h)ideology" was the great principle of slave life, as it has been, historically, of the lives of all dominated peoples.

All these actions had, it is argued, two objectives and effects. First, they enabled slaves, usually without great risk to themselves, concretely to impede and impair the smooth functioning of the plantation and so hit Massa where it hurt him most: in his pocketbook. Second, they permitted slaves to assert, in a concealed and roundabout way, their subjectivity in the face of the uniquely objectifying character of slavery. To the extent that such acts were endemic in plantation life, Michael Craton (1982:25) is right in insisting that "there was no such creature as a genuinely docile slave." Even accommodation to the system becomes a devious act of resistance to the extent that it is willed, whence the extreme ambiguity of the whole "Quashie phenomenon" first explored by Orlando Patterson (1967:174–81): by voluntarily becoming the smiling, fawning dullard that Massa or Busha believed him to be, the slave could adroitly turn the stereotype against them, preserving an inner freedom beneath the mask of compliance. And appearances to the contrary, the slave plantation was *not* a panopticon. The Whites saw the slaves only in the fields

3. The Whites obviously knew they were being lied to, stolen from, and made fun of behind their backs (or sometimes to their faces), but they were incapable of doing anything about it: "Instead of choosing panegyric for their subject-matter [in their songs], they generally prefer one of derision, and not infrequently at the expense of the overseer, if he happens to be near, and listening: this only serves to add a poignancy to their satire, and heightens the fun" (Long 1774:2:423; see also Edwards 1806:2:293). Phillippo (1969:201) records the story of a drunken planter who chances to see "a negro personifying his own gestures and habits when in a state of intoxication, amidst the convulsive laughter of the multitudes of men, women, and children gathered around him. The whole scene had such an effect on him that he never again indulged in similar excesses."

and in other "professional" contexts and remained largely ignorant of the nighttime and weekend lives they led in their villages, where from the earliest days "plays" and similar rituals became the major focus of *cultural* resistance to slavery. And as we shall see, Massa not only saw and knew much less than he thought but was constantly seen and known, often to the depths of his being, by slaves to whom in his blindness he often denied the very capacity to see. The "visual politics" of the plantation were in reality the very opposite of what they appeared on the surface.

This chapter retains the conventional distinction between "physical" and "psychological" or "cultural" forms of resistance but gives them different names, derived from the work of Michel de Certeau. In an article titled "On the Oppositional Practices of Everyday Life" (1980), de Certeau proposes a distinction between what he calls "resistance" and "opposition" that, while giving it much greater theoretical precision, conforms very closely to the standard "physical"/"psychological" contrast outlined above. In very general terms, de Certeau argues that a given sociopolitical system can be *resisted* only when it is possible for the dominated group or dominated individuals to place themselves entirely outside the system in question. Resistance requires an "elsewhere" from which the system may be perceived and grasped as a whole and from which a coherent *strategy* of resistance may be elaborated. *Opposition*, on the other hand, has no space it can properly call its own. It takes place of necessity *within* the system, on ground defined by the system, and in the absence of any concerted strategy of resistance it operates, says de Certeau, "blow by blow," moving from one *tactical* maneuver to another within and against the system. It utilizes "the gaps which the particular combination of circumstances open in the control of the proprietary power. It poaches there. It creates surprise. It is possible now for it to be where no-one expects it. It is wile. In sum it is an art of the weak. Cracks, glints, slippages, brainstorms within the established grids of a given system: such are the style of these tactical practices, which are the equivalent in the realm of action of wit and witticism in the realm of language" (de Certeau 1980:5–7). The relevance of this distinction to the study of slavery should be evident. It enables us to retain and refine the distinction between "physical" and "psychological" forms of resistance—all slaves, we might say, *opposed* slavery at all times, but only some slaves *resisted* it some of the time—and also to clarify the conditions that made it possible to move from opposition within the system to resistance to the system as such. The distinction opposition/tactics:resistance/strategy also helps us pinpoint the kinds, and timing, of the activities involved. Opposition characteristically involves turning the system against itself by deceit and dexterity, using the means and materials the system offers to outwit and subvert it, whereas before it becomes possible even to consider resistance, there must be some chance of escaping entirely from the system. Opposition takes place when the strong are strong and the weak know it; resistance becomes possible when the weak sense both their own strength and the weakness of the strong. Opposition, in short, belongs to periods of pessimism when all outlets seem blocked; resistance belongs to periods of hope, above all of hope deferred or frustrated,[4] when, in de Certeau's terms, the possibility of an "elsewhere" appears. In the concrete case that concerns us, this happened when slaves began to feel that slavery would soon be abolished or even to believe that it already had been.

I have also used in this chapter some of the ideas developed with reference to Malayan peasant society by James C. Scott in *Weapons of the Weak* (1985) and applied more generally to systems of oppression in *Domination and the Arts of Resistance* (1990). In these studies Scott examines what he calls "the infrapolitics of subordinate groups," that "wide variety of low-profile forms of resistance that dare not speak in their own name"—Scott lists, among others, "rumor, gossip, folktales, jokes, songs, rituals, codes, and euphemisms," in fact "a good part of the folk culture of subordinate groups"—that collectively make up "a politics of disguise and anonymity that takes place in public view but is designed to have double meaning or to shield the identity of the actor" (1990:19). I have in particular made use of Scott's conception of "public" versus "hidden transcripts" to explore the ambiguities of relations between masters and slaves recounted by one such master, M. G. Lewis, as operating on his plantation in Jamaica just after the end of the Napoleonic wars: this is the subject of the section that follows. I have also drawn on the Greek idea of *mētis* (cunning intelligence) as expounded by Marcel Detienne and Jean-Pierre Vernant. To the extent that *mētis* is "not one, not unified, but multiple and diverse," that its "field of application is the world of movement, of multiplicity and of ambiguity," and that, operating as it does through disguise and duplicity, it is its "way of conniving with reality which ensures its efficacity" (Detienne and Vernant 1991:18–21), it describes precisely the everyday opposition and accommodation that enabled thousands of slaves to survive their ordeal. They narrativized the practice in the stories they told each other of the spider-trickster Anancy, the subject of the second section of this chapter. The third section discusses the slaves' oppositional culture as embodied in just one oppositional ritual, the Jamaican Christmas festivity known as Jonkonnu, and the chapter concludes with the passage from opposition *from within the system* to resistance *to the system itself* as evinced in the circumstances that precipitated and made possible the greatest of all slave revolts in the British Caribbean—the Baptist War of 1831–32.

---

4. Thus Beckles (1987:6–7) maintains that slave revolts were linked with "rising expectations unfulfilled" and occurred most frequently "at the specific junctures when, within matured creole societies, rapid social changes were taking place."

## Massa and Quashie: "Monk" Lewis in Jamaica, 1816–1817

When on the morning of 2 January 1816, the day after his arrival from England, Matthew Lewis made his first long-heralded appearance on his estate near Savannah-la-Mar, the life of the plantation was transfigured as by the sudden materialization of a god:

> The works were instantly all abandoned; every thing that had life came flocking to the house from all quarters; and not only the men, and the women, and the children, but "by a bland assimilation," the hogs, and the dogs, and the geese, and the fowls, and the turkeys, all came hurrying along by instinct, to see what could possibly be the matter, and seemed to be afraid of arriving too late. Whether the pleasure of the negroes was sincere may be doubted; but certainly it was the loudest that I ever witnessed: they all talked together, sang, danced, shouted, and, in the violence of their gesticulations, tumbled over each other, and rolled about on the ground. Twenty voices at once enquired after uncles, and aunts, and grandfathers, and great-grandmothers of mine, who had been buried long before I was in existence, and whom, I verily believe, most of them only knew by tradition. One woman held up a little naked black child to me, grinning from ear to ear;—"Look, Massa, look here! him nice lilly neger for Massa!" Another complained,—"So long since none come see we, Massa; good Massa, come at last." As for the old people, they were all in one and the same story: now they had lived once to see Massa, they were ready for dying to-morrow, "them no care."

For the rest of the day the slaves "shouted and sang me into a violent headache. It is now one in the morning, and I hear them still shouting and singing. I gave them a holiday for Saturday next, and told them I had brought them all presents from England; and so, I believe, we parted very good friends" (Lewis 1834:60–63). And so it continues during the days that follow. One after the other slaves, or more often whole delegations of slaves, come to the Great House to pay homage to their master from England, to assure him of their love for him and their undying loyalty, and to shower him with promises of hard work and good behavior. By 19 January Lewis is fully "accustomed to see every face that looks upon me, grinning from ear to ear with pleasure at my notice, and hear every voice cry 'God bless you, massa,' as I pass" (119). "Je ne vois que des yeux prêts à me sourire," he quotes, and concedes that, although "all this may be palaver," "I find it quite impossible to resist the fascination of the conscious pleasure of pleasing." Even manumitted slaves who once worked on the plantation join in the ritual "because, as they said,—'if they did not come to see massa, they were afraid that it would look ungrateful, and as if they cared no more about him and Cornwall, now that they were free.' So they stayed two or three days on the estate, coming up to the house for their dinner, and going to sleep at night among their friends in their own former habitations, the negro huts; and when they went away, they assured me, that nothing should prevent their coming back to bid me farewell, before I left the island" (89–90).

Not for one moment during Lewis's three-month stay on the plantation does the slaves' public enthusiasm abate. Two slaves "'beg massa hard, quite hard'" that, when he departs, he should "leave his picture for the negroes" so that "they might talk to it, just as they did to massa." When one is produced— a very approximate likeness drawn by a slave, with a long red nose and huge pair of whiskers—the slaves' delight ("'Dere massa coat! and dere him chair him sit in!'") is such that they break the frame in their frenzy: fortunately it can be repaired, and the slaves go away well contented, declaiming that they will talk to it every morning "all one as if massa still here" (120, 185–86). Another slave, an Eboe (Ibo) named Strap, "never can express his gratitude sufficiently" for being nursed back to health by Lewis in person, and, at every opportunity, accosts him to declare, "'oh massa, massa! God bless you, massa! me quite, *quite* glad to see you come back, my own massa!' And then he bursts into a roar of laughter so wild and so loud that the passers-by cannot help stopping to stare and laugh too" (187). On another occasion Lewis asks a group of slaves why they had missed the previous Sunday's prayer meeting and is told "that they wished very much to come, 'because they wish to do *any thing* to oblige massa'" (230–31). When in an excess of generosity Lewis grants the slaves three new annual holidays, the latter throng into the Great House and chant "'Since massa come, we very well off,' which words they repeated in chorus, without intermission (dancing all the time), for hours together; till, at half-past three, neither my eyes nor my brain could endure it any longer, and I was obliged to send them word that I wanted to go to bed, and could not sleep till the noise should cease" (193). The final apotheosis comes on the morning of Lewis's departure:

> With their usual levity, the negroes were laughing and talking as gaily as ever till the very moment of my departure; but when they saw my curricle actually at the door to convey me away, then their faces grew very long indeed. In particular, the women called me by every endearing name they could think of. "My son! my love! my husband! my father!" "You no my massa, you my tata!" said one old woman (upon which another wishing to go a step beyond her, added, "Iss, massa, iss! It was you");* * * * * * * and when I came down the steps to depart, they crowded about me, kissing my feet, and clasping my knees, so that it was with difficulty that I could get into the carriage. And this

was done with such marks of truth and feeling, that I cannot believe the whole to be mere acting and mummery. (240–41)

Needless to say, when Lewis returns the following year the whole ritual of welcome begins over again, though, as we shall see, with somewhat more unfortunate consequences than on the initial occasion.

This, then, is the public transcript, in Scott's terms, of the slaves' relationship with their master, and it would be a serious misreading to interpret it as wholly devious and insincere, as "simply" a classic case of "puttin' on ole Massa." For it is quite plain that the slaves *are* pleased to see Lewis, and for two very good reasons: they know that Massa means presents and a chance of getting one back on the subordinate Whites who have mistreated them in his absence. Throughout his stay, but particularly during the first two or three weeks, Lewis, anxious among other things to live up to his self-image as a liberal and munificent master, is notably generous with his gifts of cash, clothes, food, and days off: virtually every slave who approaches him, for whatever reasons, comes away with a piece of salt fish or salt beef, some item of clothing, or a "maccaroni" (a small donation of money) without being required to do anything other than smile and be grateful. Often the gifts are unsolicited and essentially unmotivated, like the "handful of silver" sable Psyche receives for her dance (77) or the "couple of my dollars" given to "a little way of a negro boy" for performing an impromptu Jonkonnu dance (75) on Lewis's arrival. Sick slaves regularly receive gifts of food to speed their recovery and duly thank Massa not just for the food but for "him kind words too . . . , kind words do neger much good, much as good food" (218). Sometimes idle or recalcitrant slave receive gifts to encourage them to work, and in a still more self-interested way, each mother of a newborn child that survives its first week is given "a present of a scarlet girdle with a silver medal in the centre" that she is instructed to wear on feasts and holidays, "when it should entitle her to marks of peculiar respect and attention, such as being one of the first served, and receiving a larger proportion than the rest." Should she "sin," producing the girdle will earn an indulgence, and "on every additional child, an additional medal is to be affixed to the belt, and precedence is to follow the greater number of medals" (125). But the greatest number of gifts are a result of slaves' wheedling, and Lewis recounts, not without pleasure, numerous occasions when a satisfactory performance of loyalty or need elicits from him the expected "charitable" gesture. Each such occasion is a drama in miniature in which giver and receiver conform to fixed roles—"they begged, and lifted up their folded hands, and cried, and fell on the ground, and kissed my feet—and, in short, acted their part so well, that they almost made me act mine to perfection, and fall to blubbering" (153–54). But finally master relents, and the slaves are rewarded for their patience, resourcefulness, and self-abasement, or else they give up and "laugh themselves at their own unreasonable-ness" (201), in which case, like as not, they get something in return.[5] Massa is out-maneuvered but is scarcely displeased, since his image of both other and self is confirmed by the reward of performance with gift. On the one hand, the gift implicitly subverts the relationship between master and slave because the master acknowledges his property as subject and, in a derisory way, as property owner. On the other hand, the power relationship survives its manip-ulation by the slaves, who emerge both enriched and impoverished, and quite possibly corrupted, by the pseudoperformance they have engaged in. Each party to the "exchange" is both winner and loser, as is always the case in the oppositional game.

But it was not just prospect of presents that led the slaves of Cornwall estate to welcome their master. Unknown to Lewis, in his absence the estate's attorney had left it in the hands of an overseer while he got on with running other properties elsewhere on the island. The overseer had seriously abused his powers, causing Lewis's slaves to run away en masse, leaving the estate "nearly ruined, and absolutely in a state of rebellion" (116). Order is restored by the magistrates to whom the remaining slaves appeal, but when Lewis arrives he is forthwith confronted with complaint after complaint concerning the conduct of the white personnel on the estate. Lewis resolves almost all the complaints in his slaves' favor and makes a number of dismissals; after one he is "kept awake the greatest part of the night by the songs and rejoicings of the negroes, at their triumph over the offending book-keeper" (197). It is not long before slaves from neighboring plantations start bringing him *their* grievances, "requesting me to represent their injuries to their trustee here, and their pro-prietor in England"; more than one runaway slave from other estates ask him "to write a few lines to his master, to save him from the lash" (144). Soon rumors circulate that Lewis intends to set his slaves free "in two or three years" and even that "'good King George and good Mr. Wilberforce'" have "'given me a paper' to set the negroes free . . . , but that the white people of Jamaica will not suffer me to show the paper, and I am now going home to say so" (226, 232). Not only are the slaves playing one White against others to their own advantage, but they have forged a powerful oppositional myth setting the "Good White Man from England" (Lewis, Wilberforce, the king) against the evil Buckras at home, whose counterparts can readily be found in other slave colonies at the time. It is a classic instance of what Scott calls the apparently "naïve monarchism" of subordinate peoples (1990:96–101)—the belief that

5. The self-justifying, ludic character of such exchanges is noted by Lewis: "This 'talking to massa' is a favourite amusement among the negroes, and extremely inconvenient: they come to me perpetually with complaints so frivolous, and requests so unreasonable, that I am persuaded they invent them only to have an excuse for 'talk to massa'; and when I have given them a plump refusal, they go away perfectly satisfied, and 'tank massa for dis here great indulgence of talk'" (186–87).

the king or the czar is "really" on their side against tax collectors and land-lords—and we shall see it operating again in Jamaica in 1831, 1865, and 1938, both inspiring acts of resistance and setting crucial limits to their range and effectiveness.[6] Clearly, by 1816 the slave system has been delegitimized in the eyes of the slaves of Cornwall estate.

All the time that Lewis has been acting out his roles as provider, protector, and righter of wrongs, his slaves have been pursuing their own individual and collective agendas. The *Journal* provides us with a unique opportunity to observe the hidden transcript at work behind the public as at every turn slaves, their inner lives secreted behind a bland mask of compliance, systematically resort to all the classic "weapons of the weak": pilfering (155), malingering (122), "sauntering along with their hands dangling" and "stopping to chat with every one they meet" (101), reopening old wounds and rubbing dirt into them to get off work (204), performing the simplest of tasks, like opening windows, inefficiently (393), and so on and so on, day after day after day. Not surprisingly, it is the slaves Lewis attempts to suborn with favors and gifts who prove the most obstinate and perverse, slaves like the notorious idler Nato, who receives "a piece of money" as a reward *for spending a whole week in the fields* and then promptly reports sick to the hospital (204–5), or like the compulsive runaway Epsom, who is given "a maccaroni" for having stayed put on the plantation for two years and forthwith takes to his heels; recaptured, and "all rags, tears and penitence," he begs Lewis's forgiveness, "wondering 'how he could have had such *bad manners* as to make massa fret'" (347). Still more striking is the case of the slave from another plantation for whom, as we have seen, Lewis is cajoled into writing a "reference":

> About two months ago, a runaway cooper, belonging to Shrewsbury estate, by name Edward, applied to me to intercede for his not being punished on his return home. As soon as he got the paper requested, he gave up all idea of returning to the estate, and instead of it went about the country stealing every thing upon which he could lay his hands; and wherever his proceedings were enquired into by the magistrates, he stated himself to be on the road to his trustee, and produced my letter as proof of it. At length some one had the curiosity to open the letter, and found that it had been written two months before. (236)

6. "[In 1831] white missionaries are considered by the rebels to be friends of the blacks and enemies of the white planters; [in 1865] the white royal family are perceived to be friends of the black peasants and enemies of the white members of the Assembly; and [in 1938] a near-white labour leader [Alexander Bustamente] is heralded as the sole voice of the black working class" (Bakan 1990:7–8).

All such maneuvers have a predictable outcome: the output of the plantation falls from thirty-three hogsheads of sugar a week before Lewis's arrival to twenty-three two weeks later and to a mere thirteen after three months (231). In addition, just two months into his residence, Lewis reports that no fewer than forty-four adult slaves, a fifth of his workforce, are in the hospital, seven or eight at the most with anything wrong with them, as the slaves themselves admit with impunity when "on Sunday morning they all walked away from the hospital to amuse themselves, except seven or eight" (204). Yet as Lewis wryly comments, "they are not ungrateful" for his various indulgences toward them; "they are only selfish: they love me very well, but they love themselves a great deal better." There is not a slave on the plantation who is not "extremely anxious that all should do their full duty, except himself" and who does not "represent the shame of neglecting my work, and the ingratitude of vexing me by their ill-conduct; and then each individual—having said so much, and said it so strongly, that he is convinced of its having its full effect in making the others do their duty—thinks himself quite safe and snug in skulking away from his own" (231–32). On at least two occasions (206, 321–22), the second being Lewis's return to the plantation in 1817, the slaves' extravagant celebration of their master leads to major mishaps in the running of the plantation, with cattle being allowed, through (deliberate?) oversight by the pen keeper, to escape and trample on Lewis's best cane pieces, leading to the inevitable cri de coeur from their owner: "And so much for negro gratitude! However, they still continue their eternal song of 'Now massa come, we very well off'; but their satisfaction evidently begins and ends with themselves. They rejoice sincerely at being very well off, but think it unnecessary to make the slightest return to massa for making them so" (208).

Lewis, of course, is new to plantation life, a "liberal" by Jamaican standards, and no doubt a "soft touch" as far as his slaves are concerned. The newly arrived "hero" of *Marly, or Life in Jamaica* likewise spends his first days on the plantation "acknowledging bows and curtsies, and hearing the same cuckoo song of, 'Happy to see him Massa, and him hopes that Massa will lib long on Water Melon Valley'" (Anon. 1828:37)—and he is only a bookkeeper. The slaves' welcome is, as we have seen, both "genuine" and deeply self-interested, and by his second visit to the Cornwall estate Lewis has learned that "when I see a mouth grinning from ear to ear with a more than ordinary expansion of jaw, I never fail to find, on enquiring, that the proprietor is one of those who have been punished during my absence." When Lewis reveals what he knows, "away goes the grin, and down falls the negro to kiss my feet, confess his fault, and 'beg massa forgib, and them never do so bad thing no more to fret massa, and them beg massa pardon, hard, quite hard!'" (341). Whatever he says or does, and even if he says or does nothing, Lewis's room for maneuver is impeded by the vastly superior maneuverability of his slaves: he has but one role he can play, that of Massa, while they have a whole repertoire at their disposal and can switch, as circumstances demand, from one false self to another. The net result is that, for all his power, Lewis is always on the defensive. From his vantage point on the Great House veranda he seems to enjoy a panoptic view over the whole plantation. Buildings, vegetation, animals, and slaves blend in a single picturesque panorama over which he the owner, the artist, enjoys an apparently Godlike control:

> On three sides of the landscape the prospect is bounded by lofty purple mountains; and the variety of occupations going on all around me, and at the same time, give an inconceivable air of life and animation to the whole scene, especially as all those occupations look clean,—even those which in England look dirty. All the tradespeople are dressed either in white jackets and trousers, or with stripes of red and sky-blue. One band of negroes are carrying the ripe canes on their heads to the mill; another set are conveying away the *trash*, after the juice has been extracted; flocks of turkeys are sheltering from the heat under the trees; the river is filled with ducks and geese; the coopers and carpenters are employed about the puncheons; carts drawn some by six, others by eight, oxen, are bringing loads of Indian corn from the fields; the black children are employed in gathering it into the granary, and in quarrelling with pigs as black as themselves, who are equally busy in stealing the corn whenever the children are looking another way: in short, a plantation possesses all the movement and interest of a farm, without its dung, and its stench, and its dirty accompaniments. (85–86)

In reality, though, Lewis's vision and power are as circumscribed as those of the slave children minding the pigs—indeed, perhaps more so because, on the evidence of the *Journal*, *his* charges are engaged in all kinds of oppositional activities even as he looks at them and they smile back at him. Moreover, as Lewis painfully records, not only does he not see everything, but he himself is constantly seen, even when in the apparent security of the Great House. It is "the being obliged to live perpetually in public" that weighs especially upon him: "The houses are absolutely transparent; the walls are nothing but windows—and all the doors stand wide open. No servants are in waiting to announce arrivals: visitors, negroes, dogs, cats, poultry, all walk in and out, and up and down your living-rooms, without the slightest ceremony." Even the most intimate actions are painfully public, for "the Temple of Cloacina" is "as much latticed and as pervious to the eye as any other part of my premises; and many a time has my delicacy been put to the blush by the ill-timed civility of some old woman or other, who, wandering that way, and happening to cast her eye to the left, has stopped her course to curtsy very gravely, and pay me the passing compliment of an 'Ah, massa! bless you, massa! how day?'" (150).[7]

Such, then, were the day-to-day negotiations between a master and his slaves on a fairly typical Jamaican plantation ten years after the abolition of the slave trade and twenty years before the abolition of slavery itself. It was clearly no hotbed of *resistance* (in de Certeau's sense), and on the surface Lewis is entirely right when, at the end of his journal, he states that he "could not have wished to find a more tractable set of people on almost every occasion." But what he fails to realize—or realizes only imperfectly, for he certainly does not lack intelligence—is that it is precisely the cultivation of such tractability that enables them to *oppose* slavery (again in de Certeau's sense) every hour of the day, every day of the week, every week of the year. What Lewis calls "the negro principle that 'massa can do no wrong'" (404–5) is the slaves' principal tactic in an oppositional "game" that they must win if they are to survive the rigors of their condition and that enables them, beneath a mask of bland compliance, to steal, malinger, and otherwise subvert, through idleness, inattention, or deliberate inefficiency, the smooth functioning of the plantation. If for any reason the mask should drop or their *mētis* fail, the consequences for the slaves are dire indeed, witness the fate of a slave on a neighboring plantation, cold-bloodedly shot through the head by his master for pilfering a small quantity of coffee (335), or of two female slaves of Lewis himself who, while pregnant, are kicked in the belly by white overseers, resulting in one case in the crippling of the mother and in the other, that of the child (388–89). For the most part, though, at least while Lewis is present, the slaves succeed in both producing less sugar and obtaining more food, "maccaronis," and additional holidays. But this raises two questions. First, although the slaves are in material terms indisputable winners, do they lose morally by their very success? Are they corrupted by the game of deceit and self-abasement they must daily resort to in order to survive? Does the Quashie mask finally usurp the personality of the slave who adopts it and take over the very core of the self? Second, although power is successfully manipulated by the slaves, it is patently not destroyed and may even have been strengthened by their constant preoccupation with survival at all costs. At the end of the *Journal* as at its beginning, the structures of power are intact, and the slaves' perpetual maneuverings have done no more than nibble away at its edges, yielding a tactical

7. Spying on Massa and Mistress as they engaged in their toilet seems to have been a widespread slave occupation, if the experience of an English lady recounted by Lady Nugent is at all typical: 'The old woman attending the bath was very anxious to see her, but her pokey bonnet covered her face, and her dressing-gown concealed her person; but as the lady was stepping out of the bath, in a perfectly undisguised state, she heard a voice near her, and perceived, under the door, a pair of black eyes, and indeed a whole black face, looking earnestly at her; for the door was half a yard too short, and the old woman's petticoat had been applied to the breach; this she had shyly removed, and laid herself down on her stomach to peep. The Governor's Lady gave a great squall, and away ran the old woman" (Nugent 1907:91).

gain here, a deft advance there but leaving the source of their subjection essentially unscathed. Power manipulated is power accepted, however reluctantly, and even consolidated by the manipulator's success.[8] It is a paradox that shapes both West Indian history and the culture that reflects it and that gives a particular pungency to the endless maneuverings of the spider-man Anancy to whom we now turn—that personification of slave *mētis* in all the strength of its weakness, and also the weakness of its strength.

## Mystification and *Mētis:* Anancy's Score

Our stories and storytellers date from the period of slavery and colonialism. Their deepest meanings can be discerned only in reference to this fundamental epoch of . . . West Indian history. Our storyteller is the spokesman of a fettered, famished people, living in fear and in the various postures of survival. . . . If their ludic function is undeniable, (what more fertile ground for hope than laughter when one must live in a kind of hell?), creole stories as a whole constitute a dynamic pedagogy, a form of apprenticeship in living, or more precisely in surviving, in a colonized land. The creole story says that fear is there, that every last fragment of the world is terrifying, and that it is necessary to live with it. The creole story says that open force is the harbinger of defeat and retribution, and that the weak, by dint of cunning, evasion, patience, by manipulating the system in a way that is never sinful [*de débrouillardaise qui n'est jamais péché*], can defeat the strong, or seize power by the throat. The creole story spatters [*éclabousse*] the dominant system of values, undermining it with all the immoralities or, better, amoralities of the weaker party. It does not, however, bear a "revolutionary" message, its solutions to misfortune are not collective, the hero is alone, egotistical, preoccupied with his own escape alone. For this reason, one may follow Edouard Glissant in thinking that what is involved here is an archetypal form of deviant, round-about behavior [*un détour emblématique*], a system of counter-values or counter-culture, in which are simultaneously manifested a powerlessness to liberate oneself globally and a determination to try to do so. The creole storyteller is a fine example of this paradoxical situation. The master

8. Thus, in his study of labor and gender relations in a Trinidadian factory published after the completion of this book, Kelvin Yelvington (1995a: 229–30) has argued that the effect of oppositional tactics "may ultimately be to further the interests of the powerful groups" and to "provide a basis of further attempts to subordinate the subordinate in the long run." The "process of making a virtue out of necessity tends in most cases to further subordinate the disempowered," so that Quashie's recourse to a whole range of oppositional tactics "may have achieved the slave's short-term ends, but it did so at a cost." This admirably summarizes the paradox I am exploring in this book.

knows that he is speaking, the master tolerates his speaking, sometimes the master even understands what he is saying: his Word thus
owes it to itself to be opaque, evasive, roundabout, its meaning dif-
fracted in a thousand sybilline fragments. (Patrick Chamoiseau, *Au
temps de l'antan*, 1988, quoted in Burton 1993a:466)

Toward the end of his journal Lewis refers to his slaves as "persevering
tricksters" (384), and it is ironic, given the way he has been continually outwitted, that as he sailed back to England after his first stay in Jamaica, he
should record in his journal, with evident pleasure, some of the earliest instances of what he calls "Nancy stories" (253) and their close relatives "Neger-
tricks," which he says "bear the same relation to a Nancy-story which a farce
does to a tragedy" (307). Lewis has evidently been told the stories directly or
overheard slaves telling them to each other, and we have already seen how
Thomas Thistlewood spent several evenings in succession listening to a slave
woman named Vine telling Nancy stories "very cleverly" and found them "entertaining enough" (Hall 1989:160). Here then is the first paradox of many in
this universe of paradox: the Anancy story may have its origin in the Negro
Village, but it can be told in the Great House, and not just with impunity, but
to the evident pleasure of at least some of the Great House's residents. The
storyteller, as Patrick Chamoiseau indicates in the passage cited above, is both
inside and outside the system of power his or her stories symbolically (or
apparently) subvert. The essential theme of the Anancy story, endlessly repeated in versions both ancient and modern, is the outwitting of the powerful
by the weak or, in the terms used in this chapter, the use of tactics, *mētis*, or a
whole repertoire of oppositional devices on the part of the weak first to evade
and then to manipulate in their favor a power that, if used directly, can and
must only destroy them. De Certeau's terminology is interestingly echoed in
one modern storyteller's description of Anancy: "Im have a lot of tactics in
him," "Bredda Anancy is a man dat is very *smart*, an im neva get in *no* trouble,
because im use im brains" and counters the powerful by "a *sharpenin* powa pon
dem" (Tanna 1984:79). Anancy's realm is the realm of the polymorphous perverse, of endless deviation, deflection, and switching of roles, and the storyteller's art is likewise one of subterfuge and multiple meanings, so that any
Anancy story operates polysemically, with one meaning, say, for children,
another for adults "in the know," and another still for outsiders, particularly
outsiders who are white. What another modern Jamaican storyteller significantly calls "de tactics of a story" (ibid., 35) goes well beyond questions of
rhythm, gesture, and knowing when to raise and lower the voice. It consists of
a particular mode of concealing and revealing, of revealing *by* concealing, of
continually switching voice and register, of leading the listeners away from
and back to the story, of hoodwinking them as Anancy hoodwinks his victims,

so that the Anancy storyteller becomes himself or herself an Anancy figure, spinning the web of a story—an *anansesem*—that delights the initiated with its display of verbal virtuosity and traps the unwary in its scarcely visible threads of deception.

At the most obvious but not necessarily the most important level, the Anancy story is both a transcription of the everyday oppositional practices of slaves—the perpetual outwitting of Massa by Neger, such as we witnessed on the Cornwall estate—and a projection onto the mythical level of a world in which the weak would always be able to confound the strong with their guile and gain as their prize unlimited access to food.[9] But to see the Anancy story simply and exclusively as an expression of wish fulfillment is to underrate both its subtlety and, above all, its realism, for Anancy does not always succeed, and many stories end with him trapped in and by his own trickery and being punished accordingly. Moreover, reading any representation collection of Anancy stories reveals that for every occasion when Anancy outwits one of the powerful, there are two or three when he outwits creatures as weak as himself or—because they lack guile—even weaker. Indeed, one of the commonest tactics of all is for Anancy to use one or more of the weak to outwit one of the strong and, particularly, to ensure that it is some creature dumber than himself—his frequent companion Takuma, or Tiger, Monkey, Dog, Rat, Goat, or whoever—who takes the punishment that rightfully is his. In short, if the Anancy story really is a transcription of everyday life on the plantation (and it certainly is that, if not *solely* that), it is not so much Massa who suffers from Anancy's guile as slaves dumber and weaker than himself. Massa may be outwitted, but his power remains, and he reimposes his authority by flogging the innocent while the culprit escapes scot-free.

It is factors such as this that make Jamaican Anancy often seem rather more sinister, and considerably more limited, than the Ashante prototype he derives from and whom Robert D. Pelton has so ably characterized as an emblem of "mythic irony and sacred delight," a scrambler of structures and crosser of boundaries who ultimately draws from the disorder he creates an order more human, and more life-enhancing, than the old sclerosed order the story began with. Ashante Ananse "renews by the power of anti-structure," he "transforms disruption from a destructive into a creative force"; a "metamorph, an embodiment of liminality," he is "a living connection between the wild and

9. A classic instance of the slave as Anancy is the distinction all slaves seem to have made between "taking" (from Massa) and "stealing" (from another slave), as in the argument advanced by a slave woman in *Marly* to the effect that "'him no tief from Massa, him take from Massa,' meaning the proprietor; and therefore, as she was his property, she formed part of himself, argal, what was his was hers; argal, she could not steal from him without stealing from herself, though she might take from him part of the conjunct property in communion between them, which, however, in her opinion did not amount to theft; but was only her share of the common goods belonging to them" (Anon. 1828:41).

the social, between the potentially and the actually human" (Pelton, 1980:50–57), a figure of "sacred multivalence" (227–28) whose "sacred ribaldry or serious triviality" (254) has the power, quite simply, of renewing the cosmos itself. In his exuberance and resourcefulness, Jamaican Anancy is, or seems to be, all these things, though in the course of being transported across the Atlantic and socialized into the plantation he seems to have lost most, if not all, of his original sacred dimension: for better or worse, Jamaican Anancy is human—all too human. Moreover, though like his African parent creolized Anancy is a great disrupter of structures, all his trickery seems to operate, ultimately, in favor of the *existing* order of things, which he has partly subverted but also confirmed by virtue of the very limited nature of the subversion in question. Anancy is before all else an individualist. He cares nothing for creatures on the same level as himself or lower, cares nothing indeed for his wife and family, whom he repeatedly manipulates to his own advantage and to whom he routinely denies the fruits of his trickery. Finally, never once in all the tales I have read does he even consider the possibility of *collective* action against the rich and powerful: Anancy is most assuredly a rebel, not a revolutionary. It is perhaps for this reason that, as Orlando Patterson has suggested (1967:253), Anancy operates as both folk hero and scapegoat for the slave community and its successors. On the one hand, he possesses on a properly heroic scale the capacity for ruse and disguise every slave had to have in some degree in order to survive. On the other hand, he embodies to an almost parodic extent the "toadying attitude towards force," "the smile-and-shuffle role with Whiteman" (Tanna 1984:79) that, as we have seen, was the daily stuff of life on the Cornwall estate. Even the most sophisticated and cold-blooded role player must, Patterson suggests, have felt humiliated by the self-abasement involved, and to that extent Anancy becomes "an object upon which the slaves displaced a great deal of their self-contempt and self-hate" and thus performed "two basic psychological functions." "First, by objectifying all the unpleasant features of Quashee, Anancy made it possible for the slave to reprimand and censor the undesirable part of himself without a sense of self-persecution. Secondly, having censored this part of himself, the slave could then find it possible to laugh at it and even learn to live with and accept it." Finally, that Anancy is so often punished for his excess suggests two other censoring processes at work: the slave community's fear and resentment of slaves whose individual greed threatened the well-being of the whole (and specifically the well-being of their families) and of others—or quite possibly, the same—slaves whose ability to manipulate the system in their favor placed additional burdens, above all the threat of unmerited punishment, on those they seemed not to recognize as their brothers and sisters (see Prince 1984: 27).

Hero, scapegoat, and object of opprobrium, Anancy is, in short, a polyvalent symbol of the strengths and the weaknesses of the slave community, and it was no doubt this very polyvalence that enabled the Anancy story to satisfy imaginatively everyone, or almost everyone, on the plantation, from Negro Village to Great House. The slaves could identify with Anancy as a mythical manipulator of the mighty and vicarious avenger of the humiliations of their everyday life; project onto him the shame they consciously or unconsciously felt for their role-playing complicity with the system; and issue through him a reprimand to those members of the slave community whose individualism threatened in one way or another the well-being of the whole. On the other hand, those Whites who, by design or by accident, were present at the telling of an Anancy story would take pleasure in a protagonist whose bowings and scrapings before authority caricatured the already caricatural act the slaves played out daily before them; in a set of comical maneuverings, cleverly told, that ultimately left power unscathed; and in a set of situations and characters that confirmed them in their patronizing view of their charges. The two sets of fantasies did not of course coincide, but neither were they wholly discordant, it being the paradoxical character of the Anancy story to subvert and confirm *both* the discourse of power and the attempted counter-discourses of the subordinate group (Prince 1984:49–50). Each party to the exchange receives its imaginative satisfactions, and finally, the fictive character of the whole occasion is affirmed with the uttering of the cryptic formula "Jack Mandora me no chuse none" that signals the end of the story and the return of the Real.[10] The existing order has been challenged, manipulated, and finally restored: what pleases in the Anancy story is its ultimate innocuousness.

All this is not to query Anancy's standing as a figure and focus of *opposition*: indeed, as a scrambler of systems, manipulator of masks, and transgressor of boundaries, he is the spirit of opposition made . . . spider. But he is not a figure of *resistance* or a leader of revolts, any more than the numerous progeny he has spawned in West Indian legend and life: the man-of-words,[11] the calypsonian, the smart man, the badjohn, all of whom, as Althea V. Prince has argued (1984:49–51), are in their contrasting ways variants of the trickster. As we shall see, all of these figures and others besides challenge and manipulate the existing order *with words* but notably fail—indeed actively refuse—to do

10. I am assuming, in the absence of any evidence for or against, that some such concluding formula was used during slavery. Its significance has been much debated, but most commentators suggest that it implies a disclaimer of responsibility by the storyteller for what the story has told: "At the end of each story, we had to say, 'Jack Mandora, me no choose none' because Annancy did very wicked things in his stories, and we had to let Jack Mandora, the doorman at heaven's door, know that we were not in favour of Annancy's wicked ways: 'Me no choose none' means 'I don't choose to behave in any of these ways'" (Louise Bennett, quoted in Tanna 1984:31; cf. the statement on the same page by Ivy Baxter and that on p. 80 by Ranny Williams).

11. On Anancy as man-of-words, see Takuma's comment on him in Ranny Williams's version of "Me Fada's Bes Ridin Haws": "Yu is a talkify man" (Tanna 1984:79).

anything that might overthrow that order. As soon as the prospect of *resistance* occurs, the trickster takes to his heels, changes disguise, and may even appear on the side of the order he used to flout. This is why so many of the Anancy figures in West Indian politics—Alexander Bustamante, Eric Gairy, and "Buzz" Butler come to mind[12]—are to be found, at the end, on the side of the powerful, while still pretending of course to be champions of the powerless. The resisters—Sam Sharpe, Paul Bogle, Maurice Bishop, Walter Rodney—are made of different moral and ideological material entirely.

### Christmas Jollifications: Jonkonnu in Jamaica, 1800–1834

Few West Indian cultural forms are more complex in their origins, evolution, and meaning than Jonkonnu, and few are more important.[13] Indeed, Jonkonnu could lay good claim to being the most ancient and most enduring non-European cultural form in the Caribbean. It is first attested, in its pristine form, in Sloane's pioneering account of slavery in Jamaica (1707) and first referred to by name in Edward Long's *History of Jamaica* (1774). It experienced an extraordinary flowering and diffusion in the last three decades of slavery, whereafter it declined, or rather retreated into rural fastnesses, during the second half of the nineteenth century pending a return, somewhat as a folkloric remnant of "old-time Jamaica," to national visibility after 1950. Moreover, unlike carnival in Trinidad, Jonkonnu is not a European cultural form taken over by West Indians and injected with a set of specifically West Indian characteristics and meanings. Its origins are without doubt African, and until the late eighteenth century it developed without significant interference from European influence. As depicted by Long in 1774, it is clearly a neo-African or indigenized, rather than creolized, cultural form,[14] though by the time Lewis (1816), Williams (1826), Scott (1833), and Belisario (1837) described it, it had indeed become overlaid with certain European features and may even have been in decline before the end of slavery. Nonetheless, Cynric Williams's description of 1826 cannot be bettered for its combination of precision and

12. On Bustamante as Anancy figure, the "supreme example of the trickster leader," see Post 1978:252; on Butler as "mixture of elusive magician and obeah man," "folk-hero, half-trickster, half-shaman pitted against those inveterate enemies of the people: the Police," see Rohlehr 1990:210; on Gairy, see Singham 1968:152–69. The Surinamese military leader Desi Bouterse has also been likened to Anancy, but to one who "wears a uniform, carries an uzi, and walks around in jackboots" (see Meel 1993:140).

13. This section was written before the publication of Michael Craton's richly documented essay "Decoding Pitchy-Patchy: The Roots, Branches and Essence of Junkanoo" (1995). Craton situates Jonkonnu within a hemispheric perspective and, in addition to Jamaica, discusses its manifestations in the Bahamas, Bermuda, St. Kitts and Nevis, Belize and North Carolina; his comments (34–37) on the "grammar" that underlies these different textual forms are especially valuable, as is his concluding discussion of the etymology of Jonkonnu (37–40).

14. On the distinction between indigenization and creolization, see Wynter 1970:34–35, 42.

indeterminacy: "The custom is African and religious, although the purpose is forgotten" (Williams 1826:26). An African cultural form rapidly indigenized in Jamaica and only belatedly subject to surface creolization, Jonkonnu functioned as the core of the oppositional culture of Jamaican slaves, at first in isolation then increasingly as part of a much wider cultural phenomenon: the extraordinary "Negro Carnival" (Scott 1852:247) that was Christmas in Jamaica during the last thirty or forty years of slavery.

Many etymologies—some of them fanciful in the extreme[15]—have been proposed for the term Jonkonnu, the most plausible being Cassidy and Le Page's suggestion (1967:249) of an amalgam of two Ewe words, *dzono* (sorcerer) and *kúnu* (something deadly, a cause of death): this would certainly point to the sacred, and possibly magical, origins of the dance. Most nineteenth-century observers believed the dance was of African origin, though most equally believed it had been combined or overlaid with elements derived from European forms of mumming and masquerade. Lewis (1834:51) characteristically likens "John-Canoe" to "a Merry-Andrew dressed in a striped doublet," and equally characteristically, Michael Scott makes comparisons in *Tom Cringle's Log* with "morrice-dancers," "May-day boys in London," and "Jack-in-the-Green" (1852:250). The best-informed modern interpreters of Jonkonnu (Patterson 1967; Wynter 1970; Ryman 1984; Bettelheim 1988a) are united in stressing its African or neo-African character, with only late and comparatively minor European accretions: all agree that the masquerades of West African secret societies such as the Egungun and the Poro are the most likely African prototype. Jonkonnu has also been linked, with varying degrees of plausibility, to African yam festivals (Patterson 1967:245–46), to Myalism (Wynter 1970: 41), and even to the Shiite Muslim festival of Hosein (Ryman 1984:51); some connection with Obeah is also a distinct possibility.[16] Many of the most popular figures of "modern" Jonkonnu—the Indian Babu, Chinih (Chinese) Man, Cowboy, Doctor, Drunkard, Executioner, Belly Woman, Sailor, Whore Girl—were probably added after the end of slavery and in many cases reflect postemancipation changes in the composition and character of Jamaican society.[17] But Jonkonnu began as a theriomorphic ritual, and it is this earliest form of the

15. For a discussion of the dubious claims of "John Conny" (proposed by Long), "gens inconnus" (Belisario), and others, see Cassidy 1961:256–59.

16. Ewan, the Jonkonnu dancer Martha Beckwith interviewed in 1919, was said to be "a notorious *myal* man in Lacovia" who was able to "summon the spirits of the dead to work mischief upon an enemy": "Mavis Campbell, his leading singing girl at the time, told me that he always look the cap [the Jonkonnu "house"] out into the graveyard on the night before it was to be brought out upon the road, and performed the songs and dances there among the dead" (Beckwith 1923:11). The figure of Pitchy Patchy (who may have existed during the slave period) is traditionally linked to "the vegetal costumes that the Maroons wore for camouflage during guerilla warfare" (Bettelheim 1988a:50).

17. For a full discussion of the postemancipation development of Jonkonnu, see Ryman 1984:51–53 and Bettelheim 1988a:48–56.

dance that Sloane is referring to when he describes how slave dancers "very often tie Cows Tails to their Rumps, and add such other odd things to their Bodies in several places, as gives them a very extraordinary appearance" (1707:1:xlvii–xlix). When (almost three-quarters of a century later) Long provides the next description of the dance, animal masks still predominate, but already Jonkonnu has taken on its crucial character as a *Christmas* ritual:

> In the towns, during Christmas holidays, they have several tall robust fellows dressed up in grotesque habits, and a pair of ox-horns on their head, sprouting from the top of a horrid sort of vizor, or mask, which about the mouth is rendered very terrific with large boar-tusks. The masquerader, carrying a wooden sword in his hand, is followed with a numerous crowd of drunken women, who refresh him frequently with a sup of aniseed-water, whilst he dances at every door, bellowing out John Connú! with great vehemence; so that, what with the liquor and the exercise, most of them are thrown into dangerous fevers; and some examples have happened of their dying.

Long goes on to say that "in 1769, several new masks appeared: the Ebos, the Papaws, &c. having their respective Connús, male and female, who were dressed in a very laughable style" (Long 1774:2:424–25), strongly suggesting that at this stage it was African rather than creole slaves who were most heavily involved in Jonkonnu. By the early nineteenth century, when other human masks, notably Koo Koo or Actor Boy, had been added to the dance, Jonkonnu was still notably more "African" than the other great Jamaican Christmas ritual, the parade of the Set Girls, which was tending more and more to engulf it, at least in the towns. Kelly's description of 1831 not only indicates a clear tension between the African and creole modes of celebrating Christmas—the Creoles dance to fife and drum in the center of the hall, while the Africans sing and dance to gumbay music on the margins—but also suggests that the different African ethnic groups were *competing with each other* as well as against the Creoles as a whole.[18] Scott partly confirms this when he contrasts, in highly ethnocentric fashion, "the barbarous music and yelling of the different African tribes" to "the more mellow singing of the Set Girls," though the John Canoe who most attracts his attention is "a light, active, clean-made young Creole negro" (1852:247); in *Marly*, both John Canoe and his "wife" are "of true African extraction" (Anon. 1828;294), and Williams (1826:27) adds the useful intelligence that on the plantation where he wit-

18. "The Margolas, the Mandingos, the Eboes, the Congoes, &c., &c., formed into exclusive groups, and each strove to be loudest in the music and songs . . . peculiar to their country" (quoted in Epstein 1977:87). Philippo (1969:242) adds that at Christmas "each of the African tribes upon the different estates formed itself into a distinct party, composed of men, women and children."

"'Queen' or 'Maam' of the Set-Girls." From I. M. Belisario, *Sketches . . . of the Negro Population of the Island of Jamaica* (1837–38). Reproduced by permission of the Syndics of Cambridge University Library.

nessed Jonkonnu in the early 1820s, "the mulattos kept aloof, as if they disdained to mingle with the negroes; and some of the pious, the regenerated slaves, also objected to participate in the heathen practices of their ancestors." The evidence, while inconclusive, tends to suggest a tension, in the final period of slavery, between a number of different forms of Jonkonnu: most notably between a neo-African rural (plantation) Jonkonnu probably dominated by Africans but supported by most, if not all, of the creole slaves and a more creolized urban form still dominated by Africans but from which creole slaves (and still more, Free Coloureds and Free Blacks) were tending to distance

"French Set-Girls." From I. M. Belisario, *Sketches . . . of the Negro Population of the Island of Jamaica* (1837–38). Reproduced by permission of the Syndics of Cambridge University Library.

themselves in favor of the parades of the Set Girls and associated processions and displays.[19]

Most foreign visitors to Jamaica between 1800 and the end of slavery tended to conflate Jonkonnu and the Set Girls into a single carnivalesque Christmas extravaganza, but though the two coexisted on the streets of Kingston and other towns and on some plantations, it is clear that they were wholly distinct in both origin and character. Whereas Jonkonnu is by almost universal consent of African origin and clearly established as a Christmas festivity by the 1770s at the latest (and probably long before that), the Set Girl parades are generally considered to have been "imported" into Jamaica during the 1790s and early 1800s by French planters fleeing with their slaves from the

19. The distinction between urban and rural forms of Jonkonnu survives to this day, according to Luther Cooper, a masquerader from Savannah-la-Mar interviewed by Judith Bettelheim (1988a: 53): "Yes, there is people who play Cowhead but not in town here. You don't play Cowhead in town. The masks from the country generally play Cowhead and Horsehead." According to Beckwith (1923:9), "until recently both Horse and Ox-head dancers begged for money at Christmas-time in the streets of Kingston and other large centers, but their antics have finally banished them from city streets, and even in country districts the terror is so great at the appearance of the Ox-head that he is now forbidden by law."

great slave insurrection in neighboring Saint-Domingue. Bearing names such as "Royalists," "Mabiales," and "Americans" (Dirks 1987:7), the earliest "French sets" clearly owed something to the French creole carnival tradition,[20] though Lewis (1834:53) suggests that the rivalry of the Red Girls and the Blue Girls that he saw enacted on the streets of Black River on New Year's Day 1816 went back to rival balls given "many years ago" to the "Brown Girls" of Kingston by two British admirals, the "Admiral of the Red" and the "Admiral of the Blue," who had a score to settle between them, in consequence of which "all Kingston was divided into parties: from thence the division spread into other districts: and ever since, the whole island, at Christmas, is separated into the rival factions of the Blues and the Reds (the Red representing also the English, the Blue the Scotch), who contend for settling forth their processions with the greatest taste and magnificence": this crucial aspect of Jamaican Christmas as ritualized contest and conflict will be discussed in detail shortly. Whatever the origins of the competing processions, it is clear from Stewart's account of 1808 that they appealed more to the creole sections of the population than to the African born, that they were primarily but not exclusively an urban phenomenon,[21] and that they were predominantly, but again not exclusively, a form of female rather than male self-assertion and display. The music that accompanied the Jonkonnu dance was the classically African combination of gumbay, rattles, and (female) voice, while that of the Set Girl parades was perceptibly more creole with its inclusion of fiddles, kettledrums, and fifes. Writing in 1825, Henry de la Beche was not alone in predicting the imminent demise of the old-style music in the face of the attractions of the new: "Joncanoe himself," he claimed, "is getting out of fashion" (quoted in Epstein 1977:86).[22] Finally, Lewis's account of Christmas at Black River makes it clear

20. This is a widely held view, though William Beckford's account of 1790 (2:389–90) suggests that a wholly Jamaican origin is equally plausible: "At Christmas, the negroes upon neighbouring estates are divided, like other communities, into different parties; some call themselves the blue girls, and some the red: and their clothes are generally characteristic of their attachment." It is more than likely that the sets began as an imitation by free colored women of the white society balls in Spanish Town at which, according to Long (quoted in Barnett 1978–79:29), the (white) women "[vied] with one another in the richness of their dress, and everyone [made] a point of exhibiting a new suit or finery"; Stewart 1808:303: "On all occasions the brown ladies emulate, and even strive to excel the whites in splendour, taste and expensiveness of dress, equipage, and entertainment." Urban-based slave women would in due course imitate the free colored women imitating the white women and would in *their* turn be imitated by slave women on the plantations.

21. Stewart (1808:263–64) writes that on New Year's Day it was customary "for the negro girls of the towns (who conceive themselves far superior to those on the estates, in point of *taste, manners, and fashion*) to exhibit themselves in all the pride of gaudy splendor, under the denomination of *blues* and *reds*—parties in rivalship and opposition to each other, and distinguished by these colours." The girls would sing songs "which they had learned for the occasion, or those which they had caught up from the whites, in a style far superior to the negresses on the plantation."

22. According to Barclay (1826), the "rude music" of the African slaves would soon be "altogether exploded among the creole negroes, who show a decided preference for European music" and

that "John-Canoe made no part" of the Set Girls' procession, being engaged "upon quite an independent interest" that involved him and a fellow mask going "about from house to house, tumbling and playing antics to pick up money for themselves" (Lewis 1834:56). That Jonkonnu and the Set Girls' parades were separate cultural forms—separate in origin, personnel, and meaning, the first neo-African and only superficially creolized, the second creole in both form and content—seems beyond doubt: it is even possible that they were engaged in a struggle for preeminence by the time Lewis described them as differentiated elements of a single Christmas ritual.[23]

On the estates, however, Jonkonnu still reigned supreme and still, in the 1820s, remained essentially what it had been fifty years before: a neo-African rite, now incorporating some incidental European features, through which slaves, both African and creole, expressed some submerged, unconscious, or forgotten sense of otherness and participated along with their masters, mistresses, and other plantation Whites in a complex oppositional game whose meaning is likely forever to remain obscure, so ambiguously does it combine self-assertion on the part of the slaves with a celebration, real or feigned (or both), of plantation unity. In many ways the annual Christmas extravaganza was an extension, elaboration, and intensification of the crop-over celebrations that, about August each year, marked the successful termination of the sugar harvest. On this occasion, wrote Barclay (1826:10), the slaves assemble in the evening "in their master's or manager's house, and, as a matter of course, take possession of the largest room, bring with them a fiddle and a tambourine. Here all authority and all distinction of colour ceases; black and white, overseer and book-keeper, mingle together in the dance." The contemporaneous account in *Marly* (47–48) stresses the coming together of masters and slaves, but also the limits to their "fraternization." The slaves do not come to the Great House until invited, the "black belles" arrive bedecked "in all the finery which they possessed" knowing that "there could be no ball without them," and they are accompanied by "the sable fops of the estate, in their gala dresses, of which a white neckcloth forms a prominent part." White men dance with black women—there appear to be no white women on the es-

---

for dances such as the Scotish reel; he does, however, stress that this kind of "extreme" Europeanization is largely "confined to those who are, or have been, domestics about the houses of the whites, and have in consequence imbibed a fondness or their amusements, and some skill in the performance" (quoted in Epstein 1977:85).

23. Set Girl parades certainly existed on the estates, where they seem to have combined without problem with Jonkonnu: 'The young girls of a plantation, or occasionally of two neighbouring plantations leagued, from what is called 'a sett.' They dress exactly in uniform, with gowns of some neat pattern of printed cotton, and take the name of Blue Girls, Yellow Girls, etc., according to the dress and ribbon they have chosen. . . . A matron attends who possesses some degree of authority, and is called Queen of the Sett, and they have always one or two Joncanoe-men, smart youths, fantastically dressed, and masked so as not to be known" (Barclay 1826:11).

tate—and then watch as "saple fops" join "black belles" to "display their prowess in dancing." When supper "calls the Buckras from the hall," the slaves dance on by themselves until, supper over, the Whites return and dancing continues until the early hours of the morning, whereupon "all departed, if not happy, at least well pleased, and thus the black ball terminated"—in short, an enjoyable if less than ecstatic occasion during which, some minor infractions apart, the essential social and racial boundaries are observed by both sides.

Christmas has an altogether more transgressive character, though once again everything happens with the permission and complicity of the Whites and once again the essential structures of plantation are in due course restored after their brief symbolic flouting by the Blacks. By far the best account of Christmas on a Jamaican slave plantation is that provided by Cynric Williams in his *Tour through the Island of Jamaica* of 1826, and it is worth quoting here in its entirety:

> I was grumbling in imagination at the incessant clamour of the cocks on the morning of Christmas-day, when my ears were assailed with another sort of music, not much more melodious. This was a chorus of negroes singing "Good morning to your night-cap, and health to master and mistress." They came into the house and began dancing. I slipped on my dressing-gown and mingled in their orgies, much to the diversion of the black damsels, as well as of the inmates of the house, who came into the piazza to witness the ceremonies. We gave the fiddler a dollar, and they departed to their grounds to prepare their provisions for two or three days, and we saw no more of them till the evening, when they again assembled on the lawn before the house with they gombays, bonjaws, and an Ebo drum made of a hollow tress, with a piece of sheepskin stretched over it. Some of the women carried smaller calabashes with pebbles in them, stuck on short sticks, which they rattled in time to the songs, or rather howls of the musicians. They divided themselves into parties to dance, some before the gombays, in a ring, to perform a boléro or a sort of love-dance, as it is called, where the gentlemen occasionally wiped the perspiration off the shining faces of their black beauties, who, in turn, performed the same service to the minstrel. Others performed a sort of pyrrhic before the Ebo drummer, beginning gently and gradually quickening their motions, until they seemed agitated by the furies. They were all dressed in their best; some of the men in long-tailed coats, one of the gombayers in old regimentals; the women in muslins and cambrics, with coloured handkerchiefs tastefully disposed round their heads, and ear-rings, necklaces, and bracelets of all sorts, in profusion. The entertainment was kept up till nine or ten o'clock in the evening, and dur-

ing the time they were regaled with punch and santa in abundance; they came occasionally and asked for porter and wine. Indeed a perfect equality seemed to reign among all parties; many came and shook hands with their master and mistress, nor did the young ladies refuse this salutation any more than the gentlemen. The merriment became rather boisterous as the punch operated, and the slaves sang satirical philippics against their master, communicating a little free advice now and then; but they never lost sight of decorum and at last retired, apparently quite satisfied with their saturnalia, to dance the rest of the night at their own habitations. (Williams 1826:21–23)

The following day the slaves return, and this time they perform the Jonkonnu dance proper, led by "a man dressed up in a mask with a grey beard and long flowing hair, who carried the model of a house on his head"—our first glimpse, so far, of the enigmatic and incongruous structure that is often itself referred to as Jonkonnu. The mask "first saluted his master and mistress," accompanied by "eight to ten young girls" who "also danced without changing their position, moving their elbows and knees, and keeping tune with the calabashes filled with small stones"; the "African" character of the dance is so blatant that one of the dancers is reprimanded by the others for her *imperance* (impertinence?). While an "incessant hammering" is kept up on the gumbay drum and a Windsor chair that the slaves requisition as a secondary drum, "the Jonkanno's attendant went about collecting money from the dancers and from the white people" (ibid., 25–26), whereupon the slaves depart, presumably to display and disport themselves on neighboring plantations. Williams's account of a plantation Christmas is replicated, with only minor variations, by Stewart (1808:262–64) and by the anonymous author of *Marly*, the latter stressing, as he had already in his description of crop-over, the limits of the welcome the Whites extend to their scarcely unexpected visitors, whom before long they find "tedious and troublesome. To get rid of them, they therefore had recourse to sending them to the overseer to receive their Christmas present [of salt fish, rum, and sugar]. And it proved an effectual excitement to get quit of their officious, though well meant and sincere kindness, for in a very short time they had all disappeared." Clearly, though for a few days "the bonds of slavery are loosened," the radically inegalitarian structures of the institution remain in place (Anon. 1828:288–89).

It is in the towns, however, says Marly (289), that "the suspension of slavery for this very limited space shows itself in all its glory—where the bond servants seem as if they were electrified with joy, so happy do they appear." Here the behavior of the Jonkonnu masqueraders seems distinctly more aggressive than on the plantations, with one writer describing how the "negroes dress themselves in bulls" hides, with the horns on, into which they are sewn

Jonkonnu troupe from Duheney Pen, St. Thomas, Jamaica (1976), depicting (left to right) Warrior, Amerindian, Amerindian, and Cowhead. Photo by Judith Bettelheim.

and go bellowing about the streets, butting all the people they meet" (Chambre, 1858, quoted in Cassidy and Le Page 1967:250), while the hero of *Tom Cringle's Log* is moved to anger by one "Device" who, bouncing and leaping before him as though "possessed by a devil whose name was Legion," sings a song about "Massa Buccra's" preference for "brown girl" over "buccra lady" that is all too close to the mark: "'Get away, you scandalous scoundrel,' cried I; 'away with you, sir!'" (Scott 1852:249–50).[24] But in Kingston as in Black River, it is the Set Girls rather than Jonkonnu that occupy center stage, and Lewis, Scott, and the author of *Marly* all provide invaluable, if not always intentional, insights into the meaning of this more recent, and more obviously creolized, form of Christmas celebration. The key elements in the Set Girls' parades are clearly competition and display or, since the two elements are inseparable, *competitive display*, setting against one other associations of women, not all of them necessarily young and beautiful, who correspond to, or represent, the principal social or racial categories in the colonies: "There were brown sets, and black sets, and sets of all the intermediate gradations of colour. Each set was dressed pin for pin alike, and carried umbrellas or parasols of the same

24. The hero also has his face wiped with a "dirty handkerchief" containing "sundry moppings and mowings" but, aside from exclaiming "murder, what a flavour of salt fish and onions it had!" does not seem at all put out (Scott 1852:248).

colour and size. . . . They sang, as they swam along the streets in the most
luxurious attitudes. . . . But the *colours* were never blended in the same set—no
blackie ever interloped with the browns, nor did the browns in any case mix
with the sables—always keeping in mind,—black *woman*—brown *lady*" (ibid.,
251–52). But at Black River no such divisions of race or complexion seem to
set off the Blue Girls from the Red, whose "mutual jealousy and pique" and
"scornful animosity and spirit of depreciation" Lewis compares to the rivalry of
the Guelphs and Ghibellines as they "examined the efforts at display of each
other" (1834:53). Perhaps, if free, the women came from different parts of
Black River or pursued different trades or professions; perhaps, if slaves, they
belonged to different plantations. Perhaps, more fundamentally still, it was the
sheer desire to assemble and compete that brought them together in "sets"
whose raison d'être was to that extent wholly gratuitous. Perhaps, finally, it
was the ludic, agonic principle per se that caused Black River, like Kingston
and every other substantial town in Jamaica, to explode once a year in a
display of collective effervescence based on conspicuous consumption and ritualized conflict that neither had nor needed any meaning beyond itself. "I
never saw so many people who appeared to be so unaffectedly happy," wrote
Lewis of Black River, "nothing was thought of but real pleasure; and that
pleasure seemed to consist in singing, dancing, and laughing, in seeing and
being seen, in showing their own fine clothes, or in admiring those of others"
(58).

But while Lewis was particularly struck by "the excessive rapture of the
black multitude" (ibid.), he and other observers provide sufficient evidence of
white participation in the rituals of Christmas to support Robert Dirks's judgment that "the masters were involved as deeply as the slaves in the saturnalia;
in a way, it was as much a white saturnalia as it was a black one" (1987:x).
That involvement was in the first instance an economic one. Although much,
perhaps most, of the money needed for the purchase or making of Christmas
finery came from the slaves' own "alternative" economy,[25] all observers stress
the part played by contributions from slaveowners and other Whites (not to
mention certain "rich negroes"; see Lewis 1834:75) on the plantation and from
"the opulent among the white and brown population" in the towns, "the negroes," according to "Marly" (295), "contributing very little among themselves,
but their own exertions and labour, which, as has been seen, they esteem as
the very acme of pleasure." Some of these contributions were without doubt
self-interested, and Lewis (75–76) describes how the wealthy slave sponsors
of Jonkonnu "afterwards share the money collected from the spectators during

25. See Williams's description (1826:3–4) of the town of Falmouth just before Christmas: "I
was surprised to see so many negroes purchasing finery for the approaching holidays, and laying
down pieces of money that I had never thought to see in the hands of slaves; for some changed
doubloons, gold pieces, worth here five pounds six shillings and eight pence of the island currency."

[the John Canoes"] performance, allotting one share to the representator him-self." But for most of the white and brown contribution it was prestige, not profit, that was involved, and *Marly* in particular provides fascinating insights into the "species of competition which yearly occurs among the native born ladies of the Island . . . relative to who would show on their girls the greatest profusion of jewels on these slave gala days."[26] Thus, when "black Luna" is elected "queen" of her set, her owner, a Miss Strutt, is anxious "to show that she was possessed of jewels in abundance, to enable Luna to act with honour and dignity on such a momentous occasion" and goes to great lengths to ensure that "her" girl outshines Miss Pindar's Quasheba and Miss Goodly's Clementina. Likewise "Snowball," the set "king," sports a hat "grandly deco-rated with the towering ostrich feathers, which his mistress had that morning withdrawn from her bonnet" and is further bedecked with "his Massa's gold watch and chain, to which was appended a very large bunch of seals; and to make him appear still more grand, his Massa, who was Senior Warden of the Lodge in the Parish, clothed him with his sash of office." "The dress of the townspeople's negroes bespoke the vanity of their owners," "Marly" concludes (290–93), as if the point needed underlining: if the slaves attain to a regal or mythic identity for a day, it is because their masters and mistresses *wish* them to do so in order to enhance their own standing in colonial society. The slaves are their masters' surrogates, charged with vicariously displaying their wealth: to emphasize this is not to exhaust the significance of Christmas or to down-grade the part the slaves played in it, but to remind ourselves that Christmas in Jamaica was a two-sided (or three- or four-sided) ritual and that as such its meaning is necessarily ambivalent and certainly far more complex than a straightforward—or even roundabout—assertion of identity by the slaves.

What, then, *was* going on when the slaves thronged into the Great House on Christmas morning, singing and dancing and beating their gumbays, or flaunted themselves in all their finery—theirs or their owners'—on the streets of Kingston, Black River, or Montego Bay? In the first and most obvious in-stance, the Black Saturnalia was a brief "sacred" interlude in the profane order of plantation society, a rupture lasting two or three days in a world dominated by work, exploitation, and oppression, during which slaves and masters min-gled in conditions of at least apparent equality, squandering resources that, in their different ways, they had been accumulating during the rest of the year: a feast, in short, in the Durkheimian sense of the word. To the extent that work was suspended for two or three days, Christmas and the New Year were, as "Marly" says, "truly holidays of freedom, happiness, and merriment," and the

26. The emotional investment of whites in the success of "their" set is well brought out by partisan behavior of the hotel owner Miss Edwards in Lewis's account: "'For the love of Heaven, only look at the *Red* lights! Old iron hoops, nothing but old iron hoops, I declare! Well! for my part!' and then, with a contemptuous toss of her head, away frisked Miss Edwards triumphantly" (1834:59).

slaves responded accordingly: "Attired in their best and gayest apparel, they seemed all life and glee, joyous gladness sparkled in their dark coloured eyes, and smiled on their black and glossy countenances, for at length the happy period had arrived" (288). In similar vein, and still more evocatively, Stewart (1808:262–63) describes how at Christmas "these poor people appear as it were quite another race. They show themselves off to great advantage, by fine clothes, and a profusion of trinkets; . . . they address the whites with greater familiarity; they come into their masters' houses and drink with them—the distance between them appears to be annihilated for the moment . . . ; they seem as a people recreated and renewed." On entering the Great House en masse and playing the instruments and dancing the dances that most announced their otherness, the slaves crossed—with their masters' permission—the threshold between "us" and "them," and for a period of perhaps four or five hours the plantation plunged into a liminal state in which customary boundaries and constraints were nominally suspended. The slaves saluted and praised their masters and mistresses and received gifts in exchange. Blacks and Whites danced together to the most "African" of music. There was some mockery and satire from the slaves, which was expected and probably enjoyed by the Whites, provided it did not go beyond certain mutually understood limits—as, in the cases we have examined, it clearly did not. And that, on the surface of things, was that as in due course the slaves moved out, either back to their village or on to another plantation to salute, serenade, and confront both its masters and its slaves.

How "sincere" were the slaves when they greeted the Whites with cries of "Good morning to your night-cap, and health to master and mistress" and wished them "long life and crosperity"?[27] Were they confirming paternalism or undermining it, or somehow both confirming and undermining it at the same time? That there was *some* kind of identification by slaves with their masters—necessarily ambivalent—seems beyond doubt, even if it was not the identification of "sons" and "daughters" with their "father" that planters such as Long liked to imagine. Slaves, writes Long (1774:2:410), are "extremely vain in reflecting on the connection between them" and their masters for, he says, the following reason: "Their master's character and repute cast, they think, a kind of secondary light upon themselves, as the moon derives her lustre from the sun; and the importance he acquires, in his station of life, adds, they imagine, to their own estimation among their neighbour Negroes on the adjacent estates." More than a century after Long wrote these words, but at a time when the memory of "old-time" Jonkonnu had not been entirely forgotten, a black Jamaican, J. H. Reid, provides a further clue when he states that "the object of a Jancoonoo play originally was praise of the master or owner of the slaves

27. That is, a prosperous crop; see Dirks 1987:3.

concerned and the condemnation of all others" (*Jamaica's Jubilee*, 1888, quoted in Bryan 1991:211). Adding these and Long's words to the descriptions of Williams, "Marly," and others, can we not say that the slaves' celebration of their masters was a roundabout celebration and assertion of *themselves*? Slaves had, as we have seen, every material reason for flattering their masters' self-image at every opportunity and at Christmas they do this with a vengeance. But they also go further: they take symbolic possession of the locus of white power, the Great House,[28] eat, drink, and dance with its owners, and, having taken some of that power into themselves, move on to a neighboring estate where they assert themselves ludically before a rival group of slaves and affirm their solidarity with them through the rituals of eating, drinking, and dancing.[29] In this way, the endless crisscrossing of visits from plantation to plantation that took place at Christmas and the New Year (see *Marly*, 295) becomes both an assertion of self by the slaves of each individual estate and an affirmation of a broader and far more important community, the community of the island's slaves as a whole.[30] Christmas, in short, was the weekend "play" transformed into an islandwide feast. For two or three days, what Long (1774:2:414) called the "general correspondence carried on, all over the island, amongst the Creole Blacks" was raised, through the shared rituals of eating, drinking, and dancing, into a shared sense of social and racial community that seems for once to have brought *plantation* Creoles and Africans together as one.

In the towns things were more complex and, not unexpectedly, more divided. Here it is noticeable that the different sections of society do *not* eat, drink, or dance together but remain resolutely apart as they engage in ritualized combat. "Brown girls" and "black girls," "Reds" and "Blues," defy each other with their finery, pomp, and "luxurious attitudes" as they "swim," in

28. Patterson (1967:246) notes that members of the Egungun secret society go to the chief's house and perform plays there and suggests a link with "what took place in Jamaica where the 'chief's house' was replaced by the house of wealthy merchants and planters."

29. This competitive element continues in towns after emancipation when, according to Judith Bettelheim (1988a:45), "bands from different districts would converge at special intersections where certain members would battle for right of way. The rules of the game required the team captains to step out in front and spar verbally. 'And they decide who can pass. Me don't go to your town, and you don't come here. Then the captain makes a sign and you can pull through. And that's the rules of it.'" The parallel with carnival bands in Trinidad is striking and will be discussed further in chapter 4.

30. The element of ludic combat, so central to Trinidadian carnival, is also attested at Christmas in Jamaica in the "plays" performed on plantations, such as the "rude representation of some passages of Richard III" witnessed by Alexander Barclay (1826:12) on the Dalvey estate at Christmas 1823: "The Joncanoe-men, disrobed of part of their paraphernalia, were the two heroes, and fought not for a kingdom, but a queen, whom the victor carried out in triumph. Richard calling out 'A horse! a horse!' &c. was laughable enough." The following year Henry de la Beche witnessed a nearly identical performance that ended, however, with "Richard killing his antagonist, and then figuring in a sword dance with him" (quoted in Hill 1992:238). It is highly likely that the rival Jonkonnus were the "champions" of neighboring plantations doing battle for the honor of their respective supporters, or specialist performers in whom we can recognize the ancestor of Actor Boy.

Scott's evocative phrase (252), along the streets of Kingston, Falmouth, or wherever, music, banners, and symbolic effigies at the fore. In Kingston all the different trades and professions—butchers, gardeners, workhouse guards— have their own "Gumbi-men, Horn-blowers, John Canoes and Nondescript" (Scott 1852:250), and if Scott is to be believed, there is even a "white man's John Canoe party" led by a "John Canoe with *black* face, which was all in rule, as his black counterparts wore *white* ones" (ibid., 254). To this extent the sets and other Christmas societies are just as segmented and hierarchical as the militia that parades with its separate cohorts, ranged in sociological and on-tological order, of Whites, Jews, Free Coloureds, and Free Blacks (ibid., 252– 53). Christmas, then, does not suppress differences but dramatizes them and, by allowing tensions and hostilities to be given stylized and ludic expression, brings a semblance of unity to a sorely divided society. But at nightfall the Whites and Mulattos retire to their houses, leaving the Blacks to attend "a negroe ball, at which, however, no white person is allowed to be present" (*Marly*, 293).

What, finally, was the significance of the extraordinary array of masks, items of clothing, and other appurtenances worn or carried by the various Jonkonnus we have encountered? What, for example, are we to make of the amazing patchwork figure who confronts the hero of *Tom Cringle's Log* on the streets of Kingston?

> The prominent character was, as usual, the John Canoe or Jack Pud-ding. He was a light, active, clean-made young Creole negro, without shoes or stockings; he wore a pair of light jean small-clothes, all too wide, but confined at the knees, below and above, by bands of red tape, after the manner that Malvolio would have called cross-garter-ing. He wore a splendid blue velvet waistcoat, with old-fashioned flaps coming down over his hips, and covered with tarnished embroidery. his shirt was absent on leave, I suppose, but at the wrists of his coat he had tin or white iron frills, with loose pieces attached, which tinkled as he moved. . . . His coat was an old blue artillery uniform one, with a small bell hung to the extreme points of the swallow-tailed skirts, and three tarnished epaulets, one one each shoulder, and . . . the biggest of the three stuck at his rump, the *point d'appui* for a sheep's tail. He had an enormous cocked hat on, to which was appended in front a white false-face, or mask, of a most Methodistical expression, while Janus-like, there was another face behind, of the most quizzical description, a sort of living Antithesis, both being garnished and over-stopped with one coarse wig, made of the hair of bullocks' tails, on which the *chapeau* was strapped down with a broad band of gold lace. (Scott 1852:247–48)

One's first reaction is to cry out "What a *mélange!*" as Lady Nugent did when first confronted by Jonkonnu dancers and one of their "plays" (Nugent 1907: 66).[31] But if one looks closer and reads the Jonkonnu's costume *as a text*, it becomes nothing less than a résumé in code of the history of Africa in Jamaica: African origins surviving almost parodically in the tails of the sheep and the bullocks, enslavement metonymically represented in the "tin or white iron frills, with loose pieces attached" that hang from his wrists like handcuffs and chains, captivity in a heavily militarized colony (the old blue artillery coat),[32] the Europeanization of the few (the blue velvet waistcoat with its tarnished embroidery) and the Christianization, voluntary or involuntary, of the many (the "white false-face, or mask, of a most Methodistical expression"), and so on. All this the Jonkonnu both embodies and mocks in his dress: like the grotesque Janus mask he wears on his back, he is in Scott's brilliant expression "a sort of living Antithesis," an antithesis of order, wholeness, and harmony, a patchwork being, an assemblage of borrowed bits and pieces who nonetheless contrives to be uniquely and ineffably himself—in a word, a *Creole.*[33]

One thing only is lacking—the Jonkonnu itself, described by Williams (1826:25) as simply "the model of a house," by Barclay (1826:11) as "a castle or tower surrounded with mirrors," by "Marly"—misled, like so many, by false etymologies—as "an imitation of a canoe" (Anon. 1828:294), and by Lewis (1834:51) more elaborately as "a kind of pasteboard house-boat, filled with puppets, representing, some sailors, other soldiers, others again slaves at work on a plantation, &c." The house could, of course, have some as yet unspecified African prototype, but that it is absent from Long's detailed description of 1774 (and does not, in addition, feature in every early nineteenth-century account of the dance) suggests that it was a comparatively recent *creole* addition to Jonkonnu's "armoury" and, as Belisario suggested in 1837, "an evident attempt (however humble) at West Indian architecture" (quoted in Cassidy 1961:261). If this is the case, then the Jonkonnu's accoutrement becomes even more semiotically charged. Jonkonnu was, as we have seen, originally a theriomorphic rite, and the animal hides, complete with horns, tusks, and tails, in which the dancers were concealed may be interpreted as signs of power

31. The "play" in questions "starred" Henri IV of France and the children of Tippoo Saib, sultan of Mysore, who had opposed British rule in India and was killed in 1799. The children appear to kill "Henry IV" in revenge for the killing of their father, and "after the tragedy" the actors "all began dancing with the greatest glee" (see Hill 1992:237). It is, to say the least, an extraordinary "anti-colonial" play to perform before a British colonial governor and his wife just two years after the events in question.

32. Errol Hill (1992:232) rightly stresses the visibility of military activity (and uniforms) in Jamaica during the period in question, namely the French revolutionary wars. Cf. Geggus 1987:297.

33. Cf. Belisario's description in 1837 of Jonkonnu as "a non-descript compound, in half-military, half-mountebank attire" (quoted in Bettelheim 1988a:48).

over the animal world. To these, as Errol Hill has suggested (1992:236), the slaves gradually added further emblems of power—the wooden sword mentioned by Long, the fragments of military uniform recorded by Scott—until finally, probably in the last quarter of the eighteenth century, they began to make effigies of the ultimate expression of power in plantation society, the Great House itself.[34] We know that Jonkonnu dancers took the names of prominent Whites—Admiral Rowe, General Campbell—as their "gala-day" names (Wynter 1970:43), not, it now seems, in servile imitation or submission, but to invest themselves symbolically with the power of their bearers.[35] We know too that in the words of "Marly" (1828:290) the "Negro sets" had "during their short span of freedom . . . their king, and queen, and court, to rule over them, and mimic, so far as they are able, a kingly state of society."[36] But, as *Marly* reveals, the slaves *elected* their kings and their queens, just as the wearer of the Jonkonnu mask was *chosen* by his fellows (Williams 1826:25), and if the set hierarchies mimicked those of established society, it was perhaps once again less in a spirit of submission or flattery than as a way, briefly and fictively, of replacing them and appropriating their power: thus "Snowball," festooned in his master's sash of office, is "elevated by his high situation and sounding appellation of King, in supporting which character he looked and strutted as if he had been one in reality, and probably had a more royal and dignified appearance than any of their sable majesties of Africa" (Anon. 1828: 291). Now, finally, the slaves construct a model of the Great House and mount it on the head of one of their number. Playing their most "African" music and dancing and singing in their most "African" style, the slaves throng, *with the complicity of the Whites*, into the Great House itself and, for some hours effectively make it their own. The order of the plantation is symbolically reversed, and the power of the Great House passes, as it were, into the model house the slaves have constructed. Having absorbed the Whites' power by

34. Kamau Brathwaite (1990:105) suggests that *all* the apparently secular objects worn or carried in Jonkonnu have a ritual significance as "fragments of God." It is an impressive list: "raffia, straw, tatters, cowries, beads, calabash, animal horns on head, heart-shapes on breast or carried as costume or accessories, roses rose-shapes rosettes stars pentacles whips knives garden tools . . . flags, rivers of cloth, iconographic aprons, & ritual-substitutes that have become ritual objects (sequins, feathers, flowers, playing-cards, mirrors, bits of glass, sticks, whips, umbrella sticks)."

35. It is worth stressing, in this respect, "the Maroon custom of adopting the names of gentlemen of the island" that, according to Dallas (1968:1:116), was "universally practised among them." The same author also draws attention to the fact that the captain of the Maroons "wore a kind of regimentals, perhaps some old military coat finely laced, which had been given to him by a gentleman whose name he had assumed." Name, title, uniform: it is as though the Jonkonnu dancer became a Cudjoe or a Quao for the duration of the Christmas holiday.

36. Phillippo (1969:242) says that each separate African tribe on the estates had its own king or queen at Christmas, "who was distinguished by a mask of the most hideous appearance, and attired from head to foot in gaudy harlequin like apparel."

eating, drinking, and dancing with them, the slaves then move on to cement their ties agonistically with the slaves of neighboring plantations, still singing and dancing, but *leaving the structures of their own plantation intact*.

That Jonkonnu possessed a subversive potential was of course recognized by the masters, who, according to Scott (1852:252), always ensured that the militia was on hand "in case any of the John Canoes should take a small fancy to burn or pillage the town, or to rise and cut the throats of their masters, or any little innocent recreation of the kind." On the other hand, they also recognized the value of Jonkonnu as a "safety valve" for their slaves' repressed feelings, and Cynric Williams's host probably spoke for many when he said that "there would be a rebellion in the island if any attempt was made to curtail the enjoyments of blacks, even on religious principles' (1826:29). Indeed, when such an attempt *was* made, in 1840 and 1841, the result was riots in Kingston and the loss of two lives (Wilmot 1990:72). Accordingly, no single meaning can be attached to Jonkonnu and the associated (but distinct) rituals of Christmas. Its subversive potential was considerable, its subversive effect almost nil. A ritual of opposition rather than of resistance, it was not so much "the world turned upside down" as the world skewed somewhat sideways, momentarily and figuratively challenged by the slaves (with the consent of their owners), then set once more aright on its normal foundations (with the consent of the slaves). For the duration of the feast all the oppositions in colonial society (masters versus slaves, above all, but also Africans versus Creoles, [Free] Coloureds versus Blacks, Whites versus Mulattos, Whites versus Whites, town versus country, the slaves of this plantation versus the slaves of that, and so on) are both dramatically heightened and fictively resolved, creating as great a sense of social unity—perhaps even a sense of protonational identity—as was possible in a colony founded on the ontological division of master and slave. For both Massa and Quashie, Christmas was a time of fantasies symbolically fulfilled. For Massa it was the fantasy that, a childlike primitive at heart, Quashie really did wish him and Missis "long life and crosperity," that he really did love him as a son loves his father. For Quashie it was, in the first instance, the fantasy of food and drink without limit but also, as he and his fellows streamed into the Great House, the fantasy less of equality with Massa than of appropriating his power. The two fantasies met in the main hall of the Great House as Quashie and Quasheba danced before Massa and Missis, and perhaps Massa took a turn with Quasheba and, somewhat more gingerly, Missis with Quashie. Gifts of salt fish, salt meat, rum, and sugar were given, confirming Massa and Missis in their role as providers, and perhaps giving Quashie and Quasheba the pleasure of feeling that they had outwitted them *again*. Then, after more singing and dancing, eating and drinking, set off perhaps by some innocuous mocking by the slaves of their masters, the two fantasies diverged, as Massa and Missis and Quashie and Quasheba returned to their own worlds until the ritual resumed the following year. But Quashie and Quasheba continued to dream, and there came one Christmas—that of 1831—when it seemed that their fantasy could be fulfilled *for real*. Unknown to Massa and Missis, they and twenty thousand of their fellows moved imperceptibly from opposition to slavery to outright resistance, and the outcome was the greatest single slave uprising in British West Indian history.

## "Upon Yonder Gallows": Samuel Sharpe and the Baptist War, 1831–1832

The Baptist War (or Christmas Rebellion) of December 1831 to January 1832 was not, of course, the only attempt by Jamaican slaves during the last period of slavery to actively resist the regime that many—perhaps most—of them now believed to be doomed in the long run. Two factors above all prompted the slaves to revive the project, largely abandoned since the crushing of Tacky's revolt in 1760, of actually overthrowing rather than merely opposing the source of their misery: the knowledge, first, that in neighboring Saint-Domingue slavery had been destroyed and political independence achieved by the actions of the slaves themselves, and second, the belief that, after the abolition of the slave trade in 1807, the abolition of slavery itself could not long be delayed, and indeed that it had already been decreed by the king and his ministers in England but was being withheld from the slaves in Jamaica by the local Whites acting on their own pernicious initiative. Concerning the first, Lady Nugent (1907:254) records how the Jamaican Whites unwittingly encouraged their slaves by discussing the Saint-Domingue uprising in their presence, praising the "splendour," "superior strength," and "firmness of character" of its leaders so openly over dinner that "the blackies in attendance . . . hardly change a plate, or do any thing but listen."[37] With regard to the second, there can be little doubt that by the early 1820s there existed, in the words of one local magistrate, "a general Expectation among the negroes of freedom being given shortly by Government at home" (Samuel Vaughan, 1823, quoted in Hart 1985:2:237).[38] But discussing the progress of abolitionism openly before slaves, Whites created the impression that its momentum was irresistible, and by communicating their despair, they encouraged the slaves in the belief that slavery had already been abolished or shortly would be. Not only could slaves see and hear, but by 1820 many of them

37. For a full discussion of the impact of the Saint-Dominique uprising on Jamaica, see Geggus 1987.

38. According to one Free Black, Samuel Borwell, interviewed after the Baptist War, "their owners and bushas (overseers) knock into their teeth that they are going to get free, but they will sweat them first" (Bleby 1853:132). Bleby cites a dozen or so cases of Whites' blithely digging their own graves in this way.

could read and write, thanks in large part to the activities of the missionaries. Samuel Sharpe, leader of the 1831 uprising and a deacon in the Black Baptist Church, regularly read newspapers he had obtained at Montego Bay out loud to slaves on his and other plantations and thus actively spread the incendiary idea that slavery had already been abolished in law if not yet in reality) Hart 1985:2:252). The creature that the owners saw as just an object was, in other words, in reality a subject seer. The slaves knew that their masters were threatened and sometimes felt strong enough to reveal it, like the nominally submissive slave boatman who looks Lady Nugent straight in the eye and grins the night it is learned that a French fleet is heading for Jamaica (Nugent 1907: 289).

Before the generalized uprising of Christmas 1831, there were a number of attempts by slaves to organize local movements of resistance, all of them originally timed to coincide with Christmas. In 1816 a conspiracy was discovered at Black River that, according to Lewis (1834:227–28), involved only slaves of Eboe (Ibo) origin, but in whose organization "a *black* ascertained to have stolen over into the island from St. Domingo" and "a *brown* Anabaptist missionary" were said to have played a leading part. The conspirators elected a "King of the Eboes" and two "Captains," the plan being "to effect a complete massacre of all the whites on the island, for which laudable design His Majesty thought Christmas the very fittest season of the year." His captains, however, thought otherwise and urged immediate action, thus perhaps contributing to the undoing of the plot, which was discovered when an overseer (also from Saint-Domingue) on the Lyndhurst Penn estate happened to observe "an uncommon concourse of stranger negroes to a child's funeral, on which occasion a hog was roasted by the father" and, stealing closer, heard in addition to details of the plot being discussed, the following song sung by the "King of the Eboes" while his fellow conspirators joined in the chorus:

> Oh me good friend Mr. Wilberforce, make we free!
> God Almighty thank ye! God Almighty thank ye!
>   God Almighty, make we free!
> Buckra in this country no make we free:
> What Negro for to do? What Negro for to do?
>   Take force by force! Take force by force!
> CHORUS: To be sure! to be sure! to be sure!

In December 1823 another plot was discussed in the parish of St. Mary when a fifteen-year-old slave boy let slip to his master that the latter would "have a bad Christmas" were he to remain in the locality. It being revealed "that the Negroes in General were to rise at the fall of Christmas," eight slaves were arrested, condemned, and executed "before the Holidays, as an example to other Negroes, and to prevent the danger of an escape, or an attempt to release them" (Hart 1985:2:228–29). At the same time, in the parish of St. George, another uprising was planned for Boxing Day but had to be postponed until early 1824. The slaves had once again elected some of their number to be "king," "governor," "second governor," and so on and had, according to one of the conspirators,[39] met under cover of a slave court-cum-drinking society at which "the negroes so assembled some times made *play*, with their *sticks*, and *paraded* . . . and some of them had *wooden swords*" (2:231; italics added). The conspiracy also included a "Guinea negro" named Jack who rubbed his coconspirators "with certain Bushes at the Same time saying that such rubbing . . . would give them Strength and cause them to be invulnerable": he as also, in all likelihood, the obeah man who presided over the blood oath at which the conspirators swore loyalty to each other (2:235–36).

Taken together, the conspiracies of 1816 and 1823 show how readily the rituals of slave life—funerals, "plays," Obeah, the conferring of titles, possibly Jonkonnu—and acts of resistance could flow into each other, the first providing both inspiration and cover for the second; it is also abundantly clear that Christmas was the optimum time for launching an uprising.[40] Nor can there be any doubt concerning the role of *ideas* in the making of the 1831 rebellion, whether it was knowledge of events in Saint-Domingue (often diffused by slaves from the former colony) or news of abolitionism in Britain (overheard from the Whites, read in newspapers, or passed on by missionaries). The role of the latter, and of Christianity more generally, remains somewhat equivocal, and a number of distinctions are in order: between Black Baptists and other Christian slaves, between the leaders of the uprising and their mass following, and above all between black Christians as a whole and white Baptist and Methodist missionaries. By the 1820s, as we have seen, a very substantial proportion of the slaves of Jamaica had been baptized, though in many cases their "conversion" was nominal at best; nonetheless Abigail Bakan (1990:53) is surely right in arguing that by that time "the authority of the black Baptists was stronger than that of the myal and obeah men" and, correlatively, that "the inherent African religious tradition and the derived Baptist Christian teaching had become largely intertwined." Among the leaders of the uprising (who were preponderantly privileged, skilled, and Jamaican born)[41] the inten-

39. His name, Richard Montagnac, suggests he may have come from Saint-Domingue, as did, almost certainly, another conspirator, Jean-Baptiste Corberand; the plot also involved a Lecesne and a Baptiste, "a fine looking tall young man, black colour" who "wore a small crucifix" and "came from St. Domingo on purpose to stir up the negroes" (Hart 1985:2:233–34).

40. Linton, a colored overseer heavily involved in the 1831 uprising, stated after his arrest that "every year back at Christmas or October we were to begin, but were afraid to jump off until this year" (Hart 1985:2:250).

41. "It was the head people and the most indulged servants who were the ringleaders during the rebellion" (Hamilton Brown, May 1832, quoted in Higman 1976:227).

sity of Christian belief is not doubted, any more than the radicalism of the political conclusions they derived from it. On hearing or reading texts such as "No man can serve two masters" (Matt. 6:24), "There is neither Greek nor Jew; there is neither bond nor free" (Col. 3:11), "If the Son therefore shall make you free, ye shall be free indeed" (John 8:36), many slaves would have concluded, as did Samuel Sharpe himself, that "the white man had [no] more right to hold blacks in bondage than the blacks had to enslave the whites" (Sharpe as reported by corebel Edward Hylton; Bleby 1853:111) and that resistance to slavery—by force if necessary—was thus justified in God's eyes. The white missionaries, however, felt that slaves should *wait* until slavery was duly abolished by law, failing to understand that many slaves believed it already had been but that the "free paper" was being withheld by the planters. In his death cell, Sharpe explicitly rejected the idea, put to him by the Methodist missionary Henry Bleby (1853:117), that "even slaves are required patiently to submit to their lot, till the Lord in his providence is pleased to change it," responding: "If I have done wrong, I trust I shall be forgiven; for I cast myself upon the Atonement."

What prompted the outbreak of the 1831 uprising was a combination of internal and external events that the old order was disintegrating before their eyes and that a determined effort on their part could bring about its final collapse; for the first time since Tacky's uprising, an "elsewhere"—the prospect of *immediate* freedom from bondage—opened up before them, inspiring them to shift in large numbers from opposition to slavery to outright resistance. In May 1830 the Anti-Slavery Society in Britain at last abandoned its gradualist policy in favor of immediate abolition, a development the slaves were duly apprised of by the vociferous protests of their masters, many of whom began openly to advocate seccession from the British Empire and joining the United States. In defiance of the British government's policy of progressively ameliorating the slaves' condition, the Jamaican Assembly voted in February 1831 *to reduce the number of free days the slaves were to enjoy at Christmas.*[42] It is difficult to imagine a more provocative measure, and one may surmise that serious preparations for an uprising at Christmas began not long afterward, with Sharpe in particular using the relative freedom he enjoyed as a deacon of the Black Baptist Church to move from plantation to plantation and, under the cover of prayer meetings, "holding secret intercourse with those slaves whose co-operation he wished to enlist" (Bleby 1853:119). Sharpe's hold over the slaves of St. James, Westmoreland, and Hanover was clearly mesmeric, and Gardner, one of his closest lieutenants, must have spoken for hundreds of his fellows when

42. After the suppression of the uprising, the British colonial secretary wrote to the governor of Jamaica concerning "the danger of such innovation" given that "the slaves would attach to this very ancient privilege an importance which, to persons in a very different condition of life, might easily appear exaggerated" (quoted in Hart 1985:2:245).

he said that he was "wrought up almost to a state of madness" when Sharpe spoke on the subject of slavery (ibid., 115). Central to the slaves' morale was the belief—which Sharpe certainly encouraged, though he probably knew it was untrue—that slavery had already been abolished and that accordingly the king, in the words of Linton, another leading conspirator, "was upon our side" and "had given orders for his soldiers here not to fight against us" (quoted in Hart 1985:2:268). There can be no doubt that a powerful sense of solidarity built up among the Black Baptists, who not for nothing were known by slaves as the "Black Family" (Bleby 1853:25), with Sharpe know variously as "Daddy," "General" or "Ruler," and other conspirators assuming, in accordance with a now well-established slave tradition, titles such as "Colonel" (Johnson, Campbell, and Gardner) and "Captain" (Dehaney, Dove, M'Cail, etc.). To complete the analogy with the hierarchies and uniforms of Jonkonnu and the sets, some insurgents would fight dressed in "blue jackets and black cross belts," and an attack on Anchovy Bottom near Montego Bay on 9 January 1832 was led by a slave dressed in a "red uniform, with black sleeves, with red stripes up the seams, and blue pantaloons"; another rebel, William Hall, rode a white horse "possessing such a power of ubiquity as rendered it almost incredible how he was seen at distant places nearly at the same time" (Hart 1985:2:297, 303–4). Some uncertainty remains concerning the ultimate goal of the uprising. According to Gardner (who, after his arrest, tried to minimize his role in the revolt and to denigrate Sharpe in every way possible), the slaves took an oath "to drive the white and free people out of Jamaica; if they succeeded a governor was to be appointed to each parish" (ibid., 2:251), while the probably more reliable Hylton stated the terms of the oath as "not to work after Christmas, but to assert their claims to freedom and to be faithful to each other. If 'Buckra' would pay them, they would work as before; but if any attempt was made to force them to work as slaves, then they would fight for their freedom" (Bleby 1853:110–12). The fight was against slavery, then, but not (if Hylton is right) against property or the plantation system itself, though the slaves *may* have envisaged harvesting the cane and processing it for their own profit (see Holt 1992:15).[43] What 1831 almost certainly was *not*, however, was a revolt against British colonial rule, and this limitation on the insurgents' ambitions would have significant consequences for the future history of Jamaica.

"The Baptists all believe that they are to be freed; they say, the Lord and the King have given them free, but the white gentlemen in Jamaica keep it back" ("Confession of William Binham, a Prisoner Sentenced to Death," 1832, quoted in Hart 1985:2:245). So widespread was this belief that in June 1831

43. The slaves certainly went to great lengths, at the beginning of the uprising, not to destroy the growing cane and plantation buildings other than trash houses: this could suggest a desire to "take over" the plantations and operate them autonomously (see Hart 1985:2:264).

King William IV issued a decree disclaiming any such intention. When it was read out in churches and chapels in Jamaica on 22 December, it was greeted with "evident contempt" by the assembled slaves, for whom it was just one more ploy on the part of the owners; the slaves were convinced that the "free paper" would arrive in Jamaica at Christmas, brought by the Rev. Thomas Burchell, a well-known Baptist minister who, they believed, had been summoned to London for that purpose earlier in the year. More and more the slaves were distinguishing between the "good Englishman" (the king, Wilberforce, Burchell, and other missionaries) and "Buckra," the evil local White who, for the slaves in the west of the island, was epitomized by a Colonel Grignon, planter, magistrate, and commander of the militia, whom the slaves called "Little Breeches" and who was said to be planning a general massacre of Blacks. As Christmas approached, both Whites and Blacks were seized with a kind of *grande peur*, and the crisis of white authority was revealed when on the Salt Spring estate, just before Christmas, a driver refused to flog a slave woman caught with "a piece of sugar cane in her hand": when constables were brought in to restore order, the slaves repelled them with cutlasses drawn (Bleby 1853:3). Christmas itself passed uneasily if tensely, but on 27 December, the day scheduled for the resumption of work, thousands of slaves in the west of the island simply downed tools, declaring that "we won't be slaves no more; we won't lift hoe no more; we won't take flog no more. We free now . . . no more slaves again" (quoted in Hart 1985:2:249). The same day an attack was launched on the Montpelier estate led by "Colonel" Johnson and "Colonel" Campbell; the local militia, commanded by the detested Grignon, retreated, and "the impression became general . . . that the whites had abandoned the island and left it in the hands of the blacks" (Bleby 1853:13). In this apparent power vacuum, at least twenty thousand slaves rose in revolt.

The events of December 1831 to January 1832 have been well narrated and analyzed elsewhere and need not detain us in detail here;[44] nor, in the present context, is it necessary to do more than record the massive disparity between the number of white casualties (fourteen, all but three being militiamen) and the number of black (at least 200 killed during the uprising, with a further 344 hanged or shot by firing squad in the aftermath, usually after trials that were perfunctory at best; see Hart 1985:2:327–30).[45] What needs to be stressed is the combination of circumstances and mentalities that permitted the *rupture* of December 1831 and made possible the shift from multiplicitous, even pervasive, acts of opposition to a concerted movement of mass resistance involving one in five slaves in active roles in the west of the island, plus many thousands more giving sympathy and support. White power appeared to have

---

44. See, in addition to Hart 1985:2:291–311, Turner 1982:148–73.
45. These are the figures given by Holt (1992:14); Bakan's estimate (400 killed in combat, 376 executed) is perceptibly higher (1990:64–65).

collapsed, it was believed that slavery had already been abolished or was about to be so, and slaves at last felt able to step outside the system that oppressed them and resist it physically, by force. That said, the limits of the slaves' resistance need to be stressed: the revolt never spread to the parishes of the center and east, there was only sparse support from Free Coloureds and Blacks, and the slaves lacked a clear plan of what they would do should the insurrection succeed. Although the Baptist War undoubtedly accelerated the passing of the Abolition Act of August 1833, it also in a sense consolidated colonial rule to the extent that slaves never challenged the belief that Britain, its king, its Parliament, and its people were ultimately their friends and deliverers. Even the ship that brought Sir Willoughby Cotton's force of repression to Montego Bay on 1 January 1832 was, according to Bleby (1853:14), held by the slaves to have been sent "by the king to assist in breaking their chains." The Baptist War was rapidly recuperated by the colonial order and comprehensively erased from the "official" memory of the colony: it was only with the advent of the radical People's National Party in 1972 that Jamaica officially solemnized the sacrifice of the man who "would rather die upon yonder gallows than live in slavery" (ibid., 116), and that too might be regarded as a form of neutralization by acceptance. Thus it was that when complete emancipation came on 1 August 1838, the slaves sang "Queen Victoria gi me free dis is de year of jubalee" (Lewin 1984:21), and the churches, having been instrumental in destabilizing the old order, now seemed the predestined guarantors of the stability of the new. But no sooner was freedom proclaimed than the ex-slaves began to contest the new order with a range of oppositional practices that were both old and new, pending the outbreak of further movements of resistance in 1865 and 1938. And even more than before it was religion, understood in a sense very different from that of the white missionaries, that would be the focus of the Jamaican dream of real, rather than merely formal, freedom and equality.

# 3

## In the Shadow of the Whip:
## Religion and Opposition in Jamaica,
### 1834–1992

On the evening of 2 August 1838—day two of full freedom for the 311,000 or so former "apprentices" of Jamaica—a ceremony of thanksgiving and celebration was held on the Farm Pen estate of Lord Carrington. His own former slaves, along with those of the neighboring plantation owned by Lord Seaford, were invited to give thanks to all those responsible for the magnanimous bestowal of freedom a full two years in advance of the date originally decreed by the Emancipation Act of 1833. In the presence of the governor, Sir Lionel Smith, and "several ladies and gentlemen of the first respectability," three hundred former slaves sat down at a row of tables that, with heavy symbolism, "stretched along a beautiful lawn between the great house and the negro village," enclosed, as beneath "a spacious arcade in the Gothic style," by "a beautiful and highly-finished fabric of evergreens, adorned with chaplets and festoons of flowers" set off with "flags of different colours, on which were inscribed the names of the illustrious living characters who, under God, had achieved the glorious triumph they were met to celebrate." It was, according to the Baptist minister Rev. James M. Phillippo, a disciplined and abstemious occasion when toasts were drunk to Queen Victoria, to her ministers, and the governor and his wife. Cheers were raised for the two previous governors, Lords Mulgrave and Sligo, for Clarkson, Wilberforce, Buxton, Brougham, and Sturge, "for the ladies of Great Britain and Ireland," "for the missionaries and other philanthropists in Jamaica, and for the friends of liberty throughout the world." Thereafter the company dispersed, "each individual going peacefully and joyfully to his home," and ci-devant Massa and Missis to the Great House, and the erstwhile slaves and—for a brief but grueling four-year interlude—apprentices to

90

the Negro Village, just as of yore after Christmas or crop-over. Thus, concludes Phillippo (1969:179–85), "harmony and cheerfulness smiled on every countenance, and the demon of discord for a season disappeared." The minister's caution was only too justified. Having been put sorely to the test since apprenticeship began in 1834, the fragile bond between Great House and Negro Village would, after much stretching and twisting, finally snap in October 1865, when a major uprising, pointing back to the Baptist War of 1831–32 and forward to the labor riots of 1938 in the centenary year of emancipation, broke out at Morant Bay in the east of the island. Led by two Baptist ministers, one black (Paul Bogle), the other colored (George William Gordon), the Morant Bay rebellion gives further proof, if proof were needed, of the inseparability of religion and sociopolitical protest in Jamaica. This chapter traces that alliance from 1838 to 1938 and beyond, from Native Baptism, Myalism, Revival, and Kumina to Bedwardism, Pentecostalism, and Rastafarianism, with two questions in mind: How far has Jamaican religion, in its multiple forms, stimulated protest against the status quo? And how far has it reinforced the existing situation by diverting discontents into one or another "spiritual" outlet? To answer these and related questions, the changing socioeconomic structure of Jamaica must constantly be borne in mind, and our first task, taken up in the section that follows, is to dissipate a widespread myth concerning the "flight" of the ex-slaves from the site of their former bondage, the plantation, to the hills and mountains around it.

## Land, Family, and Culture, 1834–1865

According to tenacious legend, the slaves of Jamaica, like their counterparts in Britain's other slave colonies, had only one thought when they finally achieved full freedom on "the glorious and never-to-be-forgotten 1st of August, 1838" (Phillippo 1969:174): to break totally with the plantation and, where vacant land was available, to move as far from it as possible, establish themselves as an autonomous peasantry, and henceforth produce subsistence crops by and for themselves alone while continuing, as under slavery, to sell some staples and livestock on the alternative "protopeasant" economy that had emerged in the interstices of the plantation system itself. But from the researches of Hugh Paget (1964) and in particular of Douglas Hall (1978), it is clear that *in 1838* few ex-slaves had any such goal, the vast majority preferring to remain where they were, in the Negro Villages where they had their huts, their grounds, and more often than not the graves of their forebears, all of which, they assumed, they would continue to enjoy rent free and without harassment as they had under slavery. As Hall says (1978:24), the ex-slaves' behavior in the years *immediately* after slavery (say between 1838 and 1842) makes little sense unless due weight is given both to their "hatred of the estate" and to their "love of home on the estate." By the time of emancipation the slaves were, as we have seen, owners by custom if not in law of provision grounds their forebears had cultivated for generations, and they produced food crops and livestock that not only sustained them but allowed them to trade profitably on the thriving network of autonomous slave markets. No freedman or freedwoman in his or her right mind would willingly abandon such well-established routines for a hazardous life on the uncultivated backlands. The ex-slaves, it is now clear, did not, save in a minority of cases, leave the estate villages by choice. They were forced out by the planters, who, in a monumentally misguided attempt to constrain them to work on the plantations as under slavery, sought either to create a landless (and hence dependent) rural proletariat by driving the freedmen out of their villages or to force them into selling their labor by imposing rents or other conditions on the homes and grounds they considered their own property and that, under slavery, they had occupied rent free. In short, "the movement of the ex-slaves from the estates . . . was not a flight from the horrors of slavery. It was a protest against the inequities of early 'freedom'" (Hall 1978:23).

Once it became clear to the ex-slaves that they could not function as an autonomous peasantry within the confines of the plantation, they began to leave the estates in large numbers, either purchasing or squatting on unoccupied land or, in a very large number of cases, moving to one of the many "free villages"—200 by 1840, with 8,000 dwelling places in all—that the nonconformist churches, led by the Baptists, sponsored by buying up ruined plantations and selling individual plots to freedmen and their families. By 1845, 19,000 families—perhaps 100,000 people in all, or a third of the ex-slave population of Jamaica—had settled in such villages (Mintz 1987:3). Yet even if they moved off the plantation (and many could not or did not), the ex-slaves could not in most cases break its hold over their lives, and very few of the free villagers or those who bought or occupied land independently could be described as "peasants" in the standard sense of small landowners who managed to live solely off the yield of their land (see Frucht 1967; Fraser 1981). In general the freedmen and their families did not move far from the plantations where they and their forebears had labored since time immemorial, occupying rather what Thomas Holt (1992:168) calls "the interstitial areas among the surviving estates rather than . . . the vacant Jamaican 'outback'" where they "sought to combine provision gardening with estate work rather than depend exclusively on either" and thus evolved into an "unfinished proletariat, a semi-peasantry" (175) attempting, but usually failing, to get the best of both forms of labor. Neither "peasants" nor "proletarians," the ex-slaves were neither inside nor outside the plantation system; they belonged to a liminal domain where, classically, the tactics of opposition came into their own. The freedmen did everything they could to play plantation and plot off against one another, laboring on the former only when absolutely constrained and refusing, except at times of direst need, to allow their womenfolk and children to work on the plantations at all. Whereas male and female slaves had toiled together in the canefields, after emancipation there emerged "a strong convention that women should avoid employment, if possible, and focus their labor on 'female crops' such as oil nuts and beans." It was after 1838, not before, that "some crops and certain agricultural tasks [became] gender-defined" (171) and that, more generally, an ideology of distinct "male" and "female" sociocultural "spheres" emerged in Jamaica and elsewhere. As we shall see in the chapter that follows, this pattern is based on a strong association of male activity with the "outside" and of female activity with the "inside" or yard.[1] The labor crisis the planters faced was a result, in the first instance, of the withdrawal of female workers from the "public" world of the canefield into the "private" realm of home, yard, and kitchen garden: "Women dominated field labor forces before emancipation but not after. . . . By the end of the first decade of freedom, the wage labor force was mostly male" (Holt 1992:152–53).

Though the Jamaican "peasantry"[2] took root in what Sidney Mintz (1985:131) calls the historical and ecological "crevices" of plantation society, where it grew "like blades of grass pushing up between the bricks," its continuously embattled condition did not prevent—and may even have fostered—the development of a dynamic creole culture that formed, as we have seen, in the interstices of the slave plantation. It was to thrive in conditions of freedom until the last quarter of the nineteenth century, when a revival of the plantation system threatened the very existence of the economic, social, and cultural countersystem that the freed slaves and their descendants had forged. The core of this reconstituted peasant culture was the possession of land, and it is from the immediate postemancipation period that "freedom" and "freehold" came to be indissolubly linked in the Jamaican and more broadly the West Indian mind as the only real and permanent source of security, status, and individual prestige as well as a concrete link between past, present, and future generations (see Lowenthal 1961:4–5). As Jean Besson has shown in her studies of the free village of Martha Brae in the parish of Trelawny, for the ex-

1. On the emergence of this pattern, see the chapter tiled "Houses and Yards among Caribbean Peasantries" in Mintz 1974:225–50 and, for a more general consideration of gender roles after emancipation, Momsen 1988. According to Richard B. Sheridan (1986:170), "emancipation brought immeasurable gains to the black people of Jamaica. Health and well-being improved as the growth of a free peasantry coincided with the retreat of sugar monoculture and the establishment of a more balanced ecosystem. No doubt the greatest improvement accrued to black women who used this freedom to escape from field labour and devote their time to family life on peasant holdings."

2. The quotation marks—to be dropped hereafter—are designed to show that this is a "fictive" peasantry in Peter Fraser's sense of the word (1981:330), partaking of some of the features of a peasant class but ultimately possessing no economic or social autonomy.

slaves and their descendants land was the very opposite of an economic asset that could be bought and sold as individual interest dictated. Land was (and still commonly is) "family land" before anything else, and in the words of present-day residents of Martha Brae, is "not to be sold, *not* to be sold; *not* selling it. If me even *dead*, it can't sell. Not selling. It's fe the children: all the children" (Besson 1987:118). It is to be handed down to "children and children's children, till every generation dead-out" (Besson 1984:59). As such, family land is, in Besson's own words (1987:103–4), "the spatial dimension of the family line, reflecting its continuity and identity" as well as embodying more general values of "freedom, security, social prestige and personhood" (1984:64) for those who hold it in trust. On family land in free villages such as Martha Brae, Sligoville, Sturge Town, Refuge, Kettering, and Granville, the ex-slaves constructed homes in an emerging Jamaican vernacular style (see Green 1984) to which, no doubt for the first time in their history, they gave names such as Happy Home, Comfort Castle, Canaan, Mount Zion, Free Come, Content My Own, Thank God to See It, A Little of My Own, and most pertinent of all, Save Rent (Phillippo 1969:229). These names testify as eloquently to a new sense of identity through ownership as the Christian names and surnames taken by the slaves on baptism or emancipation testify to a new sense of self-ownership through religion. Taken together, the complex of house, yard, and family land thus represents less "a mosaic of inert survivals from colonial or ancestral cultures" than "a dynamic Caribbean cultural creation forged by the peasantries themselves in resistant response to the plantation system" (Besson 1992:202), in short, the foundation of a creole culture that, building on cultural forms developed under slavery, was now finally consolidated as a cultural *system*, as a self-sustaining tertium quid rather than as an assemblage of disparately derived "African" and "European" elements.

At the heart of the mature creole synthesis in the country lay a new sense of family that the withdrawal of women from field labor both reflected and made possible. There can be no doubt that the trend toward nuclear families we observed beginning in the final decades of slavery was enormously aided and accelerated by the advent of freedom. According to Phillippo, writing in 1843, over fourteen thousand Christian marriages had been celebrated annually since 1840, and marriage was now "associated with everything virtuous and honourable in human conduct," with "those who worthily discharge its duties and obligations" being "inevitably regarded as individuals deserving the highest respect and esteem" (1969:231–32). This impressionistic (and hardly disinterested) judgment is supported in a modified form by Orlando Patterson, who argues (1982:146) that "the vast majority of ex-slaves who became peasants developed highly stable, if non-western, mating patterns, strongly valued the institutional norm of marriage although as the life-long culmination of a successful union rather than as its initiation, and redeveloped a strong and sometimes even paternalistic husband-father role." Above all, it was during the twenty-five years after emancipation that marriage came to be the ideal (albeit an ideal that not all, or even most, could attain) to which the generality of Jamaicans aspired, and the most important indicator of respectability and status. It was also during this period that the yard, already embryonically present under slavery, as we have seen, emerged as an institution capable of binding together nuclear family units and an extended family network in a single social and physical space. As such, it became the nucleus within which popular Jamaican culture "expresses itself, is perpetuated, changed, and reintegrated" (Mintz 1974:231–32): "The yard is an extension of the house, just as the house is the living core of the yard; the outer limits of the yard came to represent the outer 'walls' of the house itself, as it were" (248). This stress on family is hardly to be wondered at, for as Nigel Bolland was written (1992a: 142), "insofar as slavery involved the natal alienation of the slave and his social death through the loss of kinship ties, the transcendence of slavery must recover or re-establish such ties." But the trend toward nuclear families united by the macrofamilial structures of the yard did not preclude the formation of strong communal ties in the free village as a whole. On the contrary, the sense of community as family was as vital for survival in freedom as it had been in slavery and found expression in the ex-slaves' "respect for old age," "love of offspring," "generous compassion for the distressed," "ordered and disciplined friendship," and not least, the "politeness and respect" they showed each other and that sometimes, said Phillippo (1969:234), "[approached] extravagance." Thus it was, according to Bolland (1992a:142), that emancipation produced not a "liberal society of autonomous citizens" but rather a "genuine community of people linked by kinship and other ties," whose sense of the collective set them against both the capitalistic values of the planters and the notion of *individual* salvation and *private* morality promoted by the white Baptist ministers who sought to control the lives of the free villagers they sponsored, for whom "personal autonomy, rather than being defined over and against the rights of others, became achievable only in connection with others."

All this is not to idealize the rural culture that emerged in Jamaica in the decades that followed the abolition of slavery or, above all, to exaggerate its extent either in space or in time. Many ex-slaves were forced to remain on the plantations, and many others, not least women and youths, in the face of grinding economic distress, were driven to the towns, above all to Kingston, where in 1865, on the eve of the Morant Bay uprising, hundreds of women were to be seen on the streets, their "tawdry gowns dangling in remnants, and fluttering in the wind, like flags hung out to intimate their trade and occupation, or as signals to emblazon their disgrace." Gangs of youths, the ancestors of the Rude Boys of a hundred years later, would hang around on the streets and, "impatient of restraints, rude, boisterous, regardless of all decency," "swear, swagger, and fight, bluster and blaspheme with a volubility and a recklessness that is most painful to witness" (*Report on the Moral Condition of the City of Kingston*, 1865, quoted in Robotham 1983:95–96, 100). Even during the supposed honeymoon period of Jamaican peasant culture in the 1840s and early 1850s, day-to-day life was almost intolerably taxing: "This Free worse than slave, a man can't put up it," one ex-slave is reported to have said in 1848 (quoted in Holt 1992:174). It would become even more so in the late 1870s when the plantation system began to revive, with bananas rather than sugar now the main crop. The last quarter of the nineteenth century witnessed a massive "fragmentation and subdivision of small holdings held by small settlers" as local and foreign capitalists bought up land, with government encouragement, for bananas, and "by 1900 the concentration of landholdings in the hands of a few large landholders had once again become a marked feature of the system of land tenure in Jamaica" (Satchell 1990:154, 2). An immediate consequence of the crisis of peasant agriculture was the departure of tens of thousands of Jamaicans, mainly men, in search of work in Costa Rica, Nicaragua, Panama, the United States, and elsewhere,[3] a movement of population that in its turn drew women back into the field labor they had renounced after slavery, so that by the end of the century "the unskilled agricultural workforce became once again predominantly female as it had been in the later stages of slavery" (Momsen 1988:151). As men and women were sucked out of the peasant sector in search of work aboard or on the resurgent plantations, so, according to Patterson (1982b:148–49), the nuclear, father-centered family of the immediate postemancipation period gave way to "unstable" matrifocal kinship forms similar to those of the eighteenth-century plantation: the modern Jamaican family, he argues, is not an inheritance of slavery but a product of the late nineteenth-century reversion from peasant plot to plantation. But, even in its pre-1860 heyday, the peasant culture of Jamaica was double-edged in its meaning, for if it was an act of resistance—or more precisely of *opposition*—to the plantation and its values, it was also as Sidney Mintz has stressed (1974:155), simultaneously "an act of westernization" as well, which drew the ex-slaves deeper into the values of the dominant colonial culture even as it gave them the resources to withstand the pressures and challenges of freedom. There is no better or more important instance of this deep-seated ambivalence than the ex-slaves' religion, the subject, in all its multifarious complexity, of the section that follows.

3. Twenty-four thousand Jamaicans left for Panama in 1883 alone. For a useful summary of nineteenth- and early twentieth-century emigration from Jamaica, see Thomas-Hope 1986:15–18.

## Missionaries, Preachers, and Myalmen, 1838–1865

As we saw in chapter 1, by 1838 the vast majority of Jamaican slaves had become at least nominal Christians, thanks more to the proselytizing of *black* Baptist preachers than to that of their white counterparts, who began serious missionary work in the colony only in the 1820s, almost forty years after the first waves of slave converts had been made by black missionaries such as Liele, Gibbs, and Baker.[4] In fact the real impact of white missionaries came more after emancipation than before (see Curtin 1968:34, 114; Austin-Broos 1992:222), and the years between 1838 and 1865 in particular were marked not merely by a conflict for economic and social survival between ex-slaves and ex-masters but also by a cultural (and by extension social and political) struggle between the white missionaries on the one hand and, on the other, the freed community and its black preachers over the *kind* of Christianity that was to hold sway in Jamaica. What had emerged from half a century of primarily black proselytism was an unstable compound of Myalism and Christianity that we may call Afro-Christianity, provided we recognize that the relative proportions of the "Afro" and the "Christian" were always in flux, that the African substrate was forever threatening to break through the Christian, and that until well into the twentieth century, and perhaps even today, Afro-Christianity remained an amalgam of potentially discordant elements rather than a fully achieved and "stable" synthesis of different religious traditions. The Afro-Christianity of the ex-slaves and their black ministers contained a multiplicity of elements—dancing and drumming, "prophesying," speaking in tongues, spirit worship, trance, and possession—that were inimical to the Euro-Christianity of the white missionaries. Beginning in 1838, the latter would attempt to extirpate them in the name of a Christianity that was individualistic, moralistic, and thoroughly "middle class" in orientation.[5] Neither "side" can be said to have triumphed definitively in this struggle. The ex-slaves resisted incorporation by the white missionaries but, even as they did so, were drawn deeper than ever into the hegemony of white colonial values. The missionaries accepted—within certain limits—the Jamaicanization of Christian belief and practice in the interests of making converts and of retaining their power over their flocks, which might otherwise have been rejected completely. The result was a necessarily ambivalent creolized Christianity that was

4. The following account leans heavily on the standard work by Curtin (1968, first published 1955), reinforced by Stewart 1992, Murphy 1994, and above all the outstanding article by Austin-Broos (1992), which has greatly influenced my overall argument.

5. Thus William Knibb told his flock that "to be free you must be independent. Receive your money for your work; come to market with money; purchase from whom you please; and be accountable to no-one but the Being above, whom I trust will watch over you and protect you" (quoted in Austin-Broos 1992:224).

capable of challenging and reinforcing the existing sociopolitical order more or less simultaneously, dousing with one hand the revolutionary fires that it stirred up with the other. The two variants of Christianity clashed head on in the 1850s and 1860s and would do so again between 1890 and 1920 during the heyday of Bedwardism (see below), whereafter the radical potential of Afro-Christianity would be progressively neutralized by the spread of Pentecostalism and the increasing introversion of Revival, pending the emergence in the course of the 1930s and 1940s of a new form of religious radicalism (Rastafarianism), this time non- and even anti-Christian, that by 1980 would itself be largely recuperated by the existing order. Having sketched the overall trajectory of my argument, let me begin by focusing on the religious crisis that accompanied and reflected the social and economic crisis of postemancipation Jamaica and that would culminate in the Morant Bay uprising of 1865.

No one reading Phillippo's *Jamaica, Its Past and Present State* (1843) would guess that the society he purportedly was describing was already, four or five years after emancipation, in the throes of a serious conflict between rival versions of Christianity that would be regularly repeated over the next twenty-five years. On the surface of things, the "white" version of Christianity has successfully implanted itself throughout the freed community, driving into the background what remained of the ex-slaves' "heathenish" beliefs and practices and binding white ministers and black "praying people" closely together in a single, and massively popular, evangelical enterprise. "The attendance at all places of worship favoured with an evangelical ministry is astonishingly great," Phillippo writes (1969:287–88): 2,000 "hearers" each Sunday at "King" Knibb's chapel at Falmouth, 2,200 on average at Burchell's at Montego Bay, and 2,500 at Oughton's on East Queen Street in Kingston, with a further 700 present at weekday evening services. Moreover, based on Phillippo's interviews with supposedly representative black Christians, the beliefs of these converts met all the requirements of evangelical orthodoxy. "All black pusson is sinner, as same as white pusson" (365), yet all can be saved not by their own merits but by God's grace alone, with Jesus as the sole mediator between man and God. "None care for me poor neger like Jesus," says one of Phillippo's black Christians (407), while another (389) prays that there may be a "full Heaven and an empty hell; that they may be saved from going to that place where no sun shine, no tar twinkle," "What is your greatest enemy?" one interviewee is asked (311), and replies: "Me own heart." "If the spirit of God don't touch we," says another (320), "we is a dark and ignorant people, dow we know plenty a tings else." One believer after another expresses the desire to "steal away to Jesus" (407) or voices fear lest "precious blessed Jesus turn away from me," only to assert reassuringly, "but him promise; and me hold upon de promise" (310).

And so on and so on for page after page of evangelical orthodoxy as one sanctified Quashie after another gives voice to beliefs of reassuring passivity in which reverence for "precious Massa Jesus" consorts easily with reverence for his representative on earth, the smiling, benevolent white missionary: it was above all Phillippo's book that created the stereotype of the Christian Black against which, as Diane Austin-Broos has said (1992:227), Jamaican Christians would struggle until well into the twentieth century (see also Russell 1983). Nor is there any reason to doubt the sincerity of the convictions Phillippo's interviewees express or, above all, the intensity with which, in the minister's own words (1969:368), "they emphatically regard each other as belonging to the family of Christ, and as being *members* one of another." The problem is that Phillippo's account is "not so much a description as a blueprint for the Christian black" (Austin-Broos 1992:232), and that such impressively orthodox black evangelicals were probably a minority even among the 232,000 Jamaicans of all races who in 1840 are said to have belonged to one or another Christian church, to say nothing of the remaining 163,000—almost all of them black—who had no formal church affiliation whatever.[6] Thanks to the so-called ticket system (see Curtin 1968:37), the white missionaries had a measure of control over who could approach the communion table in the churches and chapels where they officiated, but they could do little to enforce orthodoxy at the far more numerous religious meetings presided over by Native Baptist ministers on plantations and elsewhere, and they had no influence at all over the Myalmen who, with little or no admixture of Christianity, remained active among the substantial minority of Jamaicans who belonged to no formal church. Even Phillippo cannot conceal the existence in the colony of other forms of religion, no more than superficially Christianized, admitting that "in some districts, it is true, Myalism has recently revived" under the cover of Christianity, "the priests of this deadly art, now that religion has become general, [having] incorporated with it a religious phraseology, together with some of the religious observances of the most popular denominations" (1969: 263). The reference is clearly to the "outbreak" of Myalism in the parishes of St. James and Trelawny in 1841–42, which will give us our first detailed insight into that "zone" on the religious continuum, corresponding to basilectal Creole (see Alleyne 1988:91), where the "Afro" is barely overlaid with the "Christian" and that forms the bedrock and *materia prima* for all the varieties of Afro-Christianity discussed in this chapter.

Like Obeah and the belief in the existence of duppies (see Leach 1961), with both of which it is clearly if ambiguously connected, Myalism often had as its physical focus the cotton tree (*Ceiba pentandra*), which with its "great outspreading branches" and "massive bulging steel-grey trunk" supported by huge buttresses, forms so imposing a feature of the Jamaican landscape (Rash-

6. Phillippo takes his figures from Candler and gives the following breakdown (1969:296): 108,000 Baptists, 50,000 Methodist, 46,000 Anglicans, 11,000 Congregationalists, 7,000 Moravians, 7,000 Presbyterians, and 1,000 Roman Catholics. He also lists 5,000 Jews.

ford 1985:49). It was at the foot of one such cotton tree that in 1842, near Blue Hole in St. James, the Presbyterian minister Hope Waddell witnessed the following scene:[7]

> There we found them in full force and employment, forming a ring, around which were a multitude of onlookers. Inside the circle some females performed a mystic dance, sailing round and round, and wheeling in the centre with outspread arms, and wild looks and gestures. Other hummed, or whistled a low monotonous tone, to which the performers kept time, as did the people around also, by hands and feet and swaying of their bodies. A man who seemed to direct the performance stood at one side, with folded arms, quietly watching the evolutions. (Quoted in Murphy 1994:117–18)

Attempting to quiet the "mad women," Waddell is informed in no uncertain fashion that "they are not mad," "they have the spirit," "you must be mad yourself, and had best go away," "let the women go on; we don't want you," "who brought you here?" "what do you want with us?" and so on (Stewart 1992:140). In another account J. H. Buchner (*The Moravians in Jamaica*, 1854), quoted in Murphy 1994:118) relates how "some would perform incredible evolutions while in this state, until, nearly exhausted, they fell senseless to the ground, when every word they uttered was received as a divine revelation. At other times, Obeah was to be discovered, or a 'shadow' was to be caught, a little coffin being prepared in which it was to be enclosed and buried." Finally, toward the end of the century, but still referring to the 1841–32 "outbreak," the Reverend Thomas Banbury (*Jamaica Superstitions, or The Obeah Book*, 1894, quoted in Murphy 1994:119) describes an "Obeah-pulling" session that took place on a plantation in the presence of the owner, his attorney, overseers, bookkeepers, and an English member of Parliament and quotes a song that shows the "Afro" and the "Christian" to be thoroughly entangled one with the other:

> Lord have mercy, oh!
>   Christ have mercy, oh!
> Obeah pain hot, oh!
>   Lord, we come fe pull he, oh!
> A no we come fe pull he, oh!
>   You fada want you, oh!
> Boy, you fada want you, oh!

---

7. The following account is based on a conflation of Stewart 1992:136–48 and Murphy 1994:116–24. In order not to overburden the text, I have kept references to a minimum.

From these and similar accounts, it appears that, though Myalism incorporated certain elements of Christianity, it was felt by its practitioners to be distinct from, and perhaps opposed to, the Euro-Christianity represented by such as the Reverend Mr. Waddell; that it involved inspiration by "the Spirit" rather than possession by "the spirits" as in Afro-Catholic cults such as Vodou, Shango, Santería, and Candomblé (see chapter 5 below); that dancing, singing, and drumming played an integral part in the experience of trance, glossolalia, and "prophecy" it revolved around; that it was "not a perfect Afro-Christian syncretism, in spite of the Christian claims and terminology of the Myalists, but manifested elements that were almost purely of African traditional religion" (Stewart 1992:140); that women were central to its ritual practices but probably not leaders; that it was intended, among other things, as some kind of counter to Obeah; that it was not intrinsically anticolonial or antiwhite but might readily become so; and that the Myalmen, otherwise known as "faith men" or "angel men," exercised considerable authority over their followers, even though Phillippo's claim (1969:263) that they "[accomplished] their purposes by *violence* as well as by terror" remains to be proved. The relation between Myalism and Obeah has aroused much speculation, with some writers arguing, after the Jesuit ethnologist Joseph John Williams (*Psychic Phenomena of Jamaica*, 1934), that the two are radically antithetical one to the other (see Stewart 1992:136–37), though Waddell's almost structuralist insistence that they are "corresponding parts of one system" (quoted in Murphy 1994:226) seems much more consistent with the essentially nondualistic character of the Afro-Jamaican worldview. Although Obeah "flourished outside the rule of law as an alternative system using different technologies of power and other modes of domination and resistance" and in certain circumstances undoubtedly "united and empowered slaves against masters and made group resistance possible" (Lazarus-Black 1994:47), it could also be directed against other members of the slave (and ex-slave) community and indeed against that community as a whole: as "empowering knowledge and enabling practice . . . , it may be directed against an exploiting class, but the justice it expresses also permeates relationships between neighbors, lovers, and kin" (259). It may be that Obeah and Myalism confront each other less as absolute opposites than as private and public manifestations of the same magicospiritual power (see Murphy 1994:120–21). As power and counterpower neither is inherently political, but given the appropriate context, both can be redirected from the "enemy within" to the common "enemy without." It is this, I argue, that has made religion such a powerful vehicle of sociopolitical protest throughout the history of Jamaica.

In the relatively propitious conditions of 1841–42, the appropriate context did not exist, and the first postemancipation explosion of Myalism soon abated, thanks not least to the "several hundreds of special constables" who were drafted in "to punish numbers of these deluded people for disturbing the peace." Six years later a Myalman calling himself "Dr Taylor"—an early example no doubt of the "Convinced Doctors" of the end of the century (see below)—"gave much trouble to Manchester and Clarendon, drawing great crowds after him," for which "crime" he was sent to the penitentiary, where he was "accidentally" killed. In 1852, after the terrible cholera epidemic of 1850–51 when 32,000 people (one in thirteen of the population) were killed, "the delusion again appeared: some now gave themselves out to be prophets, and saw visions, but the firmness of the missionaries soon put an end to these practices." At the same time, after the death of Knibb in 1845, the mainstream Baptist Church was itself stricken with "a spirit of worldliness on part of those whose religious convictions had never been very deep" (all quotations in Gardner 1971:460–62), and in his overview of the West Indies written in 1862, the Reverend Edward B. Underhill lamented that, though "people are not getting rid of religion," "it is not as it was twenty years ago . . . at the time when 'free come'"; in particular, young people "do not listen as formerly to the old people 'to stick to the gospel'" (quoted in Mintz 1987:8). Underhill's pessimism is all the more noteworthy for coming hard on the close of the so-called Great Revival of 1860–61, which many white clergymen initially supported for what Gardner (1971:465) called "the quiet, purifying influences" it brought in its train, namely the boost that expectation of the Second Coming gave to Christian marriage and to Bible reading—37,000 copies were said to have been sold in eighteen months—and the effectiveness with which fear of the Lord drove "multitudes" of Jamaican men from rum shop to chapel. But "like a mountain stream, clear and transparent as it springs from the rock, but which becomes foul and repulsive as impurities are mingled with it in its onward course, so with this most extraordinary movement." "In too many districts there was much of wild extravagance and almost blasphemous fashion," especially where Native Baptist ministers—whom Gardner almost, but not quite, identifies with the Myalmen—"had any considerable influence." According to the *Freedman* (quoted in Stewart 1992:146), there was "pandemonium" in the chapels of Jamaica by early 1861, what with the "simultaneous singing, shouting, groaning, praying, thumping, stamping, tumbling, rolling, dancing round and round in wildest frenzy"; "there was no getting round it," comments Philip Curtin (1968:171), "the Great Revival had turned African." By 1862 the white Baptists' influence over "their" flocks had noticeably waned (Austin-Broos 1992:233), and for the first time since their arrival in the colony, they were being regarded as part of, rather than apart from, the white-dominated order of society (Curtin 1968:172). As the influence of white preachers subsided, that of their black rivals correspondingly grew, and with social and economic distress mounting throughout the whole island, the formerly "apolitical" religious enthusiasm took on a radical and, still more alarmingly, overtly racial dimension. According to one Methodist minister, writing on the eve of the Morant Bay uprising,

> In almost every Parish a number of uneducated, and I fear unprincipled men, have risen up us native Preachers, chiefly of the Baptist persuasion. They have formed churches and become their ministers. Most of them are utterly incapable of instructing the people in the great principles of Gospel Truth; and it is highly probable that they have dwelt much on the claims of *classes*, and have represented the Black as an oppressed race, who ought to defend themselves. I have heard of language like the following as used by a black preacher—"You are black and I am black, and you ought to support your own colour." "The blacks are seven to one of the others, and they ought to have the island." (Rev. Jonathan Edmondson, quoted in Stewart 1992:166–67)

On 3 May 1865 a Native Baptist preacher named Crole declared before his congregation in Kingston that "the Bible says we are not to obey an immoral Government, therefore we are not bound to obey the Government of this country, for it is immoral, and no man should make you do it" (quoted in Elkins 1977:1). About the same time, a proclamation signed "A Son of Africa" was posted on a wharf gate at Lucea in Hanover demanding an end to oppression "by Government, by Magistrates, by Proprietors and by Merchants" and telling "the sons and daughters of Africa that a great deliverance will take place for them from the hand of opposition" (quoted in Heuman 1994:86). The road to Morant Bay was open, but before we go down it, we must first consider a curious phenomenon, linked to religion, that tended to run first with and then finally against the very radical current we have so far discerned in Jamaican Afro-Christianity.

## The Good White Man and the Great White Queen

On 29 September 1839, having come to the end of his tour of duty, Sir Lionel Smith, the governor who had overseen the whole process of emancipation in Jamaica, left the colony to return to England. Emerging from his official residence in Spanish Town, he was greeted by a crowd some two thousand strong waving banners proclaiming "We Mourn the Departure of Our Governor" and saluting him as "The Poor Man's Friend and Protector," and as he drove off in his carriage a "whole mass" of those present ran alongside it "until ready to faint with fatigue, uttering lamentations and invoking blessings on his head" while "mothers in almost every instance exhibited their infants as trophies—trophies of the blessings and advantages of freedom." The whole six-mile road to Port Henderson was similarly lined with grieving ex-slaves, and when the carriage reached its destination, "an immense number, nearly all of whom were in deep mourning, or wore black riband in some conspicuous part of their dress, had drawn themselves up in two parallel lines at the entrance, and as Sir Lionel and his *cortège* had proceeded to the middle of the lines the whole mass surrounded them, and declaring that their 'Governor and friend' should not leave them, began to effect their purpose, by taking the horses from the carriage to draw him back again to the seat of government." Dissuaded from so doing, "they then insisted on drawing him to the beach, as the last act of kindness they might show him," but, once there, Sir Lionel found himself hemmed in once more by "an impenetrable barrier, as though determined he should not advance." With some difficulty Sir Lionel and his party got to the water's edge, at which point "the sobs of the multitude, hitherto half-stifled, now burst forth like a torrent" and "as the boat receded from the shore Sir Lionel rallied sufficiently to bow to the assembled crowd, and cries and lamentations, intermingled with invocations, followed him until he was out of hearing" (Phillippo 1969:254–56).

We have witnessed equivalents of this before, above all in the joyous reception given to M. G. Lewis on his arrival(s) on his plantation, and in the no less fulsome expressions of grief from his slaves when he left, behavior that, as we have seen, is to be partly explained by their self-interest and from which an element of deception and "puttin on Ole Massa" is assuredly not absent. In a similar vein, though without obvious satirical intent, we have repeatedly seen evidence, in the buildup to the 1831–32 uprising, of the slaves' conviction that they had already been freed by "the Lord and the King" but that "the white gentlemen in Jamaica keep it back" (William Binham, quoted in Hart 1985:2:245); the belief that their "free paper" was being withheld from them by the planters was, as we have seen, instrumental in propelling many slaves from opposition to slavery to outright resistance. During the apprenticeship period from 1834 to 1838, the nominally freed slaves remained convinced that "the King had sent out their free, and they would have it" (Wilmot 1984:3), and when they protested against the planters' attempts to curb the few freedoms and rights they possessed, would continually ask "Is it the King's law?" "Would you swear that the King put his name to it?" or invoking a still higher authority, "Could you swear it is the law of Jesus Christ?" (5). When William IV was succeeded by Victoria in the year before "full free" was granted them, the ex-slaves acquired an even more charismatic protector of their rights and persons, and there must have been many who, like the ex-slave Edward Barrett, speaking at the celebration banquet at Falmouth on 1 August 1838, felt they owed their final and complete emancipation to the personal intervention of the queen herself: "Let us lift our hearts and bless God, let us bless Queen Victoria . . . , yes, Kings did sit on the throne, but Kings could not do it,

*Victoria* did" (9). Finally on 13 August 1838, a ninety-year-old African-born ex-slave sent Sir Lionel Smith the following letter:

> I, Robert Peart, baptized in that name in Jamaica, but in my country I was named Mahomod Cover: I was born at Bucka. For myself, my Countrymen and my Countrywomen, who may be alive in Jamaica, return thanks to Almighty God, and next to the English nation, whose laws have relieved us from the bondage in which we have been held. God bless and grant long life to our Queen Victoria, and repose to the soul of her uncle King William the Fourth, in whose good reign was passed the law which this day has made us free people. God bless Sir Lionel Smith, our governor, father and friend, whom we all love and will obey. (10)[8]

In none of the instances cited does there seem any *necessary* reason to doubt the sincerity of the ideas and feelings expressed. None of those concerned had anything concrete to gain from their utterances, which likewise contain no discernible trace of mockery and guile. In the absence of compelling reasons to do otherwise, let us take them at face value and state, in the face of much received opinion, that the slaves really did believe that they had been freed by the king and queen of England, acting either unilaterally or at the behest of abolitionists, missionaries, and the English people as a whole, and that they were grateful from the bottom of their hearts for the "gift" of freedom they had received. Equally important is the split these utterances reveal in the slaves' and ex-slaves' perceptions of white people. Worst of all were the overseers and bookkeepers they encountered day to day, against whose cruelties and malpractices they would appeal to the attorney, who in his turn could be made answerable to Massa. Above Massa was a still greater Massa, the governor, and above him, the Super Massa or Missis in England who appointed him; above him or her was the Law, and capping the whole hierarchical edifice there reigned the Massa of Massas in heaven. Quite simply, the farther the white man was from the canefield the "better" he was, and as we have seen, slaves played white men against one another as a matter of policy to improve their position and gain room for maneuver, setting Massa against Busha, the missionary against Massa, and so on up the chain. But though the figure of the "Good White Man" undoubtedly had a tactical basis, it seems equally clear that it involved not just affection but reverence on the part of the (ex)-slaves that both prompted resistance and placed significant limits on it, inciting them to counter the "Bad White Man" (the local planters

---

8. Extraordinarily, the letter was written by Peart in Arabic characters and translated before it was sent by Smith to the Colonial Office in London (Wilmot 1984:10).

and their allies) in the name of the "Good" and so drawing them deeper into the overall colonial hegemony even as they struggled against its particular embodiments in the colony itself. The revolts of 1831–32, 1865, and even 1938 may have been revolts against the status quo in Jamaica, but they were in no way (save, very perhaps, in the case of 1938) revolts against colonialism *as such*.

The Jamaican (and more broadly West Indian) cult of the "Good White Man," or more accurately the "Powerful White Man,"[9] is manifested in many ways, not least in the foundational act of *naming*.[10] When slaves were baptized, they commonly took as their surname either that of their owner or that of the missionary who baptized them—not, I suggest, in a spirit of servility, and still less as recognition of ownership or patronage, but as a quasi-magical attempt to arrogate some of the white man's mana and power by taking over his name.[11] The practice continued in a modified form after emancipation in the taking over of the first names and surnames of British prime ministers or generals (Gladstone, Balfour, Winston, Orde, Attlee, etc.), of colonial governors,[12] and even, it seems, of touring English cricketers, at a time when English cricket meant power.[13] The effect of such names was both to empower the bearer "magically" and to imprison him (or more rarely her) in the mental structures of colonialism, just as the effect of the struggle against slavery, conducted in the name of the "Good White Man" (Wilberforce, Clarkson, Burchell, Knibb) was to draw the ex-slaves still deeper into the colonial mind-set. Thus, according to Sidney Mintz (1987:15–16), the missionary became for the (ex)-slave a "substitute—an altogether preferable substitute—for the estate owner, the overseer, the slave driver, the judge, and the custos" and frequently acted, though not without encountering severe opposition, as a "strong force for the Europeanization or westernization of the slave" and in general for "the 'de-

9. For a discussion of the cult of the "Bon Blanc" in Martinique (where it is, or was, centered on the figures of the abolitionist Victor Schoelcher and General de Gaulle), see Burton 1994:119–27. On the cult of "true great Buckra" in Demerara before the 1823 uprising, see Viotti da Costa 1994:221.

10. On the complex and intriguing subject of naming in West Indian and, more generally, Afro-American societies, see De Camp 1960, 1967, Price and Price 1972, Genovese 1972:444–50, Manning 1974, and Dillard 1976.

11. Cf. the Maroon practice of taking over the name of the ex-master, discussed in chap. 2, n. 35 above.

12. Thus the Trinidadian calypsonian Hollis Liverpool (Mighty Chalkdust) is named after Sir Claude Hollis, the former governor general of Trinidad, and the large number of Hughs in Jamaica presumably owe their name to Sir Hugh Foot, the highly popular governor general just before independence.

13. According to Sir Learie Constantine, n.d.a:78, recalling the 1920s and 1930s, "when visiting M.C.C. teams come to the West Indies, so great is the admiration for their prowess that hundreds of little black babies are named after them, sometimes using the white players' Christian names, but often using their whole name."

Africanization' of the believer." More broadly, it is possible to attribute the success of white or near-white populist politicians in the Caribbean (Cipriani, Bustamante, Michael Manley, Edward Seaga) partly to the lingering influence of the mythical Good White Man.[14]

Finally, there remains the ex-slaves' conception of God. Although, as Diane Austin-Broos has said in her searching discussion of religion in postemancipation Jamaica, "Christianity came not as a permanently alien phenomenon but a negotiated one, in which Jamaicans themselves have sought to reinterpret the nature of its message and the values it decrees" (1992:222), it remains that "Jamaicans have *only partly* redefined the captor's God" even as they have "radically localized the Christian tradition" (240; italics added). Linked to the image of White Massa, White Governor, and White King or Queen, the White God continued to hold Quashie and perhaps still more Quasheba in his thrall, even as he inspired them to assert themselves over and against the negative image Whites had of them. It is for this reason that in the professions of faith of Phillippo's black Christians, at least three Massas (God or Jesus or both, the missionary [Phillippo himself], and the ex-master) seem to lock together to form a complex superego construction to which the ex-slave remains slave:

Ah me sweet massa, we all wish fo pray to we sweet Massa Jesus long before, but Massa Buckra prosecute we so. (Phillippo 1969:348)

Me can't leave off to lub Massa Jesus for please Massa Buckra. (ibid.)

Beggen massa pardon, God's angry worsen dan massa's angry, an me soul wants more feed dan me body want feed. (349)

Me bin waiten-boy for Buckra once, an me bleedge to wait for massa time; now me servant for Massa Jesus, and me can't patient wait for him time? (405)

Thus while on one level the White Man's God empowered and liberated, on the other he bound and alienated, and it would be more than a century after emancipation before the white superego the ex-slaves had internalized would be seriously challenged by a new and radically *anti-Christian* religion, Rastafarianism. We may be quite sure that when Leonard Howell and his early fol-

14. On the role of the "Good White Man" in Jamaican popular protest movements, see the summary by Abigail Bakan (1990:7–8) quoted in chap. 2, n. 6, above. According to Sir Murchison Fletcher, governor of Trinidad during the labor riots of 1937 and himself an embodiment of the "Good White Man," "the secret of Cipriani's influence lies, not so much in any personal ability, as in the colour of his skin. . . . Labour, formerly accustomed to cringe before the white slave-driver, found in their strong and forceful white champion as it were a demi-god, and they placed him upon a pedestal accordingly" (quoted in Singh 1994:127).

lowers rose to sing "God Save the King" at Trinityville in St. Thomas in 1933, it was not to George V or to any epigone of "King" Knibb that their words were addressed, but to Haile Selassie, King of Kings and Lord of Lords, who was God, King, and prophet rolled into One (see below and R. Hill 1983:33).

## "War Is at Us, My Black Skin": The Morant Bay Uprising, 1865

In the circumstances, therefore, it is wholly characteristic that the events of 1865[15] should have been set in train by a letter sent by one "Good White Man," the Reverend Edward Underhill, secretary of the Baptist Missionary Society, to another, the British colonial secretary Edward Cardwell, depicting "the extreme poverty of the people" of Jamaica, which left them no alternative but to "steal or starve," and predicting the "entire failure of the island" unless something was done to create employment, to lower taxes, and in general to alleviate "the ragged and even naked condition" of "vast numbers" of the formerly enslaved population (quoted in Heuman 1994:45). Equally symptomatic is that, even before the Underhill letter was made public, the people of St. Ann directly petitioned "our Gracious Lady Victoria our Queen" that she rent them Crown lands at low rates so that they could "put our hands and heart to work, and cultivate coffee, corn, canes, cotton and tobacco and other produce" that they would sell to an agent she appointed for the purpose. These pleas were echoed in the numerous "Underhill meetings" that, prompted by the missionary's letter, were held throughout Jamaica in the early months of 1865 (49–52). In response the British government, in the person of its senior colonial official, Henry Taylor, drafted the "Queen's Advice," which in the name of the queen herself urged on her Jamaican subjects the necessity of "working for Wages, not uncertainly, or capriciously, but steadily and continuously, at the times when their labour is wanted." This, and not "any such schemes [such as redistribution of land] as have been suggested to them" was the only way they might effect "an improvement in their condition"; they could rest assured that "her Majesty will regard with interest and satisfaction their advancement through their own merits and efforts" (quoted in Holt 1992:277–78). Delighted, the new governor, Edward Eyre, ordered fifty thousand copies of the document distributed throughout the colony to be read out loud at church services and public meetings, where it caused "an amount of irritation most painful to observe" among those who heard it and who refused, quite rightly, to believe that the queen herself could have so addressed "the suffering poor without one kind word of sympathy for them in their distress brought upon them by circumstances over which they had no control" (Revs. Henderson, Dendy, and Reid, quoted in Heuman 1994:55). There was a fur-

---

15. The following account is based essentially on Heuman 1994, supplemented where appropriate by Holt 1992. To avoid overburdening the text, I have kept references to a minimum.

ther rumor that the queen had sent clothes and money to her suffering Jamaican subjects, only to have them commandeered by planters to pay and clothe the Indian indentured laborers whom many Afro-Jamaicans held responsible for further depressing wage levels in the colony (36). As in 1831–32, a split had opened up in the popular perception of Whites, setting the "Good White Man" (or Woman) in Britain against the "Bad White Man"—the planters, but also increasingly the governor—in Jamaica, a split that, as had happened thirty years earlier, would both provoke sections of the Jamaican population to radical action and also confine that action within certain significant limits, as well as ensuring that the attitude of the bulk of the island's population did not go beyond sympathetic neutrality toward the insurgents' cause when they did not actively oppose it.

When, on 11 October 1865, in circumstances we need not examine here, violence finally erupted in the town of Morant Bay in St. Thomas in the East, it took on forms in which we can discern some of the deepest traditions of Jamaican popular protest as well as certain new features that point to future patterns of opposition and resistance. Issuing from a number of outlying villages, principally from Stony Gut, where their leader, the small farmer Paul Bogle, was also deacon of the local Native Baptist Church, several hundred men and women moved into the center of Morant Bay "like a mob, dancing and blowing horns" according to one account or, according to another, "packed together close behind each other, not at all straggling" but advancing "slowly and deliberately," cutlasses, sharpened sticks, and an occasional gun at the ready, and flying a red flag as an emblem of their newfound solidarity and strength of purpose (Heuman 1994:3). Throughout the week or so of the revolt's duration, drums, fifes, conch shells, and horns would provide a continuous obbligato to the action in progress, suggesting once more a continuity between forms of sociopolitical protest and ceremonial rituals such as Jonkonnu, while the assumption of military titles by the uprising's leaders—General Bogle, Colonel Bowie, plus numerous captains—and the flying of flags pointed to links with both the titles and insignia of the Maroons (whom Bogle had unavailingly sought to recruit to his cause) and, as we shall see in the chapters that follow, with the military-style hierarchies and uniforms of carnival and other ceremonial societies in Trinidad, Haiti, and elsewhere. It is as though, in the Caribbean, protest is unthinkable without some minimum of ritual, just as Caribbean rituals or ceremonies of all kinds—be it Jonkonnu, carnival, cricket, or whatever—always carry with them at least an undercurrent of social or political protest that in certain circumstances may erupt.

In October 1865, however, it is clear that the crowd was intent on violence from the outset. Marching "with a blowing of shells or horns, and a beating of drums" toward the Morant Bay courthouse, shouting "Colour for colour!" and "War, war!" they confronted the custos (chief magistrate) of St.

Paul Bogle, Baptist deacon and leader of the Morant Bay uprising in Jamaica (1865). NLJ photo. Courtesy of the National Library of Jamaica.

Thomas, the German-born Baron von Ketelhodt, flanked by a number of fellow vestrymen and a small contingent of white and colored militiamen. To von Ketelhodt's pleas for "Peace in Her Majesty's Name!" the crowd replied with cries of "No Peace! Hell today!" and engaged forthwith in hand-to-hand combat with the representatives of colonial law and order, forcing them back into the courthouse, from which they would eventually be driven by fire (Heuman 1994:8–10). By the end of the day eighteen officials and militiamen had been killed along with seven members of the crowd, which, having captured the town, fanned out into the parish of St. Thomas in the East, "marching in ranks with flags flying, drum beating, and a horn blowing" (20) in what seems to have been a semisystematic settling of accounts with Whites (and to a lesser extent Coloureds) who were deemed to have treated them unjustly. Violence took place against both persons and property, but crucially, the insurrection failed to attract the true mass support it needed even among the distressed farmers and laborers of eastern Jamaica. It probably at no time numbered more than two thousand, less than one-tenth the number of slaves actively involved in the uprising of 1831–32. Without a clear strategy or definable objective, the uprising lost momentum and, once the forces of law and order were able to regroup, was crushed with a systematic use of violence and terror that even today beggars belief. Insurgents and bystanders alike were flogged (often with whips threaded with wire), raped, shot, or hanged at random or after the most rudimentary of trials, and huts, even whole villages, were put to the torch as a mixed force of British troops with memories or images of the Indian Mutiny ablaze in their brains, local white and colored militiamen, black soldiers of the British West Indian Regiment, and not least Maroons ran riot with their officers' consent or encouragement. At the very least, 439 actual or imagined insurgents were killed in the aftermath of the uprising, including Bogle (hanged after being captured by the Maroons he had hoped to win to his cause) and George William Gordon, the colored assemblyman for St. Thomas in the East whose ally and agent Bogle had been but who, for all his championing of the popular cause in the face of the opposition of planters and colonial administration combined, seems to have played no active role at all in the uprising. If any experience introduced the concept of "Dread" into the Jamaican lexicon, it was surely the "Killing Time" of October–November 1865 (Heuman 1994:143).

Thus summarized, the events that took place in St. Thomas in the East in late 1865 may seem out of proportion to the importance they came to assume, then and subsequently, in the eyes of Jamaicans and non-Jamaicans alike. Although not essentially different in its causes from earlier disturbances that failed to develop beyond the riot stage,[16] the Morant Bay uprising highlighted, through the number and violence of its participants (neither of which should, however, be exaggerated), the disparity between the formal freedom the ex-slaves had acquired in 1838 and the concrete, meaningful freedom—freedom, above all, from high rents and taxes, low wages, and arbitrary acts of injustice—to which they legitimately aspired. It offered further evidence, if further evidence were needed, of the symbiotic relationship in Jamaica between sociopolitical protest and Afro-Christianity, especially in that indeterminate zone

16. For a discussion of disturbances in Jamaica between 1838 and 1865 (notably in 1848 and 1859), see Heuman 1994:39–41.

where Christianity, Myalism, and Obeah shaded into each other.[17] And it revealed the presence in the minds of perhaps thousands of lower-class black Jamaicans of an apocalyptic worldview in which the conflict of peasants versus planters assumed the dimensions of the Endtime struggle of Christ and Antichrist foretold in Revelation. "War is at us, my black skin, war is at hand from to-day to to-morrow," wrote Bogle in his remarkable call to arms of 17 October (quoted in Heuman 1994:91), words echoed in the numerous anonymous or pseudonymous letters that continued to be sent to prominent Whites and Coloureds well after the uprising was over. "I going raise War I will be a Second Paul Bogle," wrote one such "correspondent," while another letter signed "Thomas Killmany, and intend to kill many more" vowed to destroy the town and inhabitants of Port Maria: "You will see blood running through the bay like river." "Take warning, warning, warning, take it, this is it, our cutlass is now ready," threatened "Anancy Green." "Judgment, judgment," declared another letter, "We will bring judgment to Jamaica at once, at once" (102–4). Nor can it be doubted that the war the insurgents envisaged was some kind of racial Armageddon, even though not all their victims were white or colored and though they spared the lives of many Whites whom they deemed to have done them no harm. "Skin for skin," proclaimed Bogle's letter of 17 October, and attacks on Whites were regularly accompanied by cries of "Colour for colour; kill them all" (11), "We don't know one buckra from another, we will kill them all" (18), and so on. Consciousness of race was clearly the strongest, if not the only, mobilizing force among the insurgents, and it was symptomatic that just before the uprising broke out, a black policeman was instructed on pain of death to "cleave from the whites and cleave to the blacks" (5). As we have already seen, a Methodist missionary reported having heard a Native Baptist preacher tell his flock, "You are black, and I am black, and you ought to support your own colour." But as the same missionary wrote, such preachers "dwelt much on the claims of *classes* and represented the Blacks as an oppressed race who ought to defend themselves" (Rev. Jonathan Edmondson, quoted in Stewart 1992:166–67; emphasis in original). Race and class, in short, were entangled with each other in principle but separable in practice; the two categories blurred in the killing of the insurgents' one black victim, a local builder, member of the vestry, and political ally of Baron von Ketelhodt named Charles Price, on the grounds that "he has got a black skin and a white heart" and "because you got into the Vestry, you don't count yourself a nigger" (quoted in Heuman 1994:9). Race and class now converged,

17. At least one accredited obeah man, Arthur Wellington, took part in uprising and was shot and decapitated (Heuman 1994:122), and an obeah stick covered with blood and hair was found at Amity Hall, one of the Great Houses attacked by the insurgents (24). The oath taken by the insurgents—kissing the Bible and drinking a mixture of rum and gunpowder (6)—suggests a characteristic mixture of Christianity and Myalism.

now diverged according to individual case and circumstance, producing a confusion of categories, together with a fundamental ambivalence toward Jamaicans of mixed race that would be carried over into the still more explicitly
race-centered worldview of Rastafarianism in the century that followed.

Curiously, however, this very marked racialization of social and political
categories seems to have coexisted in the insurgents' minds with a continuing
sense of loyalty to the queen herself, raising a series of questions concerning
the overall objectives and motivation of the uprising. Many of the insurgents
clearly had only short-term, practical goals, notably the acquisition of "backlands" (Crown lands) at modest rent, but even they must have realized that to
secure a reduction in rents and taxes, or to obtain an increase in plantation
wages, would require a fundamental transformation of power relations in the
colony. Some insurgents envisaged taking over the plantations "to make sugar
for ourselves," as one put it, or even putting Whites to work in the canefields
(90). Others seem to have sought a wholesale replacement of white and colored officials by people of their own race, like the rebel Charles Mitchell who,
pointing to a colored customs officer's chair, told him that it was "the place of
a blackman, and if you don't quit it quietly we will have your head cut off."
Some went even further. "Colonel" James Bowie asserted that "we want to beat
all the brown and white off the island," and another rebel leader, George
Craddock, told the people of Stony Gut "that this country would belong to
them, and they were about getting it . . . ; it had long been theirs, and they
must keep it wholly in possession" (88–89). Yet it is doubtful that Craddock
or any other insurgent had in mind anything resembling *political* independence.
Bogle always insisted he was not rebelling against the queen (xvii), and though
Gordon was alleged to have told a crowd to "do what Hayti does" (59), there
is no evidence that he envisaged any kind of break with Britain. Indeed, if the
report of a black shoemaker from Manchioneal is to be believed, the planned
extermination of local Whites assorted very well with a continuation, even a
strengthening, of colonial ties with Britain, since it would oblige the queen to
send "fresh gentlemen from England and we and those gentlemen will quite
agree" (90). Likewise, other Blacks were said to believe that Eyre would be
hanged and that "a new Governor had come out with new laws from the
Queen to give them rent free land and land free" (166). Finally, if the aims of
even the insurgents stopped well short of political independence, the vast
majority of Jamaicans, Blacks as well as Whites and Coloureds, "remained
loyal to the government and were horrified by the events at Morant Bay"
(Heuman 1994:99). Like the Baptist War before it, the Morant Bay uprising,
to the extent that it led directly to the abolition of the old planter-dominated
Assembly and its replacement by direct Crown Colony government, actually
strengthened the colonial ties binding Jamaica to the "Motherland," a development not every black or colored Jamaican may have deplored; not for nothing

John Eyre, governor of Jamaica at the time of the Morant Bay uprising and responsible for its repression. NLJ photo. Courtesy of the National Library of Jamaica.

did a group claiming to speak for "hundreds of the negro inhabitants of Kingston and its neighbourhood" inform the Royal Commission of 1882 that "without the protection of the [British] government our fellow colonists [presumably the white elite] would not permit us to enjoy the breath we breathe" (quoted in Augier 1993:180). But Morant Bay was not forgotten, and it bequeathed to future generations of Jamaicans the archetypal figures of the black martyr (Bogle), the colored redeemer (Gordon), and the white ogre (Eyre) with, presiding over them all, a far-off tutelary king or queen, figures whose later manifestations we shall have cause to study in the sections that follow.

Revivalists, Bedwardites, Pentecostals: Christianity and Social Change
in Jamaica, 1865–1980

In the decades that followed the Morant Bay uprising, the colonial state,
in alliance with the denominational churches and the expanding public education system, made strenuous efforts to curb the religious excesses to which the
Afro-Jamaican masses were by now believed to be congenitally subject. Under
the energetic leadership of Bishop Enos Nuttall (d. 1916), the Anglican
Church, disestablished since 1870, increased its number of churches from 89
in 1868 to 212 in 1900, with places for other 70,000 worshipers, two-thirds of
them regularly filled; in addition by 1900 there were 96 mission stations in the
fourteen parishes (Bryan 1991:61). The other mainline churches—Methodists,
Moravians, Baptists, Presbyterians—made similar efforts and strengthened
their hold on the existing colored middle class and the emerging black lower
middle classes as well as making some inroads into the Afro-Jamaican masses.
In their vast majority, however, the black lower classes remained outside but
not uninfluenced by the mainstream churches, participating in one or more of
a variety of popular religious forms ranging from the wholly non-Christian
Kumina, an African ancestor cult practiced by African indentured laborers and
their descendants,[18] through the barely Christianized Convince cult, to the
overlapping forms of Revivalism that in time would be given the names
Pocomania (Pukumina), Revival Zion, and Tabernacle. It was, as ever, on the
interface between Myalism and Christianity that the most extreme and potentially subversive varieties of religious belief and practice took shape, as in the
"Convinced Doctors" operating in the parish of Hanover in 1896, who were
said by the *Daily Gleaner* to be teaching that God had "raised them up as
prophets and doctors for the good of the oppressed negroes of the island to
deliver them from the slavery and oppression of the white doctors and par-
sons" (quoted in Elkins 1977:4). About the same time, a black preacher styling
himself Rev. Captain Charles C. Higgins, B.A.E. (British and American Evan-
gelist), or "Warrior" Higgins for short, began teaching that "white men murdered the son of God, and God damned them for their wickedness" (quoted in
Elkins 1977:23) and, according to a convert to Rastafarianism who heard him
as a child, that Jamaicans should reject Queen Victoria and all she stood for
("get under Missis Queen shift and drawers and cuss," as he allegedly put it)
and "turn them eyes and them heart to Africa and . . . stretch forth them hand

18. For a useful overview of the range of religious forms in twentieth-century Jamaica, see
Morrish 1982. For Kumina see Warner-Lewis 1977, Brathwaite 1978, and above all Bilby and Bunseki
1983. Convince is studied in Hogg 1964 and Revival in Chevannes 1978, Wedenoja 1988, and
Murphy 1994:114–44.

to Africa" (quoted in Chevannes 1994:90).[19] In 1904 the self-styled "Royal Prince Thomas Isaac Makarooroo of Ceylon"—actually plain Isaac Uriah Brown, who had emigrated from Jamaica in 1891—announced on his return to Kingston from London that he had "come to lift up the black people of Jamaica" and urged them not to pay taxes on the grounds that the laws of Jamaica were "no good," having been made "to uplift the white man and to crush the poor man." When he further declared that he had written to the king of England, "and if he does not put a stop to the oppression, I will make a revolution in this island," "Makarooroo" was arrested and imprisoned, and he was last heard of in Grimsby in England, calling himself the prince of Zululand and claiming, most significantly in the light of future religious developments in Jamaica, that he was the nephew of King Menelik of Abyssinia and heir to the Abyssinian throne (Elkins 1977:33–35).[20]

Apocalyptic and potentially subversive religious beliefs thus were more or less commonplace in Jamaica between 1890 and 1920,[21] but it took the career of the remarkable Alexander Bedward (ca. 1859–1930) to bring the radical energies of Jamaican Afro-Christianity to their peak, whereafter it was superseded as the main challenge to the colonial order by the newly emergent millennialist cult of Rastafarianism. An early member of H. E. Shakespeare Woods's Native Free Baptist Church at August Town near Kingston, Bedward returned from Panama in 1891 and began baptizing and healing followers in the Hope River to the accompaniment of the chant "Dip dem Bedward, Dip dem / Dip dem in the Healing stream" (quoted in Bryan 1991:43). Such was his charisma that no fewer than twelve thousand followers from across the island were allegedly present at one of his Wednesday morning gatherings in 1893, and true to the inner dynamic of Myalized Christianity, it was not long before a radical social and political message was added to the spiritual radicalism of Bedward's teaching. In 1895, after urging his followers to "remember the Morant War," Bedward made the following incendiary declaration: "There is a white wall and a black wall, and the white wall has been closing around the black wall; but now the black wall has become bigger than the white wall, and they must knock the white wall down. The white wall has oppressed us for years; now we must oppress the white wall" (quoted in Post 1978:7; see also Bryan 1991:45). Arrested but found not guilty, Bedward spent three weeks

19. On Queen Victoria and her well-known statue in Victoria Park, Kingston, as a symbol of imperialism in later Rastafarian rhetoric, see Homiak 1987:237–40.

20. Cf. Shrevington Mitcheline, who arrived in England from Jamaica in 1924 claiming to be crown prince of Abyssinia and son of the prince of Kenya (Elkins 1977:38).

21. As during the Great Revival of the 1860s, protracted drought offered ideal conditions for the creation and reception of millennialist beliefs, as in the case of the followers of Solomon Hewitt (he staged his own crucifixion and "rose from the dead" in Smith's Village, Kingston), who declared in 1914, "Christ is coming. Him is sending Him signs and wonders. We have earthquake, we have hurricane, we have dry" (quoted in Elkins 1977:43).

Rev. Alexander Bedward, radical revivalist preacher in Jamaica, ca. 1870–1930. From *Black Roadways: A Study of Jamaican Folk Life,* by Martha Warren Beckwith. Chapel Hill: University of North Carolina Press, 1929.

The crowd at one of Bedward's revivalist meetings at August Town, near Kingston, ca. 1920. From *Black Roadways: A Study of Jamaican Folk Life*, by Martha Warren Beckwith. Chapel Hill: University of North Carolina Press, 1929.

in the Kingston Lunatic Asylum, from which he emerged proclaiming the "end of the law" and prophesying that "Jesus is going to burst the prison and mash the asylum and do away with all churches." Thereafter little is heard of him and his followers until 1920 when Bedward, allegedly now claiming to be Jesus, announced that he would ascend to heaven in a flaming chariot on Friday, 31 December, and return three days later to carry his followers to glory before raining down fire on the earth; the white race, he declared, "would be destroyed and there would be a new heaven and earth in which blacks would become whites and Bedwardism would reign for a millennium."[22] On the appointed day, thousands of Bedwardites converged on August Town to witness the ascension of their savior-leader, who, after remaining obstinately earthbound on this and three subsequent occasions, announced that God had commanded him to remain on earth for seventeen years more, until 1938, the centenary of the final abolition of slavery. Later in 1921, Bedward attempted to lead his followers from August Town into central Kingston but was prevented by the police, to whom he allegedly introduced himself as "the Lord Jesus Christ" and asked, "Must I obey you and disobey the command of my father?" (see Wedenoja 1988:110; Elkins 1977:15–16). This time, with both the colonial administration and middle-class Kingston traumatized by the

22. On Bedward's apparent acceptance of whiteness as the supreme value and his belief that God was white, see Chevannes 1994:28, 109.

possibility of some kind of reprise of Morant Bay,[23] there was no escape and Bedward was arrested, found guilty, and interned in Kingston Lunatic Asylum, where he died in November 1930 just a few weeks after the coronation, in Ethiopia, of Prince Ras Tafari as Emperor Haile Selassie I. Thus not only do Bedward and Bedwardism provide "a vital link in the continuity of protest from Morant Bay onwards (Post 1978:8),[24] they also prepare the way for the still more subversive worldview of Rastafarianism.

The events of 1920–21 mark both the climax—an anticlimactic climax, as it turned out—of radical Afro-Christianity in Jamaica and the beginning of its progressive domestication and recuperation by the existing order. Two factors account for its gradual depoliticization: first, the emergence of Rastafarianism in the 1930s offered a more potent vehicle of protest and self-affirmation to the more radical and displaced (male) sections of Jamaican society, and second, Afro-Christianity was itself profoundly transformed by a new wave of missionaries, not Baptists or Methodists from Britain but Pentecostalists, both black and white, from the United States.[25] Beginning with the founding of a Jamaican branch of the Holiness Church of God in 1907, Pentecostalism rapidly became "the dominant religion of poor Jamaicans, especially of working women" (Austin-Broos 1992:237) over the decades that followed, with the Church of God alone increasing its membership from 1,774 in 1921 to 43,560 in 1943, 191,231 in 1960, 305,412 in 1970, and 400,379 in 1982 (official census figures). In 1982 one in four Jamaicans (513,929 out of a total population of 2,172,879) claimed membership in one or another Pentecostalist church, as against 154,548 Anglicans, 217,839 Baptists, 68,289 Methodists, 107,580 Roman Catholics, and 150,722 Seventh-Day Adventists (Austin-Broos 1987:4–5), and it was estimated at the time that Pentecostal membership would equal denominational membership by about 1990 (Wedenoja 1980:31). Despite first resisting the Pentecostalist incursion and then incorporating Pentecostalist elements into their services, both the mainstream churches and the Revivalist sects lost substantial numbers of followers to the new churches, with Revival in particular tending to become more and more confined to the elderly and to country dwellers; by the late 1970s, one well-informed observer was already speaking of Revival as a "disappearing religion" (Chevannes 1978). Pentecostalism, like Rastafarianism, owed much of its success among lower-class Jamaicans to the resources it offered them in the face of the massive transformations undergone by Jamaican society since 1920, as expressed most

23. On fears of "another Morant Bay" in Jamaica after 1865, see Bryan 1991:275.

24. Cf. the Jamaican who told Martha Beckwith in the early 1920s how he remembered the Morant Bay uprising and the Great Revival of 1860: "It was taken up by the whole world. Now today there is Bedward" (quoted in Murphy 1994:125).

25. On the role of returning Jamaican migrants to the United States in the spread of Pentecostalism, see Wedenoja 1980:35.

graphically in the doubling of the population of Kingston between 1921 and 1943, its further rise by 86 percent between 1943 and 1960 to almost half a million, followed by a further doubling (at least) since independence. Not for nothing has Pentecostalism been described as "a mass form of supportive psychotherapy for casualties of the modernization process" (Wedenoja 1980:40). Many of these "casualties" were women driven by the transformation of Jamaican agriculture to seek domestic work in towns (above all in Kingston),[26] and it was they who, often bringing up children alone in the absence of a partner, provided Pentecostalism with its earliest, most numerous, and most committed recruits. They drew strength and solace from its marked emphasis on personal salvation through a personal relationship with Jesus, derived support from its ethic of self-discipline and respectability for the daily tasks that confronted them, and not least, found companionship with women like themselves through belonging to close-knit and usually small-scale, locally based church communities.[27] Although men held, and continue to hold, the main positions of power in the Pentecostalist churches (as of course they do in their denominational rivals), women soon dominated, and still dominate, the intermediate positions between the leadership and the generality of worshipers, themselves predominantly women. There was nothing absolutely new in this prominence of women in Jamaica's already "feminized religious world" (Austin-Broos 1987:8), but in "[celebrating] the spirituality of women" and in offering them spiritual and social satisfactions of a particularly "feminine" kind, Pentecostalism, it is claimed, gave a still more "markedly feminine orientation" to "the Jamaican sense of a spiritually animated world" (Austin-Broos 1992:238). Thus, though all Jamaican religious groups, with the notable exception of Rastafarianism, showed an excess of female over male adherents in the 1982 census, the bias was far more marked in the case of the Church of God (225,239 women to 175,140 men) and other Pentecostalist churches (65,596 to 47,924) and would be heavier still in terms of actual participation in their activities (Austin-Broos 1987:4–8). Jamaican Christianity was apparently becoming more and more the preserve of the "respectable" middle-class men and women who provided the bulk of the membership of the denominational churches and the "respectable" lower-class women who flocked to their Pentecostalist rivals. The lower-class male, particularly the *young* lower-class male, was tending more and more to be left outside the fold of Christianity in both its mainstream and its charismatic forms.

26. In 1921 there were 125,400 women employed in agriculture, in 1943 only 45,600 (see French 1988:53); by the same time, domestic work had become the largest single employer of women in Jamaica.

27. On the theological differences between the Old Testament, possession-oriented worldview of Revival and the New Testament, Christocentric, and salvation-oriented worldview of Pentecostalism, see Wedenoja 1980:38–39. The specific appeal of Pentecostalist Christocentricity to women is illuminatingly discussed in Austin-Broos 1987:24–28.

All this proceeded pari passu with a perceptible deradicalization of the churches' social message. The denominational churches continued to underwrite the spiritual, social, and political values of their mainly middle-class members. Revival focused more and more on the spiritual and physical well-being of its followers rather than on their social and political aspirations, while Pentecostalism, besides acting as "a major medium of American hegemony," does not "contest Jamaica's class structuration" (Austin-Broos 1991–92:311–12), promotes "a moral order in which issues of race are neutralized" (Austin-Broos 1992:238), and in general acts as "a significant force for conservatism in Jamaica's electoral politics" (Austin-Broos 1991–92:310). All it (allegedly) offers its predominantly female members is the ambivalent experience of being "born again, and again, and again," while the concrete situation of their lives remains essentially unchanged (Austin 1981:244), the born-again experience being "overwhelmingly understood by women as a process of being delivered out of the sexually predatory circumstances of their everyday lives into the care of the benign and feminized Jesus" (Austin-Broos 1991–92:309). Whereas Afro-Christianity in its various overlapping forms formerly held lower-class men and women together in common opposition to the status quo, Pentecostalism binds lower-class women to the existing order and tends to marginalize lower-class men completely until middle age or pressure from their partners, or both, brings them back into the fold. In short, popular Christianity, once the main threat to the colonial order in Jamaica, has (so it is claimed) become a principal bulwark of the postcolonial order that has supplanted it.

At the same time that lower-class women were beginning to monopolize the middle-ranking positions in the expanding Pentecostalist churches, so the Jamaican educationalist Errol Miller has argued (1986, 1988), lower-middle-class women were beginning to establish themselves in a range of middle-ranking occupations in the wider society, thanks to a combination of better educational qualifications than black men had and to white and colored elite males' willingness to admit black women to subordinate posts of authority that they continued to deny to black men. "Unknowingly," Miller has written (1986:68), "the black woman was being recruited by the ruling minority as an ally against the black man." Just as female teachers became *numerically* preponderant at both elementary and secondary levels by the 1930s, and overwhelmingly so by the 1960s, Miller argues, female students began to outstrip their male counterparts at all levels, so that by 1985 girls outnumbered boys in high schools by an incredible 58.5 percent to 41.2 percent (55,536 to 32,681). At the Mona campus of the University of the West Indies in 1986–87, the gender distribution was 55.3 percent female (2,820) to 44.7 percent male (1,559), with women dominating every faculty of study except natural sciences (where they nonetheless made up 47.7 percent of the students), medicine (44.3 percent), agriculture (46.2 percent) and engineering (8.3 percent); no less than 61.3 percent of law students at Mona that year were women (Miller 1988:5–10). Not only is Jamaica "one of the few countries in the world in which there are more illiterate men than women in the population" (1986:4), it is also one in which women are better qualified generally than men, earn higher first incomes, and are more than twice as likely as men (27 percent to 12 percent) to hold middle-ranking positions in society. The top positions remain dominated, however, by men of the long-standing white, near white, and colored upper middle class (1988:14–15). Based on such evidence, Miller hypothesizes that the existing matrifocal structure of Jamaican society is in the process of evolving into an actual matriarchy or, better, gynocracy, as upwardly mobile black women, "so far sponsored by the dominant group, turn against their sponsors and exploit the prevailing social circumstances to their advantage." This leaves lower-class, and even some middle-class, black males increasingly liable to marginalization, unemployment, deviance, violence, and symbolic castration; in short, "the end of patriarchy has already begun in the Caribbean" (1988:18). As a sex, the argument implies, Jamaican women are closer in their values, behaviors, and aspirations to the dominant "European" or, better, "North American," norms of the society than are Jamaican men, whence the alleged tendency of the latter to define black lower-class and lower-middle-class women as "not entirely loyal, the thinly disguised Achilles' hill of the Black struggle": "their propensity to respectability is made the ultimate immorality, for through it they became the betrayers of the people" (Austin-Broos 1991–92:307). It is against this background of the apparent "feminization" of Jamaican Christianity, of the Jamaican educational system, and of whole sections of Jamaican social and economic life that the discussion of Rastafarianism that follows takes place and shape.

## Opposing the Shitstem: Rastafarianism and Jamaican Society, 1932–1992

How it was that Leonard Howell, Robert Hinds, Joseph Hibbert, Archibald Dunkley, and others, drawing on the converging strands of Afro-Christianity, Ethiopianism, and Garveyism, came separately but more or less simultaneously to acclaim Ras Tafari, crowned Emperor Haile Selassie I of Ethiopia in October 1930, as the black king from Africa allegedly prophesied by Garvey has been well described by Robert Hill (1983) and Barry Chevannes (1994), and need not further detain us here; nor is the content of Rastafarian beliefs and practices the present focus of attention.[28] My concern is rather

28. The basic argument of this section was formulated before the publication of the important collection of essays edited by Barry Chevannes, *Rastafari and Other African-Caribbean Worldviews* (1995). The essays by Chevannes himself, and above all the outstanding study by John P. Homiak ("Dub History: Soundings on Rastafari Livity and Language," 127–81) add substantially to our knowledge of the evolution of Rastafarianism and broadly confirm the course of my original argument; I have as

with the highly ambivalent way that, from the very origins of the movement in the early 1930s, Rastafarians have related to Jamaican society, with the no less paradoxical way that Jamaican society has reacted to Rastafarians and their beliefs, and with how, finally, Rastafarians, although *in theory* engaged in all-out warfare with Babylon and all it stands for, have *in practice* been forced to accommodate to it. They have done so by creating for themselves a liminal psychological, cultural, and other physical space that is neither wholly inside nor wholly outside established society, a space from within which they can, in de Certeau's terms, *oppose* society as it is without being able to move entirely outside it in order to *resist* it. The liminal or oppositional character of Rastafarianism can be observed in the first instance in the physical movements of its earliest adherents between Kingston and the parishes, and within Kingston itself, and this discussion begins with the characteristically nomadic career of the remarkable Leonard Perceval Howell (1898–1981), to whom, if to anyone, the title of founding father of Rastafarianism belongs.

Like Bedward before him,[29] and like virtually every other charismatic religious or political leader that has emerged in the English-speaking Caribbean, Howell was a returning migrant, having worked in Panama and the United States, where he seems to have had contacts not only with Garveyism but with Pan-Africanism and communism in the person of George Padmore. The Jamaica he returned to sometime between 1930 and 1932 was already in the grip of an upsurge of Revivalism or "Shakerism" that we can attribute at least indirectly to the social and economic distress unleashed in the colony by the Wall Street crash of 1929. Howell held his first public meetings on the subject of "Ras Tafari, King of Abyssinia" in Kingston in January 1933 but, failing to attract the community of followers he had hoped for, soon shifted his center of activities from the capital to the countryside, and specifically to that heartland of the Afro-Creole countertradition, the parish of St. Thomas in the East, to which he moved in April 1933. It was here, in a human and cultural crucible where the traditions of Afro-Jamaicans meet and merge with those of the descendants of Maroons and African and East Indian indentured laborers,[30] that Howell made his earliest converts. And it was here that, after a meeting

---

far as possible incorporated their principal conclusions into the text and footnotes of the revised version of this section.

29. The whole of this paragraph is based on Hill 1983:28–35.

30. Each of these traditions may have left its mark on Rastafarianism: the Maroons through their physical self-removal from the world of the plantation, the African indentured laborers through their Kumina drumming, from which Rastafarian drumming is primarily derived (see Bilby and Leib 1986), and the East Indians through their use of ganja (marijuana) and perhaps through certain similarities between Hindu concepts of the identity of self and God and the "I-and-I" oneness of selfhood and godhead taught by Rastafarianism. Significantly, Howell at one time styled himself "Gangunguru [or G. G.] Maragh," meaning great king in Hindi, and it is possible that his later title of "Gong" derived from this (see Hill 1983:35). For further details on possible East Indian influences on Rastafarianism, see Friday 1983 and Mansingh and Mansingh 1985.

The only known picture of Leonard Perceval Howell, early
Rastafarian preacher and prophet, ca. 1935. *Gleaner* photo.
Courtesy of the National Library of Jamaica.

held at Trinityville on 18 April 1933, he first attracted the attention of the authorities when, as we have already seen, he urged his audience to "sing the National Anthem, but before you start, you must remember that you are not singing it for King George the Fifth, but for Ras Tafair [sic] our new king" (police report, quoted in Hill 1983:33). Following further incendiary meetings in St. Thomas and Portland, Howell was arrested on 1 January 1934 along with his associate Robert Hinds, and though both were sentenced to prison, the content of their teaching continued to spread among what the *Daily Gleaner* of 20 August 1934 described as "the small producer and labouring class in eastern St. Thomas" who, the newspaper averred, had come to believe "that the land belongs to the black people: no longer are they accountable to Government or property owners" (34).

Released from prison at different times, Howell and Hinds seem to have split up, with Howell returning at least temporarily to St. Thomas and Hinds, a former Bedwardite, founding his King of Kings Mission in downtown Kingston. His combination of Rastafarian doctrine and Revivalist-style ritual attracted a large number of followers, most of them probably displaced migrants from the parishes; as Diane Austin-Broos has written (1992:236), both Rastafarianism and Pentecostalism are "modes of response, in a somewhat different vein, to the crumbling norms and mores of a self-contained rural life," the latter appealing mainly to women and the former, as we shall see, overwhelmingly to men. The mission also attracted the attention of the police, especially when in 1937 Hinds claimed in public that the new British king, George VI, had not been properly and legitimately crowned and that, accordingly, Haile Selassie was the true sovereign of Jamaica, as he was of all Africans "at home or abroad" (see Chevannes 1994:126–44). Galvanized by the Italian invasion of Abyssinia in 1935,[31] which Britain had utterly failed to forestall, and by the determined fighting back by the emperor and his people, the nascent cult was moving in the direction of a confrontation with the colonial state. Whether, or to what extent and how, it was involved in the islandwide labor riots of April–June 1938 (briefly discussed in the section that follows) remains hotly disputed, with Robert Hill claiming (without much evidence to hand) that it played a significant if not decisive part in events and Ken Post stating categorically that what he calls Ethiopianism "provided no basis for effective political action, threw up no lasting organizations" either in 1938 or he implies, at any time in the future (Post 1978:205). Writing from a rigidly Marxist standpoint, Post further asserts (193–94) that by 1937–38 Rastafarianism, having built itself up "through a series of verbal confusions, implicit assumptions, mistaken identities and wishful thinking," was already inward

---

31. On Rastafarian and, more broadly, West Indian reactions to the Italian invasion of Abyssinia, see Hill 1983:27–30 and Weisbord 1970.

looking and "retreatist" in its orientation, as from his point of view is only to be expected of a movement that he characterizes as "a product of cumulative false consciousness, incorporating as it did elements of biblical interpretation, pseudo-history, and even white racist fantasy." In the absence, at present, of clinching evidence one way or the other, it seems prudent to conclude with Post that there was no specifically Rastafarian *activity* in 1938 and with Hill (1983:34) that "Rastafarian millenarian ideology" functioned—along with other more important factors such as trade union organization—as "an active catalyst in the developing popular consciousness that led to the labour uprisings of 1938 by virtue of its radical vision of black dominion." From the outset, in other words, there was a tension within Rastafarianism between the extremism of its language and the comparative moderation, or ineffectiveness, of its actions. Allied to this was a tension between the urge to withdraw from Babylon physically (through repatriation to Africa or migration within Jamaica), or at least spiritually, culturally, and psychologically, and the counter-urge to transform it by radical and if necessary violent means. As we shall see, these and similar tensions have continued to divide the movement and its members right up to the present.

Howell and his followers moved to Kingston in the late 1930s and survived for a time by baking and selling bread. In the face of continual police harassment, however, Howell decided in true Maroon style to "put foot" into the hills, where, in the vicinity of the former "free village" of Sligoville in the parish of St. Catherine, he and his so-called Ethiopian Salvation Society established the community of Pinnacle, which lasted, with interruptions, from 1940 to 1954 and even, according to some accounts, until 1981.[32] The community—which was explicitly compared to a Maroon settlement in the *Daily Gleaner* and *Jamaica Times* in July 1941 (Hoenisch 1988:445)—survived several police raids in the early 1940s. In the course of one of them Howell was against arrested, along with sixty-seven of his followers, but the community continued to retain a quasi-autonomous existence more on the margins of established society than completely outside it. It was at Pinnacle that the ritual use, and widespread cultivation, of ganja seems to have begun—it was the commune's main cash crop—and there that self-sufficiency in food, clothes, and artifacts emerged as the ideal to which many subsequent Rastafarian settlements would aspire, usually, as at Pinnacle itself, in vain (see Chevannes 1994:122–23). Styling himself "Gong," "Counsellor," or "Prince Regent," Howell seems to have regarded himself, and to have been regarded by his followers, as (in the words of one Howellite interviewed by Barry Chevannes) "a

32. The account of Pinnacle is based on a conflation of Hoenisch 1988 and Chevannes 1994:121–24. In a recent study, published after the completion of this book, Frank Jan Van Dijk (1995:75) has argued that "notwithstanding its importance in the early days or its great symbolic significance, Pinnacle was perhaps far more marginal to Rastafari than generally assumed."

man on him throne like Nebukadnezzer" holding authority, in Haile Selassie's name, over an independent nation-state within the confines of the colony and not hesitating to use the totemic weapon of the slaveholder to impose his will on his "subjects": "Suppose you disobey him, him order you fi get lash, and if is in yu hand, you have fi take it. If is twenty, take the twenty in you hand. If you violate what him say, you get flogging, and if you refuse, you was sent out of the compound" (124). I will return to the question of authoritarianism and violence in Jamaican popular religion in the concluding section of this chapter.

When the Pinnacle community finally broke up in 1954, Howell and his followers returned to Kingston to confront a highly divisive situation that had emerged in the slums of Trench Town, the Dungle, Back-o-Wall, and Ackee Walk, which would henceforth constitute Rastafarianism's physical and spiritual epicenter. While the Howellites had been living in semireclusion outside Kingston, the movement within the city had expanded considerably beyond the original nuclei provided by the various missions set up by Hinds, Hibbert, Dunkley, and others, in the process precipitating a conflict between the early adherents, who in certain respects remained close to the traditions of Afro-Christianity and Revival, and a new generation of converts who in 1949 constituted themselves semiofficially as the Youth Black Faith. The latter wanted to "purify" the movement of the Revivalist vestiges that clung to it and in general to heighten its separation from the world of Babylon into which—so they argued—it risked being reabsorbed. It was during the conflict between the "purifiers" and the "accommodationists" of the early 1950s, only recently revealed by Barry Chevannes (1994:152–70, 1995a, 1995b) and John P. Homiak (1995), that the most radical forms of Rastafarian "livity" were elaborated and defined, as members of Youth Black Faith and similar groups such as the House of Boanerges sought to distance themselves in every way possible not just from Babylon but, perhaps more urgently and immediately, from "de 'old-man-style Rasta vibes'" (Ras I-rice I-on, quoted in Homiak 1995:135) and particularly from "poco-ism"—that is Pocomania or Revival—which they clearly saw as a set of "female" cult practices that threatened to contaminate the "male" purity of "true" Rastafarianism (Chevannes 1994:130).[33]

Whereas Howell had sought, ultimately without success, to remove himself and his followers physically from the clutches of Babylon, the younger generation signaled its rejection through what Homiak (1995:136) calls "a process of signifying upon the authorized social codes that upheld the everyday commonsense legitimacy of the system"—in other words, by systematically scrambling, inverting, and *playing with the* system's norms while remain-

---

33. See also Yawney 1989:198: "The identification of Pocomania and spiritual emotionalism with women is clear in the minds of the brethren."

ing more in the interstices of the system than, after the manner of Pinnacle, on its margins. Thus it was during the 1950s in Kingston rather than, as was once thought, during the 1940s at Pinnacle that Ital (<(v)ital) dietary practices, based primarily on the avoidance of meat and salt, were formulated as a way of marking the true believers' rupture from the "bellyswangers" (meat eaters; Homiak 1995:149) that made up the bulk of Jamaican population. Many radicals eschewed even the cooking utensils and tableware of Babylon: "We were so I-tal we doan use spoon or even bowl . . . maybe we just eat off a leaf" (Headful, quoted in Homiak 1995:145). Other fundamentalists—the term does not seem misplaced—renounced not just meat but the flesh, believing that "I-n-I is not people wha lust" (I-rice, 141) and that "after dealing wid a ooman in a 'creational' [sexual] form, she takes a certain amount of strength out of your mind, out of your *goody* [body], and she interrupt your meditation most time" (Headfull, ibid.). Others again marked their rejection of Babylon by "trodding in Higes Knots"[34] (walking barefoot in the middle of the street clad only in crocus bags and wielding a rod or staff; see Homiak 1995:151–56) in order, Brother Hyawhycuss recalls (151–52), "to let de enemy know dat Rasta would stand regardless what dem try to do we. Dis was to show Babylon dat de Righteous would never bow . . . fo' we went to de last stage of sackcloth." But the most visible and contentious sign of the radicalization of Rastafari was the purists' insistence that brethren should not cut or comb their hair, both in obedience to supposed scriptural authority (the example of Samson's devirilization by Delilah was frequently and significantly invoked)[35] and as a way of maximizing the distance between the Rastas who rejected Babylon outright ("Dreadlocks") and those who were prepared to compromise or even to collaborate with it ("Combsomes").[36] "Plenty of de old time Rastaman couldn't tek de message of de Locks-Dread Nyahman . . . couldn't tek de message!" says one of Homiak's informants (Sister Merriam Lennox, 134), and another recalls how "since I-n-I ages Rasta arise, is de Dreadlocks yout rise and stamp out de neo-Revival "ting" (Ras-I-mes, 147). Each of these developments, and others related to them, will be further treated later in this section, but it is clear from the detailed reconstructions of Homiak and Chevannes that by the mid-1950s the radicals had won a decisive victory over their rivals, whereupon the purified movement embarked on a ten-year period of head-on conflict with what a somewhat later generation of Rastafarians would call the "shit-

34. "Knots" refers to the "Bags Knots" or crocus bags worn by the brethren, "hige" being "an archaic term in Jamaican English meaning 'to torment'" (Homiak 1995:151).

35. Cf. the Ethiopians' ska hit "The Ring" (quoted in Constant 1982:83): "Samson was a dread / And Delilah took his hair."

36. Chevannes (1994:201) cites a case of a barbershop in Kingston being burned down because the red, white, and blue of its sign was too close a reminder for some brethren of the red, white, and blue of the British Union Jack.

stem" (Constant 1982:33)—"is spiritual warfare we is on," recalls one participant in the confrontational march in downtown Kingston in April 1954 (Chevannes 1994:161)—that in 1959–60 would lead to outright violence and briefly threaten the stability of the whole existing Jamaican order as it moved hesitatingly through the federal interregnum to full political independence in 1962.

In the course of the 1950s Rastafarianism became closely associated for the first time with "youth" and its problems and gained numerous converts, or at least sympathizers, among the Rudie subculture of Kingston and other major towns. It was, however, a veteran of Jamaican millennialism, the Reverend Claudius Henry (born ca. 1900), who precipitated the sequence of events that would bring Rastafarianism and the Jamaican state into collision, whereafter, as in the earlier case of Afro-Christianity, relations would gradually be resolved into grudging, and still highly suspicious, acceptance and accommodation on both sides.[37] Arrested as early as 1929 for attacking the Anglican Church as an agent of British colonialism, and adjudged to be insane, Henry had a series of religious visions before migrating during World War II to the United States, whence he returned, in paradigmatic fashion, in 1957, now styling himself "the Repairer of the Breach" and bringing with him pictures of the "true Jesus" and his virgin mother, both of whom, of course, were black. Announcing himself further as "God's Approved Prophet and Israel's Leader," "Another 'Moses' leading Israel's Scattered Slaves Back Home to Motherland Africa," "Implement of the Holy Trinity," and "God's Watchman over the Nations," Henry quickly attracted a core of about two hundred supporters, many of whom lived together as a commune in a yard on Rosalie Avenue in downtown Kingston that had been offered by Sister Edna Fisher, leader of a local branch of the Ethiopian World Federation. In March 1959 Henry distributed large numbers of blue cards to members of the public in Jamaica that purportedly would take "Pioneering Israel's scattered Children of African Origin back home to Africa, this year 1959, deadline date Oct. 5th."[38] At least five hundred hopeful "emigrants" turned up at Rosalie Avenue on the appointed day, and in the affray that followed when it became clear that no Africa-bound boat or plane was going to arrive that day or any other, Henry was arrested, fined, and bound over to keep the peace for a year. When he failed to do so the police raided his Kingston headquarters on 6 April 1960 and, to their amazement, discovered an arms cache consisting of several sticks of dynamite, over

37. The following account is based essentially on Chevannes 1976, supported where appropriate by Morrish 1982:73–76; For further details see Van Dijk 1995:81–94. Chevannes 1995a:30 argues that many Rastas viewed Henry "with suspicion, because he wore neither dreadlocks nor beard," and he should perhaps be regarded as a radical Ethiopianist closer to Revival than Rastafarianism.

38. For the full text of Henry's "passport" see Morrish 1982:73–74.

five thousand detonators, a shotgun, some twelve-bore cartridges, a revolver, and an array of swords, clubs, batons, and a spear, whose symbolic significance will become clear in due course. Still more astounding, they discovered a letter addressed to Fidel Castro (who, to the dismay of the Jamaican establishment, had entered Havana in triumph on January 1959) announcing an imminent "Invasion on the Jamaican Government" and promising that "Jamaica and the rest of the British West Indies will be turned over to you and your Government, after this war which we are preparing to start for Africa's freedom is completed." The "conspirators" themselves announced that "we do not want Jamaica, but to go home" (quoted in Chevannes 1976:277). At this point Rastafarianism and communism merged in the increasingly paranoid Jamaican establishment's mind, and Henry and twelve of his followers were found guilty of conspiring to "subvert, overawe and intimidate the government of Jamaica," Henry himself being sentenced to ten years' hard labor. In the meantime the police had discovered a further arms cache in Red Hills just outside Kingston, where Henry's own son Ronald had withdrawn, Maroon-style, with several followers, two of whom had apparently been executed for disobedience of the younger Henry's orders. A shoot-out took place, and two British soldiers were killed; Ronald Henry and four of his followers were hanged for their murder and that of the two dissident rebels. The association between Rastafarianism, subversion, and savagery was complete.

In the wake of the "Claudius Henry Affair," the Jamaican government commissioned a report on Rastafarianism by three prominent local academics (Smith, Augier, and Nettleford 1960) that, in retrospect and to the extent that it advocated a sympathetic approach to the movement, marked the beginning of the neutralization by accommodation that took place over the decades that followed.[39] So effectively was this process accomplished that one Jamaican scholar writing in 1980, could state, without fear of contradiction, that "Rastafarianism is now a part of the taken-for-granted landscape" of Jamaica (Callam 1980:43). This "recuperation" or "domestication" of Rastafarianism came about as a result of adjustments in policy and attitude on both sides of the "breach" that Henry and his followers had so signally failed to repair. Most Rastafarians (including the group of which Henry resumed leadership on release from prison) implicitly if not explicitly abandoned their belief in actual physical "repatriation" to Africa, and as they did so, "the physical withdrawal which would have landed them in Africa was internalized into an ethic of heroic withdrawal" (Callam 1980:32). Focusing now on the task of surviving in Babylon without becoming part of it (see Breiner 1985–86:33) or, in the case of an activist minority, of striving to transform the Jamaican Babylon into a

39. But not before there had been a further violent confrontation between Rastafarians and police at Coral Gardens in Montego Bay in 1963, resulting in eight deaths (see Lacey 1977:84–85). On the "routinization" and "secularization" of Rastafarianism in the 1980s, see Chevannes 1995a:15.

surrogate Zion, Rastafarians in practice entered into one or another modus vivendi with the prevailing order of things in Jamaica. As most "orthodox" Rastafarians tended more and more to withdraw into their individual and collective selves, their ideas, mentalities, symbols, and language, ironically, began to be diffused throughout the whole Jamaican society and beyond, thanks in large part to the closer and closer association between Rastafarianism and the various forms of popular music—ska, rocksteady, reggae—that succeeded one another in course of the 1960s and early 1970s.[40] (The further co-option of Rastafarian themes and rhetoric into politics by the People's National Party in the general election of 1972 is discussed in greater detail below). It became difficult, if not impossible, to define any clear cutoff point between Rastafarian and non-Rastafarian as Rastafarianism became Jamaicanized and Jamaica became Rastafarianized to a significant if superficial extent (see Albuquerque 1979:22). The most influential and typical Rastafarian groups of the 1970s and 1980s, the Bobo (see Chevannes 1994:172–88) and the Twelve Tribes of Israel (see White 1983:279–81; Van Dijk 1988), both reached an accommodation with the wider society in contrasting ways. The Bobo live in amicable symbiosis with the people of Bull Bay, on whose outskirts their principal commune, headed by Prince Emmanuel, is situated; the Twelve Tribes created a cell-based pyramid structure under their "Gadmon," Vernon Carrington, and encourage members, many of middle-class origin, to infiltrate Babylon in quest of converts. Established Jamaican society danced to the music of the Wailers, wore dreadlocks, and "colours" as fashion accessories,[41] bought Rastafarian pictures and sculptures to adorn uptown Kingston homes, and dispatched Count Ossie and the Mystic Revelations of Rastafari to countless international cultural events abroad. By the mid-1970s the clash of worldviews that had brought Rastafarianism and Jamaican society into conflict in the late 1950s and early 1960s had been in large part defused as a result, perversely, of the widespread diffusion of at least the superficial elements of Rastafarian belief and lifestyle, prompting calls by one group of orthodox Rastafarians known as Nyahbinghi[42] for an "effort at countermissionization" (Yawney 1993:165) to prevent the dilution of the pristine Rastafarian faith through acceptance by Babylon. In short, Rastafarianism, if not individual Rastafarians themselves (who continue to be discriminated against in a variety of ways), has become "respectable," and the reconciliation of Rasta and Babylon was solemnized at

40. On the "attenuated version of the Rastafarian message" transmitted by reggae, see Yawney 1979:160. For general studies of the interaction between Rastafarianism and Jamaican popular music, see White 1983 and Waters 1985.

41. Whence the expression "Fashion Dread" coined by Gregory Stephens (see Chevannes 1994:274).

42. There have been various Rastafarian groups calling themselves Nyahbinghi (supposedly meaning "Death to the Whites"), some of them apparently real, others plainly popular or elite inventions. See Post 1978:173 and Chevannes 1994:43, 164–65.

the state funeral of reggae star Bob Marley in May 1981. The lesson was read by that ultimate pillar of the Jamaican establishment, Governor General Florizel Glasspole, and eulogies were given by Michael Manley and Edward Seaga, leaders of the bitterly opposed People's National Party and Jamaica Labour Party, whom Marley—looking, it was said, like Christ on the cross between the two thieves—had vainly brought together on stage at the celebrated "One Love" Peace Concert held at the height of Jamaica's interparty violence in April 1978 (see White 1983:27–28 and 300–301). Two months before Marley's death, in February 1981, Leonard Howell had also died in Kingston, totally forgotten save by a handful of followers, having, like Bedward before him, spent much of the last thirty years of his life in a mental hospital, apparently believing, again like Bedward, that he was Christ. Bedward, Howell, Marley: one Christ figure after another had come and gone, to say nothing of any number of Moseses and Joshuas, and still the sufferers of Trench Town and Back-o-Wall suffered on.

It should be clear from the account above that, despite its militant separatist ideology, Rastafarianism has at no time during its sixty-year history been able to create for itself a space outside Jamaican society from which it would be possible to resist, in de Certeau's sense of the word, Babylon and all it stands for. Given the self-evident failure of its strategy of "repatriation" to Africa, the movement has in practice had to resort to a variety of oppositional tactics that have enabled it to survive within Babylon without in any way liberating it and its members from the institutions, mentalities, and values of the dominant order. Rastafarianism's oppositional character is manifested in the first instance in its early adherents' continual to-and-fro movements between town and country, seldom establishing themselves permanently in one or the other, removing themselves at intervals from urban centers but—like Maroons and the postemancipation "peasantry," constrained to remain in a relationship with the plantation economy and society they rejected—never so far as to suspend contact and exchange with them entirely, and then moving back into towns as economic circumstances or harassment by authorities required.[43] Once in the towns, especially in Kingston, (male) Rastafarians have commonly lived interstitial rather than marginal lives, locating their holiest sanctuaries in the very "colon of Babylon," as Carole Yawney (1979:162) so strikingly puts it, and using all manner of "Ethiopian diplomacy"[44] to retain,

43. According to Chevannes (1994:190), "a significant section of the Rastafari comprises people with one foot in the city and the other in the country," many of them owning small plots of land to which they periodically repair and that permit them to survive without a regular job, within the interstices of the "official" economy, like so many "scufflers" in Jamaica (see Post 1978:135). On the significance of Rastafarians' movements between country and town, see Post 1981:189.

44. "Ethiopian diplomacy" is an expression used by the brethren themselves and alludes to the legendary sagacity of the Ethiopian (see Yawney 1979:163).

Anancylike, their room for maneuver in a society they at least partly reject and that, until the 1970s, rejected them totally. But as Yawney shows elsewhere (1983:196–97), many male Rastafarians contrive to divide their lives between men-only "camps" or cult centers and mixed-sex "yards" (see chapter 4 below) that remain in symbiotic relation with Babylon. Playing off camp against yard, tacking and tracking this way and that between the Zion of the mind and the Babylon of reality, most Rastafarians remain ultimately dependent for their material survival on the very "shitstem" they repudiate.

But this parasitism is also encountered in other, nonmaterial aspects of Rastafarian belief and practice. Curiously for a religion that so totally rejects Christianity, Rastafarianism has originated no sacred scriptures of its own[45] but contents itself with a "verbal manipulation of authoritative texts," principally Exodus, Leviticus, the Psalms, and from the New Testament, the Book of Revelation, in such a way that "the authority of the Bible is retained, but by a few critical reinterpretations its significance for the black-white polarization is reversed" (Cumper 1979:12; see also Breiner 1985–86:31–33). The Rastafarian faith, in other words, rests on a deconstructive reading of the enemy's canonical text that reproduces that text's underlying assumptions even as it reverses its explicit message. With regard to ritual, Barry Chevannes has argued (1994:145) that despite their desire to "purify" Rastafarianism of the numerous Revivalist elements it still contained, the reforming Dreadlocks "only went halfway in their elimination of Revival retentions," with the result that contemporary Rastafarian ritual consists, he claims, of "a mixture of innovations and traditional elements from Revivalism"; it is a compromise symptomatic of the broader "dilemma of the Dreadlocks: determined to break with the peasant world view, but forced to remain within the mainstream of that tradition" (170). The same might be said of other aspects of Rastafarian behavior. By eschewing certain widely consumed Jamaican foods—notably salt pork and salt fish, both deemed to be "slave food"[46]—in favor of a largely vegetarian "Ital" diet, Rastafarians have certainly distanced themselves from the eating habits of Babylon (or rather of its victims); but their smoking of "the herb," even when raised to the level of a religious sacrament, no longer sets them radically apart from a society in which ganja use is now all-pervasive and in practice tolerated by the state (see Rubin and Comitas 1975). Moreover, what Carole Yawney (1976:240) calls Rastafarianism's "paracabalistic verbal activity"—above all the systematic replacement of the phonemes of Standard En-

45. On the various pseudobiblical texts (the Holy Piby, the "Maccabee Version," etc.) that have supplemented but not supplanted the Old and the New Testaments, see White 1983:9–11 and Chevannes 1994:117.

46. On the broader question of salt avoidance in Rastafarian diet, see Warner-Lewis 1993:114–16 and Chevannes 1994:35. On the gender implications of the preparation of Ital food, see Homiak 1995:145.

glish by the phoneme "I" to produce such characteristic formulations as Idrin (brethren), Inity, Ireator (Creator), Iternal, Itheopian, and Ital—reveals, when examined, a similar parasitic relationship with the language of Babylon that the Rastafarian subdialect (Chevannes 1994:167) simultaneously invokes and subverts. Thus "downpression" depends on "oppression" for its meaning and force, as does "overstand" on "understand" or, for that matter, the more sibylline "Blinago," "blingaret," and "ublin" on the systematic substitution of "blin(d)" for "see" in Seaga, cigarette, and university (< U.C. < University College [of the West Indies]).[47] The supposedly subversive "Dread Talk" of the Rastafarian man-of-words[48] cannot signify unless the dominant language it opposes is simultaneously present in the mind of speaker and hearer alike. Emerging in the early 1950s, alongside the wearing of dreadlocks and the formulation of Ital dietary practices, Dread Talk had, like them, a decidedly antifemale significance to the extent that, in Homiak's words (1995:164), "'I,' for the Rastaman, is first person singular, masculine gender," the systematic use of "I and I" being "typically reserved for exchanges among *male* speakers."[49] "I" may well be "foundational," as one of Homiak's informants memorably puts it (172), but what it founds is primarily, and perhaps even exclusively, an individual and collective *male* identity. Thus it is just as much the language of Babylon's victims as the language of Babylon itself that is the target of Rastafarian troping and punning, the ritualistic use of "I and I" as collective subject pronoun uniting God, self, and community (see Owens 1976:65) challenging less the monadic "I" of European individualism than the supposedly objectified "Me" of standard Jamaican *patwa*. Just as, in the name of "Africa," the reformist Dreadlocks opposed creolized religious cults such as Revival as expressions of "female" passivity, so they sought to define themselves linguistically over and against both the agents of Babylon *and* the average "downpressed" Jamaican who failed to "overstand" the source of his or her misery and continued to eat "slave food" like ackee and salt fish. But some Creole

47. For these and similar examples of how Rastafarians have "morphemically segmented English words so as to tease out meanings which the original word-unit does not bear or use homophony to derive analogical meaning" (Warner-Lewis 1993:121), see Pollard 1980:36 and, above all, Homiak 1995:160–73.

48. On the concept of the man-of-words, see chapter 4 below. Carolyn Cooper (1993:136) illuminatingly describes the word games of the Rastaman and the contemporary DJ as "forms of verbal maroonage" and supplies the other essential cultural referent when, speaking of Bob Marley's lyrics, she evokes the "tricky, Anansi-like mutability of the oral/scribal literary continuum in Jamaica" (117). Still more tellingly, one of Homiak's informants (1995:175) says that Rasta comes to "destroy powers and principalities not with gun and bayonet, but wordically."

49. According to one of Homiak's informants (1995:172), "I" is "a personal pronoun, in a maxilin [sic] gender, carrying a nominative case, having a subject of its own," while another (163–64) specifies that it was "by keeping away from ooman" that "de *I-tesvar* [Dread Talk] came into our mind": "After a certain amount of years of expanding ourself in de emotional powers of His Majesty [Haile Selassie], we leave out de ooman altogether."

linguists derive standard West Indian "Me" not from English but from the Twi first person pronoun *mi* (see Cassidy 1961:54). It may be, ironically, that the Dreadlocks' would-be subversive "I and I" is closer etymologically to English than "Me," just as (equally ironically) their desire to purge Rastafarian ritual of any Revivalist taint may have brought it back toward Christian, and specifically nonconformist Protestant, practice, as in its emphasis on scriptural exegesis and "reasoning" and its parallel rejection of possession by the Spirit or spirits in the name, precisely, of *self*-possession and *self*-expression.[50]

It was, however, above all though the wearing of dreadlocks[51] that Rastafarianism's eponymous purifiers sought to maximize and consecrate their separation both from the world of Babylon and of its passive, unredeemed victims and perhaps most significantly of all, from the world of women.[52] But in a cogently argued discussion titled "Black Hair/Style Politics," Kobena Mercer has maintained, using terms that recall de Certeau's distinction between opposition and resistance, that dreadlocks, like the 1960s Afro they somewhat resemble, ideologically if not physically, did *not* mark a complete break, as is sometimes claimed, with European-derived notions of what constitutes "good hair" but were only "a *tactical inversion* of the chain of equivalences that structured the Eurocentric system of white bias" (Mercer 1987:40). Seeking to invert "the symbolic order of racial polarity," to transpose "nature" and "culture" and so "turn white bias on its head," wearing dreadlocks nonetheless remained, and remains, within "a dualistic logic of binary oppositionality (to Europe and artifice)." The "moment of rupture" it supposedly marked was in reality "delimited by the fact that it was only an imaginary 'Africa' that was put into play"; the further fact that, like the Afro, dreadlocks "operated on terrain already mapped out by the symbolic codes of the dominant white culture" explains the ease with which, even as they inverted those codes, they could be neutralized and absorbed back into the mainstream (41). And so it has proved with every other "counter-hegemonic tactic of inversion" (ibid.) by which Rastafarians have sought to set themselves apart from the dominion of Babylon. Because their diet, dress, hairstyles, language, and ultimately their faith

---

50. On this important distinction, see Breiner (1985–86:37): "Possession requires a voiding of personality to make way for the god. . . . Rastafarianism instead insists on the authoritative individuality of the prophet. . . . The Rastafarian speaks with his own voice, not that of his God."

51. And beards, which in 1950s Jamaica were widely seen as the distinctive sign of the "batty man" (homosexual). In the early 1950s Rastafarians were routinely referred to as "Beards" in the Jamaican press ("Beards Besiege Court," "Howling 'Beards' Jailed," etc.), the term "Locksmen" becoming current only by the end of the decade (see Chevannes 1995c:100).

52. In his important studies of the origins and significance of dreadlocks, Barry Chevannes (1995c:123) has argued that wearing matted hair was symbolic not only of "stepping beyond the control of White-oriented society" but also of its wearers' "total ascendancy over the female, who was viewed as a force used to contain them within society." For fascinating details on the gendered significance of combs and combing, see Chevannes 1995c:116–17.

are in no way "African" but are all oppositional products of the very "shitstem" they hate, every protestation or would-be expression of Africanness is of necessity self-deconstructive and merely proves and reinforces their actual non-Africanness. Unable to get outside the shitstem, they can only reproduce it even as they symbolically oppose and invert it: it is an aporia inseparable from the fact of being Afro-Creole, not African.

But it is in their attitudes toward and treatment of women that male Rastafarians most reveal their continuing bondage to Babylon.[53] Long a taboo subject, Rastafarian misogyny can now, thanks to the research of Diane Austin-Broos, Carolyn Cooper, Carole Yawney, and others, be seen as a constitutive rather than coincidental or contingent feature of the movement's worldview and practice. Such has been the traditional subordination of women in the Rastafarian movement[54] that it was as though, protested one female member, Sister Ilaloo, in 1981, there were no such person as a Rastawoman, only a Rastaman woman (quoted in Chevannes 1994:260). The "queen" or "empress" derived not only her value but almost her very identity from the relationship to her "king-man" or "emperor": after all, as Rastamen say, and some Rastawomen repeat, "the dread is the head" (Sister Faria, quoted in Yawney 1989:200), and it is through him, and only through him, that the "daughter" can relate to God. But Rastafarian misogyny has deep historical, cultural, and psychological roots. Taking over wholesale a familiar set of biblical stereotypes, Rastafarian men often represent Woman—"Woe to man"—as a quasi-diabolical force who seduced Adam—"A Damned"—into error and sin (190–91) and routinely symbolize the existing order as Babylon the Whore, the Fallen Woman of Saint John's Revelation who must be systematically reviled and "chanted down" (see Cooper 1993:121). In Rastafarianism, Carolyn Cooper has written (127), "woman, in both her literal and symbolic manifestations, is intrinsically evil, a seductive, malevolent force enticing the morally innocent Rastaman from the path of righteousness into slackness," so that it is hardly surprising if in many of Bob Marley's songs, for example, "the Adamic Rastaman, susceptible to the wiles of Babylonian Eve, becomes the passive victim of female cunning" (130).[55] Now fear of female "trickifying" and of being "tied" by female guile is, to say the least, common among Jamaican men (see Sobo 1993:229), and it may be that Rastafarianism supplies no more than a "theological" gloss to a widespread male perception of women. Similarly, the widely attested Rastafarian taboo

53. The present discussion is based primarily on Austin-Broos 1987 and Yawney 1989, with additional reference to Rowe 1980, Cooper 1993, and Lake 1994. Contemporary changes in the position of women in Rastafarianism are discussed in Chevannes 1994:256–62.

54. Significantly, Rastafarianism is the only religious grouping that in the Jamaican census of 1982 shows more male (11,661) than female (2,588) affiliates (quoted in Austin-Broos 1987:4).

55. For similar themes in Trinidadian calypso, see chapter 4 below.

against menstruating women (see Yawney 1989:197, etc.)[56] exists throughout a society in which "bloodclot" ( = blood cloth or menstrual "rag") rivals "rass-clot" ( = arse cloth) as the most offensive obscenity, and it is not just Rastafarian men who, fearing a white genocidal conspiracy, are opposed to birth control and abortion.[57] But not only does Rastafarianism not challenge these "Babylonian" phobias and fantasies, it actively reinforces them and gives them a kind of supernatural sanction: it is the heaviest irony of the movement's history that its challenge to the racial hierarchies and prejudices that still bedevil Jamaican societies should be inseparable from an acceptance, even an accentuation, of the sexual stereotypes that, arguably, cut even deeper.

In one respect, however, Rastafarian sexual practice goes diametrically against the Jamaican norm, and that is the *patrifocal* orientation of its family structures. Rejecting the matrifocal household as a product of slavery, Rasta-farian men counter it, in the name of "Africa," with a strong preference for father-centered family structures that, ironically, "[duplicate] an image of the Jamaican middle-class family where men, due to greater financial security, tra-ditionally have been able to care for their children and control a wife" (Austin-Broos 1987:18). More ironically still, they "mirror the culture of the European colonizers to whom they are ideologically opposed" (Yawney 1989:190): it is as though whenever Rastafarianism opposes the creole in the name of the African, it is fated in reality to move closer to the European. Not only is Babylon a woman, but woman is Babylon, and as Diane Austin-Broos has writ-ten (1987:21), "her subordination is in fact an integral component of the male's leonine identity." "Woman is a coward, man strong," Bob Marley al-legedly told an interviewer in 1975 (quoted in Cooper 1993:131), inadver-tently revealing that fear of the female, perhaps of the female in themselves,[58] which, at least since the advent of the Dreadlocks in the late 1940s,[59] seems to have powered male Rastafarians' faith just as much as hatred of the shitstem and all its works. Unable to generate an authentically revolutionary strategy,

56. In the Bobo commune described by Barry Chevannes (1994:176–78), menstruating women are described as "sick" and are confined to the "sick house" for no fewer than *sixteen* days each month. On Jamaican menstrual taboos generally, see Sobo 1993:229–33.

57. According to Sobo (1993:142), "male control over female sexuality is limited by 'the plan-ning,' and men are its most vocal opponents." Women who use "the planning" are said to be "walking cemeteries" (ibid.), and men commonly prick condoms before use (212). On Rastafarian opposition to birth control and abortion, see Yawney 1989:199.

58. "[Jamaican] men fear the feminine aspect of themselves much more than women fear the masculine sides of themselves. Men's gender identities are so much more conditional and tenuous. Their genitals—so different in both form and function from the female's—take on great symbolic potency for expression of manliness" (Sobo 1993:151).

59. Chevannes (1994:130) argues that women were strongly represented, and held positions of importance, in the early Revivalist-influenced communities of Leonard Howell and Robert Hinds; the growing prominence of women in contemporary Rastafarianism may be linked to its growth among the Jamaican middle class (see Chevannes 1995c:124).

reduced in practice to a series of tactical inversions of significant but limited import, Rastafarianism has precipitated a great movement of minds without being able to find or show a way out of the Babylonian impasse. It has imposed as much as it has opposed, and its legacy for contemporary Jamaica is paradoxical in the extreme.

It is perhaps because they sensed Rastafarianism's actual or imminent sclerosis that, since the mid-1980s, many young lower-class Jamaicans, both male and female, seem to have moved decisively away from it.[60] The 'de-Rastafarianization' of Jamaican youth culture—if that is what it is—is inseparable from the shift in musical styles from reggae to ragga/dance hall, from dreadlocked prophet-singer to the immaculately tonsured, designer-dressed DJ, from ganja to cocaine, and from Ital to McDonald's. The shift from reggae to ragga, which many commentators consider to have been "consecrated" by the pelting of Bunny Wailer (since Bob Marley's death the keeper of the reggae-Rastafarian faith) with Red Stripe bottles at the annual "Sting" reggae concert at Kingston on Boxing Day 1990,[61] has been variously interpreted as the triumph of "slackness" (obscenity, the celebration of sexuality) over political consciousness, as a symptom of the growing Americanization of Jamaican life, and perhaps most significantly, as a sign of the growing liberation of teenage Jamaican girls not only from their respectable church- and school-oriented upbringing but also from the sexism of Jamaican males to which Rastafarianism gave a measure of "philosophical" justification and that, more recently, the violently antifemale lyrics of DJs such as Shabba Ranks, Ninjaman, and Super Cyat have pushed to some kind of pathological climax. Certainly, on the evidence of the lyrics so ably discussed by Carolyn Cooper (1983), there are few signs in contemporary ragga of the political, or even the racial, preoccupations that powered the music of the Ethiopians or the Wailers:[62] at first glance it is *punaani*, *glamiti*, and *glibiti*,[63] and not much else, that raises the modern Jamaican DJ to action. Cooper (161) sees the "erotic maroonage" of slackness—corresponding to the "verbal maroonage" (136) of the DJ's manipulation of language—as "potentially a politics of subversion," as a "metaphorical revolt against law and order," and finally as "an (h)ideology of escape from the authority of omniscient Culture" (141).[64] This may be so—though one notes

60. The present discussion is based primarily on Cooper (1993), supported by two articles that appeared in the *Independent* in early 1991: "The Ghost of Marley" by Joseph Gallivan (11 April) and "'Bankrupt' Jamaican culture cuts loose from its moral roots" by David Adams, the exact date of which I have mislaid.

61. "When Bunny Wailer made his exit under a hail of Red Stripe bottles at last Boxing Day's 'Sting' Festival in Kingston, the reggae establishment knew its time was up. The fans wanted to hear Shabba Ranks [the new star of raggamuffin], and that was that" (Gallivan, "Ghost of Marley").

62. For a useful discussion of politics and reggae in the 1960s and 1970s, see Brodber 1985.

63. These are all *patwa* terms for the vagina.

64. Cooper quotes (147) in this connection the chorus of Josey Wales's "Culture a Lick," which,

that "potentially"—but the same had already been said of every other form of real or metaphorical maroonage from the actual runways of the seventeenth and eighteenth centuries, through the Anancy figures who manipulated the slave system without destroying or escaping from it, to those largely imaginary twentieth-century Maroons, the Rastafarians. The trouble with maroonage, be it "erotic," "verbal," or whatever, is that it is *always* "symbolic"; in other words, it leaves the structures of the plantation essentially intact. What *is* important and indeed "potentially subversive" is that it is now *women*, as much as men and perhaps even more, who are now flouting the canons of respectability, primarily through the unrestrainedly erotic form of dancing known as "waining" or "wining,"[65] which, characteristically, women perform alone or with other women in what Cooper rightly calls a celebration of their own sexual and economic independence. It is hardly coincidental that wining came to dominate the dance halls of Jamaica at precisely the time that the proportion of female graduates from the Mona campus of the University of the West Indies rose to an incredible 67 percent.[66] Much the same style of female dancing exploded at about the same time in Trinidad (see chapter 4 below), and in both countries the male reaction was fear disguised by an exacerbated misogyny and machismo that the lyrics of ragga reflect and confirm. Wining is directed as much for and against West Indian men as against "Culture" of the "Eurocentric" variety, and it is this that makes it, and the social forces it embodies, one of the most important, and also one of the most paradoxical, cultural developments in the contemporary Caribbean. I will return to this subject in chapter 4.

## "The Word Is Love": The Hero and the Crowd in Jamaican Politics, 1944–1980

Although Jamaican religion, or at least its Afro-Christian core, became increasingly depoliticized after Bedward's demise, this does not mean that Jamaican politics, when they emerged in their modern form in the late 1930s, were entirely secular in character. On the contrary, politics itself rapidly took on a "religious" dimension, with two secular "churches"—the People's National Party (PNP) and the Jamaica Labour Party (JLP)—confronting each other like

---

though she does not say so, comprehensively inverts the traditional association, must discussed by Caribbean anthropologists (see chapter 4 below), of yard and respectability and, contrariwise, of street and "slackness": "Slackness in di backyard hidin, hidin, hidin / Slackness in di backyard hidin, hidin from Culture."

65. For an early use of the term wining (< winding), see chapter 4, n. 18 below.

66. This figure is given by David Adams in the article cited in n. 60. I have not been able to confirm it, but it is consistent with the figures provided by Errol Miller (1986, 1988) for the sexual distribution of students at UWI.

two massive Revivalist bands, each regarding itself as chosen by God and the other as the agent of the devil. Both saw themselves charged with the mission of leading the Jamaican people (frequently and explicitly likened to the Children of Israel) to an undefined and perhaps undefinable Promised Land under the aegis of a leader whose prophetic, charismatic nature was systematically proclaimed and built up. Like everything else in Afro-Creole culture, the cult of the leader has its origins in slavery, partly in the highly ambiguous cult of "Massa" that we have observed in operation on M. G. Lewis's estate in the early nineteenth century and that evolved, under the impact of the missions and the spread of abolitionist ideas, into the cult of the "Good White Man" outlined above. But it also draws on the tradition, itself African derived, of the priest-cum-magician-cum-political leader that produced Tacky in the mid-eighteenth century.[67] In a Christianized form, it also produced "Daddy Ruler" Sharpe in the early nineteenth century, whence it was diffused throughout the whole religious culture of Afro-Jamaicans in the form of the "Daddies" of Native Baptism, the "Shepherds" of Revival, the "Convinced Doctors" of a barely Christianized Myalism, and so on. In their different ways and with varying intensity, all these figures were objects of reverence to their followers, and it frequently happened, as it clearly did with Bedward, that adherence to the leader's vision or message slipped imperceptibly into a personalized cult of the leader himself, who in his turn was sometimes transformed, in the eyes of his followers and perhaps in his own, from an apostle of Christ into a Christ figure in his own right. If a song reported in the *Daily Gleaner* on 15 March 1934 (quoted in Post 1978:165) is to be believed, Leonard Howell was almost instantly promoted by his followers from prophet to redeemer, to whom the believer had only to abandon himself or herself in order to be saved and transported forthwith to the Promised Land:

> Leonard Howell seeks me and he finds me,
> Fills my heart with glee;
> That's why I am happy all the day,
> For I know what Leonard Howell is doing for my soul,
> That's why I am happy all the day.

Beginning as the bearer of a vision, the prophet-leader soon becomes a charismatic mediator with the God who, in Jamaican Revival, always appears "as a stern, punitive and distant 'master' or 'father'" (Wedenoja 1980:38) or who, in Rastafarianism, is figured as a hieratic emperor, more white than black,[68] who

67. On the charismatic, Myalist origin of Tacky's power over his followers, see Chevannes 1994:17–18.

68. Haile Selassie is commonly represented as light skinned, and certainly not as "black," in Rastafarian images. See, for example, the painting by Ras Dubrick reproduced in Nicholas 1979.

dwells far away in the Holy Land of Ethiopia, whence he keeps his guardian's eye and hand over his lost children in Jamaica. Both God figures transpose the severe, distant but ultimately love and protective king (or queen) of England who, as we have seen, so exercised the Jamaican slave imagination in the last years of slavery and whose image the descendants of slaves long continued to invoke in their repeated struggles against the plantocracy. More pertinent still, "Massa God" or "Big Massa" presents all the features of Massa himself, aggrandized and spiritualized (see Chevannes 1994: 22–23). Massa is usually hidden, unseen but all-seeing, in the Great House (or still farther away in England), controlling things from afar through his attorneys, overseers, and drivers, but then suddenly manifesting himself epiphanically to his slaves, just as the God of Revival manifests himself by possessing his adepts or as Jah "grounds" himself in the midst of the Rastafarian brethren. Thus the prophet-leader is he who has privileged access to the Big Massa in the Great House of heaven, who takes or is given some of Big Massa's power and transmits it to the suffering masses below, whence the almost irresistible appeal of Afro-Jamaican religion: Surrender yourself to "Daddy" or "Ruler" or "Shepherd," and you in your turn—provided you *obey* his teaching and orders—will enter the Promised Land where, as in the Great House, you will be fed milk and honey (or, if you prefer, jerked pork with rice and peas) for all eternity.

The traditional Jamaican prophet-messiah presents certain almost paradigmatic features, many of which will in due course be transferred to the contemporary political messiah. He is always of humble origin, though, like the skilled slave Sam Sharpe or the small landowner Paul Bogle, he has sometimes attained an intermediate position by the time his career as a prophet is launched; he is usually black, though colored or even white prophet-leaders are not unknown;[69] female prophets, known as Warners,[70] are also encountered but do not seem to become the object of cults. The prophet has often, like Moses or Jesus, spent some years in the wilderness away from "his" people—Bedward in Panama, Howell and Henry in the United States—to whom he at some point "returns," bringing with him a revolutionary spiritual vision vouchsafed him abroad. He has usually suffered disease, injury, imprisonment, or oppression at the hands of Whites and on his return commonly presents himself, and is perceived by his followers, as a "Moses" or "Joshua"[71] and gives

69. Thus the Salvation Army owed its early success in Jamaica to a local White named Raglan Philipps, who by 1894 had recruited over eight thousand members. In 1906 he formed his own Revivalist movement, which became the City Mission Church in 1924 (see Wedenoja 1988:108).

70. On Warners, see Bryan 1991:36 and Chevannes 1994:82–83. The "Mada" (Mother) of the Revivalist balmyard is a very different figure and does not assume prophetic or messianic dimensions (see Wedenoja 1989).

71. Thus Bedward is said by his supporter A. A. Brooks (1917:4) "to combine in himself the faith of Abraham, the meekness of Moses, the patience of Job, and the love of St. John"; his teacher, the Reverend H. E. Shakespeare Woods, passed his mission on to him "like Moses upon Joshua," and

himself titles such as Shepherd, Watchman, Warrior, Doctor, Daddy, Fada, Gangunguru Maragh or . . . Repairer of the Breach. His insignia are of regal or military power and authority (swords, flags, scepters, rings, staffs, rods),[72] of guidance and protection (the omnipresent shepherd's crook of Revival), of access (keys),[73] and of healing: according to one former disciple of Howell, "the Gong" "had his instrument [probably a stethoscope] like a doctor when him perform "pon the people, just like a doctor up at U.C. [University College of the West Indies]" (quoted in Chevannes 1994:124). Like the suffering servant of Isaiah, the prophet-figure is "despised and rejected of men" and offers himself up sacrificially for the salvation of his pilgrim flock whom, at the price only of their total faith and obedience, he undertakes to "march home" from Babylon to Zion, from bondage in Egypt to the Promised Land of Israel.

The first secular prophet to be endowed with this complex of attributes in modern Jamaican history was Marcus Garvey on his "return" to Jamaica in 1928 after many years spent in the "wilderness" of Central America, Europe, and the United States, whence his political activities had caused him to be deported by the authorities back to the island of his birth. Described at the time as a "political Bedward" by one of his enemies (Rev. Ernest Price, quoted in Lewis 1987:62), Garvey was seen by many Jamaicans as the blend of Moses and Messiah that his middle name—Mosiah—declared him to be (Chevannes 1994:39). He was variously perceived as "a mysterious man like a superman" whom the colonial authorities had tried to kill in a poisoned herb bath in Spanish Town jail lest he "preach and turn the people heart back to Africa" (early Rastafarian, quoted in Chevannes 1994:100–01); as the John the Baptist of a future Black Christ (102); as "the forerunner to the King" (ibid.); as sublime man-of-words (the "Demosthenes of the Negro people," according to one veteran Jamaican Garveyite, quoted in Hamilton 1988:95); and as friend, redeemer, shepherd, and standard-bearer of his race (102):

---

he and his associate Dawson are now "linked together as Moses and Aaron in the congregation of Israel" (7).

72. On the use of swords in Revival, see Wedenoja 1988:96, and in Rastafarianism, see Homiak 1987:229. For flags, see Wedenoja 1989:79, Homiak 1987:229, 234, and Chevannes 1994:172–73. For rings, see Homiak 1987:229. For staffs, rods, and prayer sticks, see Homiak 1987:234, etc., and 1995:156, where members of the "Higes Knots" movement (see previous section) recall "walking wid tall rod" through the streets of Kingston in the early 1950s.

73. On the symbolism of keys in Rastafarianism, see Homiak 1987:237, 240. In 1935 Howell published a book titled *The Promised Key*, heavily based on the Reverend Fitz Balintine Pettersburgh's 1926 *Royal Parchment Scroll of Black Supremacy* (Chevannes 1994:42), and a number of Chevannes's informants refer to a movement called the Seven Keys, one of whose prophets, a 'tall, strapping man, him mout' red, big hand, big lip, big nose," possibly "from foreign," who accosted Kingstonians in the streets in the early 1930s, urging them to "take seven key to breathe God's word, Deuteronomy to seal" (Chevannes 1994:89).

Veteran Rastafarian Timothy (otherwise Fuzzy or Bongo) Hill (1904–85) at a Rasta camp at Nine Miles, St. Thomas, Jamaica, with his ceremonial key, to which "scientific" powers were widely attributed. Photo by John P. Homiak, 1980.

All around the world our Negro Leader's been
All around the world he called to Negro men
All around the world now he's back here again
The Red, the Black and Green is waving
All around the world.[74]

It is noticeable that many of Chevannes's informants refer as to a talismanic emblem to the "crook stick" that he carried everywhere with him while in Jamaica and that he would stick into the ground and top with his black felt hat whenever he spoke. This, and his bow tie, white shirt, jacket, and cloak, was enough to convince one future Rastafarian that Garvey was "an honorable man from God and you must have a great respect for persons like these" (1994:92–93, 102).

All this prepared the way for the cult of Alexander Bustamante, which would begin at the time of the 1938 labor riots and gain momentum after his imprisonment by the British authorities that year and again under wartime Defense Regulations between 1940 and 1942 until he emerged from Jamaica's first fully democratic elections in 1944 as "Busta" or "the Chief." As leader of both the Bustamante Industrial Trade Union and the victorious Jamaica Labour Party, he held the destiny of the whole island colony in his hands. A near-white Jamaican of mysterious origins,[75] Bustamante had, in the now almost obligatory fashion, spent many years away from Jamaica in Cuba, Costa Rica, the United States, and possibly Spain before returning to the island of his birth in 1934 and building up a network of strong personal loyalties and dependence among lower-class Kingstonians through his activities as a money lender. During the 1938 riots—which had almost none of the explicit religious tonality of the 1865 uprising[76] but nonetheless took place in a climate of

74. Cf. another Garveyite hymn quoted by Hamilton (1988:103):

> Listen to the voice of Garvey, the Negroes friend
> Hear him telling the people everywhere to unite
> Sing the song of New Negroes till we obtain our land
> Garvey comes to lead his people home again.

75. Or rather of origins he sought to render mysterious. He was in fact the son of a near-white planter named Clarke and, as such, a cousin of his archrival Norman Washington Manley. He claimed to have been adopted by a Spanish seaman named Bustamante and taken to Spain as a youngster (see Bakan 1900:101).

76. Ken Post's exhaustive discussion (1978) of the riots contains virtually no evidence of Revivalist or Rastafarian (as opposed to Garveyite) involvement in events, though the words of one striking dockworker, W. A. Williams, do suggest the presence, beneath the strikers' concrete laborist demands, of the characteristic Afro-Christian thematics of bondage and delivery: "We have suffered under this slavery system for many generations. And now the time has come to shake ourselves from our captivity. . . . Now that we have seen that Jehovah has placed this great knowledge in our heads today we are not going to let one another down" (290). Strikers are reported to have marched to the strains of "Onward, Christian Soldiers" (Bryan 1991:273), but they also sang "God Save the King,"

Norman Washington Manley (left) and Alexander Bustamante addressing a crowd during the Jamaican labor riots of May 1938. *Gleaner* photo. Courtesy of the National Library of Jamaica.

heightened if not millennialist expectation, partly linked to 1938's being the centenary of emancipation—Bustamante emerged improbably as both spokesman and embodiment of the "small man." His ambivalent position in Jamaican society placed him closer to the "reputation culture" of the lower-class Jamaican male (see chapter 4 below) than to the "respectability culture" of the colored middle classes epitomized by his ally and rival, the Rhodes scholar and British-trained lawyer Norman Washington Manley, who had himself "returned" to the island of his birth a few years before. Splitting in 1942 from the People's National Party he and Manley had jointly launched in 1938, Bustamante founded the Jamaica Labour Party and in the 1944 elections was systematically promoted—and no doubt systematically promoted himself—as a

and unlike Howell's early followers, they undoubtedly meant George VI and not Haile Selassie (see Post 1978:290). For an authoritative study of the 1938 labor riots in Jamaica, published after this section was drafted, see Bolland 1995:132–66. Bolland's comments (154–55) on the way "the martyred hero [Bustamante] became the dictatorial leader soon after the labour rebellion" are especially pertinent in the present context.

Alexander Bustamante, the archetypal political man-of-words, taking the salute (date and whereabouts unknown). NLJ photo. Courtesy of the National Library of Jamaica.

Revivalist-style leader who would shortly march his flock to an unspecified Promised Land of full employment and, not least, full stomachs. One JLP song of 1944, sung to the tune of a well-known Revivalist hymn, declared that "The Conquering Busta shall break every chain / And give us the victory again and again" while, according to another, "Busta power working just like a magnet / It moving me, it moving you—jus' like a magnet" (quoted in Post 1981:489); no less significantly, the Revivalist-Rastafarian leader Robert Hinds urged his followers to "pray to God for somebody to assist us with food, and when Busta rise up, him say, 'This is the man'" (quoted in Chevannes 1994:147).[77] *Ecce Homo*—but what an improbable Christ figure he was, sitting at the inaugural meeting of the JLP at the Ward Theatre in Kingston in 1943 "attired in brown shorts, a grey coat and a preacher's white tie . . . with a bandaged leg perched on a camp stool" (Paul Blanshard, quoted in Post 1981:354), a patchwork creature straight out of pantomime, the Actor Boy in the Jonkonnu dance of Jamaican politics, an irresistible and ultimately fatal mixture of trickster and messiah, Anancy and pseudo-Christ rolled into one,[78] whose mesmeric hold

77. According to the same informant (Chevannes 1994:147), "when Busta first win the election in 1944, him kill 11 head of cow at Union Hall and give it to poor people free."

78. On Bustamante as Anancy, see chapter 2, n. 12 above.

over the minds of black Jamaicans[79] in the 1940s and 1950s is brilliantly summarized by Ken Post (1981:63):

> Bustamante was a living contradiction, money-lender and labor leader, genuine sympathiser with the oppressed and luster after personal power, brilliant mass orator and dabbler in intrigue. His personal dominance over the minds of so many of the poor was a perfect expression of their level of consciousness . . . Bustamante was the sigh of the oppressed creature, the heart of a heartless world and the soul of soulless conditions. But, like revivalism, he was no less the opium of the people.

Faced with a performer and man-of-words of such prowess, the PNP labored in vain to project its would-be messiah as some kind of Moses in collar and tie. But Moses had a Joshua in the form of his son, and it would be Michael Manley, succeeding his father as leader of the PNP in 1969, who would be the next and, so far, the last (as well as the most charismatic) manifestation of the savior figure so deeply embedded in Jamaican political psyche. Almost as light skinned as his father's archrival Bustamante, Michael Manley "returned" to Jamaica in the early 1950s after wartime service in the Royal Canadian Air Force and studies at the London School of Economics and swiftly gained an islandwide reputation as a trade union negotiator for the PNP-backed National Workers Union, apparently receiving the title-nickname "Joshua" for the dynamic part he played in a strike of Jamaica Broadcasting Company employees in 1964 (see Levi 1989:112). But it was during the general election of 1972—that extraordinary mixture of Revivalist meeting, Rastafarian reasoning, and reggae splashdown, never to be forgotten by those who witnessed it[80]—that the millennialist undercurrents of Jamaican politics came absolutely to the fore. While the leader of the JLP, Hugh Shearer— "Pharaoh" Shearer, inevitably, to his opponents (Waters 1985:118)—tried to project his party as the party of Christianity, Manley comprehensively outbid him by appealing simultaneously to the Christian churches, both denominational and Pentecostalist, and to the diffuse but potentially very large Rastafarian or Rastafarian-influenced constituency, enlisting a whole galaxy of sympathetic reggae stars—Bob Marley, Peter Tosh, Junior Byles, Max Romeo,

79. Though—or because?—it was led by someone phenotypically almost white, the JLP was, from the outset, the party of the black masses, for "while the masses voted 'Bustamante' they voted 'Black'" (E. S. Barrington Williams, *Progress of a People*, quoted in Post 1981:489). The PNP would long be perceived by black Jamaicans as the "brown man party," even though its platform was considerably more radical than that of the deceptively named JLP, at least until the purge of the "4 Hs" (the Marxists Richard Hart, Arthur Henry, and Ken and Frank Hill) in 1952 brought the two parties into virtual ideological convergence (see Munroe 1972:75–84).

80. This account is based primarily on personal recollection and on Waters 1985:111–31.

Clancy Eccles, Ken Boothe, and Dennis Alcapone, some of whom had had records banned by the JLP[81]—to broadcast his message to the nation. Two motifs, repeated hypnotically by Manley and other PNP speakers, dominated the campaign: "Love," epitomized in Manley's salutation "The Word Is Love," an obvious and deliberate echo of the Rastafarians' "Peace and Love," and "Power," as in the slogan "Power for the People"—not, it should be noted, "Power *to* the People," a different concept entirely (see Waters 1985:121)— and in clenched-fisted cries of "Power!" that were everywhere to be heard before, during, and after the elections.[82] Allying Power and Love in an irresistible compound, Joshua would shortly march the Children of Israel into the Promised Land: "Better *Must* Come," as Delroy Wilson's reggae confidently blared from every PNP loudspeaker in Jamaica.

Facing annihilation at the polling booths, the JLP had recourse to an electoral ploy that, though perhaps trivial in itself, takes us to the core of the relation between power, politics, and religion in contemporary Jamaica.[83] It was known or rumored that, in the buildup to the elections, Michael Manley had been in contact with the Reverend Claudius Henry, who from prison had instructed his followers to cut their dreadlocks, shave their beards, abstain from ganja, and jettison their back-to-Africa beliefs. On release, after serving seven years of his ten-year sentence, Henry had reestablished his renamed "Peacemaker's Church" on Revivalist-cum-Rastafarian lines, his hanged son

81. Typical of the Jamaican mood of the late 1960s and early 1970s in Junior Byles's "Beat down Babylon" (quoted in Waters 1985:131), banned by the JLP government but to be heard on informal sound systems throughout the country:

> Said me nah like the kind of Babylon,
> Said me nah dig them wicked men
> For I'm a righteous Rastaman,
> And I'm a dread dread one I-man,
> I and I go beat down Babylon
> I and I must whip them wicked men
> What a wicked situation
> I and I dying for starvation
> This might cause a revolution
> And a dangerous pollution. . . .

82. Cf. also Max Romeo's "Let the Power Fall on I," sung to the tune of a well-known Revivalist hymn, another of the campaign's unofficial theme songs (quoted in Waters 1985:131):

> Let the Power fall on I, Fari,
> O let the Power fall on I . . .
> O let the wicked burn in ash, Fari,
> O let the wicked burn in ash. . . .

83. The following account is based on a conflation of Jacobs 1973:35–42 and Chevannes 1976:280–88.

Ronald being, according to some accounts, venerated as the Holy Spirit proceeding perichoretically from the Father (Haile Selassie) and the Son (a black
Christ) (see Chevannes 1976:281). In late 1969 Henry distributed a pamphlet
in which he hailed Michael Manley as Jamaica's secular savior, saying that
Manley's father Norman (who had been prime minister at the time of the
original "Claudius Henry Affair") "should have built the house of God in Jamaica; but did not; as he did not meet God's approval; hence God has appointed Michael his son, to finish his work" (quoted in Chevannes 1976:283).
A new hymn (quoted in Waters 1985:121) began to issue from the new Peacemaker's Church that, along with a bakery, a school, and other buildings, Henry
had constructed with his followers in the Green Bottom district of Kingston:

> Haile Selassie I is our God
> Claudius Henry is our King
> Michael Manley is our Joshua
> What a peace of mind
> Our Joshua has come.

At about the same time, both Manley and Shearer, also anxious to capture the
"Rastafarian vote," made separate visits to Ethiopia, each receiving a personal
gift from His Imperial Majesty: for Shearer, allegedly, a cigarette lighter (presumably not for a spliff) and for Manley a carved ebony rod complete with an
ivory handle and ivory tip (see Jacobs 1973:41). This talismanic object, rich
with both Revivalist and Rastafarian associations and redolent also of Massa's
whip and the stickfighter's baton (see below chapter 4), not to mention
teacher's cane and mother's or father's switch, was immediately dubbed the
Rod of Correction by PNP supporters and celebrated in song by Clancy Eccles, who urged "Joshua" to set about "Pharaoh" in no uncertain manner and
"Lick im wid di rod of correction, Faada / Lick im wid di rod of correction"
(quoted in Chevannes 1976:284). The rod began to be displayed ritualistically—indeed almost fetishistically—at PNP election meetings, panicking the
JLP into a desperate countercampaign. In February 1972, a few weeks before
the election, a JLP minister obtained a copy of a pamphlet written by Claudius
Henry, bearing pictures of Haile Selassie, Manley, and Henry himself each
armed with a rod and declaring that the PNP victory the three would bring
together would be "the greatest religious Event to take place on earth since
the beginning of the creation of God": "Now the time for a change has come.
This change will be brought about by Moses [Henry], Joshua, and the King of
Kings and Lord of Lords, 'Trinity of the God-head'" (285). This clearly was a
chance not to be missed, and knowing that the memory of the original Claudius Henry Affair was still vivid in the minds of tens of thousands of Jamaicans
and believing that Henry's supposedly blasphemous pamphlet would deter a

substantial proportion of them from voting for Manley, the JLP swung its considerable propaganda resources into action.

The second Claudius Henry Affair began on 22 February 1972 with the publication in the *Daily Gleaner* of a full-page advertisement that reproduced the picture of Haile Selassie, Henry, and Manley, reminded readers of the original Henry Affair, and then declared: "Behold Claudius Henry returns. He makes common cause with Michael (who calleth himself Joshua), the son of Norman." "The Voice is the Voice of Moses but the Hand is the Hand of Joshua," repeated the advertisement in order that the point be lost on nobody, and then it delivered the punch line that would run through its campaign in the coming weeks: "The PNP believe in Michael's Rod. The JLP believe in Almighty God. Vote JLP."[84] The following evening the JLP finance minister and future prime minister, Edward Seaga (also, and not coincidentally, an early authority on Jamaican Revival), brandished a rod before his constituents in downtown Kingston, claiming that *it* was the "true" Rod of Correction that he had obtained in unspecified circumstances, and that the rod Manley was flaunting was quite simply a fake; Manley, he said, was "a shepherd without his staff, a Joshua without his rod, and a leader without power." A further advertisement deriding the Henry pamphlet's blasphemous claims regarding a PNP victory was published on 24 February, and on the twenty-eighth yet another advertisement appeared showing Seaga with "his" rod and declaring "I have it now! The Rod Rules in Central Kingston Tonight!" the constituency in question being Manley's own. In the same issue of the *Gleaner*, a PNP advertisement opposed "the rod of correction" to the "stick of deception." "Seaga's stick is not Joshua's rod," it declared, and, under a half-page picture of a tough-looking Manley, showed "the" Rod of Correction itself: "Here it is on Triumphant display. It has never been out of my possession for one day—nor will it ever be. Seaga's stick is a childish trick. It is the type of stick used in Jamaica by people who cannot help themselves. The "Rod" is made of carved African Ebony with an ivory handle and an ivory tip. It has metal clasps at the handle and the tip." At this point the JLP seems to have admitted defeat, and nothing more was heard of either the rod or the stick. Each having played its improbable part in the "licking" of Pharaoh and his drowning in a veritable Red Sea of PNP votes, they were duly consigned to an imaginary museum of Jamaican historical oddities, along with Warrior Higgins's red sash[85] and Leonard Howell's stethoscope. But for more than a week the rod and the stick eclipsed

84. This and all following quotations are taken from Jacobs 1973:36–41. Jacobs plausibly suggests (40) that "Michael's Rod," as well as referring to the Rod of Correction, is also intended to suggest Manley's well-known predilection for young, attractive women, notably the media personality Beverly Anderson with whom, as a widower, he was conducting a very public relationship at the time.

85. One of Chevannes's informants (1994:90) tellingly likens Higgins's red sash to the blood he would eventually shed for his beliefs: Higgins was severely beaten up by the police or by thugs and died of his injuries in July 1902 (see Elkins 1977:23).

every other electoral issue, presumably because Manley and Seaga—both, to say the least, intelligent men and highly astute politicians—were sufficiently imbued with Jamaican religious and political culture to appreciate the hold that the Rod of Correction could exercise over the minds of a significant portion of the Jamaican electorate. What then do the rod and, more generally, "Claudius Henry II" tell us about the psychology and anthropology of political power in Jamaica?

In the first place, the Rod of Correction saga suggests that Power—real Power, ultimate Power—is always situated *outside* Jamaica, whither an abridged version of it comes as a gift from afar and above, commonly sent by an at times severe but ultimately benevolent monarch: emancipation (1838) and Crown Colony government (1865) by a queen, full adult suffrage (1944) by a king, political independence (1962) by another queen, ironically bearing the same name as the still earlier queen in whose reign English slavery began, and the rod itself (1972) by a distant and protective emperor in Africa. The theme of the gift both expresses and distorts the fact that from 1655 to the present Jamaica has always been *acted on* from without and controlled from afar, first directly and obviously from Britain and then indirectly, and at times barely visibly, from the United States. Accordingly, it is hardly surprising if, especially in the case of emancipation and political independence from Britain, the apparently selfless gift turns out to have been selfishly motivated—indeed not to have been a gift at all or, at best, a partial and ambivalent one—for in each case it was not *real* freedom and *real* power that the receiver received, but a parody of the first and a mere facsimile of the second. Furthermore, even when the colonized or formerly colonized party contests the imposition of Power, he (or much more rarely she) tends to do so in terms that have already been defined by the colonial power itself. Thus the anticolonialist myth of the benevolent emperor reproduces while it inverts the colonialist myth of the benevolent king or queen, reminding us of the Rastafarian belief that, in Leonard Howell's own words (in *The Promised Key*, quoted in Hill 1983:33), the "Sceptre of solid gold twenty seven inches long which had been taken from the hands of Ethiopia some thousand years ago" was returned to Ras Tafari at his coronation in 1930 by none other than the English king's representative, the duke of Gloucester, whom Rastafarian image and text commonly depict kneeling in homage before the Lion of Judah.[86] Rastafarianism ultimately substitutes one distant king for another without changing the bond of dependency between the king and his subjects, just as in opposing slavery the slaves substituted "Massa God," "Missis Queen," and "King" Knibb the missionary for Massa *tout court* and so failed for the most part to liberate themselves from the

---

86. According to Howell (quoted in Hill 1983:33), "the Duke fell down bending knees before His Majesty Ras Tafari the King of Kings and Lord of Lords and spoke in a loud tone of voice and said, 'Master, Master my father has sent me to represent him sir. He is unable to come and he said he will serve you to the end Master.'"

mental structures of subordination and dependence. Finally, in passing from emperor to disciple, the *golden* scepter becomes the *wooden* Rod of Correction, just as Power becomes pseudopower when it nominally passes from colonizing nation to (ex-) colony. To summarize and repeat: the myth of the rod both expresses and conceals the fact that Power in Jamaica is ultimately *other*, and that even when the colonized receives or seizes a part or version of that Power, he remains essentially within the colonialist worldview or mind-set. It is, in short, extremely difficult for the formerly enslaved to escape the mental habitus of slavery.

The second main implication of the myth of the rod is the following. Having *descended* from above, Power, or rather the pseudopower that stands in its stead, is assumed by a male hero-cum-prophet-cum-savior, often white or near white, who exercises it in the name of the black masses. The power[87] is explicitly or implicitly phallic (see n. 84 above) and *descends* upon "the people" as from father to children or from male to female; as Michael Kaufman has brilliantly written (1985:173), in Jamaica "the state itself plays a role not unlike that of men in relation to women in the female-led household: dropping in and out with the occasional favor but holding a power and eminence that is at once aloof, magisterial, and mired in the grime of everyday life." In short, in Jamaica both Power and power *descend* from above to below, just as the Spirit *descends* on the Revivalist and Jah *grounds* himself amid the Rastafarian brethren; or as Max Romeo's election reggae of 1972 so aptly and eloquently put it, "Let the Power *fall* on I, Fari" (see n. 82). The third meaning suggested by the rod is that ultimate Power—Haile Selassie's solid golden scepter in the Rastafarian myth—normally remains hidden like Massa in the Great House or Big Massa in heaven; when Haile Selassie *descended* from his Ethiopian airliner with its Lion of Judah insignia and red, gold, and green trimmings at Palisadoes airport at 1:30 P.M. on Thursday, 21 April 1966, it was nothing less than an epiphany, the first time in history that Power, real Power, had manifested itself physically among the Jamaican people, over 100,000 of whom were present to greet its first steps on Jamaican soil with banners proclaiming "Behold the Lamb of God," "Hail the Man!" and "Lay Not Thine Hand on the Lord's Anointed" (see White 1983:210–12).[88] In all other circumstances, the scepter has been manifested in Jamaica by its substitute, the rod, or even by a substitute for the substitute, Eddie's stick for Michael's Rod: not Massa, concealed in his Great House or, more likely, absent in England, but his attorney, overseers, bookkeepers, and drivers, not the king or the queen but the colonial governor and

87. Henceforth Power in uppercase is used to designate the ultimate source of Power *outside* Jamaica, power in lowercase to designate the version of it that is manifested *inside* Jamaica.

88. A month before, Queen Elizabeth II and the duke of Edinburgh had paid a state visit to Jamaica that was greeted with general indifference by all but the middle-class elite (White 1983:210). They were no longer seen to embody real Power: had Queen Victoria visited the island in 1838 or 1865, things would doubtless have been rather different.

his officials and, come independence, not Moses but Joshua. For the most part the local holders of power are in the last (and often the first) instance the agents, puppets, or hirelings of Power, even—or rather especially—when they claim to be opposing or manipulating it on the masses" behalf: Busta, above all, was not actually "the Chief," Busta actually was Busha, acting for Massa when he claimed, even believed, he was acting against him. In the last instance (and often, again, in the first) Massa's best ally against Quashie and Quasheba is Anancy.

All this expresses, finally, the crucial fact that in Jamaica power is exercised *for* the people in the people's name, but never granted *to* the people, and still less, seized *by* the people acting on their own behalf. When the people do try to seize and exercise power (to say nothing of Power) for themselves, as they did using force in 1765, 1831–32, 1865, and 1938 and through their elected representatives between 1972 and 1980, then the real source of Power *descends* on them like an avenging angel to inflict appalling physical damage—400 victims in 1765, at least 550 in 1831–32, well over 400 in 1865[89]—or, as happened between 1972 and 1980, stands by with palpable satisfaction while the local economy bleeds to death and the people inflict scarcely less terrible suffering on each other.[90] In their pursuit of at least the appearance of Power, the Children of Israel are split into not twelve tribes but two, the PNP and JLP, each led by its Moses or Joseph figure and waging internecine war with each other—over five hundred killed during the general election campaign of October 1980—on their way to an imagined Promised Land.[91] Jamaican history is mythologized as a holocaust of victims, the vast majority of them anonymous, a heroic few named and venerated by posterity—Tacky, Sharpe, Bogle, Gordon, Garvey, and more recently Peter Tosh, Michael Smith, and Bob Marley himself[92]—who validate the people's perception of themselves as the suffering remnant, God's Chosen People inexplicably wrenched out of

89. The strikes and riots of 1938, even though they involved possibly 100,000 people in all (one in ten of the population), were repressed with the loss of "only" 8 lives, but were nonetheless violent enough; no soldiers or police were killed, but 32 strikers were wounded by gunshots and 139 more were injured by other means; in addition, 800 people were prosecuted, of whom more than half were convicted (see Holt 1992:386).

90. On political violence in pre-1970 Jamaica, see Lacey 1977, and on violence in the 1970s and 1980s, Payne 1988 passim. On specific instances of interparty violence between 1972 and 1980, see Levi 1989:170 for the "Orange Street Massacre" of May 1976 (when at least ten PNP supporters were killed when JLP gunmen surrounded their tenement building, set fire to it, and prevented them from fleeing) and p. 221 for the "Gold Street Massacre" of April 1980 when PNP gunmen killed four JLP supporters and wounded eleven others when they attacked a fund-raising dance.

91. On the "Tribalization" of Jamaican politics, see Payne 1988 and Stone 1980. On the spatial polarization of politics in Kingston, see the fine analysis in Eyre 1986.

92. Peter Tosh was murdered in September 1987, and Michael Smith was stoned to death by political enemies in August 1983. Bob Marley was wounded in a politically motivated attack in November 1976 (see White 1983:288–89), and when he died at age thirty-six in 1981 he was clearly seen as a martyr to much more than the cancer that killed him.

Zion and exiled to Babylon. All this takes place in a climate of Dread in which religion and politics feed into each other the language of bondage and delivery, sin and redemption. Moses wars with Pharaoh, Christ with Antichrist, and the messiah of yesterday becomes the Lucifer of today when, as always happens, the Promised Land is never reached and the new heaven and new earth stubbornly refuse to be born: Bustamante becomes Bustamente, Manley becomes Men-lie, "Joshua = Judas," "IMF: Is Manley Fault," "Seaga = CIAga," and so on and so on.[93] It is a climate that is at once strongly democratic and strongly authoritarian. The Children have·the right to vote and do so in massive numbers, but once they have cast their votes, power is taken away from them and often turned against them. The Rod of Correction is at once the crook of the shepherd and the staff of the prophet. In it Power and Love are thought to inhere, but it is too reminiscent of Massa's whip, teacher's cane, and Fada's belt or Moda's switch to be entirely innocent or benevolent.[94] Apparently a blessing, it can become a curse, as Junior Byles realized when, as the Manley government began to lurch from crisis to crisis, he urged "Joshua send back the Rod" (quoted in Constant 1982:114).

> Selassie I gave you the rod
> To lead and protect thy children
> You took the rod
> And you influence the nation
> And capture thy children into bondage.

The interpenetration of religion and politics both challenges and reinforces the authoritarian structures and mentalities inherited from the slave past and the colonial near-present. Thus although it is true that, as Trevor Munroe has written (1991:91–92), "Afro-Christianity has by and large been uniformly an integral part of the emancipatory tradition in the Caribbean whereas the Mainline Churches have either been ambivalent, reformist or repressive," it is also true that there is a "less evident and little discussed . . . element of conservatism within the emancipatory tendency itself":

> In both its religious doctrine and organisational structure, there have been features contributing to popular disempowerment side by side, even inextricably intertwined, with liberationism. From the standpoint of doctrine and biblical interpretation, the people are urged to resist, to fight for liberation. At the very same time, however, they are seen

93. On the transformation of Bustamante into Bustamente, see Chevannes 1994:103; a "men" in Rastafarian parlance is "an insincere person and a member or defender of the establishment." For the other nicknames, see Kaufman 1985:186 and Levi 1989:219.

94. Cf. Chevannes (1976:284), who makes these analogies and who pertinently recalls (1994: 175) the popularity in Jamaica of the maxim "Don't spare the rod and spoil the child."

to be and see themselves as objects rather than subjects of leadership. In the great project and process of emancipation, heroic prophets have to lead, the people's responsibility is to follow. The positive aspect is popular arousal against slavery, colonialism and injustice in all forms. The negative is the absence of a concept of popular empowerment, with its corollary, the dependence on a David, a Joshua, a Moses, a Messiah.[95]

We shall encounter this paradox again in the chapters that follow, where the Rod of Correction reappears in such unlikely guises as the stickfighter's baton and the flashing willow wand of Sobers and Richards. But now it is carnival time, and we leave the doom-laden Protestant astringencies of Jamaica for the greater expansiveness of predominantly Catholic Afro-Creole Trinidad, but perhaps only to rediscover in carnival the paradoxes and tensions that this chapter has sought to reveal in popular religion in Jamaica.

95. Or as the author candidly admits (Munroe 1991:92–93), on a Trevor. Munroe, founder and leader of the now defunct Workers' Party of Jamaica, found himself being transformed into a characteristic combination of hero and prophet at the time of the protracted Hampden Sugar estate workers' struggle in Trelawny between 1984 and 1988 (see Feuer 1989:56).

# The Carnival Complex

$I$n the wake of Mikhail Bakhtin's classic *Rabelais and His World*, belatedly translated into English in 1968, it has become almost routine for cultural theorists, anthropologists, and literary critics to view carnival as the liberating social ritual par excellence, as a systematic flouting and reversal of all the structures and hierarchies that govern the "profane" order of society, in which the foundational oppositions of "high" and "low," "inside" and "outside," "male" and "female," and the like are joyously and extravagantly subverted to give birth to a utopian universe of play, appetite, and unbridled sexuality and pleasure. At the heart of this widely held view is the belief that what happens during carnival is essentially *different* from what happens during the rest of the year, that the three or four days it lasts are a negation in every respect of the laws and behaviors that hold good for the remaining 360-odd, during which, it is implied, people live lives of unblemished moderation, seriousness, and decorum. Even critics of the utopian theory of carnival—those, for example, like Terry Eagleton, who regard it as "a *licensed* affair in every sense, a permissible rupture of hegemony" that, after a brief "popular blow-off," actually reinforces the order it seems to subvert (quoted in Stallybras and White 1986:13)—still accept the idea of a radical discontinuity between the "sacred" world of carnival and the "profane" world of normality that it is held in some way to turn "on its head." In both of these perspectives, social time and space are divided dualistically into carnival and noncarnival. Whether carnival is believed to subvert the status quo or reinforce it (or in the best of discussions, to do both simultaneously), it is always conceived as the realm of the other irrupting into the domain of the same, from which it withdraws in due course, leaving it undermined, strengthened, or renewed according to ideological taste.

The perspective adopted in this study of carnival in Trinidad is rather different. It incorporates aspects of both the "idealist" interpretation of carnival and its "realist" critique and argues that Trinidad carnival, like religion in Jamaica, both challenges and reinforces the status quo—that, to quote Roger Sales (Stallybrass and White 1986:13), it is more or less simultaneously "a vehicle for social protest and the method for disciplining that protest." On the other hand, I argue that what happens during the four days of carnival in Trinidad[1] is not *fundamentally* at variance with what happens during the remaining 360-plus days of the year. Carnival is viewed here less as a ludic subversion of society "as it is" than, in Victor Turner's useful term (1992:42), as a "magical mirror" of it; less as a ritual of reversal than, to use the even more apt characterization of Nancy Scheper-Hughes in her remarkable study of "Bom Jesus da Mata" in Brazil, *Death without Weeping* (1992:482), as a "ritual of intensification" in which the forces that govern "ordinary" life are expressed with a particular salience, clarity, and eloquence. Hence the chapter's title is not "Trinidad Carnival" but "The Carnival Complex"—in other words, the various strands of "normal" Trinidadian social and cultural life that knit together to form a nexus of particular intensity during carnival time. The principal hermeneutic opposition employed is not Bakhtin's opposition of "high" and "low" and the related opposition of "classical" and "grotesque" bodies that have proved so fertile in the analysis of carnival in premodern Europe. Trinidad carnival may be known locally as bacchanal, but as we shall see, it is at least as much Apollonian as Dionysiac. Indeed, it may be that Trinidad carnival is less a subversion of "high" by "low" than an attempt by the low to raise, enhance, and aestheticize themselves to the level of the high: a people whose ancestors were routinely punished by having their mouths shat in by others (see Hall 1989:72–73) are unlikely to take too much pleasure, however "transgressive," in the inversion of anus and mouth that, as Bakhtin shows, is so fundamental (if that is the word) to premodern carnival in Europe. Rather than high/low, the crucial opposition used here involves the dialectic of inside and outside and of private and public that Roberto DaMatta (1991:61–115) has used so illuminatingly in his discussions of Brazilian carnival. These oppositions are in their turn inseparable from the dialectic of "reputation" and "respectability" (and correlatively of "male" and "female"), and it is with this fertile theme in Caribbean anthropology that our discussion begins.

---

1. Strictly speaking, carnival lasts only two days (the Monday and Tuesday before Ash Wednesday), but I am including the preceding Saturday and Sunday, when important contests and processions take place.

## Inside/Outside: Respectability and Reputation in Caribbean Cultures

Much of the best anthropological writing on the Caribbean of the past twenty years takes its inspiration from Peter J. Wilson's *Crab Antics* (1973), a study of one of the region's historical-cultural oddities: the English-speaking but Columbian-owned island of Providencia, which, though it is some 160 miles off the coast of Nicaragua, is shown by Wilson to be typical in its social and cultural patterns of the English-speaking Caribbean as a whole. In particular Wilson discerns two distinct but complementary value systems in operation among the island's two thousand or so inhabitants. One—to which he gives the name "respectability"—is derived, he argues, from the values of the original colonizing power (Britain) and subsequently reinforced by the island's various (and often American-funded) Christian churches. The other— "reputation"—he sees as an internally generated value system opposed to the externally generated system of respectability. Respectability, says Wilson (1973:233), is "the normal force behind the coercive power of colonialism and neo-colonialism"; the explicit value system of the churches, it is sub- scribed to by the island's small middle class and, more generally and more vaguely, by women of all social classes, for whom the churches act as "the principal public domain of sociability" (102) and who are notably more "de- vout" than their male counterparts. For the respectable, the key values are marriage (as ideal if not as actuality), the home, self-restraint, work, educa- tion, economy, purposeful self-construction, and respect for social hier- archies—values that are opposed at every point to those expressed in the "reputation system" to which, in Wilson's account, almost the entire male population of Providencia, especially those under forty, appears to subscribe. "Reputation," says Wilson (149), represents "an existentially valid structure of relations by which men secure their identity more or less separately from women" and from the externally derived values that women are said to have internalized or assimilated. If home and church are the key institutions of the respectability system, the focus of the reputation system is the street and its adjunct and extension the rum shop, where all-male "crews" forgather at every opportunity to drink, play games (notably dominoes), and above all to talk in the way that—to the outsider at least—seems so distinctively (some, running the risk of essentialism, would say so instinctively) "West Indian." That is, noisily, competitively, plethorically, with a sense of style both lin- guistic and presentational that transforms even the most humdrum exchange— but perhaps no exchange in the Caribbean is ever truly humdrum—into a minidrama or "happening."[2] In the rum shop, on the street corner or beach,

---

2. Whence the significance of the standard West Indian (male) greeting "What's happening?"

"conversations are uninhibited, animated and intimate, full of banter, joshing and confidence, quite unlike the style of conversation in the home or in public places. Members [of crews] call each other by nickname and speak of each other in complimentary terms while at the same time feeling free to insult and playfully derogate each other" (Wilson 1973:182). If self-restraint, even self-denial, lies at the heart of the respectability system, self-affirmation, even self-dramatization, is the be-all and end-all of the reputation system. Men, in Wilson's account (149–52), affirm themselves by boasting of their prowess as drinkers, fighters, womanizers, gamblers, and sportsmen, asserting the value of self by—or so it appears—systematically devaluing the other. The whole occasion seems (again to the outsider) perpetually poised on the brink of explosion as ego grates against ego and the potlatch of boast and counterboast, insult and retort, mounts to a threshold beyond which violence surely must erupt. But, crucially, that threshold is never reached, or if it is the whole ritual of reputation collapses with its crossing. The key word in Wilson's account is the word "playfully": this is a world of stylized, not actual, aggression, and while on the surface the men are affirming, or attempting to affirm, their superiority *as individuals*, deep down what they are acting out in the form of a competitive verbal ritual is their equality *as a group*. In the course of an evening's agonic exchange, male egos are both asserted and assuaged: all ultimately emerge as winners, at which point the crew members part company, their equality affirmed, and return severally to their homes where their womenfolk—mothers, wives, or companions—await them. The male-centered world of reputation is thus ultimately resolved, and dissolved until its reformation the following day, in the female-centered world of respectability. The two worldviews both oppose and complement each other, and as they grow older many men, if not most, are absorbed into the respectability system that ultimately guarantees, in Wilson's view, the neocolonial order of society. Somewhat romantically, Wilson promotes the reputation system as "being of the true nature of Caribbean society" as opposed to the allegedly imported respectability system, and he believes it has "the evolutionary potential to transform itself into a dominant system." The attainment of "true democracy" in a thoroughly decolonized Caribbean is seen to be conditional upon the triumph of reputation and its values—self-affirmation, equality—over the contrasting values—self-restraint, hierarchy—of the respectability system. If women are indeed, as Wilson claims, a "conservative influence" and "one of the strongest forces for respectability" in West Indian societies, such a triumph would appear to equate with a triumph

---

which, according to Michael Lieber (1981:61), reflects "the readiness and anticipation with which people seek to transform the passing world into a world of encounters and events."

of "male" over "female" value systems (230–34). In the course of his polemic
in favor of reputation and its values, Wilson notably fails to confront its
implications for the sexual politics of the Caribbean.

As these comments suggest, Wilson's opposition of reputation and respectability, and his evident preference for the former, have attracted some
criticism: not only do some claim that West Indian women possess a reputation system of their own (see Besson 1993), but it may well be, as Daniel
Miller (1994:319) has recently suggested, that "it is the cult of domesticity
and respectability rather than of spontaneity and display which is most effective at countering colonial dependency" and creating a true sense of community. Nonetheless, the reputation/respectability opposition, either derived
from Wilson or independently arrived at, lies behind much of the most fruit-
ful analytic work of Caribbean cultures, particularly that concerning patterns
of male sociability as studied by Manning (1973) in Bermuda, Lieber (1981)
and Eriksen (1990) in Trinidad, and Brana-Shute (1976, 1989) in Surinam. All
these works posit a series of binary oppositions between the female-dominated world of the home and the male-dominated world of the street and the
rum shop that coincides point for point with Wilson's opposition of respectability and reputation. Each writer correspondingly sees "liming" as the West
Indian male cultural activity par excellence: the practice, commented on by
observers from the mid-nineteenth century onward,[3] of West Indian men,
particularly but not exclusively those of lower-class, African origin, of con-
gregating in public places—barbershops, rum shops, betting shops, or street
corners—for the sheer self-justifying pleasure, at once simple and complex,
of being together, talking together, drinking together, and in a specific
(cards, dominoes) or unspecific (joking, storytelling, boasting, verbal jousting)
sense *playing* together. In one way or another the rum shop and its equivalents are seen as a retreat from, and reversal of, the values of both the
workplace (if the men concerned are employed) and the home, where, it is
argued, the self-identity of the lower-class black male in particular is subject
to continual disparagement in the face of a female-centered value system that
stresses work, economy, self-restraint, discipline, and order (see Lieber
1981:55; Brana-Shute 1989:63–67). Men flee the home environment, in
which they feel marginal and undervalued, in favor of the street and its
adjuncts, where in the company of men they can affirm and enhance their

---

3. See the descriptions by Charles Kingsley, 1869, and L. M. Fraser, 1874, quoted in Trotman
1986:205–6, and the article in the *Port-of-Spain Gazette*, of 22 July 1871, also quoted by Trotman: "It is
a common thing to see robust men and tall youths playing marbles in the public thoroughfares of
Port-of-Spain in the middle of the day, and it is a reflection upon us as a community that such wilful
idleness should exist when there is ample employment of every kind to be found and when, to supply
our labour market; we have to send thousands of miles for coolies."

sense of their own value and identity. This they do through the processes of self-projection and self-dramatization outlined above in which language— power with and over words—becomes the principal instrument by which the individual affirms himself in the presence of, and over and against, others. "No conversation around here gets boring until you stop to listen to it," a Bermudan barman says memorably to Manning, underlining, as the latter puts it, that rum shop talk "is not meant to be listened to for its content but appreciated for its style, humor, and rhythm." In this perspective, boasting and insult swapping (which Manning, following African American rather than West Indian usage, variously calls "rapping," "sounding," "signifying," "scream- ing," "rhyming," "playing the dozens," or "joning") may be regarded as "spec- tator games and public performances rather than private encounters," as so many "occasions for the conventional participants to display their personality and style for the benefit of an audience as well as their competitors"—and, one might add, for the benefit of the performer himself, who becomes in some measure a spectator of his own "act" (Manning 1973:62–64). Once again the appearance of anger and aggression is ultimately deceptive: the whole object of "rapping" is precisely to *avoid* violence by sublimating it into language, to diffuse and defuse it by acting it out "playfully," which in the West Indian and, more broadly, Afro-American context does not mean any less seriously.[4] As we shall see, the "play element" in West Indian culture, whether it be the play of carnival, cricket, or rum shop braggadocio, is always *deep play*, in the manner of the Balinese cockfight so masterfully an- alyzed by Clifford Geertz (1973).

What, therefore, begins as a straightforward opposition between the "rep- utation ethic" of the rum shop and the "respectability ethic" of the home (and, where relevant, the workplace) becomes, in the extended analyses of Manning and others, a microcosm of the dual value system said to pervade the whole of West Indian culture and best summarized as a series of binary opposites as in the schema below.[5]

---

4. Discussing the phenomenon of "rapping" (or "woofing") in African American culture, Thomas Kochman (1981:58) quotes one "rapper" as saying to another: "You don't need to worry; I'm still talking. When I *stop* talking, then you might need to worry." This, says Kochman, underlines that "for blacks the boundary between words and actions is clearly marked" (46) and that the whole art of rapping is poised on "the almost indistinguishable line between being serious and mock serious: showing *and* feeling anger and fearlessness versus simply showing them" (50). It is because they fail to appreciate the subtleties of this dividing line that, according to Kochman (44), "whites *invaria- bly* interpret black anger and verbal aggressiveness as more provocative and threatening than do blacks."

5. My schema is based on a conflation of the complementary schemata provided by Abrahams 1983:151–55 and Eriksen 1990:39, with additional pairs of opposites derived from Brana-Shute 1989 and Miller 1994, plus one or two of my own.

| Home | Street |
|------|--------|
| Respectability | Reputation |
| Inside, private, yard | Outside, public, rum shop |
| Female | Male |
| Family | Friendship networks (crews) |
| Hierarchy | Equality[6] |
| Order, discipline | Chaos, bacchanal[7] |
| Work, job | Play, liming |
| Obedience | Freedom, autonomy[8] |
| Decorum | Rudeness |
| Stability, passivity | Mobility, activity |
| Honesty, truth | Trickery (Anancy) |
| Quiet, harmony | Noise, vexation, "boderation" |
| Economy | Spending |
| Responsibility | Irresponsibility |
| Self-restraint | Self-dissipation, display |
| Delayed returns | Immediate returns |
| Future-oriented | Present-oriented |
| Continuous, progressive | Episodic[9] |
| Heterotelic[10] | Autotelic |
| Standard English | Creole |
| Writing | Speech |
| Inner-directed | Outer-directed |
| Centripetal[11] | Centrifugal |
| Transcendent[12] | Transient |
| Apollonian[13] | Dionysiac |
| Christmas | Carnival |

6. See Brana-Shute 1989:48: "Although there are obvious status distinctions between the clientele, the *winkel* [rum shop] is a place where the myth of social equality is fostered."

7. See Miller 1994:49 on "bacchanal" as "almost synonymous with the concept of 'confusion'—a state which arises from gossip and mixing and is opposed to a form of respectability which focuses on privacy and aloofness."

8. See Brana-Shute 1989:52: "Life on the streets is autonomy and provides one with the sense of being in control that is so important to the men who gather here regularly."

9. See Lieber 1981:61 on "the episodic fashion in which Trinidadian men organize time and its punctuations": "Time on the streets is highly episodic, and liming reflects this episodic quality" (63).

10. See Eriksen 1990:28: "Liming is acknowledged as an *autotelic* activity . . .—it allegedly contains its own ends, and it is constantly contrasted with the *heterotelic* activities entailed by domestic and professional life."

11. See Brana-Shute 1989:21 for the centrifugal/male: centripetal/female opposition, which is applied by Miller 1994:125 to carnival and Christmas, respectively.

12. On the opposition between transcendent/centripetal/female/Christmas and transient/centrifugal/male/carnival, see Miller 1994:135.

13. "During the months leading up to carnival [Trinidadians] save in impeccable 'Apollonian' or respectable manner, only to spend everything at once in an intense 'Dyonisic' orgy, with no overt worry about paying the rent of next month" (Eriksen 1990:36).

Like all such sets of binary opposites, the schema above raises as many problems as it solves, and in the pages that follow its various terms will be subject to qualification and modification, amounting in some instances to partial deconstruction, while continuing in amended form to provide the basic framework for an analysis of the carnival "complex." One question needs to be addressed forthwith, however, and that concerns the gendered nature of the reputation/respectability opposition as elaborated by what we might call the "Crab Antics" school of Caribbean anthropology. Is it true that in the Caribbean male is to female as outside is to inside and reputation to respectability, and so on? Wilson, Manning, Brana-Shute, Eriksen, Lieber, and Miller are all white males of North American or European origin. The section that follows qualifies and complicates the picture by introducing the views of female writers, both West Indian and other, on the dialectic of inside and outside that almost all recent anthropological writing holds to be central to an understanding of Afro-Caribbean countries.[14]

## Male and Female Culture Spheres in the Caribbean

On the surface of things, the three works by female anthropologists considered in this section—Diane J. Austin's *Urban Life in Kingston, Jamaica* (1984), Lisa Douglass's *The Power of Sentiment* (1992), and Elisa Janine Sobo's *One Blood* (1993)—amply confirm the general thesis of the "Crab Antics" school that in the Caribbean men and women inhabit distinct but complementary cultural spheres, each with a value system of its own; that, in Brana-Shute's words (1976:60), "as though spinning on two separate axes distinguished by different activities, the world of men and the world of women mesh and articulate." According to another female anthropologist, Henrietta De Veer (quoted in Douglass 1992:184–85), "inside" and "outside" are among the "primary organizing principles" of the Jamaican and, by extension, the West Indian social order, in which "men are looking 'inside' from 'outside' and women are looking 'outside' from the perspective of 'in the yard'"—a situation similar to that evoked in *Crab Antics* and kindred works, but already more complex. Thus in the Jamaican village studied by Sobo "men and women rarely socialize as couples or even walk together," the demarcation of "inside" and "outside" being observed so rigorously that "while it is acceptable for men to cluster at rum shops to chat, women (who are expected to keep to their yards) can only exchange news and advice when a 'mission' such as taking washing to the river brings them out. Even so, they usually walk with related females, such as

14. A notable exception appears to be the work of male West Indian sociologists and anthropologists who, John O. Stewart (1989) apart, give the respectability/reputation question no more than passing attention. On the other hand, there is no more insightful treatment of the whole theme than Earl Lovelace's novel *The Dragon Can't Dance* (1985), discussed at the end of this chapter.

daughters or the girlfriends or wives of their brothers" (Sobo 1993:12). Similarly, Douglass argues that throughout Jamaica, but especially in Kingston, "a strong division exists between the 'inside' life of cars, offices, private homes, and shops and life 'outside' on the street," but though women are in principle meant to keep to the "inside" and leave the "outside" to men, in practice the exigencies of daily life mean that "some women of the lower class share street life with men." Whereas "uptown" women—or rather "ladies"—of the middle and upper classes shun the world of the street, "the lower-class woman lives a more public life. These women are seen all over the country at any hour of the day or night, in markets and plazas, tending to their business on foot, usually unaccompanied. Like men, these women feel free to roam. They roam because their lives and their work require knowledge of the streets and freedom of mobility" (Douglass 1992: 75–76). Nonetheless, a woman on the street is still, according to Douglass, subject to stigmatization, and it is in part because she has trespassed on male cultural space that she is exposed to routine sexual harassment by the men. Even the street woman par excellence—who in the West Indies is not the prostitute but the higgler (market woman)—is regarded with ambivalence by the wider society: admired for her "manlike" autonomy and assertiveness, she is also derided on account of her often invasive physical presence, her loud dress, and her even louder demeanor and language, which make her "a comical character, a caricature of a woman, whose reputed strength of character contrasts to her lack of power," a public woman, that is to say a man-woman, who serves as the absolute antithesis of what it means to be a "lady" (Douglass 1992:246–49). If the street-oriented woman disrupts the construction of social space, so, a fortiori, does the man who, for whatever reason, clings too closely to the "female" world of the yard (and above all to his mother) and does not assert himself in the "normal" hypermasculine manner on the street. Such a woman-man, even if not actively a "batty man" (homosexual), simply has no place in the West Indian social world: the "auntie-man" is by definition the "anti-man," the negation of everything it is to be a man, just as the higgler is the negation of everything it is to be a "lady." The stereotyping of homosexual and higgler has the function, among other things, of defending the "ideal" division of space into male/outside and female/inside that, as we have seen, is commonly infringed in practice.[15]

Douglass's analysis of the lives of upper-class Jamaican women shows that the dialectic of "inside" and "outside" in West Indian cultures is a question not just of gender but also of class. For all classes, she argues, "inside" connotes relative power, wealth, and prestige, and "respectable" women *of all classes* are

15. The stigma attached to certain forms of outdoor labor is present even in rural Jamaica, where, according to Erna Brodber (1986:38), it is "well nigh sacrilege for a woman who has a husband to take wage employment or to dig yam holes."

expected, and themselves expect, to direct their lives "inward" in such a way that any move "outward"—if, for example, a married woman is obliged by economic necessity to work—will be perceived and experienced as a serious loss of prestige. Men, on the other hand, are always free to direct their lives outward, even when they have acquired positions of power and prestige in society, which explains why, in Douglass's view (1992:253), Jamaican men's "public behavior is remarkably consistent across classes." Thus, though class is important in determining gender relations and the corresponding sexual division of space, "what is considered appropriate female behavior is not simply about class. Nor can class alone explain why men live in a way more oriented to the 'street' than women" (Douglass 1992:76). Douglass's analysis is confirmed, and carried a stage further, by Diane J. Austin's study of two contrasting neighborhoods in Kingston: the lower-class district of Selton Town and the adjacent middle-class district of Vermont. Life in Selton Town, according to Austin (1984:55), is "in the last analysis a public affair." People live cheek by jowl with each other in homes that are structurally open to their neighbors, and even though a distinction still obtains between "yard" and "street," the supposedly "private" world of the former is in fact very public. Thus "most domestic affairs are performed in the presence of others" (44), cooking and washing are commonly done outside in the yard, most homes have outdoor toilets, and the whole area is characterized by "a rich public street life where people gain immediate companionship in the course of daily life" (41). To move from lower-class Selton Town to middle-class Vermont is to "move from an externalized to an inside life of domestic facilities within the house, of private yards and private transport, of clerical employment and commercial transactions in glass fronted shops and offices" (59). In the most basic sense, "Selton Town harbours an outside life, Vermont an inside life." Not only is "the public socializing of Selton Town street life . . . absent in Vermont" (62), but only a minority of men drink at local bars, most preferring to drink with friends on the porch or veranda of their homes, a kind of compromise between "inside" and "outside" that enables them to reconcile their predominantly lower-class origins with their middle-class aspirations;[16] women sometimes sit and drink with the men but, significantly, "more often retire to another part of the house" (74). Expanding her analysis, Austin sees the whole of Jamaican (and by implication West Indian) history as a dialectic between "inside" and "outside" in which "outside" becomes "a spatial metaphor for social relations rather than a mere description" (156). Embodied first in the opposi-

---

16. The veranda, that "outside room of the uptown house," plays a similar role in the lives of the upper-class Jamaicans studied by Douglass: "Veranda talk is the middle- and upper-class equivalent of the street corner political debate or even of the discussion of travelers aboard a country bus" (1992:80). Cars likewise function as a middle-class blend of "inside" and "outside," as emblems at once of both respectability and reputation (see Manning 1974).

tion of Great House and Negro Village (152), the distinction between "inside" and "outside" has always, she argues, been about status and power. The lower-class West Indian is "born outside, lives outside and works outside only to propagate outside children and begin the chain again" (150),[17] whereas "for the middle class an inside kinship status and an inside occupation were historically the progressive stages by which one came to lead an encultured, privatized, inside life" (157). Furthermore, "those born outside are rendered incapable of anything but an outside life" (155), unless, that is, they are successful at another classic "inside" institution—school—in which case they have at least a chance of coming in from the heat of the street or the canefield to the inside world of "manners," education, relative wealth, and above all respectability.

Because class, wealth, and power as well as gender are involved in the demarcation of "inside" and "outside," it is possible and necessary to partially deconstruct the straightforward opposition of male/reputation:female/respectability on which the "Crab Antics" school of anthropology founds its analysis of West Indian cultures. In the first instance, Jean Besson has argued persuasively that West Indian women as well as men "compete for status, both among themselves and with men" (1993:19), and that it is common for lower-class women of all kinds—higglers (25), church "leadresses" (24), and mothers of many children (28–29)—to acquire and enhance their reputations with verbal skills in competition with others, especially in such everyday exchanges as "tracing" (public disputes) and "kas-kas" (cursing), these skills being just as prized among women as among men (see Abrahams 1983:3; Sobo 1993:104–5). Furthermore, as we have seen, in both Jamaica and Trinidad women, especially young women, have begun since the early 1980s to display in public some of the aggressive, extroverted behavior patterns traditionally associated with male street culture. There has been, as already indicated, a notable increase in female "slackness" in both countries, expressed above all in the highly erotic and exhibitionist style of dancing known as "waining" or "wining"[18] (see Miller 1991:324–27; Cooper 1993:156–57), and there is clear evidence, discussed below, that carnival in Trinidad is becoming more and more a female-dominated occasion; the increasingly public profile of women, and their increasingly self-assertive demeanor, have almost certainly contributed to the widely attested rise in male hostility toward women as expressed, for example, in the misogynistic lyrics of ragga and calypso as well as in the increase in

17. Cf. the widespread use of terms such as "outside woman" and "outside children."

18. The term "wine" (< wind) is attested as early as 1790 in a song sung by a Jamaican slave as she danced before her master (J. B. Moreton, cited in Cassidy 1961:272):

> Hipsaw! my deaa! You no shake like a-me!
> You no wind like a-me!
> Hipsaw! my deaa! You no do like a-me!
> You no jig like a-me! you no twist like a-me!

routine harassment of women in public.[19] The evident existence of female forms of "reputation" is matched by the equally undeniable male pursuit of respectability. According to Sobo (1993:176–78), Jamaican men are often just as concerned with respectability as with reputation, especially as they grow older or rise in society, at which point "the 'respectable' high-status man need not prove his value through 'reputation' because he has already established his unequivocal maleness by achieving social position. . . . He does need to maintain his 'reputation' to some degree and can invoke it when he needs to demonstrate his solidarity with other villagers. Nonetheless, his position 'on top' gets most emphasis because 'respect' buys more than 'reputation.'" In practice the distinction between respect and reputation becomes blurred in the case of the successful man, and only the poor man remains exclusively concerned with his "reputation" as a drinker, womanizer, or player of games or music, for the very good reason that he has no chance of ever gaining "respect." "Reputation," in other words, is no more than a pis aller for true status. In the last analysis respectability—for which marriage remains the prime requirement and expression[20]—is the supreme value for men and women alike, whatever their class, as even Wilson is ultimately forced to concede.[21]

Although, on the basis of the foregoing considerations, the straightforward equation of male = reputation = outside and female = respectability = inside needs to be qualified, there is no suggestion in the works we have studied that it should be abandoned entirely; accordingly, it will continue to serve as the principal hermeneutic thread through the discussions that follow. But the relation between "reputation" and "respectability" is considerably more complex than the original "Crab Antics" thesis and its subsequent developments imply, and some further qualifications can usefully be made at this point. In the first place, whereas Wilson argues that the reputation system is indigenous to the Caribbean, in contrast to the allegedly externally derived respectability system, it could be, as Douglass (1992:254) suggests, that *both* systems are a product of the colonial past: "Neither is more 'authentic' or 'indigenous' than the other, nor does one offer better prospects for the future." In contrast, Karen Fog Olwig, in her study of Nevis, argues that both the culture of reputation *and* the culture of respectability are ultimately of English origin—the first derived from traditions introduced into the island by the earliest farmer-

19. One Trinidadian woman has testified that though she felt secure walking alone at night in the early 1970s, "by the mid-eighties this was no longer possible": "My personal experience is that I have undergone the most obscene and degrading harassment on the streets of Trinidad than in any of the countries in which I have travelled" (Mohammed 1991:40). See also Miller 1994:178.

20. As Raymond T. Smith (1973:141) so tellingly puts it: "Marriage [in the Caribbean] is an act in the status system and not in the kinship system."

21. "The values and standards that make up respectability are subscribed to, *in varying degrees*, by everyone, so that there is a continuity; they are emphasized according to particular social circumstances and life-cycle situations" (Wilson 1973:99; his italics).

colonizers of the seventeenth century, the second imparted by nineteenth-century Methodist missionaries—but that "both sets of institutions have been appropriated by the Afro-Caribbean population as a means to negate their position of social marginality in the English colonial society and have, in the process, become infused with Afro-Caribbean culture" (Olwig 1993:133; see also 57–58). In other words, both the culture of reputation and the culture of respectability have been creolized in the Caribbean, and neither is exactly the same as it was in the parent colonial society:[22] both are mimetic cultures, and both in their contrasting ways are oppositional cultures to the extent that they enabled the colonized group to define itself over and against the colonial order. Daniel Miller goes even further in suggesting that it has been the "female-centered" culture of respectability, with its stress on family continuity and stability, work and education, that has been the most effective vehicle of opposition[23] to colonialism in the Caribbean and that, especially in the post-emancipation period, "the ideal of a nuclear family and respectability" may have been "less a continuation of colonial dominance, than the primary form by which groups were able to overturn the oppressive constraints of slavery" (1994:263). In this perspective both reputation and respectability become a succession of imitations and negations of the colonial order where it becomes difficult to see which, if any, is the primary term and which is in opposition to which. Thus the male-centered culture of reputation subverts the *official values* of colonial society but also mimics the *actual behavior* of white men in slave and colonial society who derived prestige from drinking, wenching, and gambling. The female-centered culture of respectability co-opts the official values of colonial society to turn them both against that society as it is and against the male-centered culture of reputation, thus endowing female culture with a character of "double oppositionality."[24] That is, it is opposed to a male culture that is itself opposed to the dominant culture—which, as a negation of the nega-

22. Thus "the adoption of the Methodist institution of respectability on the part of the slaves did not necessarily imply an adoption of the English values of respectability which the Methodists identified with them" (Olwig 1993:85).

23. Miller (1994:262) uses the term "resistance" (in quotation marks), but plainly what is involved here is a classic instance of what de Certeau calls opposition.

24. I owe the idea of the "double oppositionality" of female culture in the Caribbean to Roland Littlewood, who argues (1993:295) that West Indian women are "respectable, not as a fixed characteristic but relative to men" and that, in general, "Black women have been 'close' to White men in a 'double opposition' . . . , through sexual relations between masters and household slaves, and through their opportunity to enter domestic work, teaching and nursing." I do not entirely accept this explanation, nor do I think that Littlewood grasps that the culture of respectability is in fact in opposition to the colonial culture it so resembles, but the general thrust of his argument seems to me to be valid. His "polythetic chain of paired oppositions" (229)—White/Black = Black Middle Class/Black Lower Class = Respectability/Reputation = Black Women/Black Men = English/Creole = life/carnival = town/bush = God/devil = inside/outside = right/left = cold/hot = social/natural, etc.—could usefully be added to the table of binary opposites above.

tion, makes it *appear* identical, or at least close, to the colonial culture it is in fact challenging on its own terms. Having thus complicated but not abandoned the "Crab Antics" school's dualism of respectability and reputation, let us move a step closer to the phenomenon of carnival itself.

## The "Play Element" in West Indian Cultures

A crucial contribution to the understanding of Caribbean cultures has been made by Roger D. Abrahams, who, in a succession of studies collected in *The Man-of-Words in the West Indies* (1983), has raised the whole debate concerning respectability and reputation in the West Indies to a new plane, providing a conceptual framework that makes it possible to bring together a whole range of cultural activities from carnival and cricket to riddling games and spelling bees in a single meaningful pattern. Building on the "Crab Antics" school's basic dichotomy of inside and outside and accepting (with some qualifications) the parallel opposition of female-respectability and male-reputation cultures, Abrahams has explored the competitive "play element" in West Indian cultures, as manifested, for example, in tea meetings and Christmas mummings or "sports" in Nevis, St. Vincent, and Tobago, in ritual speechmaking and street arguments, and in the trading of boasts and insults in rum shops, as well as in more formalized occasions of stylized display and combat, among which Trinidadian carnival is preeminent. Each of these occasions is distinguished, according to Abrahams, by a "pattern of competitive interaction" (1983:xvii): two or more individuals, groups, or factions confront each other in public, either on the street, in a rum shop, or on more formal occasions in a public hall hired for the purpose, and engage in a form of ritualized conflict in which language ceases to be a communicative medium and becomes an instrument of power, domination, and display. Whether it is in the formalized situation of the tea meeting or in the extemporized context of the street argument, the antagonists project their selves into words, deploying ever greater verbal inventiveness and wit in an effort to face down their opponents and thereby enhance their reputation among their fellows. It is, of course, essential that these logomachic rituals take place in the presence of an audience. Abrahams introduces a distinction between informal and formal speech situations and a corresponding distinction between two kinds of "men-of-words": the broad talker and the good (or sweet) talker (21). In informal situations—typically when "giving rag," "making mock," or "giving fatigue" on the street or in the rum shop (57)—the man-of-words "talks broad" or "bad," that is, in Creole, in the hope of "capping" his opponent's "rap." Insults fly to and fro in a crescendo of noise and excitement, but words now exist in and for themselves rather than for any meaning or message they may communicate, the "non-complementarity of repetition" being in Karl Reisman's words the essential feature of "cussing" or "kas-kas" (< Twi *kasa-kasa* = to throw words) in the Caribbean. "Each person takes a point or position and repeats it endlessly, either one after the other, or both at once, or several at once depending on the number of people participating. Points of view are rarely developed, merely reasserted. . . . Noise and counter-noise, assertion and counter-assertion: everyone is on their own, listening to an inner music" (Reisman 1974:65). "Discussions" of this kind can readily last an hour or more until one voice gradually prevails and the other (or others) recede(s). The reputation of the winner is enhanced, but once aggression has been released in ludic form and thereby transmuted, the two or more opponents make peace and affirm their friendship and equality as members of the "crew" in such a way that, in Abrahams's words (1983:18), "conflict becomes a positive mode of socialization" among West Indian men.

Formal speech situations are an elaboration of this basic agonic structure. At tea meetings[25] and other formal speechmaking occasions such as weddings, church services, and wakes, the aim is to talk "good" or "sweet" rather than "bad" or "broken," in other words, in standard English or, more precisely, in some stylized hyperbolic version (or parody) of it. Deploying an ornate, plethoric English replete with elaborate syntax, multiple biblical, historical, or literary references, recondite vocabulary, and even Latin quotations, which both mimics and mocks the language of the masters, the man-of-words performs either solo or, more commonly, alongside and in competition with one or more other verbal virtuosos, the merits of their respective performances being judged, at tea meetings and similar occasions, by a "panel" of elected officials bearing mock royal or mock military titles such as King George, Hero, Conqueror, Duke of York, Prince of Wales, and many others; the importance of this "fascination with exotic hierarchies" (Abrahams 1983:5), and of the alternative names, titles, and identities that go with it, will become apparent in due course. As in the verbal joustings of the rum shop, what is important here is not *matter* but *manner*, not what is signified but the signifiers themselves and the speaker's mastery over them. The tea meeting and its analogues are the domain of performative, not constative, utterance: words do not so much communicate as compete. Or rather, what they communicate is not meaning but the power and personality of the speaker, who, by projecting his ego into language, enhances—or if he falters, diminishes—his standing in the eyes of the public. "A man-of-words is worth nothing unless he can, on the one hand, stitch together a startling piece of oratorical rhetoric and, on the other, capture the attention, the allegiance, and the admiration of the audience

---

25. Tea meetings began as church-sponsored occasions in the nineteenth century when believers met to sing hymns, eat cakes, and drink tea or lemonade, from which "inauspicious beginning rose an elaborate variety concert with competitive items promoted by community clubs and individual sponsors" (Hill 1992:257).

through his fluency, his strength of voice, and his social maneuverability and psychological resilience" (Abrahams 1983:xxx).

As the man-of-words performs, the audience interjects shouts of encouragement or deprecation, generating an intense antiphonal to-and-fro between speaker and public that itself becomes a performer in what Abrahams (38) calls "a community celebration of speech of all sorts, a revelry of talk in which the entire range of speaking acts and events are put on view and enjoyed." As in the rum shop dispute, the noise level mounts precipitously until a kind of collective effervescence grips the whole gathering. The structures and hierarchies of the everyday world are at least partially subverted and replaced, for the duration of the "rite," by the fictional hierarchies of the ludic communitas, as individuals merge with each other and with the group as a whole in a liminal condition from which they and their society will emerge reinvigorated and renewed (Abrahams 1983:74–76, 98–99 on liminality and communitas; see also Turner 1977:94–130). Once more, ritualized conflict becomes a means of binding the community together.

Abrahams links the man-of-words phenomenon to the persistence in the Caribbean of "an essentially oral, African attitude towards eloquence" (33) and quotes a number of descriptions from the slavery and postemancipation epochs that besides indicating the deep-rootedness of such linguistic rituals in West Indian culture, also suggests that much more was involved than mere mimicry or mockery of Massa's language.[26] It was, Abrahams suggests (26), essentially a question of emulating his speech in order to appropriate the power it was believed to contain. But slaves also engaged in other forms of competitive play, as Richard Ligon's account of slavery in Barbados in the late 1640s graphically demonstrates. In the first instance, there were regular Sunday afternoon wrestling bouts at which the male combatants "stand like two Cocks, with heads as low as their hips; and thrusting their heads one against another, hoping to catch one another by the leg, which they sometimes do"; significantly, "when the men begin to wrestle, the women leave off their dancing, and come to be spectators of the sport" (Ligon 1673:50).[27] Still more to the point, Ligon is greatly impressed (52) by two *"Portugal Negroes"* who, in the presence of their master and presumably at his instigation, "play at Rapier and Dagger very skilfully, with their Stockados, their Imbrocados, and their

26. Thus Hesketh Bell (*Obeah: Witchcraft in the West Indies*, 1889): "Quashie has an intense love for long words of which he does not know the meaning, and delights in using them on any occasion. . . . The more polysyllabic and highsounding senseless phrases he can remember, the more he and the company will be pleased. Passages from any book containing very long words, though having no earthly reference to the occasion, will be learnt by heart and retailed to the admiring guests [at a wedding reception]. Verses from the Bible are frequently pressed into service, and seem to afford much satisfaction" (Abrahams 1983:32).

27. According to Leslie (1740:310), *"Sunday* afternoon the Generality of them [slaves in Jamaica] dance or wrestle, Men and Women promiscuously together."

Passes." The whole passage merits citation, so closely does the combatants' demeanor prefigure that of the stickfighters of a later era:

> Upon their first appearance upon the Stage, they march towards one another, with a slow majestick pace, and a bold commanding look, as if they meant both to conquer; and coming near together, they shake hands, and embrace one another, with a chearful look. But their retreat is much quicker than their advance, and, being at first distance, change their countenance, and put themselves into their posture; and so after a pass or two, retire, and then to't again: And when they have done their play, they embrace, shake hands, and putting on their smoother countenances, give their respects to their Master, and so go off.

This tradition of mock (and perhaps not so mock) swordfighting is also present in the "plays" associated with Christmas in Jamaica, as in the "version" of *Richard III* witnessed on the Dalvey estate by Alexander Barclay in 1823 in which "the Joncanoe-men, disrobed of part of their paraphernalia, were the two heroes, and fought not for a kingdom, but a queen, whom the victor carried off in triumph" (Barclay 1826:13). The Set Girl parades discussed in chapter 2 were also clearly occasions of bravado and competitive display in which societies of women both slave and free sought to face down their rivals by the sumptuousness of their costumes and the vigor of their singing. Similarly, much slave music had a marked agonic character with, as we have seen, drummers from different African "nations" vying with each other and with creole instrumentalists and singers. Finally, it is of the utmost significance that slaves gave the name "plays" to the weekend gatherings at which they danced, drank, and commemorated their dead and which the planters did their level best to suppress, rightly seeing them as potential foci of resistance. How significant, in the circumstances, that Thomas Thistlewood (Hall 1989:186) should have punished his slaves because one Sunday they "transgressed, by beating the Coombie loud, singing high, &c." How better to convey that, under slavery, "play" of whatever kind had a potentially transgressive character, implicitly and often explicitly opposed as it was to the whole objectifying force of plantation labor? Not for nothing did the slaves call any day away from canefield or mill a "play-day" (Lewis 1834:89).

It is with this subversive ludic tradition in mind that Abrahams (1983:51) calls play "the activity by which Afro-American individuality is asserted and maintained." Play in the broad West Indian sense of the word, he argues, is opposed less to the world of work than to that of respectability: it implies noise, gregariousness, "boderation," "slackness" (rudeness), boasting, bravado, trickery, "foolishness," and the acquisition, primarily but not exclusively by men, of reputation through acting out in public the negative roles and behaviors associated with the underside of "manners," education, and culture. Perhaps, like Wilson, Abrahams romanticizes the subversive purport of the culture of play and reputation, failing to grasp the ease with which, even in the supreme instance of carnival, the ludic is absorbed and neutralized by the established order. But the ultimate recuperability of play in no way diminishes the considerable richness of the competitive element in West Indian cultures,[28] ranging from word games (riddles, Anancy stories, spelling bees), numbers games (*peaka-peow* and *drop-pan* in Jamaica, *whe-whe* in Trinidad), rum shop games (cards ["whappie" and "all fours"], dice ["sebby-lebby"], and above all dominoes), cockfighting, kite flying,[29] mock auctions,[30] beauty contests (not forgetting the "Mr Out of Sight" competitions in Bermuda; see Manning 1973:69), and all the other contests associated with carnival (see below) to established international sports: boxing, soccer, basketball, netball, and athletics. But there are two forms of contest that historically have dominated the West Indian scene: one—stickfighting—of probable African origin and now almost extinct, the other—cricket—taken over from the colonial masters and turned with a vengeance against them, as Caliban turns the language he learns against Prospero. To these archetypal forms of stylized aggression the following section is devoted.

## From Mungo the Dentist to Brian Lara: Stickfighting and Cricket in the Caribbean

Introduced into Trinidad in the late eighteenth century by slaves from the formerly French-owned (and French Creole–speaking) colonies of Grenada,

28. This section was written before the publication of *The Social Roles of Sport in Caribbean Societies*, ed. Michael A. Malee (New York: Gordon and Breach, 1995). In addition to the works on cricket cited below, Austin 1984 usefully discusses number games (52), dominoes (121–22), and soccer (123–27) in Jamaica; basketball in Trinidad and Tobago is given extended treatment in Mandle and Mandle 1988, and Olwig 1987 is virtually the only work to give attention to a female-dominated sport (netball). Cockfighting in the Caribbean still awaits its Geertz. For material on stickfighting and cricket, see below.

29. According to Bickerton (1962:16), kite flying in Trinidad is "a complex and highly aggressive sport in which contestants, many of whom were grown men, aimed, with the aid of such exotic accessories as slacking mange and zwill, at cutting loose and capturing the kites of their opponents. Occasionally, these contests degenerated into gang fights, and it was for this reason that the police tried to prevent kite-flying within the city limits." "Mange" and "zwill" are the names given to slivers of glass attached to a kite's string and tail and designed to cut opponents' kite strings.

30. On mock auctions in Jamaica, see De Camp 1968:146–47: "Competition runs high during the bidding. Jokes and good-natured insults are shouted from the floor. Bidders groan and affect exaggerated grimaces of agony when their bids are topped. Impromptu mock-heroic orations are delivered to exhort bidders to support one side or the other."

"A Cudgelling Match between English and French Negroes in Dominica," by A. Brunais (ca. 1770). Courtesy of the Musée du Nouveau Monde, La Rochelle.

St. Vincent, and Dominica, stickfighting[31]—otherwise known as *kalinda* or *calenda*—was the pivotal ritual in Trinidad carnival from emancipation until it was banned after the carnival riots of 1884 (see below), whereafter it went "underground," only to surface on exceptional occasions and in semiclandestine conditions. Not officially "unbanned" until 1951, it has undergone a limited revival in independent Trinidad, where it now has its due place in the annual government-sponsored "Better Village" competition (see Steward 1989: 143–44 for a vivid account of a recent stickfighting confrontation between "Springer" and "Mussolini"). During the heyday of stickfighting (1838–84), every lower-class district (barrack yard) of Port of Spain as well as other towns and villages had its champion *batonnier* or "kalinda king," who acted as the bearer of its honor and reputation in confrontation with other barrack yards, principally at carnival, but also at Easter and on 1 August.[32] The kalinda stick

31. The following account is based primarily on the work of the Tobagonian folklorist J. D. Elder (1966b, 1971), supplemented by Pearse (1956a, 1956b, E. Hill 1972, Brereton 1979, Trotman 1986, and Rohlehr 1990. In order not to overburden the text, I have kept references to a minimum.

32. Although the present discussion is limited to stickfighting among Afro-Creoles in Trinidad, it is clear that East Indians had their own version of stickfighting and their own equivalents of the "kalinda king" (see *Port of Spain Gazette*, 14 June 1859: "About a dozen [East Indian] men maintained a

or *baton* was between five and six feet long and about an inch in diameter, made of a local hardwood such as gasparee or poui, and often further hardened by being coated with tallow and left to "ferment" in a manure heap for up to a fortnight; sporting bloodcurdling names such as "Tamer," "Bois Sang," and "Groaning," many batons were believed to possess magical, even satanic, powers. The batonniers or *bois-men* also fought under an assortment of noms de guerre (Cobra, Tiny Satan, Bubul Tiger, Toto, Cutaway Rimbeau, and Mungo the Dentist—the last so named for his skill at "fixing" the teeth of opponents), as did the imposing band of women who, before the banning in 1884, fought both with each other and occasionally with men: Sara Jamaica, Long Body Ada, Annie Coats, and Myrtle the Turtle (who fought an epic battle in 1873 over the grave of the early calypsonian Hannibal the Mulatto), Alice Sugar and Boadicea, who fought "for over an hour for the right to the sexual favours of . . . Cutaway Rimbeau," whom Boadicea subsequently thrashed with his own baton for sleeping with Alice's stickfighting sister, Piti Belle Lily (Trotman 1986:182). Batonniers wore long-sleeved silk shirts and long trousers decorated with colored buttons, set off with a red ribbon or sash at the waist and red scarves at the wrists; metal or embossed leather breastplates were also commonly worn, and many batonniers protected their shaved heads with "a small iron pot over which a head cloth was tied" (Elder 1966b:196)—shades, one might think, of the padded, helmeted batsmen of a century later.

The stickfight itself was preceded by an elaborate ritual of provocation involving the better part of the population of two or more barrack yards, men and women alike, who, singing, chanting, and beating drums and other improvised percussion instruments (tin cans, bamboo tubes, bottles, and spoons), escorted their champion and his—or her—accompanying fighters to some liminal space between the contending yards. There, urged on by the frenzied martial chanting of female singers known as chantwells (< *chanterelle* = singing bird), the batonniers would engage in the now familiar exchange of insults and boasts, both shouted and sung. In the center of the combat zone a hole, known as a *gayelle*, was dug to receive the blood that would surely flow, and enflamed by the cries of the chantwells and still hurling abuse and defiance— "Me alone / Me alone like a man / I will face hell-battalion / Only me alone" (Hill 1972:27)—the stickfighters squared up. The aim of the fight was simple, but it needed to be accomplished with *style*:[33] to deliver one or more blows, variously known as "choppers," "soutans," "uppercuts," or "casabals," to the

---

mock fight with long clubs and with shields in attitudes varying from standing to kneeling on one knee and rolling in the mud of the public road of which there was plenty that day" [quoted in Singh 1988:43]).

33. As Errol Hill writes (1972:27): "The stick fight was both a dance and a combat." For a fascinating comparison with another Afro-American martial art, see J. Lowell Lewis, *Ring of Liberation: Deceptive Discourse in Brazilian Capoeira* (Chicago: University of Chicago Press, 1992).

head or body of the opponent and above all draw blood from his head, at which point he was required to retire, drain his wound into the *gayelle*, and shake hands with the victor, whose prestige—and of course that of his yard—would be heightened accordingly. Other contests would follow, and during the intervals "females would enter the circle and sing a very lewdly erotic song accompanied by obscene dancing" (Elder 1966a:91). Eventually one yard would be declared the overall winner, and the triumphant band, still singing, chanting, and beating their drums, would march back to their base pending the next challenge to their prowess from one or another neighboring yard, whereupon a further *bois bataille* would be fought, and so on at intervals throughout the year.

From the numerous accounts now available of nineteenth-century Trinidad, it is apparent that lower-class black life in Port of Spain, Arima, San Fernando, and elsewhere consisted of a succession of such symbolic—and many not so symbolic—confrontations between the innumerable yards that, locked together like so many pieces of a jigsaw puzzle, made up the extraordinarily variegated context of the colony's main towns. Both Andrew Pearse, in his pioneering study of nineteenth-century carnival (1956a:191–93), and Gordon Rohlehr, in his authoritative history of calypso in preindependence Trinidad (1990:6–7, 16–18), link the evident intensity of the culture of stickfighting to the demographic growth of Port of Spain between 1860 (16,457 inhabitants) and 1881 (19,468) and above all to the fact that by the latter date 40 percent of the city's population had been born outside Trinidad, principally in Barbados and Grenada. Even if one sets aside the recently arrived East Indian, Chinese, and Portuguese communities, it is clear that, especially in Port of Spain, there was intense interblack competition for jobs and living space—between the Trinidadian born and immigrants from the eastern Caribbean, between Creoles and Africans (for example, the Rada community at Belmont), between English-Creole and French-Creole speakers, and between Catholics and Protestants (themselves internally divided), to name only the most obvious distinctions. In the circumstances, each of the city's yards—Mafoombo Yard, Behind the Bridge, Hell Yard, La Cou Harpe, Italian Yard, La Trois Chandelle, Marikeet Yard, and so on—was likely to differ perceptibly in its national, linguistic, or religious composition from its immediate neighbors, creating the need to resolve and release friction short of actual interyard violence, whence the surrogate violence of stickfighting. But even within yards there would be personal and group rivalries that led to regular confrontations both between individuals and between bands whose names have come down to us. There were male associations such as the Bois d'Inde, the Bakers, the Danois, and the Cerf-Volants, some of which had their origin in secret slave confraternities or in the sodalities of the "repatriated" African slaves (Nunley 1988:113), as well as all-woman bands, akin to the Set Girls of

Jamaica, that regularly fought each other under such names as the Dahlias, Mousselines, Magenta, True Blues, Black Balls, and Don't Care Damns (Brereton 1979:167).[34] In short, the lot of the mid-nineteenth-century *jamet* or *jamette* (< *diamètre* = the "other half," i.e., the poor, the criminal, and the semicriminal) involved a constant preoccupation with individual and group reputation, with violence an ever-present threat in their lives. Sometimes that violence was directed outward against the colonial authorities, as in the Canboulay riots of 1881, 1883, and 1884, to be discussed shortly, but normally it was a question of *jamet* against *jamet*, and *jamette* versus *jamette*, to say nothing of the high incidence of intersex violence, to which I shall also return. Even with the outlet of stickfighting, life in the yards of Port of Spain was perpetually dangerous and tense; without it, inter- and intracommunity violence of a truly serious kind would surely have erupted much more frequently than it did.

An article published in the *Trinidad Guardian* in March 1919 described the practice of "breaking," which the batonniers of the previous century had used to quicken their reactions and steady their nerves. "It consisted," said the article, "in having one or two fellows stand 15 or 20 yards off and hurl stones at you in rapid succession, and it was your business—and, of course, to your interest—to 'break' (i.e. parry with stick) these stones successfully. A very proficient 'breaker' would often have three men hurling stones at him, and it was seldom, indeed, that he got hit" (quoted in Hill 1972:26). It was a remarkable description and suggests a continuity between the art of the batonnier and that of the batsman, as though, with stickfighting virtually outlawed and driven underground, the ex-kalinda kings took over the archetypal game of their colonial master[35] and his local white agents (in much the same way that their forebears had taken over carnival and transformed it), injected it with specifically Afro-Creole meanings and values, and gradually turned the game against its inventors. Finally, in the never to be forgotten Test series of 1950, the colonized got the better, Caliban-style, of the colonizer on the colonizer's own turf—Lord's no less—thanks above all to three black batsmen, Worrell, Weekes, and Walcott, born within eighteen months and twenty miles of each other in "Little England" (Barbados), and to "those two little pals of mine /

---

34. On the epic street battle of 1864 between the Mousselines (or Mourelines) and the Don't Care Damns, see Trotman 1986:181: "The women of both groups were armed with stones in their aprons and with knives and razors, and with their frocks tucked up, they battled each other in a fight that spread from George Street to an open field on the banks of the Dry River."

35. The bibliography on West Indian cricket is vast and, in addition to C. L. R. James's *Beyond a Boundary* (1983, first published 1963), the principal works used here are Patterson 1973, Manning 1981, and L. Thompson 1983; other works are cited at the appropriate points. These and other essays are usefully brought together in *Liberation Cricket: West Indies Cricket Culture*, ed. Hilary McD. Beckles and Brian Stoddard (Manchester: Manchester University Press, 1995), which appeared after this section was written. An early version of some of the ideas developed here is to be found in Burton 1985 (reprinted in Beckles and Stoddard 1995: 89–106).

Ramadhin and Valentine."[36] The first was a Trinidadian East Indian, the second a black Jamaican; when selected for the team, both were twenty years old and had played no more than a handful of first-class matches between them. In this perspective, West Indian cricket becomes the ultimate oppositional practice in which Quashie (with a little occasional help from Sammie) takes on Massa at his own game and not only wins but in time establishes himself as the virtually unassailable champion of champions; not surprisingly, it is as a ritual of inversion that, following C. L. R. James's classic *Beyond a Boundary* (1963), West Indian cricket has commonly been read by scholars and non-scholars alike.[37] There has been an understandable emphasis on the ethnic composition of the West Indian Test team, and particularly on the white exclusivism that until 1960 prevented any nonwhite player from captaining the side and gave many scions of the planter and merchant classes Test caps they scarcely deserved in preference to colored and, especially, black players who most definitely did deserve them. The tension between players and spectators of African and East Indian origin is an important subtheme, it being well known that East Indians in Trinidad and particularly Guyana commonly support the opposing team (especially if that team is India) if there are no East Indian players in the West Indies team, as was generally the case throughout the 1980s.[38] Some writers have stressed the role of West Indian cricket in fostering a sense of regional identity, even a pan-Caribbean nationalism transcending local and (to some extent) ethnic particularisms; other writers emphasize the persistence of those very particularisms. One way or another West Indian cricket, especially at Test level, is seen as a "magical mirror" of the society as a whole, heightening and highlighting the tensions between races, classes, and territories even as it brought them together, as carnival does allegedly, in a common enthusiasm.[39] These themes have been well treated by others, and the focus here is accordingly different: on West Indian cricket on

36. The reference is to the refrain of the celebrated calypso "Cricket, lovely cricket" by Lord Beginner.

37. For a comparable interpretation of baseball in the Dominican Republic, see Klein 1991:113. "The subordinate group can appear to be taking on the culture of the dominant group but may in fact be altering it to fit its needs. Hence the struggle is around cultural form and essence: if a subordinate group cannot take on the form while changing the essence, it may be acquiescing in its own domination." For a fascinating instance of power inversion through sport (the defeat of a team of United States marines by a team of Japanese students *at baseball* in 1896), see Roden 1980. On the creolization of basketball in Trinidad, see Mandle and Mandle 1988:4.

38. With the advent, in the 1994 series against England, of the remarkable Chanderpaul, the West Indies side is no longer composed exclusively of "proud African warriors," to use Vivian Richards's notorious description of his side. On the whole question of Indo–West Indian cricket, see Birbalsingh and Shiwcharan 1988 and Yelvington 1990.

39. On perhaps half a dozen occasions, usually in a context of political crisis in the country concerned, these tensions have erupted in crowd riots. For a discussion of these, see Patterson 1973 and Burton 1985.

the local as much as the international level, and on the way it too reproduces the dialectic of inside and outside, respectability and reputation, around which the "carnival complex" revolves.

Cricket in the Caribbean[40] began as the outdoor recreation of those— planters and merchants—whose power lay essentially indoors, whence it spread, via the classically indoor institutions of the Caribbean's would-be Etons and Harrows (Kingston College and Woolmer's in Jamaica, Harrison College, Combermere, and the Lodge in Barbados, Queen's Royal College in Trinidad), to the colored middle-class elite and some upwardly mobile Blacks. From there it "descended" to street and beach, where by the 1890s at the latest it became part of the everyday culture of the young, the black, and the poor.[41] The cricket that evolved at street level was, needless to say, very different in character from that played "indoors-outdoors" at socially and often racially exclusive grounds by members of the white oligarchy and the rising colored meritocracy. Two forms of street cricket stand out: "Tip and Run Firms" at which "firms" of boys would band together to monopolize the usually home-made bat and ball at the expense of their rivals, and "marble cricket," a scaled-down version of the game in which participants played on their knees with a miniature bat and marbles (Stoddart 1987:324).[42] Both games were clearly of a piece with the reputation-oriented ethos of the street, which was carried from them into the first black neighborhood and village clubs that emerged in the 1890s and early 1900s and whose style of play, though closer in form to the cricket of the elite, still reflected Afro-Creole "play" values very different from the "play up, play up, and play the game" ethos of the Anglo-Creole clubs and their colored imitators. The bowling was fast, aggressive, and aimed as much at the batsman's person as at his wicket, and the batting was stylish but in a way that contrasted sharply with the elegant strokeplay favored by the elite. The aim was to score quickly, and to do so with bravado and bravura so as to enhance individual and group reputation in the eyes of opponents and specta-tors alike. The overall goal was very definitely to win and not "to take part," not least because of the amount of money being bet on the result and the fact that the losing team was expected to entertain the winners after the match at its own expense. The home umpires, wrote Learie Constantine (n.d.a.:78), "give the most terrible decisions, with perfectly grave faces, so as to protect the legitimate interests of their pockets."[43] In short, popular cricket matches

40. On cricket under slavery, see chap. 1, n. 21 above.

41. For excellent studies of the diffusion of cricket in Barbados, see Stoddart 1987 and 1988. For Jamaica, see Soares 1989, and for Trinidad, James 1983, passim.

42. "Marble cricket" was probably as much a variation on marbles as on cricket itself. On marbles in nineteenth-century Trinidad, see n. 3 above.

43. According to Constantine (n.d.a:78), "in 1922, when Trinidad and British Guiana were racing for the Intercolonial Championship, there was such heavy betting among spectators, and

were *plays* in the classic Afro-Creole sense of the word: "The local villagers turn up in force, mostly men, but with an increasing sprinkling of women and girls, very brightly clad and very noisy. Drinks are going freely; there may be a village string band; there are usually some whistles and rattles. At night, after the match, there is dancing, more food, more drinks" (Constantine n.d.b.:33–34). Indeed, some of the early black cricket clubs—like the decidedly plebeian Stingo in post–World War I Port of Spain composed of "the butcher, the tailor, the candlestick maker, the casual labourer, with a sprinkling of the unemployed," all "totally black and no social status whatever" (James 1983: 56)—cannot have been far removed in spirit from the batonnier bands of the mid-nineteenth century. If they were not quite *jamets*, they still belonged to the streets in a way that the teachers and law clerks of Shannon, the club of the black lower middle class, clearly did not, to say nothing of the brown-skinned middle-class players of Maple, the French Catholics of Shamrock, and the overwhelmingly white Anglo-Trinidadians who belonged to the Queen's Park Club. Significantly, it was Shannon where "reputation" and "respectability" met in the form of "pride and impersonal ambition" (61) that produced the greatest Trinidadian players of the 1920s (above all Learie Constantine himself), and not for nothing does C. L. R. James say (1983:64) that what he calls "Shannonism" "symbolized the dynamic forces of the West Indies" at the time—and not just in a cricketing sense.

By the early 1900s there were black players of sufficient prowess to compel selection to the colonial teams sometimes, in the face of strong white resistance, and in a still smaller number of cases, to the interisland sides that without playing Test matches, intermittently toured Canada, the United States, and beginning in 1900, England.[44] Clubs, especially in Barbados, remained segregated on a combination of racial and class lines, but intercolonial, tour, and after 1928, Test matches brought together players of radically different lifestyles and values (as well as race), and the tensions that reigned within colonial and regional teams up to the end of the 1950s were often as much between the "respectability-oriented" values of the white and colored elites (who continued, especially the first, to furnish a disproportionate number of batsmen as well as monopolizing the positions of captain and vice-captain) and the "reputation-oriented" values of the black players who, beginning with

book-keepers stood to win or lose so much, that the players were actually warned that serious trouble might occur. I was playing in that championship, and I know some of the players regularly carried revolvers."

44. Thus, in the immortal words of *Wisden's*, the West Indian team of that year consisted of "six gentlemen and seven black men," one of whom, Lebrun Constantine, "Old Cons," was the grandson of a slave and father of the future Lord Constantine of Nelson and Marivale—perhaps the supreme instance of cricket-connected upward mobility in history.

Headley and Constantine, came to dominate both the batting and fast bowling "departments."[45] In the face of this internal conflict of values—exacerbated,
of course, by the fact that the Whites, a handful of exceptions apart, were
mediocre cricketers at best—West Indian sides only intermittently performed
up to potential and tended, in crisis, to become a collection of individuals
playing as much against each other as with, giving rise to the enduring stereotype (in England) or West Indians as "calypso" or "carnival" cricketers of limit-
less "natural talent" but lacking, quite frankly, in "backbone."[46] All this was to
change with the advent of the first nonwhite captain, Frank Worrell, in 1960
and—after the interval of Gary Sobers, decidedly a reputation-oriented player
of genius—of Clive Lloyd in the mid-1970s, the great achievement of the
latter being to combine the best of the "reputation ethos" with the best of the
values and qualities of "respectability" to produce teams that fused individual
flair and collective endeavor in a way probably never equaled in the history of
cricket.

Despite the ascent of West Indian cricket from wayward genius in the
1920 and 1930s (and even in the 1950s and 1960s) to unchallenged international supremacy from the mid-1970s onward, what strikes one is the permanence of its essential features, from style of batting and bowling to the rapport
between spectators and performers, who, as in all forms of Afro-Creole "play"
(carnival, church services, cults of possession, etc.), are separated by only the
most notional threshold, which at any moment is likely to be infringed and
transgressed. The lines of descent are direct from the early fast bowlers Cum-
berbatch and Woods, through Constantine, John, Herman Griffith, and Mar-
tindale, to Hall, Gilchrist, and Griffiths and, beyond them, to Roberts, Holding, Garner, Marshall, and Ambrose, and, among batsmen, from Headley
through the "three Ws" to Sobers, Fredericks, Greenidge, Richards, and Lara.
Always, with the bowlers, it is the same emphasis on speed and aggression:
the bowling must not just *be* fast but must *look* fast from the beginning of the
run-up to the end of the follow-through. With the batsmen it is not just a

45. "On June 28th, 1900, in a match against Gloucestershire on the Bristol cricket ground, a
West Indian fast bowler [Woods] went to his captain and asked permission to take off his boots.
West Indies captain Aucher Warner, a brother of Sir Pelham asked him why; he replied that he could
bowl properly only when barefooted. . . . Woods made a last attempt. 'Mr. Warner,' he pleaded, 'let
me take off one and I could get him—just one, sir.' 'Out of the question. You can't do that here,
Woods'" (James 1983:78–79). The batsman thus spared Woods's full fury was Gilbert Jessop, who
had scored a small matter of 157 *in an hour*. According to Constantine (n.d.a:77–78), two players
(whom he does not name) had to be omitted from the 1923 tour to England because "they could not
use a knife and fork."

46. Edward Brathwaite (1969:44) lends partial credence to this view in the refrain of his great
poetic celebration of West Indian cricket, "Rites": "But I say it once an' I say it agen: / when things
goin' good, you cahn touch / we; but leh murder start an' you cahn fine a man to hole up de side."

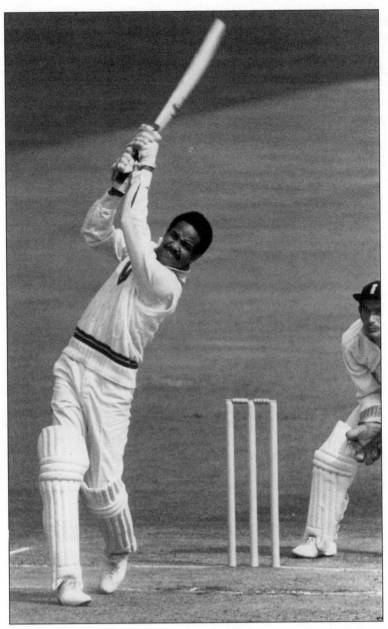

Barbadian-born Gary (later Sir Gary) Sobers, perhaps the greatest all-round cricketer of all time, batting for the West Indies against England in 1973. Photo by Patrick Eagar.

Jamaican fast bowler Michael Holding, known as Whispering Death for his virtually silent run-up to the wicket, bowling for the West Indies in 1980. Photo by Patrick Eagar.

question of scoring heavily and fast but of scoring with *style*, panache, and bravado;[47] the man-of-runs and the man-of-words belong to the same world, whether the opponent is England or the neighboring village. And in the gait and expression of the most reputation-oriented of all West Indian cricketers— who else but Viv Richards?—one glimpses something of a kalinda king's swagger, though minus the helmet, which Richards, proud and defiant to the end, disdained to wear against even the fastest of bowling.

Of course not all West Indian bowlers and batsmen conform to these types, which are always dangerously close to becoming stereotypes, and it has been the particular strength of West Indian cricket in the past thirty years to combine, in particular, "reputation-oriented" batsmen (Sobers, Richards) with more subdued and "respectable" players (Hunte, Logie, Haynes) who are able to "graft" when required. Similarly, black West Indian cricketers do not, as is often supposed, invariably come from the bottom rungs of society to rise, shamanlike, above every social and racial obstacle set before them: most are of "respectable" working-class, lower-middle-class, and even middle-class background. But all, whatever their origins, bear on their shoulders the hopes and the fantasies not just of the spectators at the match but of the tens of thousands of West Indians who, on street corners and in betting shops, barbershops, and rum shops, follow their deeds by radio commentary. All to a man (and a woman) identify with their heroes, as Edward Brathwaite captures so brilliantly in his great poem "Rites" (1969:43–44):

> "You see dat shot?" the people was shoutin';
> "Jesus Chrise, man, wunna see dat shot?"
> All over de groun' fellers shakin' hands wid each other
>
> As if was *they* wheelin' de willow
> as if was *them* had the power;
>
> . . . . . . . . . . . . . . . . . . .
> An' in front o' where I was sittin',
> one ball-headed sceptic snatch hat off he head
> as if he did crazy

47. It should not be thought that this style of batting is limited to West Indians of African origin: the example of Rohan Kanhai and his miracle shot known as the "triumphant fall" shows that this is not so (see Birbalsingh and Shiwcharan 1988:43–77). On the other hand, many of the most distinctive features of the Afro-Creole cricketing style are echoed in the "granning" (grandstanding), "showboating," "marking" (mocking), "woofing" (< wolfing[?] = insulting), and "slam-dunking" of African American basketball players (see Kochman 1981:70, 137). "Most Black ball expressions," Nelson George has written (1992:xvi), "are about elevating oneself by embarrassing others. . . . 'in your face,' the most celebrated bit of Black slang in b-ball lexicon, is about showing total disrespect for your opponent."

an' pointin' he finger at Wardle,
he jump up an' down
like a sun-shatter daisy an' bawl

out: "B . . . L . . . O . . . O . . . D, B . . . I . . . G B . . . O . . . Y
bring me B . . . L . . . O . . . O . . . D"
Who would'a think that for twenty-
five years he was standin' up there
in them Post Office cages, lickin' gloy
pun de Gover'ment stamps.

And so the crowd plays along with the players, shouting, joking, dancing, clinking beer cans, and blowing whistles and conch shells like some massive tambou-bamboo band at carnival, with its licensed jesters like the famous "King Dyal" of Barbados and "Gravy" and "Mayfield" of Antigua, in all three of whom the carnival tradition of agonic display reigns supreme.[48] The cricket match in the West Indies is the triumph of "outside" over "inside" as, laughing and *playing* out on the bleachers, the crowd flaunts itself without stint or shame, indifferent to the reactions of the powerful and respectable who watch the match from the stands or the pavilion, as though from the veranda of some cricketing Great House. But if West Indian cricket is like West Indian carnival in its noisy exuberance and extravagant display, it also partakes of the ambivalence of carnival, in that what it offers the "revelers" is the fantasy, not the reality, of power that it takes away even as it holds it before them. Cricket has enabled West Indians to define themselves over and against their colonial and ex-colonial masters, but at the price of confirming the grip of the colonial legacy over them, blurring the truly significant fact of their history: not that they regularly beat Massa at his own game and regularly make him *look foolish*, but that they are playing his game in the first place. Although West Indian cricket is routinely referred to by commentators as a "game of resistance," as one of a number of "anti-systemic resistances" to "powerful hegemonic, colonial and imperialist structures and ideas" (Hilary Beckles in Beckles and Stoddart 1995:148–49), it clearly belongs, in the terms used in this book, to a culture of opposition rather than resistance. In classic oppositional style, it challenges the dominant order on the latter's own terrain, turning its cultural

---

48. On "King Dyal" (Dundonald Redvers Dyal), see Stoddart 1987:338. On his Antiguan equivalents, see the report on the West Indies versus Australia game at St. Johns in 1985: "The most competitive contest was between the two licensed local jesters, Gravy and Mayfield. Gravy was dressed as a doctor and during drinks put his stethoscope to umpire Bucknor's heart to see if anything was beating. Mayfield hung a huge swing from one of the smaller stands and launched himself." "It was," said the disconsolate *Guardian* reporter (30 April 1985), "about the only thing that swung all day."

A section of the crowd watching the West Indies play Australia at the Kensington Oval, Barbados, in 1973. Photo by Patrick Eagar.

and ideological "weapons" against it, and while victory over the other on the other's own terms enables the dominated to get their frustration out of *their* system, *the* System itself survives—strengthened, not weakened by its merely symbolic defeat. Thus, although the West Indian victories over England in 1950 may well have the "anticolonial" meaning widely ascribed them, the plainly visceral need felt by West Indians, thirty years and more after formal independence, that their cricketers continue to humiliate the ex-colonizers match after match, series after series, could equally be read as evidence not of their liberation but of their enduring thralldom to the colonial mind-set. West Indians still apparently need the other in order to define and establish their individual and collective selfhood, and it may be that they are never so alienated as precisely when their cricketers are crushing the English at the latter's totemic sport. The paradox of West Indian cricketing prowess is that it is *at one and the same time* a conscious assertion of identity and an unconscious expression of alienation, its very triumphs evidence of a historical whitewash that no "blackwash," every two or three years, of the ex-master's batsmen and bowlers can ever fully erase.

Cricket at Bathsheba Beach, Barbados, ca. 1970. Photo by Patrick Eagar.

## The Calypsonian as Trickster and Man-of-Words

The origins of calypso,[49] like the origins of the word itself, are hotly contested, but as a song form it is almost certainly derived from what Gordon Rohlehr (1990:2) calls "the African custom of permitting criticism of one's leaders at specific times, in particular contexts, and through the media of song and story." Like stickfighting (from which it is inseparable until the late nineteenth century), it appears to have been introduced into Trinidad by slaves of French West Indian origin who were brought to the then Spanish colony by their masters after 1783, the mythical ur-calypsonian being a slave named Gros-Jean whom his Martinican-born master "Lawa" (King) Pierre Begorrat allegedly appointed as his *maît' caiso*, or master of cariso,[50] to entertain him

49. The following account is based on the authoritative history of carnival in preindependence Trinidad by Gordon Rohlehr (1990), supplemented by the valuable studies by Keith Warner (1982) and Donald Hill (1993). I have also drawn on the more personal testimony of Hollis Liverpool, alias Mighty Chalkdust (see Jones and Liverpool 1976 and Liverpool 1990). In order not to overburden the text, I have kept notes and references to a minimum.

50. The word "calypso," which is first attested in its modern form in 1900, is usually derived from *kaiso* (= "bravo" in Hausa) or *cariso* (< *carieto* = joyous song in Carib), or from a conflation of both. Both *kaiso* and *cariso* were widely used in the nineteenth and early twentieth centuries to denote the song form in question and are still encountered today (see Warner 1982:8–9 for a full discussion of the question).

with songs designed not only to flatter him and his friends and deride rival planters but also, in certain circumstances and moods, to poke fun at Begorrat himself and denounce him as some kind of devil or monster (see Pearse 1956b:253 for a specimen song). It seems that other planters also had their *maît' caiso* and that these enslaved men-of-words "would sing *mepris* or insults on each other to the amusement of other slaves, Begorrat and his friends" (Jones and Liverpool 1976:263). From the outset, then, there appears to have been an ambivalent relationship between calypso, in its primitive form, and Power. The *maît' caiso*, like the fool in medieval courtly society in Europe, is the licensed critic, the powerless one who is permitted ludically to deride the powerful, and who vies with other such jester figures to enhance the reputation of his master and patron and concomitantly his own. Just as African leaders, according to Rohlehr (1990:2), "recognized the value of such satirical songs in which the ordinary person was given the privilege of unburdening his mind while the impact of his protest was neutralized by the controlled context within which criticism was permissible,"[51] so calypso continues to this day to evince a "mixture of astringency and ineffectuality" derived from the paradoxical position of the calypsonian in the community.[52] His is a liminal realm,[53] both inside and outside society, on which he is dependent for his reputation (and increasingly his income) and that, *within certain limits*, permits him to criticize it and its members so it can enjoy the pleasure of laughing at itself but also in order to deflect or neutralize a more serious threat to its power. In short, the calypsonian occupies a classically oppositional stance vis-à-vis his society: he is Legba (Hill 1993:217), the man at the crossroads, the outsider-insider who, like Anancy, must use all his resources of verbal trickery to mock the powerful while entertaining and, above all, impressing both them and the powerless with his prowess as performer, mime, and master of words.

After emancipation, the singing of *caiso* seems to have become primarily a *female* activity brought to perfection by the "chantwells" who accompanied the batonnier to, during, and from the *bataille bois* with songs—sung in French Creole—of incitement, defiance, and derision.[54] There is also evidence, from as early as 1851, of satirical songs directed against colonial officials and other local worthies (Liverpool 1990:18). When stickfighting was banned in 1884, the male batonniers, according to Rohlehr (190:32), adopted the hitherto fe-

51. Warner (1982:38–40) also links calypso to the West African griot tradition and quotes some striking instances of griot wordplay and boasting that directly recall calypso.

52. Even the greatest and most successful modern calypsonian, Mighty Sparrow, alludes to the ambiguity of the calypsonian's position in "Outcast" (quoted in Warner 1982:86): "Calypsonians really catch hell for a long time / To associate yourself wid dem was a big crime / If you' sister talk to a steelband man / De family want to break she hand." See also Liverpool 1990:20–21.

53. On the liminality of the calypsonian, see Manning 1984:168.

54. See the testimony of Frances Richard, a ninety-six-year-old Trinidadian woman interviewed in 1953 by Elder (1966a:90). See also Rohlehr 1990:55.

male-dominated *caiso* as a substitute weapon, and over the next twenty years "the physical violence of the stickfight was to become transformed into the verbal violence of the 'single tone' (four-line) *picong* and 'double tone' (eight-line) *Sans Humanité* calypsoes."[55] In the process women—who previously had been in action not only as chantwells but also, as we have seen, as stickfighters themselves—were relegated to a subsidiary or peripheral role in carnival and its associated rituals, from which they would not decisively emerge until a century later. After 1884, as we shall see, carnival was progressively regulated and sanitized by the colonial authorities (with the support of the local middle class), and concomitantly, a fundamental change occurred in the world of *caiso*. Up to the mid-1880s, *caiso* had been sung, primarily by women, on the streets and in French Creole. By the mid-1890s, after a transitional period during which lower-class men appropriated the chantwell tradition almost without change, a new style of song (and a new style of singer) had emerged alongside, and in competition with, the old: the "oratorical calypso" sung in *English* by male singers who no longer belonged necessarily to the *jamet* class— "jacket-men"[56] like Norman Le Blanc (whose 1898 calypso "Jerningham the Governor" is traditionally, but almost certainly erroneously, credited with being the first sung entirely in English), Lord Executor (Philip Garcia), and the Duke of Marlborough (George Adilla)—and who, in the second crucial innovation, no longer performed on the street but sang in temporary structures known as "tents."[57] By 1900, according to Donald Hill (1993:5), there had emerged a clear distinction between "outdoor" and "indoor" styles of singing which, though he does not say so, corresponds almost point for point with the outside/inside dichotomy of the "Crab Antics" school of anthropology, except that men are by now dominant both indoors and out and the crucial distinction is now one of class rather than gender (Table 1).

It is clear that in the early years of the twentieth century there was something of a struggle for power in Port of Spain between the old-style chantwells and the new-style calypsonians, from which the latter eventually emerged triumphant (Rohlehr 1990:73). Singing in patois had largely disappeared by 1914, and the tradition of street singing would survive only in the much modified form of the road-march calypso with which carnival conventionally opens. In 1920 a calypsonian known as "Railway" or "Chieftain" Douglas inaugurated the practice of charging admission to his "tent" (four cents to stand,

55. *Picong* (< *piquant*) is the general Trinidadian expression for satire or mockery; the meaning of *sans humanité* (pronounced "sandeemaneetay") with which many calypso choruses conclude is disputed but may signify something like "you deserve no pity, it serves you right" (see Warner 1982:43).

56. The term "jacket-man" (*lom kamisol* in Creole) refers to "persons of a superior class who patronized the underworld heroes, playing stick with them but [keeping] their coats on to differentiate themselves" (Pearse 1956b:259).

57. "Tents" were in fact more often constructions of bamboo and thatch than of canvas; initially they had no staging or seats and were lit by open-flame torches.

**Table 1. Outdoor and indoor styles of singing**

|  | Outdoor | Indoor |
|---|---|---|
| Name | *Caiso*, chantwell | Calypso, calypsonian |
| Location | Street | Tent |
| Class | Lower | Lower + middle |
| Language | French Creole | English |
| Themes | Eating, drinking, sex | Storytelling, satire, criticism of society |
| Politics | Antiestablishment, anti-British | Praise of British Empire + some criticism of local officials |
| Style | Music more important than lyrics | Lyrics more important than music |
| Public | Carnival reveler | Ticket-buying public |

Adapted from Hill 1993:5.

six cents to sit), introduced a stage and gas lighting, substituted stringed instruments for the old-style percussion bands, and featured a whole program of calypsos sung by different singers. More and more of a commercial concern, and supported by business, which saw in it a cheap and effective form of publicity (Liverpool 1990:33), calypso gradually severed its links with street masquerade and became a performer-centered art form in its own right. The separation of "inside" from "outside" was accentuated by the gradual move, in the course of the interwar period, of "tents" from George, Henry, and Prince Streets in downtown Port of Spain to streets closer to the middle- and upper-class neighborhoods of Newtown, St. James, Belmont, St. Clair, and Woodbrook, where, according to Lord Beginner, ordinary people "used to peep through the bamboo" into what, as late as the early 1950s, Lord Superior could still call "a place for whites" where the poor entertained the rich (Liverpool 1990:11–12). Clearly the bacchanal of the outside had given way to the far more ordered and "respectable," though still intermittently turbulent, world of the inside.

The move from street to tent as we have seen, was contemporaneous with the shift from French Creole to English, which was, in its turn, proceeding apace throughout Trinidad between 1880 and 1920. As in society as a whole, the use of patois in calypso soon became an object of derision and stigma,[58] and again as in the wider society, calypsonians sought to master the resources and subtleties of English, replicating in their own sphere what one late nineteenth-century English teacher said of his Trinidadian pupils' disposition "to use long-winded words and high-flown phrases; boys and young men spend hours poring over dictionaries, simply to try and master the meanings of words which for length may be measured by the yard" (J. H. Collens, 1886,

58. According to Lord Beginner, referring to the 1920s, "people did hate to hear you when you came with a patois" (quoted by Rohlehr 1990:121).

quoted in Rohlehr 1990:56). But as in the case of the altiloquent tea meeting or wedding reception speechifier, much more was involved than a simple, and ultimately sterile, attempt to mimic the language of the colonial master. It was just as much a question of appropriating the power felt to reside in the dominant language, of using that power as a way of enhancing one's own reputation and devaluing one's rivals, and in certain circumstances of turning that language, Calibanlike, against its original owners, the English. Moreover, the "English" of the great calypsonians of the interwar years—above all, the supreme triumvirate of Attila the Hun, Roaring Lion, and Growling Tiger—was unmistakably Trinidadian in structure and tone, even though all, or almost all, of its component parts could have been found in any standard English dictionary. As in the wielding of baton and bat, what counted in the wielding of words was style as much as substance, hence the kind of verbal fireworks engaged in in a celebrated logomachic duel between Attila and Lion:

LION

On grammatical subjects I will now state
Inviting lexicographers who can debate
With Ramsomfousis asceticism
They may try to argue but are bound to run
Through the extensive alteration of anklyosis [sic]
And my encyclopaedic analysis
That makes me a man of psychology
And I can always sing grammatically.

ATTILA

From the very moment that you commence
You are singing nothing but arrant nonsense
You have your listeners in dismay
They can't understand a single word you say
You're trying to indulge in phraseology
And only demonstrating stupidity
For you are no man of psychology
And you will never sing grammatically.

(quoted in Warner 1982:31)

From the earliest times, as we have seen, *caiso* involved combat—*mepris*—between different singers, and in 1919 this ancient tradition was formalized when, as part of their circulation war, both the *Argus* and the *Trinidad Guardian* offered prizes for the best calypso of that year's carnival. In the 1920s the singers in individual tents began to compete with each other at the close of the evening's performance ("then, at the end, we had 'war,' a battle of words,

Calypsonian Raphael de Leon, known as the Roaring Lion, in 1936.

when all the calypsonians would come on stage and give each other 'fatigue'";
Lord Beginner, quoted in Warner 1982:14) and in the 1930s contests between
the different tents became an integral part of carnival. The first Calypso King
title was awarded in 1939 (to Growling Tiger for his "The Labour Situation in
Trinidad"), whereafter it continued with some interruptions until it was finally
incorporated officially into carnival in 1958 by the government-sponsored
Carnival Development Committee. A knockout competition takes place
throughout Trinidad and Tobago in the months preceding carnival, with the
final being contested on the evening of Dimanche Gras, before the opening of
carnival proper: thus the agonic principle came to embrace the whole of society, culminating in the epic—and for the winner highly lucrative—duels in
the 1960s and 1970s between Mighty Sparrow, Mighty Duke, Lord Kitchener,
Mighty Chalkdust, and others.

Calypso, then, was, and still to a large extent is, essentially about male reputation and power. The verbal cuts and thrusts of the calypsonian, like drives
and hooks of the batsman and the run-up and follow-through of the bowler,
are geared toward both effect and display: the performer's ego is fully pro-
jected into his style; he becomes one with his act, is in a sense possessed by it,
and through the mastery of his art wins the prestige and reputation (and in a
few cases the wealth) that in his everyday life would in all likelihood be
denied him. In this perspective a resounding nom de guerre becomes an indispensable part of the world of calypso. It is unthinkable that a calypsonian
would perform using his own everyday name and essential that he assume
some aristocratic or royal identity (Pharaoh, Black Prince, Julius Caesar, the
Dukes of Albany, York, and Marlborough, and all the countless Lords from
Executor and Beginner to Melody, Pretender, Caresser, Brynner, and Kitchener), that he take on the power and stealth of a predatory animal or reptile
(Alligator, Cobra, Gorilla, Panther, Viper, Growling Tiger, Roaring Lion), that
he become one of the great dictators, warriors, or generals of history (Stalin,
Montgomery, Eisenhower, Attila the Hun), that he adopt a name suggestive of
domination (Destroyer, Conqueror, Controller, Invader, Bomber, Spoiler,
Striker, and Terror), of cunning or magic (Inventory, Inveigler, Wrangler,
Houdini) or knowledge (Preceptor, Explainer), or finally, that he join the prefix "Mighty" to some second term that often connotes not power but the
resilience, trickery, and spirit of the small man: Cypher, Dougla, Chalkdust,
and—the ultimate *trouvaille*, combining the indomitability of Ti-Jean with the
resourcefulness of Anancy—the Mighty Sparrow.[59] The sobriquets are both
self-mocking and self-aggrandizing and ludically invert the power structures of

59. On the whole question of calypsonians' sobriquets, see Warner 1982:15–16. It is noticeable
that the names chosen by female calypsonians are much less flamboyant and do not entirely obliterate and transform the singer's identity: Calypso Rose, Singing Francine, Singing Diane, etc. On the
general question of nicknames in the Caribbean, see Manning 1974.

the real world, enabling, say, Raymond Quevedo to rampage through Port of
Spain like Attila the Hun or giving Hubert Raphael Charles the power to
pounce on his prey like his totemic animal, the Lion:

> The earth is a-trembling and a-trembling, and the heroes
>   are falling
> And all—because the Lion is roaring
> My tongue is like the blast of a gun
> When I frown, monarchs all have to bow down to the ground
> Devastation, destruction, desolation and damnation
> All these—I'll inflict on insubordination
> For the Lion in his power is like the rock of Gibraltar.
>                     (Roaring Lion, quoted in Rohlehr 1990:66)

In moving from street to tent, the calypsonian did not therefore in any
way renounce the reputation ethic characteristic of the former. Indeed, the
tent is probably best regarded as an intermediary space between street and
yard, an inside-outside or outside-inside, that corresponds perfectly to the
liminal position of the calypsonian in society. Something of the same ambivalence is to be found in the calypsonian's relationship to Power, both under the
colonial regime and in independent Trinidad. On the one hand, the calypsonian readily and scathingly attacks *subordinate* figures—an arrogant or incompe-
tent colonial official, a rapacious local businessman or landowner, a corrupt
government minister. On the other, he *usually* leaves untouched the supreme
embodiment of power (the governor before independence,[60] the prime minister thereafter) and for the very good reason that he knows the consequences—censorship,[61] dismissal, perhaps even legal proceedings—of attacking power at its source. In addition, in the relationship of the calypsonian to
those in authority there is something of the doubleness that obtained between
his mythic ancestor Gros-Jean and the latter's master Begorrat: a combination
of satire and flattery that ultimately leaves the position of the powerful intact,
whence the "mixture of astringency and ineffectuality" that, as we have seen,
Gordon Rohlehr (1990:2) considers inseparable from the calypsonian's condition. There are signs too of the distinction, already encountered in a number
of instances, commonly made in the colonial Caribbean between "good" and
"bad" versions of the white man, a distinction that, recalling that between the
king and his ministers, enabled calypsonians during the great labor conflicts of
the late 1930s to condemn the actions of the forces of law and order while
praising the high-mindedness and concern of the governor, Sir Murchison

---

60. For a comparatively rare direct attack on a colonial governor (Sir Claude Hollis in the
1940s)—admittedly after he had been recalled to Britain—see Liverpool 1990:45.

61. On the censorship of calypsos, particularly in the 1930s and 1940s, see Liverpool 1990:50–53.

Fletcher, and his principal aide, Howard Nankivell.[62] Similarly, though imperial *policy* is often criticized insofar as it affects Trinidad, the *principle* of empire rarely if ever comes under attack before the 1950s,[63] and especially in time of war, the identification of calypsonian with imperial motherland is almost totally uncritical. Furthermore, while attacking the manifestations rather than the sources of power, the calypsonian also confirms and corroborates certain aspects of that power—above all, as we shall see shortly, the power of men over women—and routinely endorses some of the most negative stereotypes of the various outgroups in Trinidadian society: the Barbadian or Grenadian migrant, the "Spanish" peon, Shouters and Shangoists, Chinese, Portuguese, and above all East Indians (see Rohlehr 1990:154–58, 498–500, 509, etc.). It is therefore the *limits* of the calypsonian's heterodoxy that need to be stressed

62. See Attila's "Mr. Nankivell's Speech," quoted in Rohlehr 1990:205–6:

> He spoke feelingly and strikingly
> Logically and conscientiously
> His diction was perfect, elocution great
> To describe his speech words are inadequate
> He said: "They who plant the cane and dig the oil
> And develop the estates with their sweat and toil
> While employers are living luxuriously
> They should not be dying in misery."

Thus the tribute of one man-of-words to another.

63. The closest to a denunciation of colonialism as *such* is probably Patrick Jones's (Chinee Patrick, Oliver Cromwell, Lord Pretender) calypso of 1920 that begins (Liverpool 1990:44):

> Class legislation is the order of this land.
> We are ruled with the iron hand.
> Britain boasts of democracy,
> Brotherly love and fraternity,
> But British colonists have been ruled
> In perpetual misery—sans humanité.

On the importance of the Boer War, both as a calypso theme and as an influence on the calypso form, see Rohlehr 190:45–46 and Hill 1993:119–20. A typical "imperialist" calypso runs as follows (Hill 1993:119):

> In the reign of Victoria
> We marched on Pretoria
> Under Duke of Kandahar we
> Destroyed the Boer's domination
> Now the Transvaal is mine
> Population, raise the Imperial Flag of Britannia . . .
> Sans humanité.

Needless to say, the singer in question styled himself the Duke of Kandahar, thus sealing the identity of calypsonian and imperial conqueror.

as much as its extent. He may well be, as the calypsonian Valentino has said, "the only true opposition" in Trinidad (quoted in Liverpool 1990:48–49), but condemned to oppose "the system" from within, he ultimately confirms it as much as, and even as, he challenges it, knowing like his prototype Anancy that to resist power directly is to bring power down on his head. Or in the immortal words of Mighty Chalkdust (Chalkie) in the aftermath of the 1970 "Black Power" uprising in Trinidad: I would attack the government head on, but "Ah fraid, Karl, ah fraid."[64]

If calypso is ultimately an expression of male (desire for) power, it is hardly surprising that the image it depicts of male-female relations in Trinidad is so depressingly negative.[65] The ideal place for the woman in calypso is *inside* as mother, provider, and above all as nourisher rather than as wife or companion (see Rohlehr 1990:218–19), and women who venture out into the public world of men or who try to imprison men in the private world of the yard are alike subject to scathing denunciation on the part of the threatened male singer. Women are routinely savaged for their supposed treacherousness, sexual voraciousness, recourse to magic (with the specific intention of "tying" men to themselves),[66] and lack of personal cleanliness.[67] Women are set on usurping man's power in society (see Attila's "Women Will Rule the World" of 1935; Rohlehr 1990:223–24) and will stop at nothing in their desire to outwit and dominate him:

> Some call them bats and some call them rats
> But I will call them the diplomats
> You hardly find one with simplicity
> All have the mind like Mussolini.
> (Beginner, "Second-Hand Girls," 1938;
> Rohlehr 1990:230)

When she is not a passive instrument of pleasure, woman is a devouring vampire (Cobra's "Mamaguy Me" of 1937) or cat (Sparrow's "Ah Fraid Pussy Bite Me") who threatens the male with castration, impotence, or worse, with the

64. The reference is to Karl Hudson-Philipps, the much-feared Trinidadian attorney general of the time.

65. The following paragraph is based on Rohlehr's exhaustive and highly perceptive discussion of male-female relations in 1930s calypsos (1990:213–77), supported by Warner 1982:95–110 and Mohammed 1991.

66. On calypsos treating the subject of women and Obeah, see Rohlehr 1990:258–63. Typical songs on this theme are Beginner's "The Cocoa Tea That Puzzle Me" and Growler's "I Don't Want No Callaloo" ("Young men, I am warning you / Be careful when eating crab callaloo"). On the whole question of West Indian men's widely attested fear of being "tied" by women, see Sobo 1993:229–32 and Lazarus-Black 1994:259.

67. On the figure of "unclean woman" ("stinking-mouth Doreen," "spotty-foot Pearl," "big-eye Merle," "stinking-toe Sheila," "one-breast Angela," etc.), see Warner 1982:100.

unsurprising consequence that in Rohlehr's words (1990:231) "calypso fictions often dramatise the elaborate processes of ego-retrieval by which men restore a threatened or damaged image of the Self." Marriage, and even a permanent one-to-one relationship with a woman, is often dreaded and refused as an assault on the autonomy of the male,[68] who prefers the kind of sexual eclecticism celebrated and satirized—a typical calypso combination—in Sparrow's classic "Village Ram" (Warner 1982:95–96):

> Not a woman ever complain yet wid me
> Ah ain't boasting but ah got durability
> And if a woman ever tell you that I
> Ever left her dissatisfy
> She lie, she lie, ah say she lie.

The upshot of this fear of women that calypsonian after calypsonian attempts to disguise as phallic vainglory[69] is, inevitably, physical violence:

> Every now and then cuff them down
> They'll love you long and they'll love you strong
> Black up dey eye, bruise up dey knee
> And they will love you eternally.
> (Sparrow, "Rose"; Warner 1982:103)

The calypso, in short, both dramatizes the tension between the predominantly male culture of the street and the predominantly female culture of the yard and demonstrates the ultimate dependence of the former on the latter as embodied above all in the figure of the calypsonian's mother (Warner 1982:103)

> Well for me I'm holding on to my mother
> And my wife she'll have to excuse Kitchener
> For I can always get another wife
> But I can never get another mother in my life.

One of the most significant developments in calypso since the early 1970s has been the emergence of a small number of female calypsonians, one of

68. As Sparrow put it (Warner 1982:104), "Why must I buy a cow when I know how to get milk free?" See also Attila's "Not Me with Matrimony" and "I'll Never Burden Myself with a Wife."
69. As, more wittily than most, Kitchener does in "Venezuela Maria" (Warner 1982:107):

> The wood here in Trinidad no wood could surpass
> Ah like how it thick and hard and how it does last
> Ah try Canadian Cedar, never please me good
> But the poui and the Balata, Oh Lord, dat is wood!

As can be seen, the "sweet man" is a batonnier of a kind.

whom, Calypso Rose, was crowned "Calypso Monarch" in 1978. It is too early to predict a revolution in the values and attitudes of the male calypsonian, but with Singing Francine's "Run Away" of 1979—which urged women to desert their violent partners—and above all with Singing Diane's "Ah Done wid Dat" (ironically written by a man) of the following year, a new and, it must be said, refreshing voice was introduced into the insufferable phallocratic world of the traditional calypso (Warner 1982:106):

> Leave me, don't touch me
> If ah don't leave now, is licks in de morning
> In de evening Ah can't take it, ah telling you flat
> Ah done wid dat.

The ecstatic response from women in the audience made it abundantly clear that they too had "done wid dat." Significantly, it was about the same time— 1980, 1981, 1982—that lovers of traditional carnival began to complain of the "predominance of women" in the street parades and especially of "the tendency of so many of the women masqueraders to behave vulgarly on the stage, often gyrating (or to use a popular term: wining) excessively whenever they saw a television camera" (Anthony 1989:428). I shall return to this crucial development in the section that follows.

## The Changing Content of Carnival, 1783–1990

Trinidad carnival, Daniel Miller has written (1994:130), "seems to change its implications almost each decade, facing about to address different aspects of Trinidadian society, now emancipation, now class, now gender."[70] In an attempt to describe the principal changes of meaning concerned, this section divides the history of carnival into four clear-cut periods that will be further subdivided where appropriate: first, the period from the *cedula* of 1783 to full emancipation in 1838 when carnival was dominated by Whites and, to a lesser extent, by Free Coloureds to the near-total exclusion of slaves; second, the era of the *"jamet* carnival" extending from 1838 to 1884 when, as we have seen, successive riots caused the colonial administration, backed by sections of the middle class, to subject carnival to controls that radically changed its character; third, the period 1884 to 1941 when carnival, without losing its rebellious potential, became steadily more "respectable" and began to evolve into a

70. This section is based principally on the general study of carnival by Errol Hill (1972) and the still valuable special 1956 number of *Caribbean Quarterly* (4, 3–4), particularly the articles by Andrew T. Carr (1956), Daniel J. Crowley (1956a, 1956b), and Andrew Pearse (1956a). Extensive use has also been made of Michael Anthony's year-by-year chronicle of carnival, *Parade of the Carnivals of Trinidad, 1839–1989* (1989). Notes and references have, as before, been kept to a minimum.

truly national festivity; and finally, the period of the "modern" carnival from 1945 to the present, characterized by increasing commercialization, politicization, and theatricalization. The section that follows discusses the evolution of carnival masques over more than two centuries, stressing the gradual demise of the traditional masques (*nèg jardin*, midnight robbers, Dame Lorraine, Pierrot Grenade, etc.) in favor of the massive historical and fantasy bands that have dominated carnival since the 1950s, and a concluding section attempts, through a discussion of Earl Lovelace's novel of 1979, *The Dragon Can't Dance*, the next to impossible task of bringing all of the chapter's strands together in an assessment of the significance of the carnivalesque in Trinidadian society.

### The Carnival of the Whites, 1783–1838

Trinidad carnival, like stickfighting and *caiso*, had its origins in the decision by the planters in the French or formerly French colonies of Martinique, Grenada, Dominica, and later Saint-Domingue to respond to the Spanish government's *cedula* of 1783 and move themselves and their slaves en bloc to what was at the time an underpopulated and scarcely developed backwater of the Spanish empire. The planters brought with them a form of carnival directly derived from the French carnival tradition, to which they had already added a number of creole modifications, notably the masque known as the *nègre jardin* based on their own field slaves and the ritual of what, in French, was called *cannes brûlées*, but which would become *canboulay* in Creole when, according to an anonymous account of 1881 (quoted in Pearse 1956a:182) the "pretended *nègres de jardin* were wont to unite in bands, representing the camps of different estates, and with torches and drums to represent what did actually take place on the estates when a fire occurred in a plantation. In such cases the gangs of the neighbouring estates proceed alternately accompanied with torches at night which had suffered to assist in the grinding of the burnt canes before they became sour." Trinidad carnival thus began as an imitation of Blacks by Whites, rather than vice versa, with French creole males dressing as field slaves and dancing the *bamboula* while their wives and daughters disguised themselves as *mulâtresses* and donned the *foulards* and *madras* of their female charges. After the capture of Trinidad by Britain in 1797, carnival continued to be dominated by French creole Whites who, briefly displaying themselves in public, processed by carriage from house to house in Port of Spain to eat, drink, and dance in what remained essentially private, inner-directed parties. But preemancipation Trinidad was characterized by its unusually large free colored population whose members conducted their own kind of carnival celebrations, subject to restriction, *on the streets* of the principal towns of the colony. Only the slaves, confined to their quarters both in the towns and on the plantations, were excluded from the merrymaking, condemned either to watch the Free Coloureds on the street outside or, like the proverbial *nèg dèyè pòtla* (slave behind the door), to spy on their masters and mistresses as the latter mimicked their dress, demeanor, and dances.

As in other plantation societies, however, slaves did have the right to celebrate Christmas, which they did in a manner that recalls Jonkonnu without the specific masks of the latter. They paid ritual visits to their masters and moved about with comparative freedom from plantation to plantation or, in town, from house to house, eating, drinking, making music, singing, and dancing. As Miller says (1994:131), apart, crucially, from the masques, "almost all the elements which are today associated with Carnival arose originally in Trinidad, and indeed in the Caribbean more generally, under the auspices of Christmas." After emancipation, and the systematic appropriation of carnival by the ex-slaves, the significance of Christmas in Trinidad, as Miller decisively shows (82–107), was to change radically; it became a family-centered ritual of interiority, transcendence, and respectability whereas carnival, now taken over by Blacks, was invested with the traditional values of the slave saturnalia: exteriority, transience, reputation, *freedom*. Christmas/carnival; inside/outside; home/street; centripetal/centrifugal; respectability/reputation; "female"/"male." The now familiar dichotomies impose themselves again.

### The "Jamet Carnival," 1838–1884

Emancipation in 1838 revolutionized carnival, as it revolutionized the whole of Trinidadian, and Caribbean, society from top to bottom. Even during the four-year "apprenticeship" period preceding complete emancipation (1834–38), slaves had begun to move out onto the streets at carnival time, the loudness, obscenity, and aggression of their behavior prompting a parallel but inverse movement inward on the part of the old white elite. After 1838, and until the mid-1890s, the elite would withdraw completely from public participation in carnival, abandoning the streets to the ex-slaves and former Free Coloureds, who developed an ambivalent attitude toward the new-style carnival, fearing its rowdiness, obscenity, and incipient violence but bitterly critical of attempts by the administration in alliance with the elite to curb or repress it. For more than four decades after emancipation, the *canboulay* procession would be the focus and embodiment of the so-called *jamet* carnival,[71] the carni-

---

71. According to Bridget Brereton (1983:73), there is "absolutely no evidence, for the post-1838 years, of any popular celebrations by the ex-slaves on August First" in Trinidad (as opposed to Jamaica; see Higman 1979) and above all no evidence for the widespread belief that *canboulay* processions were originally held by the ex-slaves on 1 August and then moved back, by administrative fiat, to carnival week; it is "much more likely," she claims, "that the Canboulay ceremony was always a part of Carnival and was never held on August First." On the other hand, she later shows (76) that, when *canboulay* was banned from carnival in the early 1880s, it was celebrated in some villages on 1

val of the plebs, who swiftly invested the anodyne masquerade of their former masters with a potent new meaning—freedom—that each year in February or March threatened to disrupt the structures of a postemancipation society that aimed above all at keeping that freedom within certain very clearly defined limits: Blacks imitated Whites imitating Blacks but in the process turned the Whites' representation of themselves (and society) completely on its head. Originally celebrated on Dimanche Gras and as such constituting a profanation of the Sabbath, *canboulay* was, by gubernatorial decree, shifted in the early 1840s to Monday morning where, taking place by torchlight immediately after midnight, it provided an explosive buildup to the *jouvay* (<*jour ouvert*) processions that inaugurated carnival proper.

In a memorable account in an otherwise unmemorable book, Charles Williams Day (1852:313–16) described how, at midnight on Sunday 7 March 1848, he witnessed the "squalid splendour" of a "negro masquerade"—clearly *canboulay*—at which "the primitives were negroes, as nearly naked as might be, bedaubed with a black varnish." One member of a "gang"—his word—of revelers "had a long chain and padlock attached to his leg, which chain the others pulled. What this typified, I was unable to learn; but as the chained one was occasionally thrown down on the ground, and treated with a mock bastinadoing it probably represented slavery." Each mask was "armed with a good stout quarter-staff, so that they could overcome one-half more police than themselves," while "parties of negro ladies danced through the streets, each *clique* distinguished by bodicces of the same colour": clearly all-woman bands like the Dahlias and Mousselines and equally clearly Trinidad's answer to the Set Girls of Jamaica. There were other masques in profusion—"Pulinchinellos," pirates, Turks, Highlanders, one "a most ludicrous caricature of the Gael, being arrayed in a scarlet coat, huge grenadier cap, a kilt of light blue chintz, striped with white, a most indescribable philibeg, black legs of course, and white socks bound with dirty pink ribbon," "Indians of South America, daubed with red ochre, personified by the Spanish peons from the Main, themselves half Indian" and shaded beneath "a canopy of red glazed calico, trimmed with silver tinsel" and clearly crowning the whole cavalcade, "a royal pair, who, in conscious majesty . . . , represented the Sovereign pair of England." Day notes, interestingly but unverifiably, that "every negro, male and female, wore a white flesh-coloured mask, their woolly hair carefully concealed by handkerchiefs" while noticing that "whenever a *black* mask appeared, it was sure to be a *white* man," a remark which, if true, suggests that the early

---

August, thus confirming its significance as a ritual of freedom but also reinforcing Brereton's general conclusion that "Carnival, not August First, was the major focus for popular rejoicings in the 50 years after emancipation."

"Carnival," by Melton Prior (1888), featuring black revelers wearing whiteface and devil masks, and dressed as prostitutes and sailors. The "balloons" are bladders filled with water for dousing spectators. Courtesy of the Library of the University of the West Indies, St. Augustine, Trinidad.

*jamet* carnival was a classic ritual inversion in which, as Victor Turner wrote of carnival in Rio (1992:135), "whites dress down, and blacks dress up."

After 1850 carnival became even more "disreputable"—that is, further and further from the culture of respectability and closer and closer to that of reputation—and prompted repeated ineffectual attempts on the part of the administration to curb what in 1858 Governor Keate called "the noise, tumult and barbarian mirth which fill our streets every evening" in the weeks preceding carnival and during carnival itself. Clearly referring to *canboulay*, another worthy that year deplored "the fearful howling of a parcel of semisavages emerging God knows where from, exhibiting hellish scenes and the most demoniacal representations of the days of slavery as they were 40 years ago: then using the mask the two following days as a mere cloak for every species of barbarism and crime" (quoted in Pearse 1956a:187). The lighted torches, drums, and batons so essential to the *canboulay* ritual were banned in 1868 and again in

1880, a decision that led directly to the first Canboulay riots of 1881, when a force of 150 policemen under the redoubtable Captain Arthur Baker attempted to confiscate revelers' flambeaux and sustained extensive injuries in the process. Thanks to a pact between the governor and the leading batonniers, the carnival of 1882 passed off relatively quietly, but 1883 and 1884 saw further serious clashes both between bands of batonniers and between batonniers and police; two people were killed. Similar disturbances at San Fernando and Princes Town, combined with a major riot later in the year by East Indians at their Hosay festivity (see Singh 1988), caused the colonial administration to clamp down on lower-class public celebrations in general. Drumming was banned under the so-called Musical Ordinance of 1883, and the following year stickfighting and *canboulay* itself were officially suppressed, though both continued to be celebrated clandestinely. As a *caiso* of the early 1880s put it (Brereton 1979:162):

> Can't beat me drum
> In my own, my native land.
> Can't have we Carnival
> In my own, my native land.
> Can't have we Bacchanal
> In my own, my native land.
> In my own, my native land.

The way to the eventual "sanitizing" of carnival was open.

## Toward Respectability, 1884–1941

In the decade following the repressive measures of 1883–84, the colored middle class, led by a well-known "jacket-man" named Ignacio Bodu, combined with the colonial administration to bring carnival under control with such success that "after 1895 the grosser forms of obscenity so characteristic of the jamet Carnival were no longer possible; Carnival had been purged. The way was clear for the respectable classes to re-enter Carnival, and for the festival to develop slowly into a 'national' event" (Brereton 1979:173). In 1894 the so-called *pissenlit* bands (see below) were banned, as, interestingly, was cross-dressing, and after 1892 Pierrot Grenades were required to obtain an official permit before engaging in the extraordinary feats of verbal bravado that made them among the most feared and admired carnival masques. Carnival stabilized around a cast of relatively harmless conventional figures (Indians, bats, *moko jumbies* [stilt men], *djab djabs*, sailors, and midnight robbers), and "as carnival ruction decreased and its Dionysian elements were rendered more genteel, both masquerade and calypso became media in the expression of the culture and even the political values of the [colored middle class] elite" (Hill

The 1919 carnival in Port of Spain, featuring devil bats and midnight robber with skull. The chains may be an allusion of slavery or to the "chains of souls." Courtesy of Gerry Besson, Paria Publishing Company, Newtown, Trinidad, and the Library of the University of the West Indies, St. Augustine, Trinidad.

1993:63). But the old explosiveness had not entirely disappeared, and a riot of batonniers at Arouca in 1891 caused by an attempt by the police to confiscate drums revived deep-seated fears of carnival mayhem that the famous "water riots" at carnival time in 1903 did nothing to allay.[72] Above all, carnival, even in its "domesticated" form, was still capable of generating a vast amount of *noise*, the congo drums of the *jamet* carnival being succeeded after 1890 by the so-called tambou-bamboo bands deploying a whole range of improvised tuned percussion instruments (bamboo tubes of varying lengths, bottles partly filled with water and "played" with spoons, metal scrapers, and later biscuit tins, hubcaps, and brake blocks), which have rightly been regarded as the immediate forebears of the steel bands that would erupt into prominence after World War II.

After the "Victory Carnival" of 1919, there were signs of a growing split between "downtown" and "uptown" versions of carnival, the latter centered on

72. These serious disturbances, resulting in sixteen deaths, forty-four major injuries, and the burning down of the seat of government, the Red House, were prompted by proposals to install water meters and increase water rates (see Magid 1987:106–22). In the wake of the riots, protesters sang "Jour nous cay rivay" (Our day will come); see Liverpool 1990:43.

Queen's Park Savannah and increasingly motorized floats. But the threat of such polarization appears to have been overcome by the 1930s, allowing carnival to develop into something approaching a national festivity in which all the "creole" elements of society—Whites, Coloureds, Blacks—celebrated their shared Trinidadianness; the continued nonparticipation of East Indians was made all the more patent by this public, if somewhat deceptive, show of creole unity. The presence of numerous tourists and the filming (in 1932) of carnival for foreign consumption contributed to its increasing "officalization," and by the late 1930s its potentially explosive orgiastic element had been largely neutralized by the institution of a whole series of official competitions culminating in the first Calypso King contest in 1939. With the outbreak of World War II and the suspension of carnival after 1941, the subversive charge inherent in any such mass celebration had been successfully defused—or so it seemed—by the combined action of the colonial administration and the local bourgeoisie.

*Steel Bands, Black Power, and "Pretty Mas," 1945–1990*

It was surprising, therefore, that when carnival was resumed after a four-year interlude it emerged with its radical potential renewed and with a focus and expressive form more potent than anything since the stickfighters of the nineteenth century: the steel band. Biscuit-tin and dustbin "orchestras" had already been banned under an antinoise ordinance of 1941, and craftsmen-musicians had seized on the wartime arrival of huge numbers of oil drums for the American military base at Chaguaramas to perfect a form of percussion instrument at once more powerful and more sophisticated than anything that had gone before it. When, how, and by whom the art of tuning the steel drum was perfected—Winston "Spree" Simon, Ellie Manette, and "Fish-Eyes" Ollivierre all had their advocates as the inventor of "pan"—need not concern us here as much as the impact the steel bands had when, apparently out of nowhere, they emerged on to the public stage on VE Day (7 May 1945), "timidly at first," according to a report of the time (Anthony 1989:168), "as if not sure they were allowed on the street." Indeed they were not, and confrontations with the police ensued and would become a regular feature of carnivals in the immediate postwar period, notably in the so-called Belmont Riots of 1950, justifying Gordon Rohlehr's description (1990:369) of steel bands as "social organizations similar in form and function to the legendary stick-fighting bands of the nineteenth century." True to the agonic principle inseparable from carnival and from West Indian popular culture in general, the steel bands engaged in a real and symbolic combat not just with the police but with each other, resulting in a series of clashes that have entered into the *legenda aurea* of Trinidad carnival: Invaders versus Tokyo in 1950 (nine injured), Invaders versus Desperadoes and Stromboli versus Tropitone in 1953, Desperadoes (from Laventille) versus San Juan All Stars in 1959 (thirty injured), and Sunland (Belmont) versus Desperadoes in 1961. Even the introduction of an official steel band competition (Panorama) in 1963 could not prevent further clashes between Fascinators (Belmont) and Highlanders (Laventille) in 1965 and between Highlanders and Eastern Symphony (from San Juan) in 1968, when eleven people were injured and gunshots were fired (all details from Anthony 1989 under the years in question).

During the 1950s carnival became more and more a symbol of Trinidadian identity, embodying the protonationalist myth of "all of we is one" at a time when in reality relations between Creoles (Africans) and East Indians were becoming more and more troubled by the year. Although there was now some East Indian (and Chinese) participation in carnival, it remained an overwhelmingly Black-dominated event, and its virtual co-option by Eric Williams and his predominately black People's National Movement as the epitome of Trinidadianness when they came to power in 1956 merely underlined carnival's—and the party's—restrictive racial character (see Oxaal 1968 on this whole question). The carnival of 1957 was, in Michael Anthony's words (1989:259), "the first political Carnival Trinidad has ever known"—"political" in the narrow sense that it was used as a showcase for one particular political formation—and the setting up of the government-sponsored Carnival Development Committee that same year strengthened the links between party and festival, meaning that in the future any protest against the running of carnival would be construed, rightly or wrongly, as a direct or indirect protest against government. In part an antidote to political and ethnic rivalries (in the Trinidad of the late 1950s and early 1960s they were largely conterminous), carnival inevitably became a vehicle through which disgruntled individuals and groups could express their alienation.

Many of the carnival masquerades of the 1950s could be and were interpreted as anticolonial allegories (see below), and the disputes over federation and the advent of independence in 1963 added to the growing politicizing of carnival. After a brief honeymoon period, carnival began to reflect in some of its aspects the mounting disenchantment with independence, expressed above all through a passionate identification with "blackness" and "Africa" and through a parallel rejection of "whiteness" and all its works. In 1966 there were heavily overcoded masques depicting "Bad Days of Slavery" and "The Day of Massa"—a day that seemed much less "done" in 1966 than when Eric Williams had made his celebrated speech in Woodford Square just five years earlier— and by 1968, according to Anthony (1989:331), "the feeling for things African had seeped further into carnival." In 1969 no fewer than fifteen bands featured "African" masques with titles such as "Afromania '69," "Psychedelic Afro," "Great Faces of Africa," and "Tribute to Africa," and finally in 1970 carnival protests became a prelude and preparation for the serious disturbances that would erupt in its immediate aftermath. Explicitly political masques depicted "The Truth about Blacks" and the evils of "King Sugar" ("Black blood; black sweat; black tears—white profits" was its banner's uncompromising message); one band paraded in black jerseys and jeans and gave clenched-fist "black power" salutes; there were numerous placards of Malcolm X, Stokeley Carmichael, Huey Newton, and Eldridge Cleaver; Mighty Composer sang a calypso condemning the negative use of the word "black" in "blacklist," "blackmail," and "blackball"; and banners asked, "Who owns the stores?" and "Why press your hair?" and urged revelers to "Be proud to be an African" (see Anthony 1989:343–44 and Oxaal 1971:27–29). The much-attacked choice of a light-skinned competitor as Carnival Queen was further evidence of carnival's almost preternatural, if not always intended, capacity to seize on and dramatize the tensions and susceptibilities of Trinidadian society.[73]

After reaching a zenith in 1970, the politicizing of carnival (and correlatively of calypso) has, in the view of some but not all commentators,[74] steadily receded, in part as a result of government censorship but more profoundly because of the prosperity Trinidad enjoyed between 1973 and the early 1980s thanks to the explosion in world oil prices. More and more carnival appeared to be controlled and manipulated by the People's National Movement (PNM) government through the various forms of patronage at its disposal, and it seemed to one knowledgeable observer, the Trinidadian anthropologist John O. Stewart (1986:291), that "whereas in the past the festival construed an alternative context with reflexive and rebellious potentials, in recent times it has become more openly an extension of a moderating (modernizing) process central to the overall objectives of current political leadership." Under the aegis of the PNM, and more and more impelled by considerations of profit, carnival has, Stewart contends (309), "evolved into a grand spectator event" geared as much as the visitors—many of whom are Trinida-

---

73. The failure of dark-skinned competitors to win the Carnival Queen or Miss Trinidad titles was a constant source of controversy in Trinidad, exemplified in Attila's 1955 Calypso "Guardian Beauty Contest" (quoted in Rohlehr 1990:248–49).

> This Guardian competition
> Is nothing but real discrimination
> One thing in this world will never be seen
> Is a darkskinned girl as Carnival Queen.

The calypso concludes that, for "all the passion of this world" in black women's eyes, "yet is a flat-back white woman that get the prize." It seems that it was not until 1971 that a "charming Afro beauty" (Anthony 1989:350), Elicia Irish, was elected Carnival Queen: appropriately enough, she called her gown "Colour Freedom."

74. For a dissenting view, see Rohlehr 1985. At this time I have no information concerning the refraction in carnival and calypso of the Muslimeen uprising in Trinidad in July 1990.

dian-born[75]—as at "true true Trinnies" who, he claims (291), have tended in recent years to withdraw in significant numbers from active participation in carnival because of "a feeling of encroaching emptiness in the festival."[76] Correlatively, the more significant celebrations are allegedly abandoning the street in favor of theaters, tents, and ballrooms, leaving the street a site where the population at large—or that (diminishing?) proportion of it that still bothers to attend—*watch* others reveling rather than revel themselves. In short, as carnival mutates from a popular national festivity into an international post-modern extravaganza, the active masquerader of old is giving way to the passive spectator-consumer of today. Carnival has been exoticized and commodified for foreign consumption, and Trinidadians allegedly confront it as tourists in their own land, estranged from the very festivity that is supposed to embody the quintessence of what it is to be Trinidadian or even of what it is to be West Indian, or black.

The validity of this case must be left to Trinidadians to judge: some, but not perhaps many, would agree. It is certainly true, however, as we shall see, that carnival masques have, since the late 1970s, become markedly more "spectacular" or "theatrical" than ever before, leading to complaints among die-hard aficionados that "that ain't mas, that's theatre!" (Anthony 1989:436); or in the words of the most controversial of the modern designers of masques, "Carnival is Colour" before it is anything else.[77] Moreover, the view that Trinidadians were becoming increasingly alienated from carnival during the 1980s must be qualified, though it is not necessarily refuted, by the fact that the bands themselves were becoming bigger and bigger practically by the year: Irving McWilliams's spectacle "The Rains Come" of 1978 involved 4,500 participants, Edmund Hart's "Antony and Cleopatra" of 1982 had 3,200, and Peter Minshall's remarkable "Callaloo" of 1984 included over 4,000. But the overwhelming majority of these were women (see Anthony 1989:428, 437)—over 90 percent in the case of "Antony and Cleopatra"—leading to speculation that a fundamental mutation is occurring in the structure of carnival (and in the structure of the society of which carnival functions as a "magical mirror"). Namely, it seems that its public dimension, the street, is becoming more and more female-dominated while carnival traditionalists, mainly males, are more and more seeking out and taking part in inner-oriented events and activities: a more comprehensive inversion of the "Crab Antics" dialectic of male/outside:female/inside could not be imagined.[78] As we have seen, many observers,

75. On the attachment of "salt-water Trinnies" to carnival, see Ho 1991:123–26.

76. According to Stewart 1986:309–10, many Trinidadians now watch carnival only on television, shun the main festival in favor of local street parties, or go to the beach, Barbados, or Miami, depending on resources, in an effort to avoid the omnipresence of "mas."

77. "Carnival is Colour" was the title of Peter Minshall's winning design of 1987.

78. This whole section is strongly influenced by Miller 1990, reprinted in Miller 1991:110–25.

both in Trinidad and in Jamaica, have commented on the increasingly osten-
tatious eroticism of the female dancing style known as "wining" or "waining,"
on the fact that women more and more dance alone or with each other (an
expression, Miller believes of autosexuality, not homosexuality), and that
"wining is seen more as a threat than as an invitation by men" (Miller
1994:123–24). Moreover, a new sense of women's power and aggression is
also found in typical female calypsos of the 1980s: Denyse Plummer's "Woman
Is Boss," Twiggy's "Don't Put Yuh Hand on Meh Property," and Tambu's "Yes,
Darling," in which a woman replaces her unemployed partner as breadwinner
and "Each day as a rule, she have Tommy working like a mule"—washing and
ironing (but not cooking) in the house—and "When ah say, clean dey, you
either do it, or go yuh way" (Mohammed 1991:39). Perhaps a social revolution
as profound as that of emancipation was beginning to manifest itself in carnival and elsewhere as Trinidadian women, pushed to the margins of carnival
after 1884, apparently regained, more or less exactly a century later, the central position of their infamous and illustrious forebears: Boadicea, Myrtle the
Turtle, and Long Body Ada.

## Metamorphoses of the Masque, 1838–1990

As we have seen, the "aristocratic carnival" of the old French creole elite
added at least one important masque[79]—the *nèg jardin*—to the repertoire of
figures it inherited from the French carnival tradition, and this the ex-slaves
took over and turned to their own purposes when they systematically appropriated carnival in the years after 1838.[80] It does not appear, however, that the
pre-1884 *jamet* carnival gave great prominence to individualistic masques, and
Pearse (1956a:186) is right to stress the absence from Day's account of the
1848 carnival of almost all of the most characteristic figures of the late nineteenth-century carnival. Centered on *canboulay* and stickfighting, the *jamet* carnival seems to have embodied the principle of "grotesque realism" that, for
Bakhtin, is the very stuff of carnival, what Stallybrass and White (1986:8) call
"a world of topsy turvy, of heteroglot exuberance, of ceaseless overrunning
and excess where all is mixed, hybrid, ritually degraded and defiled." Thus we
learn of a kind of pantomime called Dame Lorraine that first parodied the
dances of the old elites as the legendary *nèg dèyè pòtla* peered in amazement
through a window and then switched to a schoolroom scene in which a whip-
wielding schoolmaster (a pedagogical version of Massa himself?) attempted to

79. On the distinction between "masque" (pronounced "mas") and "mask" in Trinidad, see
Crowley 1956a:194.
80. This discussion of pre-1945 masques is based primarily on Crowley 1956a and Hill 1985.
The latter article contains (29–34) a particularly valuable catalog of the traditional masques, with a
chronology of when they are first attested.

control an unruly bunch of "pupils" whose bulging Bunteresque forms and Rabelaisian names—Misié Gwo Koko, Ma Gwo Bunda, Gwo Patat, Gwo Boudin, and such[81]—gave a creole twist to the "grotesque body" tradition of European carnival.[82] Similarly, the *pissenlit* (piss-a-bed) bands first recorded in 1858 featured body fluids and protuberances on a grand scale. Men dressed as women, or rather they undressed, for the standard "costume" was often no more than a flimsy nightdress or a menstrual cloth liberally daubed with "blood," and engaged in a variety of sexual antics with a poui stick protruding between the legs: needless to say, such bawdy transvestism did not long survive the post-1884 clampdown.

These two masques apart, the only other figures recorded before 1884 are fairly predictable: clowns, Indians, ghosts, sailors, prostitutes (*matadors* or *jamettes*), lawyers, judges, criminals and convicts, Zulus and Chinese—conventional "European" figures, then, though no doubt treated with distinctive creole *picong*. It is only after 1884 that "indigenous" masques begin to be recorded: no doubt they existed before, but amid the hurly-burly and the violence of *canboulay* and *bataille bois* they lacked the weight to attract the attention of the chroniclers. Now, with stickfighting banned, they came to the fore, and just as many ex-batonniers took over *caiso* from the chantwells, so perhaps others appropriated what had previously been second-rank carnival masques to act out the aggressive roles that stickfighting could no longer express. Thus a masque called Pierrot is first recorded in 1886, but so different was he from the commedia dell'arte figure of that name that Carr (1956:283) was almost certainly right to suggest that "Pierrot" is a false rendering of Creole *pay-wa* (country king) and that as such he linked up with and continued the tradition of the "kalinda king." Not only did he dress like a batonnier with a heart-shaped velvet breastpiece adorned with sequins and mirrors and an iron pot on his head, but he brandished a lead-lined fighting whip and confronted rival Pierrots with all the aggression and verbal bravado of a stickman. Physical aggression was systematically channeled into language as Pierrot vaunted his prowess as a warrior ("I am the King of Dahomey, but I also rule over many countries that I have conquered. Do you now visit my dominions to offer your subjugation, or do you come as an enemy to dispute my rule?" quoted in Carr 1956:282) and fired questions about British, European, and classical history at his opponents to unsettle them and humiliate them in public. Clearly, though, Pierrot's braggadocio sometimes went beyond verbal fireworks and excruciating general knowledge tests, for in 1896 he was required to obtain a license to perform his act and to leave a deposit of five pounds

81. Respectively Mr. Big Cock, Mrs. Big Arse, Fat Cunt, and Thick Prick.

82. That Dame Lorraine parodied the indoor activities of the elite may explain why it itself was performed indoors at midnight on carnival Sunday, the masques spilling out on to the streets on *jouvay* morning.

against good behavior; it was not enough to save him from enforced extinction between the wars.

Pierrot was succeeded by a somewhat milder small-island variant, Pierrot Grenade (first recorded 1923) whose carnival forte was posing and answering impossible spelling tests and charadelike conundrums that involved splitting words into syllables and switching them around or replacing them with others in a manner that seems to portend the Rastafarian with his Inity, overstand, and downpression or the rapper with his coruscating chains of phonemes. He too seems not to have survived World War II, but the man-of-words tradition is maintained to this day by the Midnight Robbers (1919) who, using aliases such as Machine Gun Kelly, Cyrano de Bergerac, King Grabbeler, Tucson Wayo (apparently a conflation of "Toussaint" and "Cetewayo"!), and Pizarro Selkirk Pattergonia, insult and challenge passers-by in familiar mock bellicose fashion and relieve them—ludically, of course—of their valuables.[83] Other masques, many of them now extinct, or almost so, deserve at least passing mention: the stiltman *moko jumbie* (1895); Barbadian cooks (1910), apparently a great favorite among white Trinidadians; Bad Behavior Sailors (1912), sometimes seen with long elephantine trunks, with enamel chamber pots fastened to their wrists or, after World War II, with elaborate headdresses representing gun turrets, complete with moving guns; *djab djabs* (1915) whose mirror- and swansdown-decorated costumes and leather carriage whips (once used to savage the costumes of rival *djab djab* bands) seem to link up with the batonniers and Pierrots of old; and *djab molassi* (1919), who, smeared from top to toe with stale molasses, tar, grease, creosote, or mud, "dance a fast version of 'winin' through the streets, threatening to touch the beautiful costumes of other masques or the clean clothes of by-standers unless they give [them] money" (Crowley 1956a:214). Finally, in rather different mode, even the most cursory chronicle of mas' should recall the individual masqueraders who for many years delighted Trinidadians with their own distinctly personal creations,

---

83. On midnight robbers, see Crowley 1956b and Wüst 1990, which valuably reproduces a number of robber speeches such as the following (47–48): Hark, hark you scrums of de earth, you twoheaded serpents, you dog of a Saxon: Stand back, for it was written in de Book of Midnight Robber that all mock men as you should be buried alive. Away down from de high class regions from de phantom graveyard comes I, de indominable son of de impregnable incredible. My name is King Grabbla, who grabbed de sun, moon and stars, created darkness, bite bits with my ivory teeth and chew, shorten de season, feeds upon wasps. At de age of one, my renowned compound was too strong for human constitution where I was placed into prison for ninety-nine years: a reward of nine thousand nine hundred and ninety-nine dollars was all for my discovery. There I studied crime-words and punishment for all mockmen as you. As de dawn of morn has just begin to illuminate de oriental horizon it seem to me as though you want to make a perfect getaway—hark, it is too late. For dese two hypnotical and magical eyes of mine have already doomed your position. At de age of two, I killed my great grandmother Izumbuma; at de age of three I drowned my mother Cecilia into a spoonful of water. So stand back mockman and tell me if it is your cowardice or bravity dat cause you to travel into dis dismal track.

above all Wilfred Strasser, whose One Penny (1948), Abraham Lincoln (1949), William Shakespeare (1951), and Humming-Bird (1958) are still remembered for their punctilious realism by aficionados of a certain age.

Although some of these traditional masques still survive, there can be no doubt that, especially since World War II, and still more since the late 1970s, the central focus of carnival has shifted more and more in the direction of the so-called historical and fantasy bands that, as we have seen, can now include literally thousands of participants. These bands had their origins in the early 1900s but did not come to the fore until the 1930s, when they took the form of parades of warriors, courtiers, and other martial, exotic, or aristocratic figures drawn, usually via the school textbook, from the classical, medieval, or imperial past: Nubians, Caliphs, Knights of the Round Table, Bedouin Chiefs, Philistine Warriors, Arabian Sheiks, Terros of the Sahara, Ancient Britons, Nebuchadnezzar and His Followers, Moorish Invaders 711 A.D., Hungarian Gypsies, Captain Morgan and His Buccaneers, Oliver Cromwell and His Ironsides, and so on and on and on.[84] No doubt it would be possible to see in this farrago of European-derived orientalist and medievalist themes evidence of the alienation of the Trinidadian "mimic man" of the interwar years: no less striking, though, is the preoccupation with power and rank that the masqueraders could be appropriating symbolically through mimesis. After World War II, the bands became larger and their presentations more stylish, extravagant, and meaningful, with—inevitably, for this is carnival—a strong spirit of competition arising among the locality-based bands and their increasingly professionalized designers. It would be possible, given some squeezing of the evidence, to see in the great contests of the late 1950s between the bands of Harold Saldenha and "Sir" George Bailey a symbolic reenactment of the struggle between "imperialist" and "anti-imperialist" images of West Indian history from which, on almost every occasion, the "anti-imperialist" Bailey emerged victorious: "The Glory That Was Greece" (Saldenha) versus "Back to Africa" (Bailey) in 1957, "Holy War" (Saldenha) versus "Of Pagan History" (Bailey) in 1958 and "Cree Indians of Canada" (Saldenha) versus "Relics of Egypt" (Bailey) in 1959.[85] Appropriately enough, the 1962 carnival featured a masque dressed as the governor-general carrying a placard that read "Lord Hailes seeing his last Carnival" (Anthony 1989:296).

Designers such as George Bailey prepared the way for the still more explicitly political masques of the late 1960s and early 1970s, when the choice

84. List compiled more or less at random from the entries on the interwar years in Anthony 1989.

85. Not too much should be made of such readings, for in 1960 Bailey's presentation was titled "Ye Saga of Merrie England" and featured Vikings, Romans, King Arthur, Robin Hood, and Saint George slaying the dragon. For an interesting if not entirely convincing "anti-imperialist" reading of Saldenha's "Imperial Rome" of 1955, see Wüst 1993:153–54.

of Band of the Year made by the official judges was frequently at variance with the "People's Choice" that had been institutionalized since 1959. As the political (and racial) tensions of 1966–72 relaxed, some commentators discerned a shift toward apolitical presentations that gave more or less unlimited scope to the fertile imaginations of a new generation of directors: Irving McWilliams, Edmund Hart, Stephen Lee Heung, and above all Peter Minshall, who between them evolved the "pretty mas'" style that has so antagonized carnival purists. Mas' gravitated perceptibly from the Dionysiac to the Apollonian, from the "grotesque body" of the *jamet* carnival that still survived vestigially in figures such as the *djab molassi* to the "classical body" apotheosized in a succession of productions by Peter Minshall and others in the 1980s. Yet if they were "apolitical," such productions were not necessarily without content, and Minshall in particular attracted both praise and obloquy for "allegorical" extravaganzas such as "Mancrab" (1983),[86] "Callaloo" (1984), and "Rat Race" (1986). Whatever else, it was clear by the mid-1980s that carnival was no longer controlled, if it had ever been, by "the people" but was increasingly the creation—and creature—of powerful designers and the economic forces that backed them, with still farther in the background a government still greatly preoccupied, as recession followed boom, with the question of public order and its own threatened survival. Both questions would come to a head in the Muslimeen uprising—a carnivalesque happening if ever there was one—of July 1990.[87]

## Subverting the Subverters: Order and Rebellion in Trinidad Carnival

Nowhere have the ambivalences of Trinidad carnival been explored with greater profundity and poignancy than in Earl Lovelace's 1979 novel *The Dragon Can't Dance*. Centered on a popular district of Port of Spain named, with heavy symbolism, Calvary Hill, the novel brings together a group of Afro-Trinidadian characters whose lives are poised, often none too firmly, at

86. At the risk of exceeding readers' credence, I suggest that Mancrab has, beneath its "official" environmental message, an unconscious subtext referring to the tension between the culture of reputation represented—how better?—by the Crab and the culture of respectability represented by Queen Washerwoman. On the Monday of carnival, Queen Washerwoman defeated Mancrab "with a soft white cloth, the white representing the purity of the river" and her allies, the white-clad River People, "celebrate by swirling across the stage, tossing white tinsel into the air" (Anthony 1989:436). On the following day, however, Mancrab gained his revenge, killing Queen Washerwoman and defiling the river with her blood, and then danced a manic dance of victory—"crab antics," indeed—all the time "issuing red umbilicus from his gut to symbolize the birth to a new dark age" (Nunley 1988:108).

87. On the Muslimeen uprising, see Ryan 1991. To describe the uprising as carnivalesque is not to deny its seriousness—after all, carnival itself *is* serious—but to underline its character as a real, if short-lived (four days, like carnival), turning of the world on its head. Ironically, the uprising collapsed on 1 August, Emancipation Day Holiday.

"Mancrab," the centerpiece of the 1983 carnival in Port of Spain. The multiarmed monster, designed and created by Peter Minshall, symbolizes the destructive power of technology. At a critical stage in the parade, blood-red dye slowly spread across the white silk canopy that surmounts the masque. Photo by Norton Studios Ltd., Port of Spain, Trinidad. Reproduced by permission of Peter Minshall.

different points along the continuum of respectability:reputation/inside:outside so often encountered in this chapter.[88] Unambiguously aligned with the reputation pole—termed "warriorhood" in the novel—are the badjohn Fisheye and his companions, whose lives are focused on the Corner, which, in Port of Spain of the late 1950s and 1960s is less the "battlefield" it had been in the immediate postwar period "than a haven, and more than a haven a vantage point, a podium from which they might view the Hill travelling up and down its main street" (Lovelace 1985:166). At the opposite pole, though not fully coinciding with it, is Miss Cleothilde, Spiritual Baptist and shopkeeper but also a former queen of the Calvary Hill band, who "lords it" over the other characters year-round and then at carnival time attempts to "become one with the yard," putting on a "friendly-friendly thing" and exclaiming at every opportunity, "Bacchanal! Trinidad! All o' we is one" (33–36). In general, all the female characters in the novel are closer than their male counterparts to the respectability pole, though there are complications and ambiguities: the rent collector Guy clearly aspires to that pole, though this does not prevent him from attempting to seduce the seventeen-year-old beauty Sylvia, who is torn between the respectability-oriented values of her mother and Miss Cleothilde and the values of the street as embodied in carnival. Poised at some median point on the continuum is the aging calypsonian Philo, son of a Spiritual Baptist mother and a failed musician father, who craves success as a singer in order to establish himself in society. Somewhere between him and the Corner society of Fisheye is Aldrick, the dragon dancer of the title,[89] who has a heavy emotional investment in carnival. He is increasingly skeptical of its value(s), however, and as well as being drawn to the world of the badjohn, he is critical of those—like Sylvia, whom he both desires and resists—who are drawn toward the values of respectability and whom he considers traitors both to themselves and to the Hill as a whole. The full continuum, then, is as shown below.

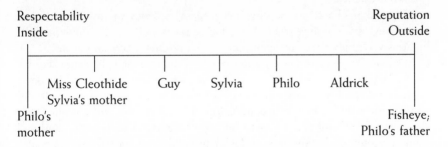

88. The important East Indian characters, Pariag and his wife, Dolly, are not included in this discussion.

89. The dragon masque is first attested in 1906 and formed a vital part of the devil bands that by the 1920s had become the most popular of all bands. As early as 1956, however, its popularity was said to be "at low ebb" (Procope 1956:280).

Except for Philo's mother at one extreme and his father and Fisheye at the other, all the characters are in flux, torn between the conflicting demands of "inside" and "outside," and it is this that generates both the action of the novel and its very considerable interest to my theme.

Carnival itself embraces the whole spectrum of positions from respectability to "warriorhood." For Miss Cleothilde, as for most of the middle class and the upwardly mobile, carnival represents the mythical ideal of "all o' we is one": an affair of three or four days, it is readily reconciled with the values of respectability that hold good for the rest of the year. At the opposite extreme, Fisheye, the son of a stickfighter-turned-preacher, and the "flagbearers of a disappearing warriorhood" (166) who cling to him in their despair, view carnival as a ritual of rebellion, an uncompromising refusal of the values of respectability, family, and work to which, Aldrick apart, all the other characters aspire, for all their misgivings about reneging on their origins in the Hill. Fisheye identifies with the "warrior carnival" of the years immediately after the war when he led the Calvary Hill steel band into battle against rivals like Red Army, Hell Yard, Desperadoes, and Tokyo, and he cannot accept the "domestication" of carnival that has since occurred in the form of commercial sponsorship, the replacement of *real* battles between steel bands by the sublimated contests of Panorama and the like, and the rise of bands with names like Merry Boys and Dixie Land that, manned by "well-off, light-skinned boys from prosperous families and good schools," and "helping to make steelband respectable" (77). In their obdurate refusal of change, Fisheye and his associates embody the old rebellious past—"We is the last ones, the last fuckin' warriors," says the badjohn (179)—from which the generality of the Hill's denizens are guiltily turning away in favor of moving onward, outward, and upward in life.[90] For them Fisheye and the Corner represent what they fear most, but also their *mauvaise conscience* at abandoning the folkways of their rebellious forebears.

The other characters occupy, once again, a series of interim positions between Miss Cleothilde and Fisheye, facing (as does Miss Cleothilde herself) first this way, then that. For Sylvia carnival represents "a scream for life" (141), a chance to "leap out of herself into her self, a self in which she could stay for ever, in which she could *be* for ever." During carnival her "whole self" becomes "a shout, a brawl, a cry, a scream, a cyclone of tears rejoicing in a self and praying for a self to live in beyond Carnival and her slave girl costume." But she is also unwilling and afraid to let go of the world of respectability and status represented by the rent collector-turned-lawyer-turned-city councillor Guy, whom she eventually agrees, with reservations, to marry—at the cost, in

90. Socially upward means physically downward, for, as Derek Walcott says in "Laventille" (1965:32), "To go downhill from here was to ascend."

Aldrick's eyes and also in her own, of betraying both her "true self" and the world of the Hill that she comes from. The failed calypsonian Philo decides to use music as a passport to status and wealth, and abandoning the "rebellious" political calypsos that have failed to win him a prize, he composes a cliché-ridden phallocratic calypso "The Axe Man" that, chiming in with the new public taste, duly propels him to fame and fortune. Rejected by Fisheye and his band as a traitor to "true" carnival, he composes another calypso denouncing their hooliganism that becomes a "statement" for those Hill dwellers who want to cut all ties with the Corner; it is also, comments the narrator, "the epitaph to their rebellion" (178).

Aldrick, the most complex character in the book, is left facing all directions at once. In the manner of Fisheye, he sees his dragon masque as "the last symbol of rebellion and threat to confront Port of Spain," about to be lost, along with the *djab djabs* and Pierrots that had been "outlawed from the city," "among the fancy robbers and the fantasy presentations that were steadily entering Carnival, drowned amidst the satin and silks and the beads and feathers and rhinestones." Still more distressing is "the thought that maybe he didn't believe in the dragon any more" (135). Painfully aware that "the power of the Dragon even to threaten was coming to an end" (178), Aldrick is in a spiritual, social, and existential vacuum. A substitute for the parents he has lost, the job he has never had, and the child he has never fathered, the dragon represents the only "personhood" (50) he has: "He was a hustler, working nowhere; and the only responsibility he was prepared to bear now was to his dragon, that presentation on Carnival day of the self that he had lived the whole year" (58). But his dragon self is becoming as empty and meaningless as his "real" self, and after a final desperate carnival performance designed to prove to the Hill dwellers (and himself) that "You is people, people. People is you, people!" he decides to abandon his dragon masque for good. He confesses to Philo just before his farewell dance that "I playing a masquerade every year, and I forget what I playing it for, what I trying to say, I forget" (124), and he wonders, as the kings and princesses drift away after the end of carnival, "What of those selves? What of the selves of these thousands? What of his own self?" (139).

In the hope of recovering that self and "the self of the people" (137), Aldrick drifts toward the Corner and toward Fisheye and his would-be "warriors," who are becoming more and more contemptuous of the "respectable" Hill dwellers who pass them on their way to and from work and more and more aggressive toward the police who are called in to restrain them. "Promoted" by Fisheye "to a kind of lieutenant in the small guerrilla band that was not so much guerrilla as the last remains of a defeated army" (178), Aldrick takes part in a deliberately engineered confrontation with the police that escalates into a parodic attempt at a revolutionary coup, with the Calvary Hill

Nine, as the press dubs them, careering around Port of Spain by car with their police hostages trying to provoke "the people" into action. Armed with a megaphone, Aldrick discovers in himself unsuspected talents as a political man-of-words as, in the name of the "People's Liberation Army," he urges "our people to rise, rise up and take theyself over; take over Laventille, Calvary Hill, Belmont, take over John John, St. James, Morvant, take power and rise to be people for our own self, take power, take Pow-er! Pow-er! Pow-er!" (189). Yet not only to "our people" fail to "rise up," still more humiliatingly, the police do not even bother to confront them, knowing as they do that the People's Liberation Army's *attentat* is absurd and will perish of its own lack of momentum. The Nine are eventually arrested and sentenced to stiff terms in jail, and Aldrick recognizes that "they wanted to destroy us in our own eyes. They wanted to kill rebellion in us, to show us that even with no police to stop us we couldn't do nutten" (199). As their defense lawyer says, they were "unable to make their frustration anything better than a dragon dance, a threatening gesture" (197), which does not prevent the die-hard warrior Fish-eye from proudly declaring that "we play a mas', eh? We really play a mas'." To which Aldrick retorts: "Even with guns in we hand, even with power, we was looking to somebody else to make a decision. . . . Even when we have power, when we have guns. Is like we ain't have no self. I mean, we have a self but the self we have is for somebody else. Is like even when we acting we ain't the actor. Know what I mean? Eh?" (200–202). Carnival, it turns out, is not revolutionary because, for all its empty ethos of "all o' we is one," the values it upholds are ultimately individualistic and spontaneous, not collective and or-ganized and, as Fisheye finally recognizes, "Alone, all a man could do is play a mas" (205). Carnival requires of its masquerades, dancers, and singers only that they be *"role* serious, not real serious" (245), whence the failure of the Calvary Hill Nine, like all the *jamets* and *jamettes*, batonniers, badjohns, dragons, Pierrots, *djab djabs*, panmen, and calypsonians who went before them to "make some dent in the real world" (76). Alas, carnival, like poetry, "makes nothing happen."[91]

And so the novel's "verdict" on carnival (and with it our own) is double-edged in the extreme. On the one hand, the "system" seems to have found a way of "subverting the potential subverters' (Scheper-Hughes 1992:483) by taking over carnival, sponsoring it, and thereby neutralizing any *real* threat to its survival by giving the people's frustrations a licensed imaginary outlet: as Georges Balandier once wrote, "the supreme ruse of power is to allow itself to be contested *ritually* in order to consolidate itself more effectively" (quoted in

---

91. The reference is to W. H. Auden's "In Memory of W. B. Yeats": "For poetry makes nothing happen."

Stallybrass and White 1986:14).[92] On the other hand, the powerful cannot *always* be sure they have diverted the powerless from their frustrations, as Eric Williams discovered at the time of the Trinidadian "Black Power" disturbances in February–March 1970 when he reputedly urged his entourage "not to worry, just give dem a little fete, a little 'pan-on-de-road' and dey will quiet down" (quoted in Ho 1991:98). And as we shall see in the chapter that follows, it was by no means fortuitous that the final collapse of Duvalierism took place in February 1986 against the background of carnival. Yet again, Williams was ultimately able to divide and absorb the challenge to his power with a little more stress, it is true, than it took to defeat the Calvary Hill Nine, and in Haiti Duvalierism survived without Duvalier, in one form or another, for eight more years: nothing, it seems, is easier to contain or deflect than a carnival-born(e) opposition movement. Similarly, despite Miss Cleothilde's endless "all o' we is one," the world of Calvary Hill remains divided against itself—Creoles against East Indians, men against women, the better-off and respectable against *jamets* and badjohns—as well as against other poor neighborhoods in the city, to say nothing of middle-class districts like Diego Martin and Queen's Park. In reality, carnival has sometimes exacerbated Creole/East Indian relations as much as it has eased them,[93] and whatever (limited) fraternization takes places on the streets, the fact remains that

> When Ash Wednesday come and pass
> The people does go back to dey race and class
> So the only thing that keep dem together is mas.
>     (Lord Valentino, quoted in Liverpool 1990:22)

Finally, until the marked "feminization" of mas' in the past fifteen years, it could be said of Trinidad carnival, as Nancy Scheper-Hughes has said of carnival in Bom Jesus da Mata (1992:491), that it is "largely designed for the pleasure of men and boys. The 'female' [is] liberated but only . . . for the purpose of titillating male fantasies of sexual abundance and erotic abandon." Whether the advent of female calypsonians and "wining" is "real serious" or only "role serious" remains to be seen.

So what is left? Perhaps only the infinite fragility of the masques, made still more beautiful by the night that surrounds them and the ashes they will be reduced to, and above all the dance: not so much the dragon dance, fine

92. Cf. Abner Cohen's assessment of the Notting Hill carnival in London (1993:132): "Carnival is a cultural mechanism expressing, camouflaging and alleviating a basic structural conflict between the state and the citizen."

93. As, for example, in 1979, when Black Stalin's calypso "Caribbean Man" precipitated a major controversy over whether the title included or excluded West Indians of non-African origin (see Deosaran 1987 and Warner 1993).

though that is, as Sylvia's Dance against Death.[94] That "scream for life" convulses the whole of her being and proclaims "a humanness unlinked to the possession of any goods or property" (165), a self in which she wishes she could stay forever but that, by definition, will be taken from her when carnival ends. And so, clad in her slave girl's costume she dances, the sister and daughter of all those slave women who danced and wined in the "plays" of the past, and whether she ends up in middle-class Diego Martin married to Guy the councillor or living with Aldrick the failed mas' man and rebel up on the Hill or somewhere else entirely, it matters not in the least, for at least once in her life she will have become the self that was her dance, in the full glory of her Afro-Creole humanness. And this neither death, marriage, nor above all Dr. Williams can ever take away from her.

94. I have taken this expression from the title of Scheper-Hughes's chapter on carnival in *Death without Weeping* (1992:480).

# 5

# Masquerade, Possession, and Power
# in the Caribbean

Toward the end of a life devoted to understanding ritual, Victor Turner wrote several essays, collected and published posthumously as *The Anthropology of Performance* (1987), concerning the analogies between carnival and the various possession cults, primarily Umbanda, that he had been able to observe firsthand in Rio de Janeiro. Both carnival and cult are said to exemplify what Turner suggestively calls "the subjunctive mood of culture" (1992:59): "its mood of feeling, willing and desiring, its mood of fantasizing, *its playful mood;* not its indicative mood, when it tries to apply reason to human action and systematize the relationship between ends and means in industry and bureaucracy" (123; italics added). Carnival and cult offer their followers—who in cities like Rio and Bahia are commonly the same—a "rich subjunctive compensation for the limited scope of their indicative lives" (68). Both are liminal institutions, "entertainments" in the literal sense (41) in that they take place *between* rather than completely outside the established structures of society that they ritualistically—that is, ludically—turn on their heads in the form of "fictitious or pseudo-hierarchies" (59) such as the Bahian *Congados* or *Rei do Congo* (not mentioned by Turner), a festive pageant "portraying a royal court of the King of the Congo, complete with richly-dressed king, queen, dukes, counts, ambassadors, warriors, and female courtiers, who parade and dance" (see Crowley 1984:16). If the Umbandist *terreiro* (temple) is a "liminal, space-time 'pod' in which [cultists] can distance themselves from immersion in the status-role structures of the present by identification with gods, ancestors, and traditions of African roots" (Turner 1992:55), so by extension the whole city becomes a *terreiro* writ large at carnival time as the masquerader, a secular version, as it were, of the Umbandist "ridden" by a guardian spirit, becomes one with his or her *fantasia* or carnival role or disguise. Thus it is that cult and carnival interpenetrate as ways of transcending, expanding, or multiplying the self, the first through trance and vertigo and the simulation of the spirits, the second as mimicry, theater, and disguise, to create a childlike condition (130) in which, in a world oblivious of original sin (137), antistructure or communitas reigns supreme before society finally returns to its indicative mood at the end of the ritual or on Ash Wednesday morning.

The continuity between possession cult and carnival and the ludic, theatrical, and agonic character of both is demonstrated in that, at carnival in Bahia (not discussed by Turner, whose focus is Rio), many *grêmios* or carnival societies are in effect extensions of local Candomblé nago *terreiros*, with many masqueraders dressing in the traditional costumes of the *orixás* (Crowley 1984:13–14), so much so that Bahians speak of carnival as *Candomblé de brincadeira* (Candomblé for fun), prompting Mikelle Smith Okari (1984:26) to write that "Carnival is a Candomblé without trance or possession by the Orixá" and Sheila Walker (1991:107) to describe it quite simply as "candomblé in the streets." But if carnival is "Candomblé for fun," Candomblé and similar cults of possession are always, at some deep level, fun in themselves, and it is not for nothing that one *iyalorixá* (priestess) uses the expression "when the Candomblé is playing" to describe the ceremonies in her *terreiro* and that dancers exclaim "A xiré Ogun o" ("We play for Ogun") as they wait for the warrior-*orixá* to come down and possess them (Murphy 1994:65–66, 69). *Xiré*, meaning "play," "gala," or "party" in Yoruba, lies at the very heart of Candomblé, enabling initiates to "be 'onstage' and the focus of attention for a time," "to outdo 'sisters' or fellow initiates with their display," and in general to enjoy "an opportunity for aesthetic and theatrical display" (Okari 1984:25) that their "indicative lives," to return to Turner's expression, probably rarely if ever afford them. Whether it be Candomblé, Santería, Vodou, or the East African Zâr cult, possession, I. M. Lewis has written (1971:196), is always in some sense "a kind of 'game.'"

As well as always being "play" in the profound Afro-Creole sense of the word, possession always involves play in the sense of simulation and acting, and the continuities between possession and theater have been illuminatingly explored by a number of writers, beginning with Nietzsche's tracing the origins of Greek tragedy to Dionysiac cults of possession. In 1958 the French poet, autobiographer, and anthropologist Michel Leiris published a pathbreaking study of the Ethiopian Zâr cult in which he argued that the spirits of the cult resemble theatrical "characters," each with its individual history, personality traits, appearance, and costume defined by tradition. Having "dispossessed" the cultists of their personal selves, these spirits use them as mediums or—to use the term found in almost every cult of possession—as "horses" through which to manifest themselves publicly to the living, speaking to them to chide, warn, comfort, and advise, and acting out the "parts" or "roles" custom assigns to them. Spirits are thus "figures belonging, properly speaking, to the domain of the theatre" endowed with "an openly spectacular allure," with the adepts through whom they manifest themselves" "playing the role of actors (*baladins*) exhibiting themselves to the crowd" (Leiris 1958:8–9). Possession is intrinsically theatrical because it "consists objectively in the figuration of a mythical or legendary character by a human actor" (100) and as such raises the question, which Leiris explores with great subtlety, of how far the state of possession is consciously willed and artfully crafted by the adept-performer and how far it happens "spontaneously" without the active collaboration of the cultist concerned. Building on Leiris's insights, Gilbert Rouget, in his magisterial study of the role of music in possession, stresses (1985:118) that "the very existence of possession cults requires that possession be public behavior," and that since possession "consists in a change of identity" that would be "meaningless if it were not recognized by the group," it follows that by definition "possession cannot function without becoming theater" (325). Possession, then, is a triadic phenomenon involving a spirit, a "horse," and spectators who may at some point in the proceedings be "ridden" themselves. It is public, mimetic, and other directed, a creation of music and dance and changes of costume, expression, and voice, founded above all on the belief that something *will* happen, that the spirit *will* appear. In short it is "Supreme Theatre," as Fernando Ortiz (quoted in Simpson 1978:94) wrote of the Cuban festival Abakuá in which, in a way quintessentially Afro-Creole, cult and carnival fuse as one.

This chapter takes up the insights of Turner, Leiris, Rouget, and others into the links between possession and theater and applies them to a range of Afro-Creole possession cults—principally but not exclusively Haitian Vodou—and seeks to link these in their turn to the dialectic of inside and outside (and, correlatively, of "female" and "male," respect and reputation) explored in the previous chapter. But it also seeks, rather more tentatively, to do more: to link the phenomenon of possession to the experience of slavery, colonialism, and the politics of the postcolonial Caribbean, to see what goes on in *hounfor, palais,* or balmyard as some kind of microcosm or "magical mirror" of the relation of the powerless to power, and of power to the powerless, in the Caribbean experience as a whole. For whether it is the power of the slavemaster, the colonial apparatus, or the charismatic political leader in the "independent" Caribbean, power, as we have seen, always *descends*, like the spirits, onto the powerless below. It may empower them—for a time—but it does so only by dispossessing them of themselves and filling them with a power that, since it is other and originates elsewhere, can be taken away as quickly and as easily as it was bestowed. The first four sections that follow deal with the interlocking questions of possession, theater, hierarchy, and power insofar as they relate to carnival and cult from slave times to the present. Progressively the images of the whip and the rod, already encountered in Jamaican electoral politics, combine with that of the Vodou spirit Ogou's double-edged sword to embody the fundamental ambivalence of power in the West Indian context, and the chapter concludes by showing how the structures of the slave plantation have fed into those of popular religion to form the highly authoritarian matrix of politics in the region from which, I argue, the Caribbean is only now beginning to emerge.

## From the Inside to the Outside: Vodou and Rara in Haiti

If, as Leiris, Rouget and others have argued, possession is before all else a *theatrical* event,[1] it should follow that the venue where possession takes place must be in some way theaterlike in its structure. That is, it is set apart from the "profane" world of society in some "sacred" space of its own and at the same time open, in theory, to all comers and not just to the regular cultists or performers. This is certainly true in the case of Candomblé, where, Mikelle Smith Okari writes in an essay from which this section takes its title (1984: 17), crossing the threshold of the *terreiro* brings "a sense of leaving urban openness and entering a rural, cloistered space"[2] in which the cult area itself is segmented into "private" and "public" domains—an inner sanctum where cult objects are stored and where the most secret rituals of initiation take place and the *barracão* where public rites of possession are celebrated and where there are banks of seats for spectators, men on the left of the public entrance, women on the right, and raised platforms set aside for drummers, for initiates, and for the *iyalorixá* (priestess) and her "court." Though usually far less elaborate, the "temples" of both Vodou and Shango conform to the same basic pattern. They are set apart from the profane world of the street or the road, usually surrounded by a wall or a fence, but their presence is signaled by the flags prominently displayed at their entrance, indicating that though they are "private," they are also public in the sense that in principle no restrictions are imposed on those who can enter; they are at once homelike and in theory open to the public as a whole.[3] Inside, the compound is divided into three distinct zones:

1. The bibliography on Vodou is massive, and I have relied principally on Métraux 1959, Brown 1991, and Desmangles 1992. For Shango, see Mischel 1957, Mischel and Mischel 1958, Bascom 1972, Simpson 1978:73–79, and Houk, 1994. References are kept to the minimum necessary.

2. In Candomblé, the annual period of initiatory rituals is known as *roça* (= country; Okari 1984:17).

3. The same distinction exists in Santería between the *igbodu* (inner sanctum) and the rest of the *ilé*. Even when the "temple" consists of a single room or apartment (as is commonly the case among Haitians and Cubans in the United States), an inside-outside distinction remains, with sacred altars and objects being located (in the case of Santería) in a multishelved cabinet called a *canastillero* (see Murphy 1994:110–11).

the private home of the priest or priestess or both, one or more inner sanctuaries or storerooms (*djévo* and *case-mystères* [or *bagi*] in Vodou, *chapelle* in Shango) where initiatory rituals are conducted and sacred objects stored, and finally a "public-private" area called the *peristil* in Vodou and the *chapelle* in Shango where what Karen McCarthy Brown calls "possession-performances" (1991:6) take place and that is, in structural terms, both "open" and "closed." Usually there is a thatched roof supported by several poles of which the central one, or *poteau-mitan*, plays a crucial part in the ceremonies, and, very often, a waist-high wall that both encloses the cultists and permits them to be seen from without (Houk 1994:198–99). The most important power thus resides in the innermost part of the cult area, appropriately enough since, as we have seen, power is always located *inside* in the West Indies but is brought out, in the form of flags, costumes, and other cult accessories into the public-private domain when ceremonies take place. Possession cults are, to repeat Victor Turner's expression, an *entertainment* that, suitably, takes place in an intermediary zone *between* the wholly private (the home) and the wholly public (the street). This intercalary space is doubly appropriate since, as we shall see, it is above all *women* who display themselves in the cult place, who gain reputation through the facility and expressiveness with which they "manifest" the spirits, and for whom the *hounfor* and its equivalents function socially as the rum shop functions for men. A woman may not display herself on the streets (unless she is a higgler or prostitute), but she may do so on the public-private stage of *peristil* and *palais*.

The "theatrical" character of Vodou and Shango is well known and has been brought out by all the best writers on the subject. Possession consists not—except sometimes during its inaugural phases—of some uncontrolled frenzy or trance but of a conventionally codified and crafted performance in which the "horse" impersonates or mimes the character, appearance, and gestures of the *loa* (Vodou) or *orisha* (Shango) that "rides" her or him. Significantly, in Vodou all "horses," male and female alike, are known by the female term *hounsi* (Métraux 1959:69) and will accordingly be designated hereafter by female pronouns. Once it becomes clear (or is made clear by the officiating priest or priestess) which spirit has "mounted" (*chevauché*) which horse, the horse is dressed up in the costumes and accessories traditionally associated with the role: a crutch and pipe for Legba, the limping guardian of the crossroads where sacred and profane intersect (Desmangles 1992:108–14); pink and blue dresses, necklaces, earrings, wedding rings, expensive perfumes and soaps, silk handkerchiefs and lingerie, and imported wine and liqueurs for that amorous lover of the high life Ezili (132–33); a straw hat, blue denim shirt, hoe, machete, and knapsack (*macoute*) for the peasant *loa* Zaka (118–19); a sword or machete for the warrior spirit Ogou (145), a frock coat and striped trousers like those worn by undertakers at funerals for Baron Samedi, one of the numerous Gede *loas* associated with cemeteries and death (117), and so on. Equipped thus with her costume and props, the horse then acts out the part traditionally assigned to the spirit possessing her. If that spirit is the snake *loa* Dambala, the horse writhes hissing on the *peristil* floor, dances the serpentine *yanvalor* dance, flicking her tongue in and out like a snake as she does so (Desmangles 1992:125–26), or even hangs from the beams of the *peristil* like a boa constrictor or python (Métraux 1959:105). If the spirit of Legba is discerned, the horse limps around with her crutch; if Zaka, she moves with a yokelish gait and speaks in (supposedly) peasantlike grunts, all the time wielding machete or hoe with one trouser leg rolled up to the knee (Desmangles 1992:118–19). "Every possession has a theatrical aspect," says Métraux (1959: 126–27), though "in the eyes of the public a possessed person is never really an actor. He does not play a character part, he *is* the character as long as the trance lasts." Sometimes horses act out "playlets" with each other, and the spectators—who, as we have seen, are vital to the whole possession performance—cry out in encouragement, "Play, cousin Zaka, play!" (128). Most of the possessed, says Métraux (135), apparently gain nothing more than "the approval of the congregation," "measured by the amount of attention it devotes to his words and actions"—which is to say the horse gains reputation and respect, a precious reward for any black West Indian, but especially for a black West Indian *woman*.

The Vodou pantheon is divided, as is well known, into a number of *nanchons* (nations) of *loas*, of which only two need concern us here: the Rada *loas* and their complementary opposites, the Petro. As well as being (or so Vodouisants believe) of different origin—Rada from Africa, Petro from Haiti itself[4]—the two *nanchons*, according to Brown (1989:67–70), express "contrasting views of the world" whose basic opposition is surprisingly familiar. On the one hand, the Rada *loas'* "way of being-in-the world is defined by family," and they set group consciousness and the preservation of the group above all other concerns; they "delineate and reinforce familial bonds" and accordingly are "treated as family and, in time, treat their devotees with the indulgence and nurturing accorded to family members." On the other hand, the Petro *loas* "embody the individualism, effectivity, and power of foreigners," "a way of being-in-the world which puts stress on the use of coercive power and the pursuit of self-interest"; Petro *loas* are served with fire, gunpowder, cracking whips, and shrill police whistles, and they are commonly interpreted as "an expression of rage against enslavement, or an attempt to imitate the slavemas-

4. The term "Rada" derives from the Dahomean town of Arada; "Petro" is usually, if somewhat fantastically, said to derive from the name of an eighteenth-century Vodou priest from the Spanish part of Hispaniola (see Moreau de Saint-Méry 1958:69).

**Table 2. Rada and Petro *loas***

| Rada | Petro |
|------|-------|
| Insiders | Outsiders |
| Family | Foreigners |
| Protective | Severe, fierce, uncompromising |
| Collectivity | Individualism |
| Right hand | Left hand |
| Gentle, nurturing | Bitter, aggressive |
| "African" | "Creole" |
| Water | Fire |

ters." On the basis of Brown's characterization of the *two nanchons*, it is possible to draw up a set of binary opposites that correlates closely with the dialectic of inside/outside, female/male, respect/reputation we have been exploring.

Métraux (1959:88) likens the opposition between Rada and Petro to that between Olympian and chthonic deities in ancient Greece: it is not so much that some *loas* belong to one *nanchon* and some to another, but that each *loa* has its "Rada" and "Petro" dimensions or aspects, each being the inverse of the other so that when they "mount" their "horses" they necessarily "present themselves by turns, or even sometimes simultaneously, as beneficent or terrible, as creative and destructive" (Desmangles 1992:97). The two pantheons, says Brown (1989:69), "cannot be allowed to touch or mix"; their altars and sacred objects are kept well apart, the dancing styles associated with each differ markedly, and according to Wilcken (1992:33), the Petro drums, which are played with the hands, stand in "binary opposition" to the Rada drums, which are played primarily with sticks. Although there are a number of *loas*—notably Ogou, to whom I shall return in the penultimate section of this chapter—who mediate between the two *nanchons*, it is clear that their opposition corresponds to some deep tension within Haitian history and culture, perhaps ultimately beyond that of inside/outside and its correlates to the family- or group-centered values inherited from Africa and the violent and disruptive forces unleashed by the experience of slavery. It may be, as Brown argues (1989:68), that the Petro *loas*, and the rituals associated with them, represent "an attempt to expropriate the power of slaveholding and its contemporary transmutations—oppression, prejudice, economic discrimination—to use that power against itself." The relevance of this statement to my overall argument will become clearer as I proceed.

Significantly, it is the Petro *loas* that come to the fore during and after carnival in Haiti. Although carnival as such in Haiti has long been a comparatively staid occasion, dominated by the mulatto elite, once carnival ends a new set of rituals known as Rara[5] begins, and the people come into their own. There is no clearer evidence of the continuity between cult and the carnival-esque in the Caribbean than the way Rara, without itself being properly speaking a ritual of Vodou, nonetheless emerges from Vodou[6] or from one dimension, the "Petro dimension," of Vodou and represents, so to speak, the passage of the *loas* from inside to outside, from the *hounfor* out onto the street, the road, and the countryside in general. Rara is both an extension of and deflection from Vodou, and though possession as such rarely occurs during Rara processions, "mass hypnotism and catharsis might be said to be the strongest elements of organization in these bands" (Dunham 1983:35). Significantly, during the period when Rara is celebrated (essentially from the end of carnival to Easter Sunday), no Vodou ceremonies are held in Haiti. Rara begins at midnight on Mardi Gras with the ritual of *brulé-carnaval* when the carnival masques are ceremonially incinerated, and the Rara dancers make a black cross on their brows with the ashes. Then, beating drums that have previously been dedicated to the Petro *loas* in ceremonies in the *hounfor*, the bands move off and, for the duration of Lent and the Easter triduum, process noisily and aggressively—"Rara" probably comes from the Yoruba word for "loudly" (Yonker 1988:16)—along country roads, accosting and defying other bands with which they engage in a series of combative rituals, notably a Haitian version of stickfighting known as *jonc* after the metal-tipped staff that is often left to "sleep" overnight in *hounfor* or cemetery to enhance the magic powers it is believed to contain. Clad in "vivid assemblages of paper, cloth, mirrors and sequins"—shades of Jonkonnu![7]—and sporting a cape in the colors of the band's patron *loa*, the champion *major-jonc* of one band confronts the champion *major-jonc* of another, the object being, of course, to *krasé Rara* to "crush" the rival band ludically, ritualistically, and perhaps physically as well and so enhance the band's reputation in the eyes of opponents as well as in those of society as a whole.

Rara, in other words, embodies the familiar carnival phenomenon of ritual combat between bands, and it would not detain us further but for two things. First, as Harold Courlander wrote (1960:109), Rara so clearly ties in with Vodou. Second, it so clearly reaches out to the construction of political power in Haiti, with its well-documented links to the secret societies discussed in the next section and, through and beyond them, to the networks of *chefs de section*,

5. The present account of Rara is based primarily on Yonker 1988, supplemented by Courlander 1960:105–9 and Dunham 1983:13–35. I have also used Davis 1988:282–84, but with caution. References are kept to a minimum.

6. According to the well-known Vodouisant Max Beauvoir, all Rara bands come out of the *hounfor*, while another *houngan* insists that "the mysteries [i.e., the *loas*] demand Rara. . . . Rara is a mystic obligation with an ancient meaning" (quoted in Yonker 1988:155).

7. On the possible connection, perhaps expressed etymologically in *jonc*, between Jonkonnu and Rara, see Craton 1995:38.

Haitian Rara band, showing *majors-jonc* displaying their *joncs*. Photo by Dolores M. Yonker.

houngans, and *tontons macoutes*—often, under the Duvaliers, the same person— that back them locally and nationally. Rara is, I suggest, a "magical mirror" for the operations of power in Haiti, not just in the sense that it evinces "the 'combative compulsion,' the motivation to compete violently for dominance" and that just beneath its surface lurks "the threat of violence and vengeance controlled by military discipline" (Yonker 1988:154), but that it is situated at the crossroads[8]—that truly "crucial" site in the imagery of Vodou—where the road leading from cult to carnival intersects with the road leading from slavery to modern political power. That this is so is suggested by the following apparently random images and facts whose interconnections will, I hope, be clear by the end of this chapter:

1. In addition to the accouterments mentioned above, the *major-jonc* wears dark glasses, the identifying emblem of the Gede *loas* of death (Yonker 1988:148) before they were co-opted by the *tontons macoutes* as their insignia.

8. On the symbolism of the crossroads in Vodou and, in particular, on Kafou (*carrefour*) Legba as the guardian of the crossroads where *loas* and humans meet, see Desmangles 1992:108–13.

2. It is common in Rara processions to see a *"bokor* [magician] driving before him a band of zombies, wielding a whip, and barking out weird ravenous commands" (Courlander 1960:106) as well as, at the head of the procession, a "menacing figure, wielding a sisal whip, flaying at the crowd" (Davis 1988:282).

3. The fall of Jean-Claude Duvalier took place in the immediate lead-up to carnival (6 February 1986, Mardi Gras being on 11 February), and it is reasonable to assume that the rural and urban bands that helped precipitate his departure and initiated the violent *déchoukaj* ["uprooting"] of Duvalier supporters that followed would have been closely connected to Rara (see Desmangles 1992:57).

Furthermore, many Rara dancers wear "comic ancient military attire, replete with swords, epaulets, medals, and outlandish beards, representing 'the Generals'" (Courlander 1960:106), and the leaders sport an assortment of titles, though, this being republican-military Haiti, generals and brigadiers, presidents, ministers, and senators are at least as common as kings, queens, and princes (Yonker 1988:151; Paul 1962:188). We have encountered these titles and uniforms before, in slave uprisings, Maroon bands, Jonkonnu, tea meetings, and Trinidad carnival: the time has clearly come to examine in detail the whole Afro-Creole obsession with "fictitious or pseudo-hierarchies" (Turner 1992:59).

## The Names of Kings

When the massive Antiguan slave conspiracy of 1736 was discovered, Whites were stunned to learn that what they had taken as a piece of innocent masquerade by the slaves had in reality formed both the organizational basis and the means of concealment for the attempted overthrow of white rule on the island and its replacement by an independent Akan-style kingdom run by the slaves. On 3 October 1736 the slave who subsequently turned out to be the leader of the conspiracy, an African-born washerman (re)named "Court," was publicly crowned "King of the Coromantees" in the presence of over two thousand slaves and not a few Whites, for throughout the slaves made no attempt to conceal what they were doing; this, said the judge later charged to investigate the affair, was the "Masterpiece of the plot," namely that Whites "might be spectators, and yet ignorant of the meaning; The Language and Ceremonys used at it, being all Coromantee" (Gaspar 1985:251). On the day of his coronation, "Court" was seated beneath "a Canopy of State, Surrounded by his great Officers," wore "a particular Cap, proper to the Kings of his Countrey" made of "green Silk imbroidered with Gold, with a deep border either of black Fur, or black Feathers, and three plumes of Feathers in it." He "walked in Procession as King, and had all the Homage and Respect of a King paid to him," and later in the day, surrounded by his "Generals," he danced the celebrated shield dance or *Ikem* of the Akan, again in the presence of Whites who failed utterly to discern the dance's significance—a declaration of war (249–52). The coronation was the culmination of many months of lesser ceremonies and gatherings during which slaves had taken "Damnation Oaths" together and drunk potions containing "Oath Ingredients" (grave dirt and cock's blood) at what the judge called "Entertainments of Dancing, Gaming and Feasting . . . coloured with some innocent pretence, as of commemorating some deceased Friend by throwing water on his Grave, or Christening a House, or the like, according to the Negro Custom" (245–46). It was, in short, a highly elaborate and formalized version of the slave "play" that we have encountered so often, but this time organized as a surrogate court complete with its queen (248), its princes and princesses, and a military hierarchy that assumed "Gentlemans Names" throughout the festivities, "Mingo" becoming "Major Nanton" and other slaves "Major Vernon," "Colonel Gilbert," "Captain Clarke," and so on (249). Although "Court" and some of the other conspirators were African born, the bulk of the leaders were Creoles (though of probable Coromantee parentage), and most of them, as skilled slaves, lived, in the judge's view, lives "as easy as those of our White Tradesmen and Overseers," not to mention of "our Common Whites, who were looked upon by some of them, for their Poverty and Distress with Contempt" (227–28). "Lately baptized" and able in some cases to read and write, "Tomboy," "Hercules," "Jack," "Scipio," "Ned," "Secundi," and "Toney" had, under the inspiration of "Court," created the lineaments of an African polity under the very noses of the Whites (232). In a carnivalesque inversion of the hierarchies of the plantation, the slaves had transformed themselves into an African aristocracy under its king, and it was only at the very last minute that their gloriously open subterfuge was discovered and eighty-eight of their number were executed, five broken on the wheel, six gibbeted, and an incredible seventy-seven burned to death (227).

The Antigua conspiracy was remarkable for its scale, bravura, and sheer effrontery, but it was by no means the only one of its kind. In 1675 a plot was discovered in Barbados in which the conspirators, Coromantees in the main, planned to crown Coffee, an "Ancient Gold Coast Court Negro" as king of Barbados and enthrone him upon a "chair of state" in keeping with long-established Akan tradition (Beckles 1987:37). The great 1760 uprising in Jamaica seems also to have involved the creation of a surrogate Akan-style court, with one female slave being crowned queen of Kingston by her Coromantee "courtiers" (Craton 1982:132), and as late as *Christmas* 1805, a plot was discovered in Trinidad in which slaves had organized under the cover of drumming and dancing bands with names such as the Régiment Danois (presumably composed of slaves from the Danish West Indies), the Régiment Macaque, and the Couvri de Sans Peurs, each with its king and its queen, its dauphin and dauphine, and general judge (ibid., 235). Maroon societies too were organized along aristocratic-military lines, with the various "colonels" and "captains" commonly adopting "the names of gentlemen of the island" (Dallas 1968:2:116), a practice of empowerment by appropriating the names of the powerful that is also attested in the French West Indies.[9] Finally, during the Saint-Domingue uprising, it was common for insurgent bands to elect titular heads, a king and queen whom "they treated with great respect," like the Free Black Jean-Baptiste Cap, whom his followers had "crowned" king of Limbé and Port-Margot (Fick 1990:103), while the ten to twelve thousand slaves who formed the independent "Kingdom of Platons" elected "a titular ruler whom they designated as king" (ibid. 151). In the circumstances, it might be more appropriate to praise "King" Henry Christophe for his reinvention of *African* monarchy in independent Haiti than to deride him and his all too well known Ducs de Marmelade and Limonade for their sterile mimicry of European courts.

Nor did slave "kingdoms" necessarily disappear with the abolition of slavery. In Trinidad it is practically certain that slave sodalities like the Régiment Danois referred to above mutated, in 1838, into the batonnier bands and other fraternities (and sororities) that dominated the *jamet* carnival, and *jamet* life in general, up into the 1980s, just as, in Martinique the famous Société des Oeillets and Société des Roses, having functioned as surrogate "courts" under the slave regime, evolved into mutual aid organizations after abolition in 1848 (see Debbasch 1959). In independent Haiti the Maroon bands did not merely survive but increased in numbers if not in power as ex-slaves fled from the forced labor system instituted by Toussaint L'Ouverture and his successors, and they may have formed the organizational basis for a succession of nineteenth-century peasant uprisings (1807–19, 1843, 1867, and 1883) and even for the maroonlike Caco War against the American occupying force in 1918–19 (Laguerre 1980:157). More specifically, according to both Michel Laguerre (1989:71) and Wade Davis (1988:215–31) there is a direct affiliation between the Maroon bands (themselves based on, or strongly influenced by, African secret societies) and the much-discussed secret societies of contemporary Haiti,[10] shadowy organizations sporting names such as the Zobop, the San

9. Thus the leader of the principal Maroon band in mid-seventeenth-century Martinique, Francisque Fabulé, had taken over the name of his former master (Debien 1974:413), and the leaders of the Guadeloupe Maroons in 1726 appropriated the names of the governor general, Général de Feuquières, and the military commander, the Comte de Moyencourt, charged with their destruction (Abenon 1987:251). See also Campbell 1988:255.

10. This account of the secret societies is based on Davis 1988:241–90, whose somewhat sensationalist nature does not impair its basic veracity.

Manman and San Poèl, the Galipotes, Makandals, Vinbindingues, and Bizango, which patrol the streets and roads of Haiti at night and compete with each other for power and influence over the citizenry as a whole, interlocking in complex ways with the worlds of Vodou, Rara, and the *tontons macoutes* and their post-Duvalierist descendants. Each secret society has its own quasi-aristocratic, quasi-military structure, with the Bizango outdoing the rest with a complex hierarchy of at least thirty ranks ranging from empereur at the top through first, second, and third queens, *reien drapeau, mère la société, général, prince, premier ministre, préfet de discipline,* and not least, *bourreau* (executioner) to simple *sentinelles* and *soldats* (Davis 1988:250). The Bizango has its distinctive flags, uniform (black trousers or skirts, red shirts or blouses marked with a black cross on the back), passwords and even passports (267). As the list of officers suggests, women play a prominent part in the life of the society, which not for nothing is known as *la fanmi (famille) bizango* (Laguerre 1980:153), its different branches encompassing, allegedly, the whole of Haitian society.[11]

Still more evocative for our purpose are the *cabildos* of Cuba[12] that emerged in the late sixteenth century as church-sponsored confraternities for the religious instruction of urban-based slaves but in the course of the seventeenth and eighteenth centuries evolved into all-purpose associations that offered Afro-Cubans both slave and free a continuum of activities ranging from the worship of the *orishas* of Africa under the guise of the Catholic saints (*santería*) at one end to music, dancing, and carnival processions (*comparasas*). Named after a specific African *nación* but not necessarily recruiting its members from just one ethnic group, each *cabildo* elected a king (*rey*), overseer (*capataz*), and other officers[13] and had as its principal public occasion the annual festival of Epiphany (Día de los Reyes) when, an observer wrote in 1884, "each tribe, having selected its king and queen, paraded the streets with a flag, having its name, and the words *viva Isabella*, with the arms of Spain, painted on it. Their majesties were dressed in the extreme of fashion, and were very ceremoniously waited on by the ladies and gentlemen of the court," while all the time African drums could be "heard far and near, and their sonorous sound, now falling now rising on the air, seemed like the summons to a general insurrection" (J. G. F. Wurdemann, quoted in Brandon 1993:73). After the abolition of slavery in 1868, *cabildos* came under pressure from the Spanish authorities as hotbeds of nationalist fervor. They were prohibited from celebrating the Día de

11. According to one Bizango official interviewed by Davis (1988:249–50), "it is women who constitute societies. . . . Without women you cannot have societies."

12. The following account is based on Brandon 1993:69–85, supplemented by Bettelheim 1988b and Murphy 1994:81–113.

13. When *actual* African princes and chiefs belonged to *cabildos*, as was not uncommon in nineteenth-century Cuba, they remained clearly subordinate to the *elected* king of the society (Brandon 1993:75–76).

los Reyes in 1884, and after some efforts to organize them federally in the 1890s, they disappeared as such in the early 1900s, their unique role as the focus of both carnival and cult being assumed by two separate institutions, the *casa templo* or *ilé orisha* (house of *orishas*) for the saints and the spirits, and the *comparsa* (for the celebration of carnival). Though physically separate, *templo* and *comparsa* continued to feed into each other, at least until the 1959 revolution, by virtue of their shared roots in the community, their overlapping memberships, and above all their hierarchical structure, part royal court and part extended family with its *madrinas* and *padrinos, ajihadas* and *ajihados,* which pointed to a common origin in the heavily African-influenced world of the *cabildo* (see Bettelheim 1988b:137–39).

Elsewhere in the Caribbean the links between masquerade and possession have become distended and blurred, surviving metonymically in the shared emblems and instruments to be discussed in the section that follows. What remains constant is the hierarchical structure of both carnival and cult organizations, usually regal for the former and family-based for the latter. Of the former type, Maureen Warner-Lewis (1993:111) has written that

> African Caribbean groups always elected kings and queens: *cabildos de nación* (national societies in Cuba), *convois* (secret societies) in Trinidad, St. Lucian La Rose and la Marguerite dance affiliations, *jonkonnu* bands and Brukins dance groups in Jamaica, tea-parties in Tobago, St. Vincent and Jamaica, African and *bèlè* dances in the Eastern Caribbean, even modern Trinidad carnival masquerade bands, all of them— whether temporary or permanent sodalities, or wholly or partially secular—were/are headed by royal figures.

Turning to the cults,[14] we find that in almost all of them, whether "Protestant" or "Catholic," "family idioms are used extensively," as William Wedenoja writes of Jamaican Revivalism (1989:89), "and they are not merely metaphors" since "cultists behave according to the familial roles associated with their positions." Thus in Revival, beneath a "Father" or a "Daddy" (cf. "Daddy" Sharpe) who, says Wedenoja, is "sometimes the dominant but more often a removed but respected figure" (somewhat like the God of Revivalism himself), there is a "Mother" or "Momma," usually the dominant influence in the cult, aided by a team consisting, in descending order, of Leaders and Leadresses (or Shepherds and Shepherdesses), Armor Bearers, Captains, and Bandsmen, with, at the bottom, the "ordinary" believers, almost all of them women (Wedenoja 1988:94; see Murphy 1994:127 for a somewhat different arrangement in Revival Zion).

14. As a non-Christian religion, Rastafarianism is not considered here, though, as we have seen, its male bias is even more marked than that present in the Afro-Christian churches and cults (see Austin-Broos 1987:17–21).

In St. Vincent the Spiritual Baptists (otherwise known as Shouters or Shakers) are led by a Pointer—always a man—supported by Leaders and Captains in the Spirit (again always men) with, beneath them, Church Others—Pointer Other, Assistance Mother, and Mother Matron in that order—and so on down through Nurses and Warriors to the rank-and-file worshipers among whom, once again, women constitute an overwhelming majority (Henney 1974:29–30). Similarly, the Trinidadian spiritual Baptist Church studied by Stephen D. Glazier (1983) had no fewer than 22 ranks for its 102 regular members (83 female, 19 male), with a male-dominated elite composed of Judge, Inspector, Commander, Warrior, and Teacher-Pointer seconded by a plethora of lesser officers, bell ringers, healers, divers, nurses, mothers and sisters: not surprisingly, Glazier claims (1983:88) never to have "met a Baptist who was content with his present rank."

As one moves from Protestant-based cults to Catholic-based and syncretic ones such as Santería and Shango (Vodou is discussed later), the hierarchical and familial structure is if anything heightened,[15] though there is a *relative* shift from male to female dominance until, in the case of Brazilian Candomblé (not discussed here) one confronts what appears to be an almost wholly female-controlled cult.[16] Nonetheless caution is in order, for though fully 80 percent of Santería cultists are said to be women, "the largest *ilés*, and the leaders with the widest repute, seem to be men" (Murphy 1994:87). Similarly in Trinidadian Shango, although 75 percent of the cultists studied by Mischel and Mischel (1958:25) were women, it appears from the recent study by Houk (1994:168) that *mongbos* (priests) outnumbered *iyas* (priestesses) by as much as seven to one, though most actual shrine heads are elderly black women known as "Queens of Shango" (Pollack-Eltz 1993:19). Yet in Shango, Santería, Convince (Jamaica), Kélé (St. Lucia), Big Drum (Carriacou), Revival, Spiritual Baptism, and so on, not only do women make up the bulk of those present, but they are far more likely than men to be "ridden," "overshadowed," or "adopted" or otherwise to manifest the gifts of the spirit; indeed, when he studied the Rada community in Trinidad in the early 1950s, Andrew Carr (1953:48) was told that "no saint has come into the head of a man" since *1902!* Everywhere women are the most active members of cults and the most spiritually "gifted," but always, it seems, the titular heads of the cult, and the ultimate source of power, remain men, and the imbalance of power becomes all the more marked the "higher" one moves in the denominational hierarchy, from the cults into the "established" (i.e., Euro-American) churches: Pentecostalist, Baptist, Meth-

15. As one *iyalorixá* ("mother of the spirit" in Candomblé) puts it: "To climb the ladder of the candomblé, a person mounts one rung at a time" (quoted in Murphy 1994:54).

16. "It is almost as difficult for a man to become great in candomblé as it is for him to have a baby. And for the same reason: it is believed to be against his nature" (Edison Carneiro, quoted in Murphy 1994:53).

odist, Presbyterian, Anglican, Roman Catholic. Only the remarkable "Miss Queenie," head of the Kumina "band" studied by Warner-Lewis (1977) and Brathwaite (1978), seems to have effective authority over the fifty to a hundred people who visit her yard, but other queens of the Kumina seem at most to share power with a Master of Ceremonies and wear the black-and-white cord that symbolizes authority only when he is absent or himself possessed (Simpson 1978:99).

The question of the various hierarchies within Vodou is more complex and needs to be discussed separately. There can be little doubt that the organization of the *hounfor*, be it large or small, urban or rural, is patterned on that of à family in which the "parents," the *houngan* and *mambo*, also but more rarely known as *papa-loa* and *mama-loa* respectively (Métraux 1959:62), exercise a high degree of authority over the "servants" of the *loas* who, whether male or female, are designated by the female term *hounsi*. They are the *pititt-cailles*, the "children of the house," and they owe respect and deference to those placed above them: *M'respèté hûngâ mwê, M'respèté mâmbô mwê* (I respect my *houngan*, I respect my *mambo* [71]). When the "children" become fully initiated into the service of the *loas* through the ritual of the *pot-têt* ("head pot") in which clippings from the neophyte's hair and nails, symbolizing his or her *gros bon anj*, are placed, the *houngan*, as the custodian of the pot, "gains complete control of his *hounsis'* souls" (200). Beneath the *houngan* and the *mambo* there are, as one would expect, an array of subordinate ranks and offices. The most important of these, the *laplace* and the *confiance* appear to be male monopolies, but they also give women the opportunity of playing a significant part in the running of the *hounfor* and its ceremonies, as *houngénikon* or *reine chanterelle* (queen chorister), for example, *reine-drapeaux* or *reine-silence*, whose job it is to impose silence at certain critical points in the service, and so on (71–73). Women, in other words, have definite influence within the *hounfor* (and, as in Santería and Shango, are more likely than men to be "ridden" by the spirits), but aside from the *mambo* herself they have little real power, and even the *mambo*, especially in rural Haiti, remains ultimately subordinate to the male Master of spirits.

This description, based essentially on data collected by Métraux in the 1940s and early 1950s, needs to be qualified, however, by Karen McCarthy Brown's insistence (1991:255) that "few other places in the world rival Haiti in recognizing women's religious leadership." Although women are unable to "challenge the religious hegemony of the rural male," in urban centers, at least half of the Vodou leaders are said to be women; moreover, "the ethos within a woman's temple is like that inside the home, where the mother moves in and out of her role as an authority figure as the situation demands, whereas a man's temple usually reflects the more rigid role definitions of the public arena" (221). Despite the fact that "Haitian culture is a misogynist culture" in which "the ideology of male supremacy is fierce," Vodou, according to Brown (220), "empowers women to a larger extent than the great majority of the world's religious traditions," giving them positions of authority and influence within the cult world itself, and also strengthening their position vis-à-vis men in Haitian society at large; in this perspective "a decision to serve the spirits is a decision to stop serving men" (167). How do we square this description with that of Métraux above? Perhaps, in the first instance, by recognizing the difference between the Haitis of 1950 and 1990, and above all the massive movement of population from country to town that occurred during that time and that, among other things, caused the traditional *lakou* (yard) to disintegrate in both town and country, freeing women for more complex and independent roles, especially in the capital and other large cities.[17] In the country, Brown writes (157), men's power is "in tension with and to some degree modulated by that of women," whereas in urban centers the growing economic independence of women "threatens Haitian men." It could be, therefore, that the evident accession of women to positions of *public* power in Vodou is as significant an indicator of grassroots social change as is the heightened public profile of Trinidadian women at carnival or the growing number of female graduates at the University of the West Indies in Jamaica:[18] quite simply, the old inside/outside dichotomy is everywhere eroding. But as before it is essential not to exaggerate: women may be more "visible" in contemporary urban Vodou, as Brown says (255), and their voices may be "strong, but they do not dominate." Furthermore, although female-headed urban *hounfors* may be more "democratic," Glenn R. Smucker reports (1984:54–55), admittedly before the fall of Duvalierism and without considering the question of gender, that urban *hounfors* tend "towards greater hierarchy and an elaborated division of labor" than those in the country. It would be fascinating to know whether male-headed *hounfors* were more likely to be co-opted into the networks of Duvalierist power than their allegedly more "democratic" female-headed equivalents. Given the widely attested influence of women in at least the lower strata of the Duvalierist "machine," we should not automatically assume they would be.[19]

There is one final issue regarding hierarchy in Vodou that must be consid-

17. For a discussion of the Haitain "rural exodus," see Maingot 1986–87:77–80, above all his conclusion (80) that "the traditional distinction between urban and rural Haiti is blurring."

18. See chapter 3 above.

19. On the role of *madam saras* (market women) in the Duvalierest apparatus, see Weinstein and Segal 1984:59. The support of the women's organization Faisceau Féminin played a crucial part in the elder Duvalier's election in 1957, and its leader Rosalie Bosquet, the future wife of Max Adolphe, known in Haiti as "Madame Max," was commander-in-chief of the *tontons macoutes* at the time of Jean-Claude Duvalier's fall in 1986 (see Abbott 1988:64); earlier Sanette Balmir, described by Abbott (88) as "a convicted thief and lesbian," and been commander of the *tontons macoutes* in the southwestern city of Jérémie at the time of the infamous "Vespers of Jérémie" in 1964 when dozens of anti-Duvalierists, mainly Mulattos, were massacred (Abbott 1988:122–33).

ered. Writing just before the French Revolution and the Saint-Domingue uprising, Moreau de Saint-Méry states (1958:65) that, in a telling amalgam of
monarchy, slavocracy, and family writ large, the male and female "ministers" of
"*Vaudoux*" are known to their followers as "Roi" and "Reine," "maître" and "maî-
tresse" and "papa" and "maman" respectively: "They are, throughout their
whole life, the heads of the great family of *Vaudoux*, and they are entitled to
the unlimited respect of those who compose it. . . . To disobey or resist them
is to resist the God [of *Vaudoux*] himself and to expose oneself to the greatest
calamities." It is noticeable, however, that, in contemporary Vodou, the terms
*roi* and *reine* are used neither of the *houngan* or *mambo* nor of the *loas* themselves.[20]
On the other hand, military and political emblems, instruments, and titles pervade the whole of Vodou (see Métraux 1959:157 and Brown 1989:70) from the
parading of flags and brandishing of swords (see below) to the titles of certain
*loas*: Baron Samedi, Général Clermeil (responsible for rivers and streams), Général Brisé (protector of trees at Chardette), and so on (see Laguerre 1989:121);
even the sun is known in Haiti as Compère Général Soleil.[21] In addition, it is
not unknown for political figures themselves to become *loas*, like Empereur
Dessalines, invoked as "Désalin Désalin démâmbré" ("Dessalines, Dessalines
the powerful," Métraux 1959:49), and, not least, François Duvalier, prudently
referred to as *Loa 22os* after his supposed lucky number (Laguerre 1989:123). In
keeping with Haiti's post-1820 republican constitution the Vodou pantheon,
like the hierarchy of the *hounfor*, seems to have evolved from a royal court,
either African or French, into a military command structure or a presidential
cabinet under "Président Carrefour," with an appropriate portfolio for each of
the main *loas*: Legba (internal affairs), Zaka (agriculture), Dambala (finance),
Loko (public health), Agoué (coast guard), Ogou (army), and so on (Laguerre
1989:123). Significantly, a similar "republicanization" or "militarization" of carnival societies took place when the republican Boyer finally ousted "King"
Henry Christophe in 1820, so that during Boyer's long presidency Carnival
Kings and Queens were, it appears, displaced by a hierarchy consisting of
Président, Sénateur, Général de Division, and Commandant de la Place—this
last being, as we have seen, a Vodou official as well (Paul 1962:137). By the
twentieth century, Président, Ministre, Magistrat, and Colonel were standard,
and it became common for carnival bands to be divided into their Exécutif,
Judicaire, Législatif, and Armée sections, without this, however, leading to any
perceptible democratization: "The notion of authority is highly developed,
and the President always possesses very extensive powers" (153–54). That,
finally, the head of the Rara band is called not its king but its president (188)
suggests not only that the hierarchical structures of both Vodou and carnival

20. Though the title *reine* is used, as we have seen, for certain *subordinate* female offices.
21. See the great novel of that title by Jacques Stephen Alexis (Paris: Gallimard, 1955).

mirror and replicate and hierarchical structures of the state but that what takes place in, especially, the *hounfor* (or, mutatis mutandis, in the *palais* or balmyard in Trinidad or Jamaica) is linked, beyond its properly religious significance, to the structure of power in the colonial and postcolonial polities of the Caribbean. It is this hypothesis that we will explore in the final sections of this chapter.

## Weapons of the Weak?

For the moment, though, there can be no doubt: both cult and carnival empower, and those whose lives they most enhance are the chronically disempowered by race, class, or gender or, in very many instances, by the combination of all three. "Being a Shango woman is my life," said one Trinidadian to the Mischels (1958:258), speaking not just of the experience of being "ridden" by the *orishas* but of the whole network of friendships and associations she had found in the *palais* and of the way these, as well as the rites of Shango itself, sustained her in her sense of herself and in the eyes of her very limited society. As the Mischels show (254–55), the experience of possession is first and foremost an experience of *power* in that "the possessed is virtually in absolute control of those around him." Other cultists regard her (or more rarely him) with "awe and respect, frequently mingled with fear," moving close—but not too close—"to the power, attentive to every word, alert to any advice, warning, or recommendation that may issue." Thus it is that "the domestic who thirty minutes earlier was submissive to the whims of her British mistress is, under possession, transformed into a god; the unemployed laborer is master of an audience of several hundred people. The transition is often an almost direct role reversal—from passive impotence to central importance, dominance, power, and recognition." Much the same could be said of the carnival masque, possessed as it were by the "spirit" of the figure he or she is *playing*, commanding respect by the sheer splendor of his or her presence, lost in, but also controlling, the ecstasy of the dance. "Look at me, I am dancing!" is the ultimate message of both carnival and cult, and, for the duration of both, how *can* we know the dancer from the dance?[22]

Since carnival and cult are at their heart experiences of power, it is appro-

22. "The possessing familiar which the patient incarnates, or impersonates, expresses very clearly the frustrated demands of the dependent woman or downtrodden low class man. Women who seek power and aspire to roles otherwise monopolized by men act out thrusting male parts with impunity and with the full approval of the audience. The possessed person who in the séance is the centre of attention says in effect, 'Look at me, I am dancing.' Thus those forced by society into subservience play exactly the opposite role with the active encouragement of the séance audience" (Lewis 1971:194–95). The reference in the last part of the final sentence in this paragraph is to W. B. Yeats's "Among School Children'": "O body swayed to music, O brightening glance / How can we know the dancer from the dance?"

Jonkonnu "courtier" with ax and mace, Savanna-la-Mar, Jamaica
(1976). Photo by Judith Bettelheim.

priate that emblems and implements of power should be intimately associated
with both. Swords, axes, hatchets, flags, whips, and drums are as fundamental
to possession as they are to the contrasting worlds of Rastafarianism and carnival.[23] Thus, in both Vodou and Shango, the "horse" ridden by Ogun (Ogou)
brandishes a sword less as a symbol than as an embodiment of her—it is
almost always "her"—power, while in a distant but related religious tradition
the Revivalist uses a wooden sword to "cut and clear" the forces of "destruction" that threaten the well-being of the cultists' souls (Wedenoja 1988:96).

23. See chapter 3 and chapter 4 for discussion of Rastafarianism and carnival respectively.

An Orisha (Shango) altar in Trinidad, with the swords of Ogun and Shango. Photo by James T. Houk.

But as we have seen, the wooden sword is also wielded by the Jonkonnu dancer and by many carnival masques (see Crowley 1956a:197), just as the magic baton of the stickfighters echoes the Revivalist's rod, the crook of the Shepherd and Shepherdess in Pukumina, the staff of the *major-jonc* in Rara or, for that matter, the cricket's bat—that most emphatic expression of power in the ex-British West Indies—or as we have seen the "Rod of Correction" of the charismatic populist political leader. Similarly, flags are common to Vodou, where they are brought out of the sanctuary at the beginning of the ceremony and solemnly paraded around the *poteau-mitan*;[24] to Shango, where the distinctive flags of the major *orishes* are "mounted on bamboo poles that may reach as high as thirty feet" (Houk 1994:193); to Revival, where brightly colored "banners" identify the balmyard from afar (Wedenoja 1989:79); to Rara (Dunham 1983:35) and the nocturnal Bizango procession (Laguerre 1980:153); and of course to cricket matches and carnival.[25] Sometimes carnival bands advertise their links with the cults as in the *orisha* masques of carnival in Bahia (see

24. On the "profoundly liminal" character of flags in Vodou, see R. Thompson (1983:184): "Unfurled and paraded in *vodun* rites, they stand at the boundary between two worlds."

25. Thus the celebrated banner at a Test match at Sabina Park (Kingston, Jamaica) in the early 1970s that declared, after an extravagantly wayward over by a local fast bowler, that henceforth "Dowe shalt not bowl."

Female revivalist with shepherd's crook preaching at a Jamaican market in 1972. Photo by William Wedenoja.

Crowley 1984:13) or in Trinidad, in the wooden hatchets brandished by the Maribones band in 1871 that according to Nunley (1988:113), were "painted to resemble the scepter or dance wand used by Shango devotees," a "play" not on words but on objects that was repeated, over a hundred years later, in the "Rain Forest" masque of 1983 (see ibid., 94). Cross-dressing or the transposition of sex roles is found in both carnival and cult, as are infantile and occasionally scatological forms of behavior.[26] Above all there is *noise*, that crucial ingredient in all Afro-Creole cultures (see Reisman 1970, 1974),[27] the inevit-

26. On the exchange of sex roles in Shango see Mischel and Mischel 1958:256, and for Rara, Dunham 1983:44; cross-dressing was, as we have seen, banned at one time in Trinidad carnival. Childish behavior is commonly encountered in the initial stage of possession known as *ere* or *were*, during which incontinence can sometimes occur (Mischel and Mischel 1958:256). The scatological element is (or was) present in the *pissenlit* bands of nineteenth-century Trinidad (see chapter 4) or, combined with cross-dressing, in the *baisser-pisser* bands of Haitian carnival in which men dressed as women intermittently crouch down and imitate women urinating.

27. Reisman 1974:56 pertinently quotes George Lamming's *The Pleasures of Exile*: "So I made a heaven of a noise which is characteristic of my voice and an ingredient of West Indian behaviour." See also Cooper 1993:5 on "the politics of noise" in Jamaican culture.

able and indispensable accompaniment to all forms of Caribbean "play," whether it be the whistles and rattle of beer cans at cricket matches, the tambou-bamboo bands or their equivalents at the region's multifarious expressions of carnival—as we have seen, the very word *rara* means "loudly" in Yoruba—or the "trumping," "sounding," or "groaning," and of course the drumming and singing, in any number of popular religious cults throughout the Caribbean. As the Revivalist Martha Williston told Martha Beckwith in the early 1920s (quoted in Murphy 1994:131): "When the Spirit overflows within you, you have to shout and shout and shout. You have to shout with joy."

Almost all of the emblems and implements mentioned above—especially the swords and the axes—can be linked beyond doubt to prototypes in Dahomean or Yoruban cults of possession, as can the "checheray brooms" used so widely in New World variants of Shango (see Pollack-Eltz 1993:20).[28] But though unquestionably of African provenance, such emblems and implements gain an added power and poignancy, as well as a significant charge of ambiguity, through their frequent associations with slavery—through having been wrenched, so to speak, from the masters and placed in the hands of slaves and their descendants. There is no object more historically supercharged in the Caribbean than the whip, and the whip features everywhere in the region's festivities and cults: in Rara, where it is "cracked at entrances and exits to deflect potentially malevolent forces" (Yonker 1988:152); in Trinidad carnival, where it is (or was) wielded by any number of masques, Pierrots, *djab djabs*, and the mock schoolmaster in the Dame Lorraine mime (Crowley 1956a:195, 214); in Shango, where the eponymous *orisha* flourishes a thick vine whip called a *pessie* (Simpson 1978:75); in Vodou, where both *mambo* and *houngan* carry whips as signs (and sometimes as actual instruments) of authority (Métraux 1959:198, 201–2) and where the cracking of whips, along with the blowing of whistles and explosion of firecrackers, forms an essential part of the Petro rite. "In an ingenious twist of symbolic meaning," Lois Wilcken has written of this ritual (1992:43), "Vodou servants transform the former tools of oppression into instruments of liberation."[29] Ingenious, certainly, but as we shall see, the "weapons of the weak" can all too often be turned against them not by the powerful from whom, symbolically or in fact, they seized them but by those of their own "kind" whom they have placed (or who have placed themselves) above them, like the Spiritual Baptist Pointer mentioned by Henney (1974:33–35) who chastises a cultist for some misdemeanor with a leather

28. For an excellent discussion of the imagery of Yoruba cults in Africa and the New World, see R. Thompson 1983:33–68.

29. According to I. M. Lewis (1971:100), writing of the Somalian possession cult Zâr, the many ex-slaves who participate in the cult "carry as insignia whips which . . . enable them to present themselves not as slaves, but as masters of slaves. This striking role reversal is a crucial element in the ritual."

Jonkonnu dancer in Jamaica wearing a "house," ca. 1920. From *Black Roadways: A Study of Jamaican Folk Life*, by Martha Warren Beckwith. Chapel Hill: University of North Carolina Press, 1929.

strap, saying that if he "had not given Mistress S. the lashes, the Holy Spirit would have lashed him." The seizing by the powerless of the instruments of power delivers them neither from the ambiguity of power nor from its potential destructiveness, as we shall see from the aggressive and often finally suicidal swordplay of Ogou, discussed in the section that follows.

Finally, in this survey of the iconography of Caribbean carnival and cult, it is impossible not to be struck by the number of symbols and talismanic implements that are associated with the *head*. Thus, more or less at random, we have Jonkonnu masks, above all Cowhead, Horsehead, and the Jonkonnu "house" itself; the countless forms of headdress worn by carnival masques in Trinidad, Haiti, and Cuba; the turbans and head wraps of Shango, Revival, and Pukumina;[30] the ritual of *lav-tèt* or head washing in Vodou (Métraux 1959:200; Dunham 1983:10), Revival (Simpson 1978:114), and the initiatory rituals of the Radas of Trinidad (Carr 1953:47); the related ritual of the *pot-tèt* in Vodou (Métraux 1959:199); the glass of water that queens of Shango and Kumina balance on their heads as they dance in possession (Mischel 1957:58; Brathwaite 1978:62); to which could be added the dreadlocks, "colours," and "tams" of Rastafarians and Rudies, the afros of black power, and—at the usual risk of exciting derision—the talismanic maroon caps of the West Indies Test team.

This preoccupation with the head and with headgear clearly goes back to slavery and, beyond that, to religious traditions and practices of Africa. Thus Cuffee, the leader of the Windward Maroons in Jamaica in the 1730s, wore "a silver-laid hat and a small sword" to distinguish himself from his "subjects" (Patterson 1979:261), and when Thomas Thistlewood met the more famous Cudjoe in 1750, the latter "had on a feathered hat, sword by his side, gun upon his shoulder," and "somewhat a majestic look" that brought to Thistlewood's mind "the picture of Robinson Crusoe" (Hall 1989:14); the hat, like the sword, the gun, and the title of colonel, may be seen as part of the systematic appropriation, by Maroons, of the symbols of white power. Thistlewood also reveals (109) that at the time of Tacky's uprising (1760) "a shaved head amongst the Negroes was the signal of war" and that, among his own slaves, "Jackie, Job, Achilles, Quasheba, Rosanna, &c. had their heads remarkably shaved." Still more strikingly, two of the participants in the great Jamaican slave uprising of 1831 react to the burning of the Great House on "their" plantation by seizing those twin symbols of Massa's power, his hat and his horse: "I took up my Master's hat, and Alick took it out of my hand and went into the Stables and took Master's big mare—saddled it, and rode around the canes" (quoted in Brathwaite 1977:47). It would be difficult to imagine a gesture more charged with political, anthropological, and psychological meaning: the "horse" becomes the rider and, at last in (brief) possession of himself, flaunts Massa's "symbolic hat and hauteur" (Brathwaite) and takes magical possession of the canefields, site of his and his people's historic dispossession, by riding around them. Given the context of slavery, it is hardly surprising that hats and horses—to say nothing of rods and whips—figure so prominently as icons of power in both Afro-Caribbean religion and politics.

30. Such headgear goes back to the very origins of Afro-Christianity in Jamaica: according to W. J. Gardner (1971:460), the Myalists of 1841–42 (see chapter 3) had "their heads bound in a fantastic fashion" as they "ran about with arms outstretched, and declared that they were flying." So important is Revivalist headgear that they are commonly known in Jamaica as "wrap 'eads" (Chevannes 1995b:112).

It is in all likelihood a common African origin—probably the masked plays of secret societies like the Egungun[31]—that explains the remarkable similarity in the design of the symbolic headdresses and headgear found throughout the Caribbean, and also the fact that they are found, without significant modification of form, in both sacred and secular domains. Thus, to take just one example, the elaborate mirror-encrusted "house" of Jonkonnu appears to be echoed in all of the following: in the hat "decorated with small mirrors, bells, and ribbons of various colors and sometimes with paper flowers and birds" worn at the Fiesta de Santiago Apostal in Loíza, Puerto Rico (Alegría 1956:130); in the "fantastic straw helmet" worn by the Afro-Cuban dancer at the Dia de los Reyes festival witnessed by Wurdemann in 1844 (Brandon 1993:73); in the "huge headdress of paper flowers, mirrors, and ostrich plumes" in which the majordomo leads the Rara procession in Haiti (Dunham 1983:33); in the miter about eighteen inches high made of cardboard covered in calico, with small mirrors on front, back and both sides worn by a Jamaican healer as the "Haddo Doctor" in the 1870s and 1880s (Elkins 1977:3); and in the *reisados* of Bahia who, at the Feast of the Epiphany, don "high, curved, off the face of headdresses of cardboard covered with brightly-coloured satin and decorated with feathers, beads, and small mirrors" (Crowley 1984:16).

In Trinidad this Afro-Creole tradition of the headdress meshes with the Indo-Creole (and specifically Shiite Muslim) tradition of the *tadjeh* to create elaborate and outlandish coiffures such as the electrified headpieces of some midnight robbers in which "small light bulbs are used to decorate and illuminate the costume, or to serve as 'eyes' for the cobras, spiders, 'morocoy,' alligators, and lizards that festoon the hat and shoes of the Robber" (Crowley 1956b:266) or the post–World War II headpieces "representing gun turrets with moving guns, telecommunication equipment with lights blinking on and off, cash registers with drawers that opened" as well as "every variety of clock, and other intricate mechanical models" (Crowley 1956a:203). To say that such extravaganzas are just "play" is, of course, to say that they are very serious indeed. They are probably a reworking, in the light of Creole history, of an African prototype or paradigm, not so much a specific mask or headdress—though the masks of Egungun make an obvious "source"—as an African "philosophy of the head" to which the experience of slavery gave a particular resonance and edge.

An African paradigm readily presents itself. In the Dahomean and Yoruba

---

31. According to Harold Courlander (quoted in Simpson 1978:91), one such secret society, the Egbo Club of Nigeria, has an officer who "carries a rod or whip, the symbol of the power of the society, with which, under native law, he had the right to flog to death any nonmembers who had seriously offended against its rules." On Egungun masquerades, see the special number of *African Arts* (11, 3 [1978]) and also the study of the closely related Gelede masquerades of the Yoruba by Drewal and Drewal 1983.

religions from which Vodou, Shango, and Santería are derived, the head is the locus of the personality that, for the duration of the trance, the spirit will displace and supplant, whence the Fon expression "the vodou has come into his head" (*vodun wá ta éton me*, quoted in Rouget 1985:45). It is this that explains the frequency and intensity of head-centered rituals in Afro-American possession cults, for instance, in Candomblé, where the initiate's head is washed, shaved, painted, and lightly cut at the center point of the scalp, "literally opening a point of intersection between inner and outer worlds" (Murphy 1994:62), the object of the whole ritual being to "'fix' the *orixá* within the very center of a person's consciousness" (78). Similarly, Santería has an initiatory rite known as *kariocha* (< Yoruba *ka ori ocha* = to place the *orishas* over one's head) in which the guardian *orisha* is "set" in the neophyte's head, which thus becomes "a throne which the royal spirit can ascend" (95), whence the need, as *santeros* and *santeras* sing as they perform the rite, "to cut away the cover" (shave the head) and so "clear the headland / Impinging on its owner" (98). Finally, in Vodou, the ritual of *lav-tét*[32]—the head is first wrapped in a poultice of bread soaked in wine, cornmeal, feathers, raw eggs, and other such substances, bound in a cloth, left for a week, and then washed in an herbal liquid (Métraux 1959:200)—is designed to still the restive forces that make up the neophyte's *gros bon anj* (personality, consciousness) and prepare her to be consecrated to her *loa mait-tèt*, the spirit who will be master of her head throughout her life (see Brown 1991:351). Similar head-centered rituals are encountered in Trinidadian Shango (Carr 1953:47) and in the very different tradition of Jamaican Revival (Simpson 1978:114). Each such ritual is at once a baptism, a wedding, and—to use the Spanish term for *kariocha*—a *coronación* in which the neophyte becomes the spirit's child and wife and, thanks to the infusion of its regal force, a king or queen: "to make a saint is to make a king," says one *babalorisha* (Murphy 1994:93), suggesting once again a continuity between the worlds of cult and carnival with its intricate "fictitious and pseudo-hierarchies."

The rituals are of African origin but would have a special pertinence and potency for the slave who already had an all-too-human *mait-tèt* in his master who had, so to speak, displaced his *gros bon anj* and possessed him as a *loa* rides its horse or—to use two other images rooted deep in Afro-Creole life—as an obeah man controls his victim from afar or, in Haiti, a *bokor* (magician) manipulates his gang of *zombis* living corpses who inhabit, like that other "liminal" or "limbic" being the slave (see Patterson 1982a:46), some "misty zone" (Métraux 1959:282) on the marches of life and death.[33] This being so, possession for the

---

32. Katherine Dunham underwent the full process of initiation (*kanzo*) and describes the experience, including the *lav-tèt* and *pot-tèt* rituals (1969:97–116).

33. Like virtually everything connected with Vodou, the *zombi* originates in Africa (see Courlander 1960:102) but acquires a particular salience by virtue of the slave experience. For what (at

slave (and mutatis mutandis for his descendants) takes the form of exorcising one *mait-tèt*—the slavemaster and his postemancipation avatars—from his head and replacing him with another, the guardian *loa, orisha,* or other spirit who empowers him with its *axe* or spirit force and lifts him beyond the physical and moral barriers of his life to the level of the gods: *Attiban Legba ouvri bayé pou' moin ago! Ou wè Attiban Legba ouvri bayé pou' moin ouvri bayé!*[34] It is for this reason that possessions and allied spirit rites were often so important in at least the *initial* stages of slave revolts and postemancipation popular uprisings.[35] Possession expelled Massa's spirit from Quashie's head, filled it with the empowering energy of another master spirit and drove him, like the *zombi* awakened by a grain of salt, to deeds of violence and vengeance against his master. Thanks to possession, the slave becomes a king or queen just as in carnival, that secular version of possession, the masque propels its wearer into the subjunctive world of vicarious royalty. The head adorned, magnified, enhanced, is the sign, or rather the embodiment, of a recovered selfhood, of a self empowered by the dispossession of one self and its repossession by another.[36] And there's the rub. Only the dispossessed want to be possessed, but the new self they acquire is still the self of another, not the "true self" that they must *create* patiently *from within* rather than *receive* ecstatically *from without and above.* And so it is with West Indian politics as it is with the cults of the spirits: Power descends from above and is operated *for* the People by its Leader, and

---

least while in the canefields) was a slave if not—to use Métraux's description of the *zombi* (1959:282–83)—"a beast of burden which his master exploits without mercy, making him work in the fields, weighing him down with labour, whipping him freely and feeding him on meagre, tasteless food"? Recognizable by "their absent-minded manner, the extinguished, almost glassy eyes," *zombis* can be liberated by eating even a grain of salt, whereupon "the fog which cloaks their minds instantly clears away" and realization of their "terrible servitude" rouses in them, as in slaves, "a vast rage and ungovernable desire for vengeance. They hurl themselves on their master, kill him, destroy his property and then go in search of their tombs." The analogy between slavery, colonialism, and the process of "zombification" is a commonplace of Haitian writing; the point is, as the Haitian poet René Dépestre says, to find the "revitalizing salt capable of restoring to man the use of his imagination and his culture" (quoted in Davis 1988:75).

34. Attiban Legba, open the gate for me, *ago!* You see, Attiban Legba, open the gate for me, open the gate! (quoted in Courlander 1960:77).

35. The influence of Vodou on the Haitian slave revolution remains hotly disputed. That the ceremony at Bois Caïman in August 1791 that traditionally, if somewhat loosely, is said to have inaugurated the uprising was at the very least Vodou related seems beyond doubt (see Fick 1990:260–66; Geggus 1991:43), but whether Boukman was himself a *houngan* is far from proved. Of the principal leaders of the uprising, only Biassou and Hyacinthe were incontestably *houngans* (Fick 1990:115, 139)—Romaine-la-Prophétesse was probably a kind of (male) shaman figure (128)—and both faded from the scene when Toussaint L'Ouverture, Jean-Jacques Dessalines, and Henry Christophe—all opponents of Vodou (see Métraux 1959:48–49)—came to the fore. The Duvalierist view that "1804 est issu du Vodou" (quoted in Laguerre 1989:60) is, to say the least, not proved.

36. The dialectic of head/slavery and headgear/freedom is marvelously illustrated by the story, told by Phillippo (1969:202), of a slave who, caught in a shower of rain, takes off the hat he had purchased to prevent it from getting wet, saying "Hat belong to *me*—head belong to *Massa.*"

not *by* the People itself (see chapter 3). And though the People attain to an intense feeling of subjectivity through identification with the Leader—"Is I Time Now" proclaimed the graffiti in Kingston at the height of the Manley government's radicalism in early 1977 (Stephens and Stephens 1986:154)— that "smadyization,"[37] the sense of being *somebody*, can be taken from them just as easily as it was bestowed. It is this paradox of democratic politics in the Caribbean that will be discussed through the figure of the warrior *loa* Ogou in the section that follows.

## Ogou's Dance: Power and Powerlessness in the Caribbean

Ogou is not merely "a central figure in Haitian religion," as Karen McCarthy Brown has put it (1989:65),[38] but is literally crucial in that he stands at the crux of the dialectic of power and powerlessness in Haitian society. A warrior god of undoubted African origin, Ogou has been significantly transformed in the course of his disturbing passage through Haitian history. He takes on new and paradoxical attributes with each stage of the county's development until in his modern configuration he may be said to embody the ambiguous essence of power in Haiti and, by extension, in other Caribbean nations, where he appears either in person, as in Trinidadian Shango, or by analogy in the sword-wielding figures enumerated in the preceding section and earlier sections of this book. The defining characteristics of Ogou is his doubleness. He belongs to both the Rada and the Petro families of *loas*, and his altar room is often situated between those of the two contending *nanchons*, in clear recognition of the fact that he "mediates between two opposed ways of being represented by the Rada and the Petro patheons, allowing movement from one to the other" (69). Moreover, like most of the major *loas*, Ogou manifests himself in a multitude of forms, chief among which are soldiers—Ogou Feray (Ferraille), Sin Jak Majè (Saint Jacques Majeur), and Ogou Badagri—and politicians, Ogou Panama, Achade Bokò, and Ogou Shango. The most senior of all the Ogou figures is Sin Jak Majè, who is represented as Santiago mounted on his horse and crushing his enemy underfoot and is often greeted with the chant *Sin Jak Majè / Gason lagè ou ye*, "Sin Jak Majè / You're a warrior" (71). Heading the phalanx of soldier Ogous is Ogou Feray, whose *vèvè* is based on the Haitian coat of arms, as though graphically to convey that what is being enacted on the floor of the *hounfor* is nothing less than the drama of the Haitian nation itself. Strutting to and fro on the *peristil*, chewing their cigars, demanding rum

37. The expression "smadyization" was used by Rex Nettleford in a BBC television program on Jamaica broadcast in the early 1990s to describe the psychological evolution of the Jamaican people under the PNP government of 1972–80. I cannot give an exact reference.

38. This section is based on Karen McCarthy Brown's discussion of Ogou (1989), supported by Desmangles 1992:146–53. References are as before kept to a minimum.

with the time-honored phrase *Grèn mwê frèt* (my balls are cold), and above all brandishing their sabers and machetes (Métraux 1959:109), the various Ogous symbolize in the first instance the spirit of bellicose resistance that, in the Haitian nationalist myth, has dominated the country's history from the rebel slaves and Maroon bands of the eighteenth century through the slave uprising of 1791 and the war of independence of 1801–4 to the Caco insurgents who, under Charlemagne Péralte, defied the American invading force in 1918–19 and the Vodouisants who, in the early 1940s, withstood the so-called anti-superstition campaign launched by the Roman Catholic Church. More specifi-cally, Ogou Feray is said to represent Toussaint, Christophe, and Dessalines in their struggle against the French, and to this extent any ceremony in honor of the warrior *loa* becomes "an archetypal ritual, a reenactment of the beginnings of a nation" in which every adept participates in the epic struggles and suffer-ings that gave birth to the Haitian nation-state in 1804 (Desmangles 1992: 152). But as well as embodying the martial spirit of Haitian resistance, Ogou is also a healer—he is the patron *loa* of surgeons among others—and if he in-flicts suffering with his sword, he also suffers on his own account and is some-times represented on the walls of *peristils* slumped like a mortally wounded warrior, tears rolling down his cheeks, his arms flung limply over the shoulders of his supporters, implicitly if not explicitly like Christ at the deposition from the cross. He is, in short, both violent warrior and suffering redeemer who liberates through the wounds he inflicts and heals through the wounds he suffers. He is father to the adepts who, suffering with him, sing

> Ogou, I am wounded
> I am wounded, Ogou Papa
> I cannot see my blood is red
> I am wounded, Ogou Papa.
> (147)

Father, healer, inflicter of wounds, and symbolic bearer of his people's suffer-ings, crusher of the enemy and martyr-prophet, Ogou in his various manifesta-tions is a *général sanglant* (Métraux 1959:107) in the double sense of the word: bloodthirsty and bleeding. Like Toussaint, Christophe, and Dessalines, he kills and suffers for his people, uniting in his person the contrasting destinies that in the religiopolitical leaders Papa Doc[39] and Père Titide (President Aristide) appear to be at opposite extremes of a continuum of violence but that may in

---

39. I have nowhere seen Papa Doc explicitly identified with Ogou, but the fact that he placed himself so firmly in the lineage of Toussaint, Dessalines, and Christophe (all of whom *are* explicitly likened to Ogou) suggests that the assimilation is possible. On Papa Doc and his predecessors, see *La Catéchisme de la révolution* of 1964 (quoted in Diedrich and Burt 1969:283): "Q. Who are Dessalines, Toussaint, Christophe, Pétion and Estimé? A. Dessalines, Toussaint, Christophe, Pétion and Estimé are five founders of the nation who are found with François Duvalier."

reality be disquietingly close one to another. For if Ogou inflicts violence first upon the people's enemies, he is also capable of turning it not just against the people in whose name he acts but also, in a final suicidal gesture, against himself. Symbolizing all the ambiguities of power in action, Ogou also acts out violence in all its forms and directions.

Given this complexity, it is hardly surprising that Ogou's "horse"—it is almost always a woman—goes from one emotional extreme to another in the course of her possession, whether it be in Haitian Vodou or Trinidadian Shango. In Shango, "an expression of masculinity and fierceness" envelops the face of the horse possessed by "Ogun whose eyeballs are terrible to behold."[40] Breaking away from the other dancers, she dons a red head tie and waistband and seizes a machete or sword that, her anger and violence mounting, she brandishes "near the genitals of other participants, with both a menacing and sexual effect" (Mischel and Mischel 1958:250–55). In Vodou, she "fetches a sabre and jams the hilt of it against the *poteau-mitan* and the point against her stomach" and, pushing with all her strength, causes the blade to bend. Then, "in a sudden frenzy," she attacks the *laplace*, who is also armed with a sword, and engages him in a combat that becomes to ferocious that the other *hounsis* have to part them. "Seized by another wave of bellicose frenzy," the horse then "hacks the *poteau-mitan* with her sabre and chases the *hounsis* who flee in terror" until she corners them and beats them violently with the flat of her saber, after which she appears to be soothed. She smiles, smokes a cigar (like a general after a victorious combat), eats, and distributes what remains to the chastened *hounsis*; then, speaking in the voice of Ogou, she lectures them on how they should behave themselves in future. One little girl who had previously been beaten with the flat of the sword is forced to prostrate herself before Ogou (Métraux 1959:125–26): it is as though, having asserted her power over the *hounsis*, Ogou takes her "children" under her wing to succor and protect them—always provided they obey her instructions. Sometimes, however, Ogou in her frenzy turns her sword against herself (Brown 1989:78): directed first against the external enemy, the oppressor, aggression is then visited on the oppressed and finally, though not invariably, turned against the self. Acted out week after week on the floor of the *hounfor*, the cycle of violence and self-violence will end only with the deaths of both Ogou and the people.

Brown convincingly interprets the different phases of Ogou's dance as a metaphor of political power in Haiti, which was born when the slaves turned the master's violence successfully against him but was forthwith wrested from their hands and turned against them in the name of the nation by those— Toussaint, Dessalines, Christophe, Pétion, and their successors—who had led

---

40. This Shango designation of Ogun is quoted in Houk 1994:213.

them to victory against the French. And so, year after year, regime after regime, it goes on: "Time and again the Haitians have experienced their leaders turning on them. They are deeply ambivalent about their own military and political history, and that is why Ogou, who moves between constructive and destructive uses of power, has become a natural vehicle for making their history comprehensible" (Brown 1989:76).[41] Ogou's sword may thus be seen as the Haitian version of the Jamaican Rod of Correction. Both are variants on Massa's cane and Busha's whip, and both are wrested from their original owners only to be turned, often in the name of "freedom" itself, against the collective self of the people by leaders who are often driven to actual suicide (Henry Christophe) or effective self-destruction (Jean-Claude Duvalier) by their headlong pursuit of power or their unwillingness to share it. In Haiti as in Jamaica, power always descends loa-like[42] from above onto the people below, even though in the Haitian case it was the people who, through their ancestors of 1791–1804, first seized that power from their slave and colonial masters. Ogou's sword, like the Rod of Correction, both empowers symbolically and disempowers in fact, just as the loas, in mounting their horses, dispossess them of freedom even as they possess them and endow them with might. That Haitians clearly perceive Vodou and politics as "two poles of the same continuum" (Laguerre 1989:102), interlocking with and reinforcing each other at every point, is evidenced by the well-known saying Apré Bondié sé léta (after God comes the state), by which they mean "not the goodness or the benevolence of God" but "rather his remoteness, unpredictability and power" (Nicholls 1985:220). Power dwells in the National Palace like Bondié in his heaven[43] and manifests itself not directly—Bondié never possesses an adept, any more than Papa Doc ever revealed himself on the streets and marketplaces of Port-au-Prince—but through a host of subaltern figures of authority, the

41. Brown continues as follows (1989:86): "In Haiti, Ogou's central theme is power. Ogou the revolutionary hero frees his people and puts weapons in their hands for self-protection. He intervenes on their behalf before the civil authorities. He gathers his followers to him like precious lost objects. But he also exacts strict discipline and punishes those who tire or waver. Sometimes his anger turns to blind rage, irrationally attacking those close to him or even himself."

42. The word loa is conventionally given an unspecified African derivation, but as André-Marcel D'Ans points out (1987:290), it is pronounced lwa by Haitians and is much more likely to derive from French loi, the Vodou "horse" being, precisely, under the "law" of the spirit who "rides" her. If correct, this etymology confirms the interpretation I am advancing here of Vodou as a "magical mirror" of the structure of slave society and the postindependence Haitian state.

43. The assimilation of president and God is explicitly made in the blasphemous "Lord's Prayer" appended to the Duvalierist Catéchisme de la révolution of 1964 (quoted in Diederich and Burt 1969:284): "Our Doc who art in the National Palace for life, hallowed be Thy name by present and future generations. Thy will be done at Port-au-Prince and in the provinces. Give us this day our new Haiti and never forgive the trespasses of the antipatriots who spit every day on our country; let them succumb to temptation, and under the weight of their venom, delivery them not from any evil." On the "mystical" and indeed pseudo-Christological dimension of Duvalierist ideology, see Lévêque 1971:20–22.

*chef de section*,[44] the *tonton macoute*, or this or that member of the evocatively named *classe intermédiaire*, who correspond structurally to the *loas* in Vodou. The world of the *hounfor*, like the wider world of Haitian politics and society, is hierarchical, bureaucratic, and authoritarian to the core, embodying what one Haitian calls "a sort of primitive totalitarianism" (Pluchon 1987:283).[45] But over and above Bondié in the National Palace there dwells a still greater God to the north on whose Power Bondié and his *loas* ultimately depend for their power and who on two memorable occasions (July 1915 and now September 1994) has revealed himself *directly*, in addition to the countless occasions when, like a puppetmaster or *bokor* (magician), he has controlled things invisibly from afar, imposing his will on a nation that threatened to collapse not into violence— for violence is endemic in Haiti and the source of all order—but into *chaos*. Thus, virtually from the moment of independence, it has been against a backdrop of ultimate United States control that the grotesque carnival of Haitian politics has taken place, bringing year by year one hideous dictatorial masque after another—Toussaint, Dessalines, Christophe, Soulouque, Salomon, Sam, Magloire, Duvalier *pére et fils*, and then, in accelerated succession, Namphy, Paul, Avril, and Cédras *entre autres*. Each reigns by violence for a time before being consigned, usually by violence again, to a ritual *brulé carnival* from whose ashes he is reborn like some obscene phoenix, distinguishable from those who preceded and who will follow him only by the scale and viciousness of the violence he metes out to "his" people. Thus, as Laënnec Hurbon has written (1987:18), the whole of Haitian politics since independence[46] has been conducted through and beneath a "phantasm of the Master" inherited from slavery that, in almost two hundred years, the Haitian people have yet to shake off.[47] The Master's cane passed to the general, and the overseer's whip to the sergeant, the *macoute*, the *chef de section*, and the *houngan*, who proceeded to inflict systematically on the people acts of violence that are often identical to, or instantly recall, the worse excesses of overseers against slaves.[48] Whether Fa-

---

44. The *chef de section* is the official responsible for the smallest administrative division in Haiti and is commonly referred to by Haitians as *l'Etat* (Maingot 1994:224). He is explicitly seen as a modern version of the *commandeur* (overseer/driver) in Hurbon 1987:19. Significantly, *leta* also means a bully in Haitian Creole (Michel-Rolph Trouillot, in McFadyen and LaRamée 1995:125).

45. The classic account of the structural links between Vodou and political authoritarianism is to be found in Courlander and Bastien 1966. See also Laguerre 1989:102–17.

46. Or even before independence, since, like many Haitian radicals, Hurbon (1979:106) sees the lineaments of Haitian absolutism as having been created by Toussaint between the abolition of slavery (but not of Saint-Domingue's colonial status) in 1794 and its reimposition by Napoleon in 1802 (see also Dupuy 1989:56–65).

47. "Slavery, which lasted three centuries, has left intact, after the disappearance of the master, its symbolic and imaginary networks in the heart of Haitian society and the State" (Hurbon 1987:18).

48. Thus the ritual display of Boukman's severed head in 1791 was echoed in the decapitation and public display of the bodies of anti-Duvalierist militants during the so-called Vespers of Jérémie

ther Jean-Bertrand Aristide, restored to the presidency by a complex combination of internal and external forces (see McFadyen and LaRameé 1995), can break this fantasy, and break with it himself,[49] remains unclear at this time (February 1995).

All this is to say that, like other possession-based Afro-American religions, Vodou combines a theoretical egalitarianism, in the sense that every servant of the *loas*, irrespective of class, color, or gender, is as likely to be "mounted" as another, with an indelible propensity toward hierarchy, inequality, and authoritarianism in practice. Its pantheon of spirits, like that of Brazilian Umbanda (see Brown 1986:55), is structured along quasi-military lines, and relations between servants and their spirits likewise assume "the form of a vast heavenly patronage network linking spiritual patrons and middlemen to the human clients who form its base" in such a way that the whole cosmos operates on a stratified, vertical basis: "Spiritual powers to heal and advise move downward in exchange for loyal and faithful homage and service, which move upwards" (189). It is this structural homology between the Vodou cosmos and Haitian state and society that explains the remarkable doubleness of Vodou's historical and political role. On the one hand, particularly during the early stages of the slave uprising of 1791–94, at times during the nineteenth century, and under the American occupation (1915–34) and the period of mulatto dominance that succeeded it (1934–46), it has undoubtedly functioned as a major source of opposition to internal and external oppression in Haiti. On the other hand it has also, and at the same time, reproduced the very hierarchical structures and mentalities that it periodically inverted, feeding into

---

of 1964 (see Abbott 1988:122–31). Similarly, "Père Lebrun"—the "necklacing" of known Duvalierist supporters during the prolonged *déchoukaj* (uprooting) that followed the collapse of the regime in 1986—hideously recalls the burning to death of Makandal and his followers in 1758. On the controversy concerning Aristide's endorsement (or otherwise) of "Père Lebrun," see the Americas Watch/ National Coalition for Haitian Refugees and Caribbean Rights report of 1 November 1991 (vol. 3, 12:24–25) and Farmer 1994:180. In the speech of 27 September 1991 in which Aristide is said by opponents to have given his support to "Père Lebrun," he spoke of the "beautiful tool" Haitians have in their hands—he and his supporters claim he meant the constitution—in the following terms: "What a beautiful instrument! What a beautiful appliance! It's beautiful, it's beautiful, it's pretty, it looks sharp! It's fashionable, it smells good and wherever you go you want to smell it" (quoted in Americas Watch Report 1991:25). Whether the "instrument" in question is the constitution or "Père Lebrun," it strikingly recalls both the whip and the Rod of Correction.

49. Although to my knowledge Aristide has never likened himself to Christ, Moses, or Joshua, he is known as "Msieu Mirak" (Mister Miracle) by his followers, who clearly do not hesitate to identify his *words* with those of Christ (see Maingot 1994:218–19). Since these words were written, Aristide has been succeeded by his "marasa" or twin, René Préval, the use of the Vodou term (meaning "Sacred Twins," see Brown 1991:55, etc.) suggesting the continuing salience, in the politics of post-Duvalierist Haiti, of Vodouist discourse and imagery (see Phil Davison, "Aristide's Man Heading for Landslide Win," *Independent*, 16 December 1995). Aristide significantly likened himself to a "true houngan" who "channels, orientates, revives and vivifies the community's faith in itself (*la foi communautaire)*" (see Jean-Bertrand Aristide, *Tout moun se moun* (Paris: Seuil, 1992), 87–88).

and reinforcing certain deep-seated patterns of dependence and patronage and even, as under the elder Duvalier, providing one of a series of overlapping formal networks through which a totalitarian power was imposed. Thus *all* of the *houngans* in the slum district of Upper Belair in Port-au-Prince studied by Michel Laguerre in the mid-1970s were *tontons macoutes* (Laguerre 1982:100). Truly, as Laguerre commented (117), Vodou was not "at the periphery of national, Duvalierist politics; it [was] at the center."

But as Laguerre shows, the function of such "political and spiritual brokers" (142) in the Duvalierist machine went far beyond the part they played as nodal points in the immensely complex power web by means of which, using a combination of violence, patronage, and ideological obfuscation, the Center (the Haitian elite) was able, for almost thirty years, to maintain control over the Periphery (the mass of the Haitian population, of which the slum dwellers of Upper Belair are typical). It is the experience of possession itself that, as mediated through the *houngan*-cum–*tonton macoute*, Laguerre shows to have been fundamental to the perpetuation of inequality and oppression in Haiti between 1957 and 1986. The *houngan-macoute* functioned, in Laguerre's analysis, as the center of the Periphery (the people of Upper Belair), who mediated and controlled relations with the center of the Center, understood spiritually as the *loas* and politically as the elite and, ultimately, the National Palace itself. Thus "the *houngan*, when possessed, becomes a peripheral broker in relation to two centers: the *loas* and the political elite. He is the intermediary between the *loas* and his congregation, and between the political elite and the residents of his district." Furthermore, "through possession, the center of the universe (*loas*) comes to be identified with the center of the Periphery (*houngan*). Spirit possession becomes the locus where two forms of social communication, the religious and the political, meet." So it is that, on the one hand, "the people in the center of the Periphery (Vodou priests and *tontons macoutes*) use the people in the center of the Center (elite) to maintain their rank in the slum and for upward mobility. On the other hand, the people in the center of the Center (elite) use the people in the center of the Periphery (the brokers) to exploit the community." In short, "with possession, it is the center of the universe which *descends* [Laguerre's emphasis] to identify with the center of the Periphery. Possession brings status reversal. By possession, the center of the Periphery becomes the center of the Center and the center of the Center the center of the Periphery" (Laguerre 1982:141–13, spelling, capitalization, and italics adapted for consistency).

But here, precisely, is the rub. Although the *pitit kay*, the rank-and-file Vodou cultists, may be possessed by the *loas* like their *houngan*, it is the *houngan*, the center of the Periphery, who controls their possession, so that ultimately they remain at the periphery of the Periphery, dispossessed of power by the very experience that seems to empower them: descending, the spirits invest them with power, but that power is instantly "spirited away" by the *houngan*. The *pitit kay* may *believe* that "through the relationship with the spirits, a symbolic inversion is enacted so that the Periphery becomes the Center and the Center the Periphery" (Laguerre 1982:155), but the reality is that the inversion, such as it is, is controlled by the mediator between Center and Periphery (the *houngan-macoute*), so that, like Trinidad carnival, Vodou is at the same time a subversion of the structures of society and *a subversion of that subversion* (see above, chapter 4). And so it goes on. The *pitit kay* remain peripheral to, and ultimately dependent on, the *houngan*, who, the mere center of the Periphery, himself remains peripheral to, and ultimately dependent on, the center of the Center (the elite). But that "Center" is in reality only a pseudo-Center, peripheral to, and ultimately dependent on, the "true" Center (the complex of political and economic forces in which Haiti is inserted), so that the whole phenomenon of possession becomes a game of dupes in which each party is peripheral when it believes itself to be central and dominated when it believes itself to be dominant. From its origins as an independent nation up to the present, Haitian society has been based on two parallel, interlocking, and mutually reinforcing power hierarchies—that of Vodou and the political-military "machine"—which may be represented schematically, and very approximately, as in table 3.

**Table 3. Vodou and political hierarchies**

|  | *Voudou hierarchy* | *Political hierarchy* |
|---|---|---|
| 1. "True" center | Bondié ↓ | Hegemonic power ↓ |
| 2. "Pseudo-center" (inside) | Ogou ↓ | Emperor or president[50] ↓ |
|  | Other *loas* ↓ | Generals, ministers, chief of police ↓ |
| 3. Center of Periphery (inside/ outside) | Houngans (*mambos*) ↓ Laplace, *houngenikon*, etc. ↓ | *Classe intermédiaire* *Chefs de section* *Tontons macoutes* ↓ |
| 4. Periphery (outside) | *Pitit kay* | Mass of population |

50. In the case of a supreme dictator such as François Duvalier, it is difficult to know whether he should be identified as a *loa* or as Bondié himself (see n. 43 above). In Cuba, Fidel Castro has been widely identified with the Santería spirit Obatala, messenger and "right-hand man of the god of all creation," whose symbol, a white dove, was seen to *descend* onto his shoulder as he gave a speech on the night he entered Havana in triumph (8 January 1959): "Thus, when the bird landed on Fidel, everyone watching knew that Castro was blessed; he was *El Eligio* (The Chosen One). Since then Fidel has been called *El Caballo* (The Horse), the term used to designate someone whom an *orisha* has mounted and possessed" (Elsasser and Valdès 1989:31–32).

These twin hierarchies, in their turn, replicate, and indigenize, a third hierarchy, that of the slave plantation (table 4).

**Table 4. Slave plantation hierarchy**

| | |
|---|---|
| 1. | Metropolitan power, world markets |
| | ↓ |
| 2. | Plantation owner |
| | ↓ |
| | Manager (*géreur*) |
| | Bookkeeper (*économe*) |
| 3. | Driver (*commandeur*) |
| | ↓ |
| 4. | Slaves |

In each of the hierarchies, the crucial point of transition (3) from "pseudo-Center" (2) to "Periphery" (4) or, varying the image, from "inside" to "outside,"[51] is occupied by a Black (normally but not invariably male) who, standing Legba-like at the crossroads where the worlds of the powerless and the powerful intersect, both dominates the former and is dominated by the latter. If the powerful (symbolically and almost always in fact) are male, and the powerless, whatever their gender, symbolically female, the intermediary figure is symbolically double-gendered, "male" to those below him/her, "female" to those above.[52] Furthermore, the liminal positions of *commandeur*, *houngan*, and *macoute* make them at once the visible embodiments of a normally invisible power (the "outside" expression of the "inside," as it were) and potential focuses of opposition/resistance to that power: the role of *commandeurs* and *houngans* in the great slave uprising of 1791–94 (see Fick 1990:94, 231, 244, etc.), and of *houngans* in fomenting resistance to the American occupation during the Caco War of 1918–20 (see Gaillard 1983:46, 62–66), is abundantly documented, and even *macoutes* may on occasion have become opponents of the Duvalierist machine. Finally, the very visibility of *houngans* and *macoutes* made them obvious targets (and scapegoats) for the crowd's fury when in 1986 the Duvalierist regime finally collapsed, only to be resurrected forthwith in the form of "Duvalierism without Duvalier" under the military junta: in the circumstances, it is remarkable that "only" three hundred *houngans-macoutes* succumbed to the ministrations of Père Lebrun and other instruments of torture and murder (see Dayan 1988; Bellegarde-Smith 1990:150–51). Thus, like Ogou's sword, like Ogou

51. Significantly, countryfolk in Haiti are often referred to collectively as *moun andewò* (people outside) by city dwellers (Michel-Rolph Trouillot in McFadyen and LaRamée 1995:125).

52. As we saw above, the *pitit kay*, whether men or women, are always designated by the female noun *hounsi*. There is a substantial literature on the (alleged) prominence of male homosexuals among priests in Afro-Brazilian possession cults (see Landes 1940; Fry 1982; Matory 1988), but only passing references to the subject in the literature on Vodou (see Laguerre 1982:26, 142; Bellegarde-Smith 1990:13).

himself, everything about Haitian Vodou is double-edged. A force of cohesion and resistance under slavery and of latent or overt opposition to elite or foreign domination every since, under the Duvaliers Vodou became "a tool of coercion, the whip of internal colonialism, a means for the exploitation of the Black by the Black" (Rémy Bastien, in Courlander and Bastien 1966:66). Its present situation is obscure, but the likelihood is that it will continue, as in the past, simultaneously to challenge, to legitimate, and to deflect resentment from the manifold inequalities of Haitian society: whether its egalitarian or its authoritarian dimension wins out is likely to be one of the crucial issues in the country's uncertain progress toward democracy.

## Beyond the Hero and the Crowd?

Nowhere in the Caribbean are religion and politics more closely intertwined than in Haiti, but since the end of the Second World War and the acquisition first of universal suffrage and then of political independence, most of Britain's former Caribbean colonies have witnessed their own secularized version of Ogou's dance, as one would-be charismatic leader has followed another into office or, as often as not, remained so firmly ensconced that only death, finally, could remove him from power. Almost everywhere in the Commonwealth Caribbean a mode of political leadership emerged, democratically based but autocratic in style, to which, in the late 1960s, the term "doctor politics" came to be applied first in Trinidad and then throughout the region as a whole. The paradigmatic doctor-politician was of course Eric Williams himself, but as Lloyd Best argued in a seminal article published in the Trinidad *Express* in May 1969, most British West Indian leaders of the time, whatever their level of formal education, had something of the doctor about them. Best went on to divide them into three broad but clearly distinguishable categories that the following typology elaborates and expands.[53] First come the "Sunday school doctors," Anancy figures sprung from the people whose biblical culture they share and exploit and who build their political careers on reputations acquired as trade union leaders, outwitting and outtalking the powerful in the name of the poor: typical are Eric Gairy of Grenada, Vere Bird of Antigua, Robert Bradshaw of St. Kitts, and from his anomalous class background, Alexander Bustamante of Jamaica. Then there are the "public school doctors," scions of the local Eurocentric elite, who characteristically come in father-son pairings, with the son assuming Joshualike the redemptive mission of Moses: Norman and Michael Manley (Jamaica), Grantley and Tom Adams (Barbados), and—perhaps most potent of all—the martyred son of a martyred father,

---

53. For a summary of Best's typology, see Sutton 1991:113. See also Best 1985:148–57 for a follow-up discussion of the whole question of "doctor politics" in the Caribbean.

Maurice Bishop of Grenada.[54] Finally come the "grammar school doctors" whom state education has raised from the black lower middle classes: archetypically Eric Williams of Trinidad and Forbes Burnham of Guayana. Since Best's first essay in characterization, a fourth category of West Indian leader has emerged that Paul Sutton (1991:113–14) has dubbed the "managerial doctor," an update of the grammar school doctor who "draws on US educational models, promotes economic success as the basis of achievement, and trades upon western international support as a sign of acceptability": typical of this new subspecies are Edward Seaga of Jamaica and the "Iron Lady" of Dominica, Eugenia Charles, the only woman to have achieved major office in the Commonwealth Caribbean to date.

All of these leaders are "doctors" in one or more senses of the word: as men (or in one case a woman) of knowledge and of words, as would-be healers and deliverers of their people, and also in the specifically West Indian sense of religious "doctors" (cf. "Convinced Doctors" with their particular brand of spiritual-magical "science"). Whether they belong (or belonged) to the Right, the Center, or the Left, doctor-politicians, whatever their ilk, claim to embody the will of the people but act and speak as though power flows down from them onto the people in whose interests they claim to, or actually do, rule. In this respect, if in no other, Maurice Bishop in Grenada was little different, for example, from the democratically elected but dictatorial Eric Gairy whom he and his New Jewel Movement overthrew by force.[55] No sooner is the doctor-politician established in power by popular vote or acclaim (as in Grenada) than he distances himself from the "masses," even though in appearance he often remains in their midst, linked to them by the Word that he proffers with all the eloquence of the preacher and all the cunning of Anancy. Even as they are told that "Massa day done," a new Massa, often black like themselves but wielding Massa's language with a virtuosity Massa never achieved, is spinning his spiderweb of words to entrap them. But distant from "his" people even when among them, like "Monk" Lewis in the Great House surrounded by slaves, the Caribbean leader is alone. This too is something he shares with the various Ogou *loas* of Vodou, all of whom, according to Brown (1989:81), deploy "a solitary, individual power, not the collective power of close-knit groups, not the power of the united family." "Loneliness," she says, "is the other side of power," but the solitude of the Caribbean leader

54. Maurice Bishop's father Rupert was murdered in 1974 by police loyal to the then prime minister of Grenada, Eric Gairy. For a searching discussion of the contrasting political styles of Maurice Bishop and Bernard Coard, see Heine 1990.

55. According to Manning Marable (1987:199), there were "two contradictory strands of socialism" in the New Jewel Movement, one egalitarian and democratic, the other "hiearchical, statist, command-oriented, placing power above the masses, and resembling in several administrative respects the rigid autocratic features of the Crown Colony and Gairy regimes." See also Meeks 1993:132.

is often the solitude of arrogance as he removes his hearing aid at cabinet meetings when his ministers disagree with him and barks, like a parody of the Messiah figure he once was for "his" people, "I am the one who has power here; when I say 'come' you 'cometh,' and when I say 'go' you 'goeth.'"[56]

It is at this point that the savior of yore becomes the scapegoat of today, and the people heap curses on his head just as freely and as irresponsibly as they once accepted blessings and praise from his lips and gifts from his hands. For as all the most clear-sighted commentators are at pains to bring out, doctor-politicians thrive only because their "pupils" "patients" willingly surrender their individual and collective freedom and, having installed them in power, expect all things to be given freely to them ever after:

> Annabella stocking want patching
> She want de doctah help wid dat
> Johnson trousers falling
> He want de doctah help wid dat
> Dorothy loss she man
> She want to complain to Doctah Williams
> Mighty Striker, "Annabella"

Such self-surrender to an imaginary political savior goes back to the very roots of the West Indian experience, to the love-hate relationship with Massa that, as we have seen, is so deeply embedded in the slave psyche and that resurfaces in modified form in the democratic politics of the contemporary Caribbean: "Deprived of responsibility, we degraded our own capacity. We looked for 'Doctors' whether they were benevolent planters, or cunning labour leaders, or our bright sons."[57] But it is not only the myth of the "Good Massa" (and beyond him of the Good Governor and the Good King or Queen) that lives on in the doctor-politician,[58] but also the figure of the black spiritual "shepherd" and, beyond him again, that of the Christ-Savior himself. "Massah! Massah! Big Massah!" cries out the crowd to "Montesaviour," the charismatic leader, plainly based on Bustamante, in Orlando Patterson's *The Children of Sisyphus* (1964), "Come an' give we wo'k!" "Come an' save we like you did in

---

56. The hearing-aid story was frequently told of Eric Williams in the Caribbean in the early 1970s: I cannot vouch for its authenticity. For the "When I say 'come'" speech of the 1971 election in Trinidad, see Sutton 1984:55.

57. "The Problems," *Tapia* 1 (28 September 1969). This quotation, like the verse from "Annabella," is taken from Lowenthal 1972:311, to which this argument is indebted. "Annabella" is wrongly attributed to Sparrow by Lowenthal (see Yelvington 1995a:58–59).

58. Thus in a telling detail in Earl Lovelace's *The Wine of Astonishment* (1983:5), mothers in a Trinidadian village in 1944 hold up their babies for the newly elected black local potentate, Ivan Morton, to bless with his look, exactly as slave mothers did to "Monk" Lewis in Jamaica in 1816, so "giving a thrill to all we poor women who have children and see him as the saviour who footsteps we want our boy to follow in." See above chapter 2 above.

thirty-eight!" "Save we, Big Massah! Save we!" Under Montesaviour's loving, paternal, but sometimes reprimanding gaze, each member of the crowd "[loses] his being in the collectivity, and the collectivity [kills] its being in him" (Patterson 1989:86–87): it is the same kind of ecstatic self-surrender that, in a more explicitly sexualized and masochistic form, Patterson evokes later in the novel in the relationship between the Revivalist Shepherd and his band of predominantly female followers.[59] The structures of slave plantation, colonial polity, and popular Afro-Christian or (in Haiti) neo-African religion lock together to form a psychopolitical complex that liberates and binds, empowers and disempowers, decolonizes and recolonizes at the same time. Yet though they are deeply embedded in the colonial past, doctor politics are not necessarily an immutable feature of the West Indian scene, and now that most of the last generation of colonial, and many of the first generation of postcolonial, leaders have run their "las lap," there are signs that a new generation of less charismatic politicians is taking their place—dull Lenten pragmatists, perhaps, in comparison with the carnivalesque figures of yore, who "offer themselves to the electorate as better able to 'manage dependency' than any of their rivals" (Sutton 1991:114) in the full knowledge that, ultimately, the Caribbean really is in somebody else's backyard. The reign of the doctor-politician in the former British Caribbean seems at last to be waning, and the passing of its disparate band of Joshuas and Moseses may herald the advent of a broader, if less colorful, democracy in the countries concerned. It is to this possibility among other matters, that I turn in the concluding reflections.

59. It is worth noting in this respect that at least one of the Caribbean's leading doctor-politicians, the "managerial doctor" Edward Seaga, is a noted expert on Jamaican popular religion, having published an early, and still highly informative, study of it (see Seaga 1969). On Seaga's continuing links with popular religion and on his alleged "spiritual mentor," the "widely feared Pocomania shepherd named Mallica 'Kapo' Reynolds," see the possibly sensationalized account in Gunst 1995:36.

# Conclusion

It would be easy, and certainly far from incorrect, to conclude this book by saying that the various aspects of Caribbean culture I have discussed are essentially reactions to, and compensations for, the state of chronic disempowerment to which, historically, most West Indians have been condemned. Easy, correct, and yet incomplete; for though popular religion and festivities and, more broadly, the culture of play do in an obvious sense challenge the status quo and in so doing provide those who engage in them surrogate satisfactions for the deeper dissatisfactions of their lives, they also, by their very richness, reconcile the disempowered to the political, social, and economic inequalities, inherited from the past and entrenched in their basic structure in the present, that caused the dissatisfactions in the first place. Thus there is scarcely one cultural form discussed in this book that is not at the same time a revolt against things as they are and a form of adjustment to them, scarcely one that is not at one level complicit with the structures it challenges, scarcely one that, even as it rebels against one form of domination—that of slaves by their masters, of the colonized by the colonizers—does not contain within itself the seeds of another form of domination, most notably that of women by men and of the people as a whole by a new brand of homegrown political Massa. West Indian popular culture appears to combine a perpetual rebelliousness with an inability to effect lasting changes in the structures of power it rebels against: a culture of opposition and inversion, it depends on the existence of those structures in order to exist at all. Thus, although every cultural form discussed here has at one time or another posed a threat, of varying degrees of seriousness, to the dominant social and political order—Haitian Vodou in the early 1790s, Jamaican Afro-Christianity at regular intervals between 1830 and 1930, Jonkonnu in the early 1840s, Rastafarianism almost continuously between 1933 and 1965, Trinidad carnival between 1838 and the early 1880s and again the years immediately after the Second World War, cricket (in the form of riots at Test matches) at intervals between 1953 and 1980—that threat, save in the case of Vodou in the 1790s, has never issued in a concerted contestation of the status quo and its values, still less brought about any fundamental changes in the structure of power. The dominant order first represses the cultural challenge by force and then neutralizes it by absorbing it into the structures of power (as happened with Haitian Vodou and Jamaican Afro-Christianity), by making token concessions to it and taking over and defusing its language, music, and style (Rastafarianism), by transmitting it into exotic spectacle and commodity (carnival), by making it a symbol of national union and consensus (carnival, cricket), or by elevating the heroes of the counterculture into heroes of the nation (Garvey, Marley) and thereby divesting them of the radicalism they possessed and embodied in the eyes of their followers. All this defusing does not, of course, render future disruption of public order impossible, but it suggests that such disruption, when it occurs, will be dealt with relatively easily be the structures of power: there is nothing, it seems, that cannot first be repressed and then recuperated and neutralized by the "shitstem."

But even this is true only in an obvious sense and does not capture or account for the extreme ambivalence of West Indian oppositional culture, whose radicalism and utopianism stand in such marked contrast to the pragmatism and caution that West Indians commonly display in their lives, as they have done from the period of slavery onward. Although day-to-day *opposition* was a constant feature of slavery, actual acts of *resistance*, in de Certeau's sense of the term, were comparatively rare and generally occurred on a large scale only when, as in Saint-Domingue in 1791–94, in Demerara in 1823, or in Jamaica in 1831–32, slaves knew that the structure of slave society was already seriously threatened from within and without so that they had some chance of winning. At other times slaves seem to have consciously abjured resistance in favor of opposition, knowing full well how appallingly costly ill-timed or ill-planned resistance could prove. Since the abolition of slavery, acts of resistance, especially in the English-speaking West Indies, have been rarer still and have been notable for their lack of a definable objective (the Morant Bay uprising) or, in the case of the labor riots of the middle and late 1930s, for the relative ease with which they were defused by a colonial power working in tandem with a constitutionally minded local political elite. By and large, English-speaking West Indians have preferred, through a combination of choice and necessity, to work within the political, economic, cultural, and ideological systems imposed or imparted from above rather than to reject them outright or even substantially to transform them. Thus, with the exception of Guyana (pushed toward corporatism by the intensity of its ethnic alignments), a modified form of Westminster parliamentary democracy is now firmly entrenched in all of Britain's former West Indian colonies because "quite simply, it is concordant with and expressive of a deeply conservative political culture" (Sutton 1991:109). As Eric Williams said in 1980, a year before his death, "if the Westminster model has helped Trinidad and Tobago in not producing our own barbarities and monsters, then we need not be too perturbed about the non-uprooting of our colonial structures" (quoted in Payne 1993:62). Post-independence politics have continued to be played according to rules laid down by the ex-masters, and as Paul Sutton has observed (1991:118), the parallel in this respect between politics and cricket is by no means a spurious one: in each case an English-derived form has been able to express a creole content and meaning and so has survived more or less or, in the case of cricket, wholly without external change. Similarly in both Haiti and the ex–British West Indies, the attachment to private property, often in the form of "family land," is profound. According to Haitian popular wisdom, *se vagabon qui loue kay* ("only vagabonds rent their homes"); in Barbados, "even the smallest house has a name; the name represents the emotional dimension of property ownership. The little picket fence around the house is the physical expression of the emotional dimension. That picket fence (or cactus fence in the Nether-lands Antilles) also expresses another characteristic of Caribbean peoples. In the midst of their gregariousness, they like their privacy, an expression of their intrinsic independence" (Maingot 1984:368). To this commitment to private property and Westminster-style political democracy must be added the scarcely revolutionary social and ethical values well documented in the late Carl Stone's much respected soundings of public opinion in Jamaica. At var-ious times between 1977 and 1981, 84.2 percent of respondents favored capi-tal punishment (Stone 1982:56); 41 percent in the corporate area (Kingston and St. Andrew) thought the police used "too little" violence (as opposed to 32 percent "too much" and 27 percent "just enough" [68]); 60 percent would move permanently to the United States if they could (60); and as many as 43 percent thought Jamaica would be better off as a fifty-first state (78). All these values suggest, in David Nicholls's words, that, contrary to "a widespread but mistaken belief among radical intellectuals that the masses in the Caribbean are a revolutionary force whose natural inclination to revolt is held down by force of arms or by a sinister conspiracy of school teachers, clergy and news-paper proprietors" (1985:17), "the mass of the people in Haiti—as in Jamaica, Grenada and other parts of the Caribbean—are basically conservative; the poorer they are the less ready they are to risk losing what they have for the promise of better things. Political strategies which assume the existence of a revolutionary working class or peasantry in the Antilles are bound to come to grief. Only by recognizing the force and indeed the value of tradition will constructive change occur" (285; see also Maingot 1984:365).

If Nicholls is right, then the radicalism and utopianism of the cultural forms discussed in this book appear to be less expressions of sociopolitical resistance than substitutes for it: it is as though West Indians have preferred to keep their radicalism in the cultural domain, where it can neither really threaten the power structure nor bring injury on them while permitting them to pursue pragmatic oppositional ends day to day. Profoundly conscious, like all historically oppressed peoples, of the perils of challenging the structures of power (and still more of Power) head-on, West Indians have opted to create spaces within it in where they can maneuver. On the other hand, they simulate empowerment through a series of rituals—slaves "plays," Jonkonnu, carnival, spirit worship and possession, cricket—that both sustain their spiritual, cultural, and racial identity and protect them from the dangers inherent in a direct confrontation with power. Thus, while West Indians admire the flamboyance of the culture of reputation, they are also deeply attached to the more down-to-earth values of the culture of respectability, and ultimately they will not allow the former to imperil the latter. Recognizing this, the most successful politicians in the former British West Indies have been those who have combined the utopian rhetoric of the man-of-words with a studied pragmatism in practice: Moses is followed only so long as his vision of the Promised Land does not threaten the day-to-day interests of the people. But now Moses' day, like Massa's before him, appears to be done. A "logical by-product of colonial rule," the West Indian political messiah reproduced its authoritarian character even as he opposed it, and his apparent demise in the Commonwealth Caribbean may signal that what Singham, over a quarter of a century ago, called "one of the major tasks of decolonization" (1968:329) is at last being achieved, namely "to move away from reliance on the hero, and concomitantly towards a genuine political socialization of the mass of people in the area." Henceforth the way toward greater economic and social equality is likely, at least in the Commonwealth Caribbean, to lie within "the system" rather than outside or against it, as many of the region's leading radicals themselves now readily admit.[1]

Thus it appears that the greatest strength of West Indian societies in the past has been not the outer-directed culture of reputation on which this book has principally focused, but the inner-directed culture of respectability that, historically, has concentrated energies and resources that the culture of reputation has dispersed in acts of display and aggression, often directed as much against other members of the dominated group as against the sources of their domination in the overall structure of society. As Gerald Early (1994:27) has written of the cognate African American culture of reputation, "the dozens did not save blacks from the hostile aggression of other blacks; it merely saved whites from it." When the culture of reputation has confronted the structures

---

1. See, for example, the statement by the Guyanese Marxist economist Clive Y. Thomas (1988:359): "Rights of representation and political forms of democracy do exist in the region (they were won through the heroic struggles of the masses), but are limited because they exist within a social context in which inequalities of income and wealth are systematically reproduced. . . . The task in hand is to secure economic and social rights so as to negate these limiting considerations and not to reduce their significance by caricaturing them as a 'longing for British parliamentarianism,' as certain left circles in the region are wont to do."

of power, it has not in itself been able to bring about lasting and radical changes in West Indian society, save in the exceptional circumstances that obtained in Saint-Domingue between 1789 and 1804. Otherwise its challenges to the status quo have been repressed, deflected, or defused with relative ease, though its shows of force, as in 1831–32 and 1938 in Jamaica, have often prompted the metropolitan power to introduce measures of reform, whose usual effect has been to draw the West Indies still deeper into the hegemony of western liberal-capitalist (and Christian) values. If those values now appear to hold sway in at least the Commonwealth Caribbean, it seems likely that significant progress *within the system* will depend on some new blend of the cultures of reputation and respectability that have in the past been so strongly opposed, to the very obvious weakening and impoverishment of the West Indies as a whole. Although, as we have seen, the original "Crab Antics" formulation of reputation/male:respectability/female seems increasingly untenable,[2] it is true that the culture of play and performance that has been my focus has been overwhelmingly male dominated and that it has tended to keep women to the margins, just as in consequence they have been kept largely to the margins of this book. Yet there are indisputable signs that that marginality is at least beginning to end: in the "winers" of Jamaica and Trinidad who have moved into public spaces hitherto monopolized by the performance culture of men; in the emergence of female calypsonians in Trinidad, in the Vodou *mambos* who, if Karen McCarthy Brown is right, are increasingly influential figures in modern Haitian life, especially in cities; and most important of all, in the ever-increasing number of female graduates emerging from the campuses of the University of the West Indies. The significance of such developments should not be exaggerated, but they have been enough to incite talk of a crisis of male identity in the Commonwealth Caribbean, an almost unthinkable topic even twenty years ago (see Lewis 1990). If the growing cultural and educational strength of women can be translated into concrete social, economic, and political power—and the "if" may not be as big as it first appears—it would strike at the very core of the structures and values inherited from slavery and colonialism that still bind the Caribbean in their "swaddling cerements"[3] and prevent the society part born in 1838 and part reborn in the early 1960s from attaining full human maturity. The old dialectic of inside and outside appears at last to be breaking down, and as it does so it may be possible for Caribbean men and women, combining in a new synthesis the best of the culture of respectability with the best of the culture of reputation, to move beyond opposition, which so paradoxically reinforces the structures it contests, into a world in which power, wealth, opportunity, and self-value would be far more equally distributed.

2. See above, chapter 4.
3. The reference is to Derek Walcott's poem "Laventille" (see chapter 1, n. 8 above).

# Glossary

| | |
|---|---|
| **auntie-man** | In the eastern Caribbean, a male homosexual. The term corresponds to "batty man" in Jamaica. |
| **buckra** | A white person, especially a white man. The word probably derives from Efik *mbakara, mba,* "all, the whole" + *kara,* "to encompass, master, understand." |
| **busha** | The overseer on a slave plantation. |
| **gumbey** | A round- or square-topped goatskin drum played with the hands. |
| **higgler** | A market woman or female street vendor, especially in Jamaica; the term corresponds to "Madame Sara" in Haiti. |
| **hounfor** | A temple or cult center in Haitian Vodoo. |
| **las lap** | "Last lap"; the vigorous dancing or "jumping up" in the final hours before midnight on Shrove Tuesday, ending the carnival celebrations in Trinidad. |
| **Myal, Myalism** | Terms of uncertain (though almost certainly African) origin designating a range of popular religious phenomena in Jamaica, including witchcraft, dancing, and possession; whence Myalman, Myalwoman, etc. |
| **Pocomania** | A Jamaican religious cult combining revivalism and ancestor worship, more properly termed Pukumina and known popularly as Poco. The term probably derives from Kikango *pukumina,* "to shake, to cause to shiver or tremble." |
| **rudie, rude boy** | A dissident black youth. The term gained currency in Jamaica in the 1950s. |
| **tadjeh** | Replicas of the tombs of the Muslin martyrs Hassan and Hosein, which are paraded through the streets of Trinidad and then burned during the East Indian festival of Hosay (Hosein). |
| **Ti-Jean** | A well-known figure of West Indian folklore, often partnered by his elder brothers, Gros-Jean and Mi-Jean. Ti-Jean's wit and cleverness enable him to beat opponents more powerful than himself. |

# References

Only works cited in the text are included here, and the editions are those I used.

### Primary Sources (Pre-1920)

Anonymous. 1828. *Marly, or The Life of a Planter in Jamaica*. Glasgow: Richard Griffin.

Barclay, Alexander. 1826. *A Practical View of the Present State of Slavery in the West Indies*. London: Smith, Elder.

Beckford, William. 1790. *A Descriptive Account of the Island of Jamaica*. 2 vols. London: T. and J. Egerton.

Bleby, Henry. 1853. *Death Struggles of Slavery*. London: Hamilton, Adams.

Brooks, A. A. 1917. *History of Bedwardism, or The Jamaica Baptist Free Church*. Kingston, Jamaica: Jamaica Gleaner Company.

Dallas, R. C. 1968. *The History of the Maroons*. 1803. 2 vols. London: Frank Cass.

Day, Charles Williams. 1852. *Five Years' Residence in the West Indies*. London: Colburn.

Edwards, Bryan. 1806. *The History, Civil and Commercial, of the British Colonies in the West Indies*. 4 vols. Philadelphia: James Humphreys.

Gardner, W. J. 1971. *A History of Jamaica*. 1873. London: Frank Cass.

Leslie, Charles. 1740. *A New History of Jamaica*. London: J. Hodges.

Lewis, Matthew G. 1834. *Journal of a West India Proprietor*. London: John Murray.

Ligon, Richard. 1673. *A True and Exact History of the Island of Barbados*. London.

Long, Edward. 1774. *The History of Jamaica*. 4 vols. London: T. Lowndes.

Moreau de Saint-Méry, Médéric. 1958. *Description de la partie française de l'isle Saint-Domingue*. 1797–98. Ed. Blanche Maurel and Etienne Taillemite. 4 vols. Paris: Société de l'Histoire des Colonies Françaises and Librairie Larose.

Nugent, Maria. 1907. *Lady Nugent's Journal*. Ed. Frank Cundall. London: Adam and Charles Black.

Phillippo, James M. 1969. *Jamaica, Its Past and Present State*. 1843. London: Dawson.

Scott, Michael. 1852. *Tom Cringle's Log*. Edinburgh: William Blackwood.

Sloane, Hans. 1707. *A Voyage to the Islands Madera, Barbados, Nieves, S. Christophers and Jamaica*. 2 vols. London: Printed by B. M. for the author.

Stewart, John. 1808. *An Account of Jamaica and Its Inhabitants*. London: Longman, Hurst, Rees & Orme.

————. 1969. *A View of the Past and Present State of the Island of Jamaica.* 1823. New York: Negro University Press.

Williams, Cynric. 1826. *Tour through the Island of Jamaica.* London: Hunt & Clarke.

**Other Works**

Abbott, Elizabeth. 1988. *Haiti: The Duvaliers and Their Legacy.* New York: Simon & Schuster.

Abenon, Lucien René. 1987. *La Guadeloupe de 1671 à 1759: Etude politique, économique et sociale.* Paris: Harmattan.

Abrahams, Roger D. 1983. *The Man-of-Words in the West Indies: Performance and the Emergence of Creole Culture.* Baltimore: Johns Hopkins University Press.

Albuquerque, Klaus de. 1979. "The Future of the Rastafarian Movement." *Caribbean Review* 8, 44:22–25, 44–46.

Alegría, Ricardo. 1956. "The Fiesta of Santiago Apostol (St. James the Apostle) in Loíza. Puerto Rico." *Journal of American Folklore* 69, 272:123–34.

Alleyne, Mervyn C. 1980. *Comparative Afro-American: An Historical-Comparative Study of English-Based Afro-American Dialects of the New World.* Ann Arbor, Mich.: Karoma.

————. 1988. *Roots of Jamaican Culture.* London: Pluto Press.

Anthony, Michael. 1989. *Parade of the Carnivals of Trinidad, 1839–1989.* Port of Spain, Trinidad: Circle Press.

Armstrong, Douglas V. 1990. *The Old Village and the Great House: An Archaeological and Historical Examination of Drax Hall Plantation, St. Ann's Bay, Jamaica.* Urbana: University of Illinois Press.

Augier, Roy. 1993. "Before and after 1865." In *Caribbean Freedom, Economy and Society from Emancipation to the Present,* ed. Hilary McD. Beckles and Verene A. Shepherd, 170–80. London: James Currie. (First published in *New World Quarterly* 2, 2 [1965].)

Austin, Diane J. 1981. "Born Again . . . and Again and Again: Communitas and Change among Jamaican Pentecostalists." *Journal of Anthropological Research* 37, 3:226–46.

————. 1984. *Urban Life in Kingston, Jamaica: The Culture and Class Ideology of Two Neighborhoods.* New York: Gordon and Breach.

Austin-Broos, Diane J. 1987. "Pentecostals and Rastafarians: Cultural, Political, and Gender Relations of Two Religious Movements." *Social and Economic Studies* 36, 4:1–39.

————. 1991–92. "Religion and the Politics of Moral Order in Jamaica." *Anthropological Forum* 6, 3:293–319.

————. 1992. "Redefining the Moral Order: Interpretations of Christianity in Postemancipation Jamaica." In *The Meaning of Freedom, Economy, Politics and Culture after Slavery,* ed. Frank McGlynn and Seymour Drescher, 221–43. Pittsburgh: University of Pittsburgh Press.

Bakan, Abigail. 1990. *Ideology and Class Conflict in Jamaica: The Politics of Rebellion.* Montreal: McGill-Queen's University Press.

Bakhtin, Mikhail. 1968. *Rabelais and His World.* Trans. H. Iswolsky. Cambridge: MIT Press.

Barnett, Sheila. 1978–79. "Pitchy Patchy." *Jamaican Journal* 43:18–32.

Barrett, Leonard. 1977. *The Rastafarians: The Dreadlocks of Jamaica.* London: Heinemann Educational Books.

Bascom, William. 1972. *Shango in the New World.* Austin: African and Afro-American Research Institute, University of Texas.

Beckles, Hilary McD. 1987. *Black Rebellion in Barbados: The Struggle against Slavery, 1627–1838,* Bridgetown, Barbados: Carib Research and Publications.

Beckles, Hilary McD., and Brian Stoddart, eds. 1995. *Liberation Cricket: West Indies Cricket Culture.* Manchester: Manchester University.

Beckwith, Martha Warren. 1923. *Christmas Mummings in Jamaica.* Publications of the Folklore Foundation. Poughkeepsie, N.Y.: Vassar College.

Bellegarde-Smith, Patrick. 1990. *Haiti: The Breached Citadel.* Boulder, Colo.: Westview Press.

Besson, Jean. 1984. "Family Land and Caribbean Society: Toward an Ethnography of Afro-Caribbean Peasantries." In *Perspectives on Caribbean Regional Identity,* ed. Elizabeth M. Thomas-Hope, 57–83. Liverpool: Centre for Latin American Studies, University of Liverpool.

———. 1987. "Family Land as Model for Martha Brae's New History: Culture Building in an Afro-Caribbean Village." In *Afro-Caribbean Villages in Historical Perspective,* 100–132. Kingston, Jamaica: African-Caribbean Institute of Jamaica.

———. 1992. "Freedom and Community: The British West Indies." In *The Meaning of Freedom: Economy, Politics and Culture after Slavery,* ed. Frank McGlynn and Seymour Drescher, 113–46. Pittsburgh: University of Pittsburgh Press.

———. 1993. "Reputation and Respectability Reconsidered: A New Perspective on Afro-Caribbean Peasant Women." In *Women and Change in the Caribbean: A Pan-Caribbean Perspective,* ed. Janet H. Momsen, 15–37. Kingston, Jamaica: Ian Randle; Bloomington: Indiania University Press; London: James Currey.

Best, Lloyd. 1985. "West Indian Society 150 Years after Abolition: A Re-examination of Some Classic Theories." In *Out of Slavery: Abolition and After,* ed. Jack Hayward, 132–58. London: Frank Cass.

Bettelheim, Judith. 1988a. "Jonkonnu and Other Christmas Masquerades." In *Caribbean Festival Arts,* ed. John W. Nunley and Judith Bettelheim, 39–83. Seattle: University of Washington Press.

———. 1988b. "Carnivals and Festivals in Cuba." In *Caribbean Festival Arts,* ed. John W. Nunley and Judith Bettelheim, 137–46. Seattle: University of Washington Press.

Bickerton, Derek. 1962. *The Murders of Boysie Singh.* London: Arthur Barber.

———. 1975. *Dynamics of a Creole System.* London and New York: Cambridge University Press.

Bilby, Kenneth. 1994. "Maroon Culture as a Distinct Variant of Jamaican Culture." In

*Maroon Heritage: Archaeological, Ethnography and Historical Perspectives*, ed. E. Kofi Agorsah, 72–85. Kingston, Jamaica: Canoe Press.

Bilby, Kenneth, and Fu-Kiau Kia Bunseki. 1983. "Kumina: A Kongo-Based Tradition in the New World." *Cahiers du CEDAF* 8, 4:1–114.

Bilby, Kenneth, and Elliot Leib. 1986. "Kumina, the Howellite Church and the Emergence of Rastafarian Traditional Music in Jamaica." *Jamaica Journal* 19, 3:22–28.

Birbalsingh, Frank, and Clem Shiwcharan. 1988. *Indo-Westindian Cricket*. London: Hansib.

Bolland, O. Nigel. 1992a. "The Politics of Freedom in the British Caribbean." In *The Meaning of Freedom: Economy, Politics and Culture after Slavery*, ed. Frank McGlynn and Seymour Drescher, 113–46. Pittsburgh: University of Pittsburgh Press.

———. 1992b. "Creolization and Creole Societies: A Cultural Nationalist View of Caribbean Social History." In *Intellectuals in the Twentieth-Century Caribbean, vol. 1, Spectre of the New Class: The Commonwealth Caribbean*, ed. Alistair Hennesey, 50–79. London: Macmillan.

———. 1995. *On the March: Labour Rebellions in the British Caribbean, 1934–39*, Kingston, Jamaica: Ian Randle and James Currey.

Brana-Shute, Gary. 1976. "Drinking Shops and Social Structure: Some Ideas on Lower-Class West Indian Male Behaviour." *Urban Anthropology* 5, 1:53–67.

———. 1989. *On the Corner: Male Social Life in a Paramaribo Creole Neighborhood*. Prospect Heights, Ill.: Waveland Press.

Brandon, George. 1993. *Santería from Africa to the New World: The Dead Sell Memories*. Bloomington: Indiana University Press.

Brathwaite, Edward Kamau. 1969. *Islands*. London: Oxford University Press.

———. 1971. *The Development of Creole Society in Jamaica, 1770–1820*. Oxford: Oxford University Press.

———. 1973. *The Arrivants: A New World Trilogy*. London and New York: Oxford University Press.

———. 1974. *Contradictory Omens: Cultural Diversity and Integration in the Caribbean*. Mona, Jamaica: Savacou.

———. 1977. "Caliban, Ariel, and Unprospero in the Conflict of Creolization: A Study of the Slave Revolt in Jamaica in 1831–32." In *Comparative Perspectives on Slavery in New World Plantation Societies*, ed. Vera Rubin and Arthur Tuden, 41–62. Annals of the New York Academy of Sciences, 292. New York: New York Academy of Sciences.

———. 1978. "The Spirit of African Survival in Jamaica." *Jamaica Journal* 42:44–63.

Brathwaite, Kamau. 1990. "Ala(r)ms of God: Konnu and Carnival in the Caribbean." *Caribbean Quarterly* 36, 3–4:78–107.

Breiner, Laurence A. 1985–86. "The English Bible in Jamaican Rastafarianism." *Journal of Religious Thought* 42, 2:30–43.

Brereton, Bridget. 1979. *Race Relations in Colonial Trinidad, 1870–1900*. Cambridge: Cambridge University Press.

———. 1983. "The Birthday of Our Race: A Social History of Emancipation Day in

Trinidad, 1838–88." In *Trade, Government and Society in Caribbean History*, ed. B. W. Higman, 69–84. Kingston, Jamaica: Heinemann Education Books.

Brodber, Erna. 1985. "Black Consciousness and Popular Music in Jamaica in the 1960s and 1970s." *Caribbean Quarterly* 31, 2:53–66.

———. 1986. "Afro-Jamaican Women at the Turn of the Century." *Social and Economic Studies* 35, 3:23–47.

Brown, Diana DeG. 1986. *Umbanda: Religion and Politics in Urban Brazil*. Ann Arbor: UMI Research Press.

Brown, Karen McCarthy. 1989. "Systematic Remembering, Systematic Forgetting: Ogou in Haiti." In *Africa's Ogun: Old World and New*, ed. Sandra T. Barnes. Bloomington: Indiana University Press.

———. 1991. *Mama Lola: A Vodou Priestess in Brooklyn*. Berkeley: University of California Press.

Bryan, Patrick. 1991. *The Jamaican People: Race, Class and Social Control*. London: Macmillan.

Buisseret, David, and Michael Pawson. 1975. *Port Royal, Jamaica*. Oxford: Oxford University Press.

Burton, Richard D. E. 1985. "Cricket, Carnival and Street Culture in the Caribbean." *British Journal of Sports History* 2, 2:179–97.

———. 1993a. "*Debrouya pa péché*, or *Il y a toujours moyen de moyenner*: Patterns of Opposition in the Fiction of Patrick Chamoiseau." *Callaloo* 16, 2:466–81.

———. 1993b. "*Ki moun nou yé?* The Idea of Difference in Contemporary French West Indian Thought." *New West Indian Guide* 67, 1–2:5–32.

———. 1994. *La Famille coloniale: La Martinique et la Mère-Patrie, 1789–1992*. Paris: Harmattan.

Bush, Barbara. 1986. "'The Family Tree Is Not Cut': Women and Cultural Resistance in the British Caribbean." In *In Resistance: Studies in African, Caribbean and Afro-American History*, ed. Gary Y. Okihiro. Amherst: University of Massachusetts Press.

Callam, Neville G. 1980. "Invitation to Docility: Defining the Rastafarian Challenge." *Caribbean Journal of Religious Studies* 3:28–48.

Campbell, Mavis C. 1988. *The Maroons of Jamaica, 1655–1796: A History of Resistance, Collaboration and Betrayal*. Granby, Mass.: Bergin & Garvey.

Carr, Andrew T. 1953. "A Rada Community in Trinidad." *Caribbean Quarterly* 3, 1:36–54.

———. 1956. "Pierrot Grenade." *Caribbean Quarterly* 4, 3–4:281–314.

Cassidy, Frederick G. 1961. *Jamaica Talk: Three Hundred Years of the English Language in Jamaica*. London: Macmillan.

Cassidy, Frederick G., and Robert B. Le Page. 1967. *Dictionary of Jamaican English*. Cambridge: Cambridge University Press.

Certeau, Michael de. 1980. "On the Oppositional Practices of Everyday Life." *Social Text* 3:3–43.

Chaudenson, Robert. 1992. *Des îles, des hommes, des langues: Essai sur la créolisation linguistique et culturelle*. Paris: Harmattan.

Chevannes, Barry. 1976. "The Repairer of the Breach: Reverend Claudius Henry and Jamaican Society." In *Ethnicity in the Americas*, ed. Frances Henry, 263–90. The Hague: Mouton.

———. 1978. "Revivalism: A Disappearing Religion." *Caribbean Quarterly* 24, 3–4:1–17.

———. 1994. *Rastafari: Roots and Ideology*. Syracuse: Syracuse University Press.

———. 1995a. Introduction to *Rastafari and Other African-Caribbean Worldviews*, ed. Barry Chevannes. London: Macmillan.

———. 1995b. "The Origin of the Dreadlocks." In *Rastafari and Other African-Caribbean Worldviews*, ed. Barry Chevannes, 77–96. London: Macmillan.

———. 1995c. "The Phallus and the Outcast: The Symbolism of the Dreadlocks in Jamaica. In *Rastafari and Other African-Caribbean Worldviews*, ed. Barry Chevannes, 97–126. London: Macmillan.

Cohen, Abner. 1993. *Masquerade Politics: Explorations in the Structure of Urban Cultural Movements*. Oxford: Berg.

Confiant, Raphaël. 1993. *Aimé Césaire: Une traversée paradoxale du siècle*. Paris: Stock.

Constant, Denis. 1982. *Aux sources du reggae*. Paris: Editions Parenthèse.

Constantine, Learie. n.d.a. *Cricketers' Carnival*. London: Stanley Paul.

———. n.d.b. *Cricket in the Sun*. London: Stanley Paul.

Cooper, Carolyn. 1993. *Noises in the Blood: Orality, Gender and the "Vulgar" Body of Jamaican Popular Culture*. London: Macmillan.

Courlander, Harold. 1960. *The Drum and the Hoe: Life and Lore of the Haitian People*. Berkeley: University of California Press.

Courlander, Harold, and Rémy Bastien. 1966. *Religion and Politics in Haiti*. Washington, D.C.: Institute for Cross-Cultural Research.

Craton, Michael. 1978. *Searching for the Invisible Man: Slaves and Plantation Life in Jamaica*. Cambridge: Harvard University Press.

———. 1982. *Testing the Chains: Resistance to Slavery in the British West Indies*. Ithaca: Cornell University Press.

———. 1995. "Decoding Pitchy-Patchy: The Roots, Branches and Essence of Junkanoo." *Slavery and Abolition* 16, 1:14–44.

Crowley, Daniel J. 1956a. "The Traditional Masques of Carnival." *Caribbean Quarterly* 4, 3–4:194–223.

———. 1956b. "The Midnight Robbert." *Caribbean Quarterly* 4, 3–4:263–74.

———. 1984. *African Myth and Black Reality in Bahian Carnival*. Los Angeles: Museum of Cultural History, University of California.

Cumper, George E. 1979. *The Potential of Ras Tafarianism as a Modern National Religion*. New Delhi: Recorder Press.

Curtin, Philip D. 1968. *Two Jamaicas: The Role of Ideas in a Tropical Colony, 1830–1865*. New York: Greenwood Press.

DaMatta, Roberto. 1991. *Carnivals, Rogues, and Heroes: An Interpretation of the Brazilian Dilemma*. Trans. John Drury. Notre Dame: University of Notre Dame Press.

D'Ans, André-Marcel. 1987. *Haïti: Paysage et société*. Paris: Karthala.

Davis, Wade. 1988. *Passage of Darkness: The Ethnobiology of the Haitian Zombie*. Chapel Hill: University of North Carolina Press.

Dayan, Joan. 1988. "The Crisis of the Gods: Haiti after Duvalier." *Yale Review* 77, 3:299–331.

D'Costa, Jean, and Barbara Lalla. 1990. *Language in Exile: Three Hundred Years of Jamaican Creole*. Tuscaloosa: University of Alabama Press.

Debbasch, Yvan. 1959. *Les Associations serviles à la Martinique au 19ᵉ siècle: Contribution à l'histoire coloniale*. Paris: Montchrestien.

Debien, Gabriel. 1974. *Les Esclaves aux Antilles françaises (XVIIᵉ–XVIIIᵉ siècles)*. Basse-Terre, Guadeloupe: Société d'Histoire de la Guadeloupe; Fort-de-France, Martinique: Société d'Histoire de la Martinique.

DeCamp, David. 1960. "Cart Names in Jamaica." *Names* 8, 1:15–23.

———. 1967. "African Day-Names in Jamaica." *Language* 43, 1:139–49.

———. 1968. "Mock Bidding in Jamaica." In *Tire Shrinker to Dragster*, ed. Wilson M. Hudson. Austin: Encino Press.

Deosaran, Ramesh. 1987. "The 'Caribbean Man': A Study of the Psychology of Perception and the Media." In *India in the Caribbean*, ed. David Dabydeen and Brinsley Samaroo, 81–118. London: Hansib.

Desmangles, Leslie G. 1992. *The Faces of the Gods: Vodou and Roman Catholicism in Haiti*. Chapel Hill: University of North Carolina Press.

Detienne, Marcel, and Jean-Pierre Vernant. 1991. *Cunning Intelligence in Greek Culture and Society*. Trans. Janet Lloyd. Chicago: University of Chicago Press.

Diederich, Bernard, and Al Burt. 1969. *Papa Doc: The Truth about Haiti Today*. New York: McGraw-Hill.

Dillard, J. L. 1976. *Black Names*. Contributions to the Sociology of Language 13. The Hague: Mouton.

Dirks, Robert. 1987. *The Black Saturnalia: Conflict and Its Ritual Expression on British West Indian Slave Plantations*. Gainesville: University of Florida Press.

Douglass, Lisa. 1992. *The Power of Sentiment: Love, Hierarchy, and the Jamaica Family Elite*. Boulder, Colo.: Westview Press.

Drewal, Henry John, and Margaret Thompson Drewal. 1983. *Gelede: Art and Female Power among the Yoruba*. Bloomington: Indiana University Press.

Drummond, Lee. 1980. "The Cultural Continuum: A Theory of Intersystems." *Man* 15, 2:352–74.

Dunham, Katherine. 1969. *Island Possessed*. New York: Doubleday.

———. 1983. *Dances of Haiti*. Los Angeles: Center for Afro-American Studies, University of California.

Dupuy, Alex. 1989. *Haiti in the World Economy: Class, Race, and Underdevelopment since 1700*. Boulder, Colo.: Westview Press.

Early, Gerald. 1994. *The Culture of Bruising: Essays on Prizefighting, Literature and Modern American Culture*. New York: Ecco Press.

Elder, J. D. 1966a. "Evolution of the Traditional Calypso of Trinidad and Tobago: A

Socio-historical Analysis of Song-Change." Ph.D. diss., University of Pennsylvania.

———. 1966b. "Kalinda-Song of the Battling Troubadours of Trinidad." *Journal of the Folklore Institute* 8, 2:192–203.

———. 1971. "Color, Music and Conflict: A Study of Aggression in Trinidad with Reference to the Role of Traditional Music." In *Black Society in the New World*, ed. Richard Frucht, 315–23. New York: Random House. First published in *Ethnomusicology* 8 (1964).

Elkins, W. F. 1977. *Street Preachers, Faith Healers and Herb Doctors in Jamaica, 1890–1925*. New York: Revisionist Press.

Elsasser, Nan, and Nelson Valdés. 1989. "Dancing with Fidel: Santería Gods in Cuba." *Arete* 1, 6:28–35.

Epstein, Dena. 1977. *Sinful Tunes and Spirituals: Black Folk Music to the Civil War*. Urbana: University of Illinois Press.

Eriksen, Thomas Hylland. 1990. "Liming in Trinidad: The Art of Doing Nothing." *Folk* 32:22–43.

Eyre, L. Alan. 1986. "The Effects of Political Terrorism on the Residential Location of the Poor in the Kingston Urban Region, Jamaica, West Indies." *Urban Geography* 7, 3:227–42.

Farmer, Paul. 1994. *The Uses of Haiti*. Monroe, Maine: Common Courage Press.

Ferguson, James. 1987. *Papa Doc, Baby Doc: Haiti and the Duvaliers*. Oxford: Basil Blackwell.

Feuer, Carl H. 1989. *The Struggle for Workers' Rights at Hampden Sugar Estate*. Kingston, Jamaica: Social Action Centre.

Fick, Carolyn E. 1990. *The Making of Haiti: The Saint Domingue Revolution from Below*. Knoxville: University of Tennessee Press.

Fleischmann, Ulrich. 1993. "Esclavos africanos y esclavos criollos: La lingüística como historia social." In *Alternative Cultures in the Caribbean*, ed. Ulrich Fleischmann and Thomas Bremer, 41–54. Frankfurt am Main: Vervuert.

Foucault, Michel. 1978. *The History of Sexuality*. Vol. 1. Trans. Robert Hurley, London: Allen Lane.

Fraser, Peter. 1981. "The Fictive Peasantry: Caribbean Rural Groups in the Nineteenth Century." In *Contemporary Caribbean: A Sociological Reader*, ed. Susan Craig, 1:319–48. Maracas, Trinidad: Susan Craig.

French, Joan. 1988. "Colonial Policy towards Women after the 1938 Uprising: The Case of Jamaica." *Caribbean Quarterly* 34, 3–4:38–59.

Friday, Michael. 1983. "A Comparison of 'Dharma' and 'Dread.'" *Caribbean Journal of Religous Studies* 5:29–37.

Frucht, Richard. 1967. "A Caribbean Social Type: Neither 'Peasant' Nor 'Proletarian.'" *Social and Economic Studies* 16, 3:295–300.

Fry, Peter. 1982. "Homossexualidade masculina e cultos afro-brasileiros." In *Para inglês ver: Identidade e politica na cultura brasileira*, by Peter Fry, 54–85. Rio de Janeiro: Zahar Editores.

Gaillard, Roger. 1983. *La guérilla de Batraville*. Port-au-Prince, Haiti: Imprimerie Le Natal.

Gaspar, David Barry. 1985. *Bondsmen and Rebels: A Study of Master-Slave Relations in Antigua*. Baltimore: Johns Hopkins University Press.

Geertz, Clifford. 1973. "Deep Play: Notes on the Balinese Cockfight." In *The Interpretation of Cultures: Selected Essays by Clifford Geertz*, 412–53. New York: Basic Books.

Geggus, David. 1983. *Slave Resistance Studies and the Saint Domingue Slave Revolt: Some Preliminary Considerations*. Miami: Latin American and Caribbean Center, Florida International University.

———. 1987. "The Enigma of Jamaica in the 1790s: New Light on the Causes of Slave Rebellions." *William and Mary Quarterly* 44, 2:274–99.

———. 1991. "The Bois Caïman Ceremony." *Journal of Caribbean History* 25, 1–2:41–57.

Genovese, Eugene D. 1972. *Roll, Jordan, Roll: The World the Slaves Made*. New York: Pantheon Books.

George, Nelson. 1992. *Elevating the Game: Black Men and Basketball*. New York: Harper-Collins.

Glazier, Stephen D. 1983. *Marchin' the Pilgrims Home: Leadership and Decision-Making in an Afro-Caribbean Faith*. Westport, Conn.: Greenwood Press.

Green, Pat. 1984. "'Small Settler' Houses in Chapelton: Microcosm of the Jamaican Vernacular." *Jamaica Journal* 17, 3:39–45.

Gunst, Laurie. 1995. *Born Fi' Dead: A Journey through the Jamaican Posse Underworld*. New York: Henry Holt.

Hall, Douglas. 1978. "The Flight from the Estates Reconsidered: The British West Indies, 1838–42." *Journal of Caribbean History* 10–11:7–24.

———. 1989. *In Miserable Slavery: Thomas Thistlewood in Jamaica, 1750–86*. London: Macmillan.

Hamilton, Beverly. 1988. "Marcus Garvey and Cultural Development in Jamaica: A Preliminary Survey." In *Garvey: His Work and Impact*, ed. Rupert Lewis and Patrick Bryan, 87–112. Mona, Jamaica: Institute of Social and Economic Research and Department of Extra-mural Studies, University of the West Indies.

Hancock, Ian F. 1982. "The Fate of Gypsy Slaves in the West Indies." *Journal of the Gypsy Lore Society*, 4th ser. 2, 1:75–80.

Handler, Jerome S., and Frederick W. Lange. 1978. *Plantation Slavery in Barbados: An Archaeological and Historical Investigation*. Cambridge: Harvard University Press.

Hart, Richard. 1985. *Slaves Who Abolished Slavery*. 2 vols. Mona, Jamaica: Institute of Social and Economic Research.

Heine, Jorge. 1990. "The Hero and the Apparatchik: Charismatic Leadership, Political Management, and Crisis in Revolutionary Grenada." In *The Revolution Aborted: The Lessons of Grenada*, ed. Jorge Heine. Pittsburgh: University of Pittsburg Press.

Henney, Jeannette H. 1974. "Spirit-Possession Belief and Trance Behavior in Two Fundamentalist Groups in St. Vincent." In *Trance, Healing, and Hallucination: Three Field Studies in Religious Experience*, ed. Jeannette H. Henney et al., 1–111. New York: John Wiley.

Heuman, Gad. 1981a. *Between Black and White: Race, Politics, and the Free Coloreds in Jamaica, 1792–1865.* Westport, Conn.: Greenwood Press.

———. 1981b. "White over Brown over Black: The Free Coloureds in Jamaican Society during Slavery and after Emancipation." *Journal of Caribbean History* 14:46–69.

———. 1994. *"The Killing Time": The Morant Bay Rebellion in Jamaica.* Knoxville: University of Tennessee Press.

Higman, Barry. 1973. "Household Structure and Fertility on Jamaican Slave Plantations: A Nineteenth-Century Example." *Population Studies* 27:527–50.

———. 1975. "The Slave Family and Household in the British West Indies, 1800–1834." *Journal of Interdisciplinary History* 6, 2:261–87.

———. 1976. *Slave Population and Economy in Jamaica, 1807–1834.* Cambridge: Cambridge University Press.

———. 1979. "Slavery Remembered: The Celebration of Emanicpation in Jamaica." *Journal of Caribbean History* 12:55–74.

———. 1984a. *Slave Populations of the British Caribbean, 1807–1834.* Baltimore: Johns Hopkins University Press.

———. 1984b. "Terms for Kin in the British West Indian Slave Community: Differing Perceptions of Masters and Slaves." In *Kinship, Ideology and Practice in Latin America,* ed. Raymond T. Smith. Chapel Hill: University of North Carolina Press.

Hill, Donald R. 1993. *Calypso Calaloo: Early Carnival Music in Trinidad.* Gainesville: University Press of Florida.

Hill, Errol. 1972. *The Trinidad Carnival: Mandate for a National Theatre.* Austin: University of Texas Press.

———. 1985. "Traditional Figures in Carnival: Their Preservation, Development and Interpretation." *Caribbean Quarterly* 31, 2:14–34.

———. 1992. *The Jamaican Stage, 1655–1900: Profile of a Colonial Theatre.* Amherst: University of Massachusetts Press.

Hill, Robert. 1983. "Leonard P. Howell and Millenarian Visions in Early Rastafari." *Jamaica Journal* 16 1:24–39.

Ho, Christine. 1991. *Salf-Water Trinnies: Afro-Trinidadian Immigrant Networks and Non-assimilation in Los Angeles.* New York: AMS Press.

Hoenisch, Michael. 1988. "Symbolic Politics: Perceptions of the Early Rastafari Movement." *Massachusetts Review* 29, 3:432–49.

Hogg, Donald. 1964. "The Convince Cult in Jamaica." *Yale University Publications in Anthropology* 58:3–24.

Holt, Thomas C. 1992. *The Problem of Freedom: Race, Labor, and Politics in Jamaica and Britain, 1832–1938.* Baltimore: Johns Hopkins University Press.

Homiak, John P. 1987. "The Mystic Revelation of Rasta Far-Eye: Visionary Communication in a Prophetic Movement." In *Dreaming: Anthropological and Psychological Interpretations,* ed. Barbara Tedlock, 220–45. Cambridge: Cambridge University Press.

————. 1995. "Dub History: Soundings on Rastafari Livity and Language." In *Rastafari and Other African-Caribbean Worldviews*, ed. Barry Chevannes, 127–81. London: Macmillan.

Hopkin, John Barton. 1978. "Music in the Jamaican Pentecostal Churches." *Jamaica Journal* 42:22–40.

Houk, James T. 1994. *The Orisha Religion in Trinidad: A Study of Culture Process and Transformation*. Ph.D. diss., Tulane University, 1992. Ann Arbor: University Microfilms International.

Hurbon, Laënnec. 1979. *Culture et dictature en Haïti. L'imaginaire sous contrôle*. Paris: Harmattan.

————. 1987. *Comprendre Haïti: Essai sur l'état, la nation, la culture*. Paris: Karthala.

Jacobs, W. Richard. 1973. "Appeals by Jamaican Political Parties: A Study of Newspaper Advertisements in the 1972 Jamaican General Election Campaign." *Caribbean Studies* 13, 2:19–50.

James, C. L. R. 1983. *Beyond a Boundary*. New York: Pantheon Books.

Jones, James M., and Hollis Liverpool. 1976. "Calypso Humour in Trinidad." In *Humour and Laughter: Theory, Research and Application*, ed. Antony J. Chapman and Hugh C. Foot, 259–86. London: John Wiley.

Kaufman, Michael. 1985. *Jamaica under Manley: Dilemmas of Socialism and Democracy*. London: Zed Books.

Klein, Alan M. 1991. *Sugarball: The American Game, the Dominican Dream*. New Haven: Yale University Press.

Kochman, Thomas. 1981. *Black and White Styles in Conflict*. Chicago: University of Chicago Press.

Lacey, Terry. 1977. *Violence and Politics in Jamaica, 1960–70: Internal Security in a Developing Country*. Totowa, N.J.: Frank Cass.

Laguerre, Michel. 1980. "Bizango: A Voodoo Secret Society in Haiti." In *Secrecy: A Cross-Cultural Perspective*, ed. Stanton K. Tefft, 147–58. New York: Human Sciences Press.

————. 1982. *Urban Life in the Caribbean: A Study of a Haitian Urban Community*. Cambridge, Mass.: Schenkman.

————. 1989. *Voodoo and Politics in Haiti*. New York: St. Martin's Press.

Lake, Obiagele. 1994. "The Many Voices of Rastafarian Women: Sexual Subordination in the Midst of Liberation." *New West Indian Guide* 68, 3–4:235–57.

Landes, Ruth. 1940. "A Cult Matriarchate and Male Homosexuality." *Journal of Abnormal and Social Psychology* 35, 3:386–97.

Lazarus-Black, Mindie. 1994. *Legitimate Acts and Illegal Encounters: Law and Society in Antigua and Barbuda*. Washington, D.C.: Smithsonian Institution Press.

Leach, MacEdward. 1961. "Jamaican Duppy Lore." *Journal of American Folklore* 74, 293:207–15.

Leiris, Michel. 1958. *La Possession et ses aspects théâtraux chez les Éthiopiens de Gondar*. Paris: Plon.

Le Page, Robert, and Andrée Tabouret-Keller. 1985. *Acts of Identity: Creole-Based Approaches to Language and Ethnicity*. Cambridge: Cambridge University Press.

Lévêque, Karl. 1971. "L'Interpellation mystique dans le discours duvalérien." *Nouvelle optique* 4:5–32.

Levi, Darrell E. 1989. *Michael Manley: The Making of a Leader*. London: André Deutsch.

Lewin, Olive. 1984. "Emancipation Songs and Festivities." *Jamaica Journal* 17, 3:18–23.

Lewis, I. M. 1971. *Ecstatic Religion: An Anthropological Study of Spirit Possession and Shamanism*. London: Penguin.

Lewis, Linden. 1990. "Are Caribbean Men in Crisis? An Economic and Social Dilemma." *Caribbean Affairs* 3, 3:104–12.

Lewis, Rupert. 1987. "Garvey's Significance in Jamaica's Historical Evolution." *Jamaica Journal* 20, 3:56–65.

Lieber, Michael. 1981. *Street Scenes: Afro-American Culture in Urban Trinidad*. Cambridge, Mass.: Schenkman.

Littlewood, Roland. 1993. *Pathology and Identity: The Work of Mother Earth in Trinidad*. Cambridge: Cambridge University Press.

Liverpool, Hollis. 1990. *Kaiso and Society*. Diego Martin, Trinidad: Juba.

Lovelace, Earl. 1983. *The Wine of Astonishment*. London: Heinemann. First published 1979.

———. 1985. *The Dragon Can't Dance*. London: Longman Caribbean Writers.

Lowenthal, David. 1961. "Caribbean Views of Caribbean Land." *Canadian Geographer* 5, 2:1–9.

———. 1972. *West Indian Societies*. Oxford: Oxford University Press.

McDonald, Roderick A. 1993. *The Economy and Material Culture of Slaves: Goods and Chattels on the Slave Plantations of Jamaica and Louisiana*. Baton Rouge: Louisiana State University Press.

McFadyen, Deirdre, and Pierre LaRamée, eds. 1995. *Haiti: Dangerous Crossroads*. North American Congress on Latin America. Boston: South End Press.

Magid, Alvin. 1987. *Urban Nationalism: A Study of Political Development in Trinidad*. Gainesville: University Presses of Florida.

Maingot, Anthony P. 1984. "The Caribbean: The Structure of Modern-Conservative Societies." In *Latin America: Its Problems and Its Promise*, ed. Jan Knippers Black, 362–78. Boulder, Colo.: Westview Press.

———. 1986–87. "Haiti: Problems of a Transition to Democracy in an Authoritarian Soft State." *Journal of Interamerican Studies and World Affairs* 28, 4:75–102.

———. 1994. *The United States and the Caribbean: Challenges of an Asymmetrical Relationship*. Boulder, Colo.: Westview Press.

Mandle, Jay R., and Joan D. Mandle. 1988. *Grass Roots Commitment: Basketball and Society in Trinidad and Tobago*. Packerberg, Iowa: Caribbean Books.

Manning, Frank E. 1973. *Black Clubs in Bermuda: Ethnography of a Play World*. Ithaca: Cornell University Press.

———. 1974. "Nicknames and Number Plates in the British West Indies." *Journal of American Folklore* 87, 344:123–32.

———. 1981. "Celebrating Cricket: The Symbolic Construction of Caribbean Politics." *American Ethnologist* 8, 3:616–32.

———. 1984. "Challenging Authority: Calypso and Politics in the Caribbean." In *Political Anthropology*, ed. Myron J. Aronoff, 5:167–80. New Brunswick, N.J.: Transaction Books.

Mansingh, Ajai, and Laxmi Mansingh. 1985. *Hindu Influences on Rastafarianism*. Mona, Jamaica: Caribbean Quarterly Monograph.

Marable, Manning. 1987. *African and Caribbean Politics: From Kwame Nkrumah to the Grenada Revolution*. London: Verso.

Matory, J. Lorand. 1988. "Homens montados: Homossexualidade e simbolismo da possessão nas religiões afro-brasileiras." In *Escravidão e Invenção da Liberdade: Estudios sobre o negro no Brasil*, ed. João José Reis, 215–31. São Paulo: Editora Brasiliense.

Meeks, Brian. 1993. *Caribbean Revolutions and Revolutionary Theory: An Assessment of Cuba, Nicaragua and Grenada*. London: Macmillan.

Meel, Peter. 1993. "The March of Militarization in Surinam." In *Modern Caribbean Politics*, ed. Anthony Payne and Paul Sutton, 125–46. Baltimore: Johns Hopkins University Press.

Mercer, Kobena. 1987. "Black Hair/Style Politics." *New Formations* 3:33–55.

Métraux, Alfred. 1959. *Voodoo in Haiti*. Trans. Hugo Charteris. New York: Oxford University Press.

Miller, Daniel. 1991. "Absolute Freedom in Trinidad." *Man* 26:323–41.

———. 1994. *Modernity, an Ethnographic Approach: Dualism and Mass Consumption in Trinidad*. Oxford: Berg.

Miller, Errol. 1986. *Marginalization of the Black Male: Insights from the Development of the Teaching Profession*. Mona, Jamaica: Institute of Social and Economic Research, University of the West Indies.

———. 1988. "The Rise of Matriarchy in the Caribbean." *Caribbean Quarterly* 34, 3–4:1–21.

Mintz, Sidney W. 1974. *Caribbean Transformations*. Baltimore: Johns Hopkins University Press.

———. 1985. "From Plantations to Peasantries in the Caribbean." In *Caribbean Contours*, ed. Sidney W. Mintz and Sally Price, 127–53. Baltimore: Johns Hopkins University Press.

———. 1987. "The Historical Sociology of Jamaican Villages." In *Afro-Caribbean Villages in Historical Perspective*, ed. Charles V. Carnegie, 1–19. Kingston, Jamaica: African-Caribbean Institute of Jamaica.

Mintz, Sidney, and Richard Price. 1992. *The Birth of African-American Culture: An Anthropological Perspective*. Boston: Beacon Press.

Mischel, Frances. 1957. "African 'Powers' in Trinidad: The Shango Cult." *Anthropological Quarterly* 30, 2:45–59.

Mischel, Walter, and Frances Mischel. 1958. "Psychological Aspects of Spirit Possession." *American Anthropologist* 60:249–60.

Mohammed, Patricia. 1991. "Reflections on the Women's Movement in Trinidad: Calypsos, Changes and Sexual Violence." *Feminist Review* 38:33–47.

Momsen, Janet Henshall. 1988. "Gender Roles in Caribbean Agricultural Labour." In
*Labour in the Caribbean*, ed. Malcolm Cross and Gad Heuman, 141–58. London:
Macmillan.

Morrish, Ivon. 1982. *Obeah, Christ and Rastaman: Jamaica and Its Religion*. Cambridge:
James Clarke.

Munroe, Trevor. 1972. *The Politics of Constitutional Decolonization: Jamaica, 1944–62*. Mona,
Jamaica: Institute of Social and Economic Research, University of the West
Indies.

———. 1991. "The Impact of the Church in the Political Culture of the Caribbean:
The Case of Jamaica." *Caribbean Quarterly* 37, 1:83–97.

Murphy, Joseph M. 1994. *Working the Spirit: Ceremonies of the African Diaspora*. Boston:
Beacon Press.

Nicholas, Tracy. 1979. *Rastafari: A Way of Life*. Garden City, N.Y.: Anchor/Doubleday.

Nicholls, David. 1985. *Haiti in Caribbean Context: Ethnicity, Economy and Revolt*. New York:
St. Martin's Press.

Nunley, John W. 1988. "Masquerade Mix-up in Trinidad Carnival: Live Once, Die
Forever." In *Caribbean Festival Arts*, ed. John W. Nunley and Judith Bettelheim,
85–117. Seattle: University of Washington Press.

Okari, Mikelle Smith. 1984. *From the Inside to the Outside: The Art and Ritual of Bahian
Candomblé*. Los Angeles: Museum of Cultural History, University of California.

Olwig, Karen Fog. 1987. "Sport as Secular Ritual: The Case of Netball." *Folk* 29:75–90.

———. 1993. *Global Culture, Island Identity: Continuity and Change in the Afro-Caribbean Community of Nevis*. Chur, Switzerland: Harwood Academic Publishers.

Owens, Joseph. 1976. *Dread: The Rastafarians of Jamaica*. Kingston, Jamaica: Sangster.

Oxaal, Ivan. 1968. *Black Intellectuals Come to Power: The Rise of Creole Nationalism in Trinidad
and Tobago*. Cambridge, Mass.: Schenkman.

———. 1971. *Race and Revolutionary Consciousness: A Documentary Interpretation of the 1970
Black Power Revolt in Trinidad*. Cambridge, Mass.: Schenkman.

Paget, Hugh. 1964. "The Growth of Villages in Jamaica and British Guiana." *Caribbean
Quarterly* 10, 1:38–51.

Patterson, Orlando. 1967. *The Sociology of Slavery: An Analysis of the Origins, Development
and Structure of Negro Slave Society in Jamaica*. Rutherford, N.J.: Fairleigh Dickinson
University Press.

———. 1973. "The Ritual of Cricket." In *Caribbean Essays*, ed. Andrew Salkey, 108–18.
London: Evans Brothers.

———. 1975. "Context and Choice in Ethnic Allegiance: A Theoretical Framework
and Caribbean Case Study." In *Ethnicity: Theory and Experience*, ed. Nathan Glazer
and Daniel P. Moynihan, 305–49. Cambridge: Harvard University Press.

————. 1979. "Slavery and Slave Revolts: A Sociohistorical Analysis of the First Maroon War, 1655–1740." In *Maroon Societies: Rebel Slave Communities in the Americas*, ed. Richard Price, 246–92. Baltimore: Johns Hopkins University Press.

————. 1982a. *Slavery and Social Death: A Comparative Study.* Cambridge: Harvard University Press.

————. 1982b. "Persistence, Continuity, and Change in the Jamaican Working-Class Family." *Journal of Family History* 7, 2:135–61.

————. 1989. *The Children of Sisyphus.* London: Longman. First published 1964.

Paul, Emmanuel C. 1962. *Panorama du folklore haïtien.* Port-au-Prince, Haiti: Imprimerie de l'Etat.

Payne, Anthony J. 1988. *Politics in Jamaica.* London: C. Hurst.

————. 1993. "Westminster Adapted: The Political Order of the Commonwealth Caribbean." In *Democracy in the Caribbean: Political, Economic, and Social Perspectives*, ed. Jorge I. Dominguez, Robert A. Pastor, and R. Delisle Worrell, 57–73. Baltimore: Johns Hopkins University Press.

Pearse, Andrew. 1956a. "Carnival in Nineteenth Century Trinidad." *Caribbean Quarterly* 4, 3–4:175–93.

————. 1956b. "Mitto Sampson on Calypso Legends of the Nineteenth Century." *Caribbean Quarterly* 4, 3–4:250–62.

Pelton, Robert D. 1980. *The Trickster in West Africa: A Study of Mythic Irony and Sacred Delight.* Los Angeles: University of California Press.

Pluchon, Pierre. 1987. *Vaudou, sorciers, empoisonneurs: De Saint-Domingue à Haïti.* Paris: Karthala.

Pollak-Eltz, Angelina. 1993. "The Shango Cult and Other African Rituals in Trinidad, Grenada, and Carriacou, and Their Possible Influence on the Spiritual Baptist Faith." *Caribbean Quarterly* 39, 3–4:12–25.

Pollard, Velma. 1980. "Dread Talk: The Speech of the Rastafarian in Jamaica." *Caribbean Quarterly* 26, 4:32–41.

Post, Ken. 1978. *Arise Ye Starvelings: The Jamaican Labour Rebellion of 1938 and Its Aftermath.* The Hague: Martinus Nijhoff.

————. 1981. *Strike the Iron, a Colony at War: Jamaica, 1939–1945.* Atlantic Highlands, N.J.: Humanities Press.

Price, Richard, and Sally Price. 1966. "A Note on Canoe Names in Martinique." *Names* 14:157–60.

————. 1972. "Saramaka Onomastics: An Afro-American Naming System." *Ethnology* 11, 4:341–67.

Prince, Althea V. 1984. "Anansi Folk Culture: An Expression of Caribbean Life." *Caribbean Review* 13, 1:24–27, 49–51.

Procope, Bruce. 1956. "The Dragon Band or Devil Band." *Caribbean Quarterly* 4, 3–4:275–80.

Rashford, John. 1985. "The Cotton Tree and the Spiritual Realm in Jamaica." *Jamaica Journal* 18, 1:49–57.

Rath, Richard Cullen. 1993. "African Music in Seventeenth-Century Jamaica: Cultural Transit and Transition." *William and Mary Quarterly* 3d ser., 50, 4:700–726.

Reisman, Karl. 1970. "Cultural and Linguistic Ambiguity in a West Indian Villiage." In *Afro-American Anthropology: Contemporary Perspectives*, ed. Norman E. Whitten and John F. Szwed, 129–44. New York: Free Press.

———. 1974. "Noise and Order." In *Language in Its Social Setting*, ed. William W. Gage, 56–73. Washington, D.C.: Anthropological Society of Washington.

Robotham, Don. 1983. "'The Notorious Riot': The Socio-economic and Political Bases of Paul Bogle's Revolt." *Anales del Caribe* 3:51–111.

Roden, Donald. 1980. "Baseball and the Quest for National Dignity in Meiji Japan." *American Historical Review* 85, 3:511–34.

Rohlehr, Gordon. 1985. "'Man Talking to Man.' Calypso and Social Confrontation in Trinidad, 1970 to 1984." *Caribbean Quarterly* 31, 2:1–13.

———. 1990. *Calypso and Society in Pre-independence Trinidad*. Port of Spain, Trinidad: Gordon Rohlehr.

Rouget, Gilbert. 1985. *Music and Trance: A Theory of the Relations between Music and Possession*. Trans. Brunhilde Biebuyck. Chicago: University of Chicago Press.

Rowe, Maureen. 1980. "The Woman in Rastafari." *Caribbean Quarterly* 26, 4:13–21.

Rubin, Vera, and Lambros Comita. 1975. *Ganja in Jamaica*. The Hague: Mouton.

Russell, Horace O. 1983. "The Emergence of the Christian Black: The Making of a Stereotype." *Jamaica Journal* 16, 1:51–58.

Ryan, Selwyn. 1991. *The Muslimeen Grab for Power: Race, Religion and Revolution in Trinidad and Tobago*. Port of Spain, Trinidad: Inprint.

Ryman, Cheryl. 1978–79. "The Jamaica Inheritance in Dance: Developing a Traditional Typology." *Jamaica Journal* 44:2–13.

———. 1984. "Jonkonnu: A Neo-African Form." *Jamaica Journal* 17, 1:13–23; 17, 2:50–61.

Satchell, Veront M. 1990. *From Plots to Plantations: Land Transactions in Jamaica, 1866–1900*. Mona, Jamaica: Institute of Social and Economic Research, University of the West Indies.

Scheper-Hughes, Nancy. 1992. *Death without Weeping: The Violence of Everyday Life in Brazil*. Berkeley: University of California Press.

Schuler, Monica. 1979. "Myalism and the African Religous Tradition in Jamaica." In *African and the Caribbean: The Legacies of a Link*, ed. Michael E. Crahan and Franklin W. Knight, 65–79. Baltimore: Johns Hopkins University Press.

Scott, James C. 1985. *Weapons of the Weak: Everyday Forms of Peasant Resistance*. New Haven: Yale University Press.

———. 1990. *Domination and the Arts of Resistance: Hidden Transcripts*. New Haven: Yale University Press.

Seaga, Edward. 1969. "Revival Cults in Jamaica: Notes towards a Sociology of Religion." *Jamaica Journal* 3, 2:3–13.

Sheridan, Richard B. 1976. "The Jamaican Slave Insurrection Scare of 1776 and the American Revolution." *Journal of Negro History* 56:290–308.

———. 1985. *Doctors and Slaves: A Medical and Demographic History of Slavery in the British West Indies, 1680–1834.* Cambridge: Cambridge University Press.

———. 1986. "The Maroons of Jamaica, 1730–1830: Livelihood, Demography and Health." In *Out of the House of Bondage: Runaways, Resistance and Marronage in Africa and the New World,* ed. Gad Heuman, 152–72. London: Frank Cass.

Simpson, George Eaton. 1978. *Black Religions in the New World.* New York: Columbia University Press.

Singh, Kelvin. 1988. *Bloodstained Tombs: The Muharram Massacre, 1884.* London, Macmillan.

———. 1994. *Race and Class Struggles in a Colonial State: Trinidad, 1917–1945.* Mona, Jamaica: Press of the University of the West Indies and University of Calgary Press.

Singham, A. W. 1968. *The Hero and the Crowd in a Colonial Polity.* New Haven: Yale University Press.

Smith, M. G., Roy Augier, and Rex Nettleford. 1960. *Report on the Rastafari Movement in Kingston, Jamaica.* Mona, Jamaica: Institute of Social and Economic Research, University of the West Indies.

Smith, Raymond T. 1973. "The Matrifocal Family." In *The Character of Kinship,* ed. Jack Goody, 121–44. Cambridge: Cambridge University Press.

Smucker, Glenn R. 1984. "The Social Character of Religion in Rural Haiti." In *Haiti—Today and Tomorrow: An Interdisciplinary Study,* ed. Charles R. Foster and Albert Valdman. Lanham, Md.: University Press of America.

Soares, Dave. 1989. "Cricket in Jamaica: A Brief Sketch of Its Development in the Nineteenth Century." *Jamaican Journal* 22, 2:25–32.

Sobo, Elisa Janine. 1993. *One Blood: The Jamaican Body.* Albany: State University of New York Press.

Stallybras, Peter, and Allon White. 1986. *The Politics and Poetics of Transgression.* Ithaca: Cornell University Press.

Stephens, Evelyne Huber, and John D. Stephens. 1986. *Democratic Socialism in Jamaica.* Princeton: Princeton University Press.

Stewart, John O. 1986. "Patronage and Control in the Trinidad Carnival." In *The Anthropology of Experience,* ed. Victor W. Turner and Edward M. Bruner, 289–315. Urbana: University of Illinois Press.

———. 1989. *Drinkers, Drummers, and Decent Folk: Ethnographic Narratives of Village Trinidad.* Albany: State University of New York Press.

Stewart, Robert J. 1992. *Religion and Society in Post-emancipation Jamaica.* Knoxville: University of Tennessee Press.

Stoddart, Brian. 1987. "Cricket, Social Formation and Cultural Continuity in Barbados: A Preliminary Ethnohistory." *Journal of Sport History* 14, 3:317–40.

———. 1988. "Cricket and Colonialism in the English-Speaking Caribbean to 1914: Towards a Cultural Analysis." In *Pleasure, Profit, Proselytism: British Culture and Sport at Home and Abroad,* ed. J. A. Mangan, 231–57. London: Frank Cass.

Stone, Carl. 1980. *Democracy and Clientelism in Jamaica.* New Brunswick, N.J.: Transaction Books.

———. 1982. *The Political Opinions of the Jamaican People (1976–81).* Kingston, Jamaica: Blackett.

Sutton, Paul. 1984. "Trinidad and Tobago: Oil Capitalism and the 'Presidential Power' of Eric Williams." In *Dependency under Challenge: The Political Economy of the Commonwealth Caribbean,* ed. Anthony Payne and Paul Sutton. Manchester: Manchester University Press.

———. 1991. "Constancy, Change and Accommodation: The Distinct Tradition of the Commonwealth Caribbean." In *The Fallacies of Hope: The Post-colonial Record of the Commonwealth Third World,* ed. James Mayall and Anthony Payne, 106–27. Manchester: Manchester University Press.

Tanna, Laura. 1984. *Jamaican Folk Tales and Oral Histories.* Kingston, Jamaica: Institute of Jamaica Publications.

Thomas, Clive Y. 1988. *The Poor and the Powerless: Economic Policy and Change in the Caribbean.* London: Latin American Bureau.

Thomas-Hope, Elizabeth M. 1986. "Caribbean Diaspora, the Inheritance of Slavery: Migration from the Commonwealth Caribbean." In *The Caribbean in Europe: Aspects of the West Indian Experience in Britain, France and the Netherlands,* ed. Colin Brock, 15–35. London: Frank Cass.

Thompson, L. O'Brien. 1983. "How Cricket Is West Indian Cricket?" *Caribbean Review* 12, 2:23–25, 50–53.

Thompson, Robert Farris. 1983. *Flash of the Spirit: African and Afro-American Art and Philosophy.* New York: Random House.

Trotman, David Vincent. 1986. *Crime in Trinidad: Conflict and Control in a Plantation Society, 1838–1900.* Knoxville: University of Tennessee Press.

Turner, Mary. 1982. *Slaves and Missionaries: The Disintegration of Jamaican Slave Society, 1787–1834.* Urbana: University of Illinois Press.

Turner, Victor. 1977. *The Ritual Process: Structure and Anti-Structure.* Ithaca: Cornell University Press.

———. 1992. *The Anthropology of Performance.* New York: PAJ.

Van Dijk, Frank Jan. 1988. "The Twelve Tribes of Israel: Rasta and the Middle Class." *New West Indian Guide* 62, 1–2:1–26.

———. 1995. "Sociological Means: Colonial Reactions to the Radicalization of Rastafari in Jamaica, 1956–1959." *New West Indian Guide* 69, 1–2:67–101.

Viotta da Costa, Emilia. 1994. *Crowns of Glory, Tears of Blood: The Demerara Slave Rebellion of 1823.* Oxford: Oxford University Press.

Walcott, Derek. 1965. *The Castaway.* London: Jonathan Cape.

Walker, Sheila. 1991. "Everyday and Esoteric Reality in the Afro-Brazilian Candomblé." *History of Religions* 30, 2:103–26.

Walvin, James. 1993. *Black Ivory: A History of British Slavery*. London: Fontana Press.

Ward, J. R. 1988. *British West Indian Slavery, 1750–1834: The Process of Amelioration*. Oxford: Oxford University Press.

Warner, Keith Q. 1982. *Kaiso! The Trinidad Calypso: A Study of the Calypso as Oral Literature*. Washington, D.C.: Three Continents Press.

———. 1993. "Ethnicity and the Contemporary Calypso." In *Trinidad Ethnicity*, ed. Kevin Yelvington, 275–91. London: Macmillan.

Warner-Lewis, Maureen. 1977. *The Nkuyu: Spirit Messengers of the Kumina*. Mona, Jamaica: Savacou.

———. 1991. *Guinea's Other Suns: The African Dynamic in Trinidad Culture*. Dover, Mass.: Majority Press.

———. 1993. "African Continuities in the Rastafari Belief System." *Caribbean Quarterly* 39, 3–4:108–23.

Waters, Anita M. 1985. *Race, Class and Political Symbols: Rastafari and Reggae in Jamaican Politics*. New Brunswick, N.J.: Transaction Books.

Wedenoja, William. 1980. "Modernization and the Pentecostal Movement in Jamaica." In *Perspectives on Pentecostalism: Case Studies from the Caribbean and Latin America*, ed. Stephen D. Glazier, 27–47. Washington, D.C.: University Press of America.

———. 1988. "The Origins of Revival, a Creole Religion in Jamaica." In *Culture and Christianity: The Dialectics of Transformation*, ed. George R. Saunders. Westport, Conn.: Greenwood Press.

———. 1989. "Mothering and the Practice of 'Balm' in Jamaica." In *Women as Healers: Cross-Cultural Perspectives*, ed. Carol Shepherd McClain, 76–97. New Brunswick: Rutgers University Press.

Weinstein, Brian, and Aaron Segal. 1984. *Haiti: Political Failures, Cultural Successes*. New York: Praeger.

Weisbord, Robert G. 1970. "British West Indian Reaction to the Italian-Ethiopian War: An Episode in Pan-Africanism." *Caribbean Studies* 10, 1:31–41.

White, Timothy. 1983. *Catch a Fire: The Life of Bob Marley*. New York: Holt, Rinehart and Winston.

Wilcken, Lois. 1992. *The Drums of Vodou*. Crown Point, Ind.: White Cliffs Media.

Wilmot, Swithin. 1984. "Not 'Full Free': The Ex-Slaves and the Apprenticeship System in Jamaica, 1834–1838." *Jamaica Journal* 17, 3:2–10.

———. 1990. "The Politics of Protest in Free Jamaica: The Kingston John Canoe Christmas Riots, 1840 and 1841." *Caribbean Quarterly* 36, 3–4:65–76.

Wilson, Peter J. 1973. *Crab Antics: The Social Anthropology of English-Speaking Negro Societies in the Caribbean*. New Haven: Yale University Press.

Wüst, Ruth. 1990. "The Robber in the Trinidad Carnival." *Caribbean Quarterly* 36, 3–4:42–53.

———. 1993. "The Trinidad Carnival: A Medium of Social Change." In *Alternative Cultures in the Caribbean*, ed. Thomas Bremer and Ulrich Fleischmann, 149–59. Frankfurt am Main: Vervuert.

Wynter, Silvia. 1970. "Jonkonnu in Jamaica: Towards the Interpretation of Folk Dance as a Cultural Process." *Jamaica Journal* 4, 2:34–48.

Yawney, Carole. 1976. "Remnants of All Nations: Rastafarian Attitudes to Race and Nationality." In *Ethnicity in the Americas*, ed. Frances Henry, 231–62. The Hague: Mouton.

———. 1979. "Dread Wasteland: Rastafarian Ritual in West Kingston, Jamaica." In *Ritual Symbolism and Ceremonialism in the Americas: Studies in Symbolic Anthropology*, ed. N. Ross Crumrine, 154–78. Greeley, Colo.: Museum of Anthropology, University of Northern Colorado.

———. 1989. "To Grow a Daughter: Cultural Liberation and the Dynamics of Oppression in Jamaica." In *Feminism: From Pressure to Politics*, ed. Angela R. Miles and Geraldine Finn, 177–202. Montreal: Black Rose Books.

———. 1993. "Rasta Mek a Trod: Symbolic Ambiguity in a Globalizing Religion." In *Alternative Cultures in the Caribbean*, ed. Ulrich Fleischmann and Thomas Bremer, 161–68. Frankfurt am Main: Vervuert.

Yelvington, Kevin. 1990. "Ethnicity 'Not Out': The Indian Cricket Tour of the West Indies and the 1976 Elections in Trinidad and Tobago." *Arena Review* 14, 1:1–12.

———. 1995a. *Producing Power: Ethnicity, Gender and Class in a Caribbean Workplace*. Philadelphia: Temple University Press.

———. 1995b. "Cricket, Colonialism, and the Culture of Caribbean Politics." In *The Social Role of Sport in Caribbean Society*, ed. Michael Malee, 1–40. New York: Gordon and Breach.

Yonker, Dolores. 1988. "Rara in Haiti." In *Caribbean Festival Arts*, by John W. Nunley and Judith Bettelheim, 147–55. Seattle: University of Washington Press.

# Index